Action Learning Worldwide

Action Learning Worldwide

Experiences of Leadership and Organizational Development

Edited by

Yury Boshyk

First published 2002 by
PALGRAVE MACMILLAN
Houndmills, Basingstoke, Hampshire RG21 6XS and
175 Fifth Avenue, New York, N.Y. 10010
Companies and representatives throughout the world

PALGRAVE is the global academic imprint of the Palgrave Macmillan division of St. Martin's Press, LLC and of Palgrave Macmillan Ltd. Macmillan® is a registered trademark in the United States, United Kingdom and other countries. Palgrave is a registered trademark in the European Union and other countries.

ISBN 0–333–96870–0

This book is printed on paper suitable for recycling and made from fully managed and sustained forest sources.

A catalogue record for this book is available from the British Library.

Library of Congress Cataloging-in-Publication Data
Global Forum on Business Driven Action Learning and Executive Development.
Action learning worldwide: experiences of leadership and organizational development/edited by Yury Boshyk.
     p. cm.
"This present volume originated in presentations made at the annual Global Forum on Business Driven Action Learning and Executive Development" – Pref.
Includes bibliographical references and index
ISBN 0–333–96870–0
1. Organizational learning — Case studies — Congresses. 2. Active learning — Case studies — Congresses. 3. Executives — Training of — Case studies — Congresses. 4. Leadership — Case studies — Congresses. 5. Organizational change — Case studies — Congresses. I. Boshyk, Yuri. II. Title.

HD58.82 .G545 2002   2002019086
658.4'07124—dc21

10   9   8   7   6   5   4   3   2   1
11   10   09   08   07   06   05   04   03   02

Printed and bound in Great Britain by
Antony Rowe Ltd, Chippenham and Eastbourne

Contents

Preface

This volume can be viewed as a companion volume to our previous book on action learning – *Business Driven Action Learning: Global Best Practices*. Like its predecessor, this present volume originated in presentations made at the annual Global Forum on Business Driven Action Learning and Executive Development at which practitioners from corporations, academia and other organizations come together to discuss the latest research and experiences in the field. All the different schools and approaches to action learning are represented, and so too this volume brings together some of the leading practitioners of action learning and its three major orientations: classic, action reflection, and business driven action learning. In the past, each tended to go their own separate ways, and at times were even hostile to one another. Increasingly, however, there is a realization of the connectedness and relevance of all three approaches and, more to the point, that much can be learned through a constructive sharing of experiences and concepts. Certainly, this is the spirit and intent of this volume.

In the first volume we concentrated on multinational companies. But in this work we have broadened our perspective on two fronts – by including the 'new economy' companies and their action learning experiences and issues, and by including contributions on action learning as it is practiced not only in the private sector but also in the public sector and the not-for-profit sector of social life. We have also focused this volume on worldwide examples of action learning in the three major areas of North and South America; Europe, Middle East and Africa, and Asia Pacific. While articles and books have appeared on action learning in some of these regions there is no one volume that has looked at action learning on a worldwide level. Most studies on action learning tend to be focused on experiences in the northern hemisphere and, in particular, in the Anglo-American and Nordic worlds. We also include articles on action learning in emerging markets where almost four-fifths of humanity resides and where we see extraordinary changes taking place since the end of the Cold War. It seems that these countries are undergoing a society-wide action learning experience as they build (and in some cases, rebuild) their own futures.

Those of you who have read the previous volume and other volumes with examples from the business world, know well that the number of companies and organizations using and introducing action learning has increased dramatically. This is not just another fad, as Jac Fitz-enz (2001) has pointed out in his most recent book. Action learning has been with us since the 1940s and it has a serious theoretical foundation. Its increasing popularity and usefulness has as much to do with the confluence of new realities (such as the emphasis on intellectual and human capital, and the learning organization) as it does with the solid foundations established by previous generations of practitioners. This growth and acceptance of action learning will continue, and even accelerate, for reasons which we hope will become self-evident to anyone who takes the time to peruse this publication.

Finally, it is a great pleasure to thank the many people who helped make this volume a reality: to the authors who tolerated some delays and who were kind enough to make suggested editorial changes; to the Global Forum participants who by their generosity of spirit, professional camaraderie and openness have created a wonderful foundation for stimulating discussion, dynamic research and continuous learning; to Claire Meneveau; to Stephen Rutt, Caitlin Cornish, and Keith Povey for their patience and professionalism; and to Zara, Julia, Mutti, Wally, Diane, Myron, Beth, Oleg, Samba, Milo, Chloe, D'Artagnan, and to my parents who were all part of the adventure and always encouraging; and especially to Nadia for her clarity of mind, perseverance, inspiration and love.

YURY BOSHYK

Notes on the Contributors

Carl Aspler is President of Carl Aspler & Associates, a Toronto-based consulting and training firm specializing in Change Management and Organization Effectiveness. Carl spent six years with General Electric Canada as Manager, Organization Change. Both Carl and Beverly Davids were involved in Work-Out™ and Change Acceleration Process (CAP) since their inception, internalizing both processes in GE Canada as well as working with teams throughout GE. They continue to consult with General Electric on implementing change initiatives.

Yury Boshyk (YuryBoshyk@globalexec-learning.com and YuryBoshyk@aol.com) is founding Co-Director of Global Executive Learning, a network of professionals involved in analyzing global trends that affect companies and countries, and assisting multinationals and organizations in the design and implementation of business driven action learning. Yury helps organize an annual Global Forum on Business Driven Action Learning and Executive Development, where representatives of multinational companies, public and 'third'-sector institutions come together to share experiences and the latest research in the area of executive development and action learning. He lectures widely and works in cooperation with a number of institutions, among them the J. M. Huber Institute for Learning in Organizations, Columbia University (New York, USA), where he is a member of the advisory board, and the Gordon Institute of Business Science, University of Pretoria (Johannesburg, South Africa), where he is a Visiting Professor. He has published studies, books and articles that deal with trends affecting corporations and countries, including emerging economies, as well as historical works on twentieth-century topics. His previous volume on action learning was published by Macmillan and St Martin's Press (2000) under the title, *Business Driven Action Learning: Global Best Practices*, which he edited. Formerly he was Professor of Strategy and International Business Environment at IMD, Lausanne, Switzerland. He completed his doctorate at the University of Oxford, and his Master's degree at the London School of Economics.

Charles Brassard (charles.brassard@sympatico.ca) is a consultant in the area of executive and leadership development, and also a certified professional effectiveness coach. Through his company, Impact Coaching Inc., he applies innovative learning methods to support the development of managers and executives, particularly through action learning and reflective coaching. Charles is also a consultant with San Diego-based Executive Development

Associates, a leading education and consulting firm specializing in the strategic use of executive/leadership development. Prior to starting his own consulting practice, Charles directed a programme at the Canadian Centre for Management Development (CCMD) to support the accelerated development and career advancement of high-potential executives in the Public Service of Canada. While at CCMD, he also led the development of a management and leadership learning architecture for public service managers and executives and a related web-based application to support personal learning plans. Prior to joining CCMD, Charles held various senior advisory and management positions in the public and private sectors in the areas of energy, the environment and international relations. Charles holds a Master's degree in Economic Geography from the University of Ottawa and has received extensive professional education in the field of adult learning.

Scott Byrd (sbyrd@mba1999.hbs.edu) is Manager, Global Economic Affairs, at Eli Lilly and Company where he leads a team of marketing professionals and scientists to develop and manage pricing, reimbursement and health economic strategies for Lilly's critical care products, with additional responsibility for marketing strategies related to healthcare payers and gatekeepers. Scott has an MBA from the Harvard Business School and before assuming his present position in the company he was also a strategy analyst with corporate strategic planning, and a financial analyst for planning and cost analysis. He enjoys outdoor activities, golfing, skiing, travelling, advising youth groups and reading.

Lars Cederholm (lced@aol.com) is President of CCT Inc., New York City, a consulting company established in 1981. He has been an active senior staff member of the MiL Institute, Sweden since 1986. Since 1993 he has been a Visiting Professor of Organizational Behaviour at Moscow State University. He brings 13 years of international line management experience to his organizational development practice. During the last 20 years, Lars has pursued a consulting career in the field of organizational development, providing professional services to major US and European-based national and international organizations. Among his clients are companies and organizations such as Apple Computer, Unicef, WR Grace and Grace Cocoa, Volvo Car, Volvo Truck, Himont, Pioneer Hi-Bred, Novartis Seed, Saab Aerospace, Keyspan Energy, American Management Association, Norske Bank, MiL Foundation, NYC Board of Education, AMC (American Merchandising Corporation), Brooks Fashion, Nordkorn (East) Germany and Stroypolymer in the former USSR. He has assisted top management teams with strategic planning, internal strategy development, and personal coaching of executives from these companies and others. Lars holds an MBA from the University of Lund in Sweden and an MA from Columbia University in Organizational Psychology. Following his MA he pursued additional study at The Gestalt Institute of Cleveland in Organization and Systems Development. His publications include a chapter for the book *Creating the Learning Organization* (1996) (ASTD publishers) and many articles in major US professional publications related to organization and executive development based on ARL™ (Action Reflection Learning) technology.

Sherri Cizin (Sherricizin@yahoo.com) a management and organizational development consultant and formerly Director of the Entrepreneurship Programme at the Technion Institute of Management (TIM) in Israel. Previously TIM's Programme Director, she was one of the initiators of TIM's action-learning approach to executive development for Israeli high-tech managers. Prior to returning to Israel in 1997, Sherri was President of SDM Associates, a management consulting firm, and a senior HR consultant with Exxon Co. International. Her areas of interest include global leadership, managing international growth, technology and entrepreneurial enterprises, and the utilization of management education as an organization development tool. Sherri holds an MS in Management from the Technion, the Israel Institute of Technology, and is certified in Organization Development and Consultation from the William Alanson White Institute of Psychiatry, Psychoanalysis and Psychology, New York.

Beverly N. Davids (consult@grnwch.com) is senior partner of The Greenwich Group, a Toronto-based consulting and training firm. She specializes in change management and organization effectiveness – team-building, facilitation and redesign. For over eight years, Bev was Manager, Organization Effectiveness/Change at General Electric Canada. In conjunction with GE's Corporate Leadership Development organization (Crotonville), Bev was part of the team that introduced CAP to GE Businesses in Asia. She continues to teach at Crotonville and consult to GE and other Fortune 500 companies throughout the world.

Laura Dorsey (DORSEY_LAURA_T@LILLY.COM) is a Human Resource Consultant, Eli Lilly and Company based in Indianapolis, responsible for developing new systems and programmes targeted to the development of executives and individuals with potential for executive-level leadership. These include, but are not limited to, executive mentoring, talent identification, and action learning programmes. Before joining Lilly she also worked at AT&T as an instructional technologist, AT&T National Teletraining Network, Cincinnati, where she assisted AT&T instructors in the design of technical courses for delivery via a national teletraining network, conducted curriculum analysis, developed an instructor competency model and designed an instructional model integrating the use of a student-feedback keypad system into the curriculum. Laura holds a PhD in Instructional Systems Technology from Indiana University. She has published articles in her area of specialization and has presented numerous papers at professional association conferences.

Galit Gilan is Technion Institute of Management's Programme Director, responsible for design, delivery and evaluation of TIM's programmes. Previously she was the Training and Development Manager at Tadiran Electronic Systems Ltd. Her experience includes human resources management and organizational development. Galit Holds an MA in management from Webster University in Leiden, The Netherlands. Her graduate project, on executive management programme's organizational impact, was conducted for the human resources department of AT&T Network Systems International Transmission Development in Huizen, the Netherlands.

R. Morgan Gould (rmgould@iprolink.ch) is Principal, Gould & Associates, He is a practitioner of action learning in the Suisse Romand (Geneva) region of Switzerland. In 1995 he established his practice in the implementation of strategic change with a specialization in change management, and has conducted programmes for companies or governments in China, Indonesia and Slovenia. His previous experience was at the International Institute for Management Development (IMD), Lausanne, Switzerland, as Associate Director for Research and Development and Research Fellow where he taught in several of IMD's executive programmes, and where he pursued research and writing in the area of strategic change management which led to several award-winning cases and articles – a book is near completion. He has delivered lectures to DuPont Nemours, Guinness, IBM, and Siemens AG in the area of change management, and was a guest lecturer at Chalmers University's CHAMPS programme. Morgan holds a PhD in organizational theory, where he worked with Nevitt Sanford, the distinguished American psychologist and one of the 'fathers' of action learning.

Steven Hicks (hickss@bschool.unc.edu) is Director in Executive Education at the University of North Carolina's Kenan-Flagler Business School. He works with the school's company partners to design, develop and deliver customized management development programmes that focus on improving individual and organizational performance. In addition to his administrative duties he teaches classes in leadership, coaching, learning and development strategies, and team-building. Prior to joining academia, he held management positions at Learning Resources Inc. and Westvaco Corporation, and served as a Lieutenant in the US Coast Guard. Steve received his Bachelors degree in psychology from Duke University, his Masters degree in education from the University of North Carolina, and his Doctoral degree in education from North Carolina State University. His article in this volume is based on his recent PhD dissertation (year), *Action Learning: Patterns in the Practice of Program Design for Business Education and Development.*

Dean Hopkins (dean.hopkins@cyberplex.com) is co-founder, President and Chief Executive Officer of Cyberplex, a recognized authority on Internet business strategies and solutions. Nominated in 1999 for Canada's top 40 under 40, and named Toronto Star up-and-comer for 2000, Hopkins has attracted a number of internationally recognized clients to Cyberplex, which include 3M, Handspring and Royal Bank. Headquartered in Toronto, Cyberplex has offices in Halifax, Waterloo, Austin, Boston, Connecticut, Los Angeles and San Francisco. Hopkins has positioned Cyberplex as a major player in the US market as recognized by Forrester Research, who has distinguished Cyberplex as one of the top 40 firms in the world. He speaks regularly on the subject of internet strategy and thought leadership, and has been quoted in national dailies and publications including the *Wall Street Journal*, the *Industry Standard*, the *National Post*, the *Globe and Mail*, the *Toronto Star*, *Maclean's*, and *Canadian Business and Marketing Magazine*. Prior to launching Cyberplex in 1994, Hopkins spent three years as a management consultant at McKinsey & Co. At McKinsey he advised senior managers of established Canadian corporations on a range of strategic issues. Additionally he played a leadership role within the firm's information technology division. Hopkins holds a Bachelor of Applied Science in Systems Design Engineering from the University of Waterloo where he graduated with Dean's Honours.

Brian Isaacson (bialign@iafrica.com) is a consultant to leading South African-based international organizations, state institutions and parastatal organizations on results-based alignment. He specializes in custom-designed leadership development programmes, providing action learning applications addressing the unique challenges associated with the South African situation where simultaneously corporations have to transform and perform. Brian also coaches and provides counsel to organization leaders and teaches leadership on executive programmes at leading South African business schools.

Grażyna Leśniak-Łebkowska (lebkowska@sgh.waw.pl) is Assistant Professor of Strategic Management, Warsaw School of Economics, and Director of the Warsaw Executive MBA programme, a joint project with the University of Minnesota. She is also the Deputy Director of the Polish–American Centre for Economics and Management. Among her research interests are the management of green-sector companies, managing investment in Central and Eastern European countries, and management in crisis situations. Grazyna is also a consultant on strategy, management systems and executive education. Among her clients are a number of US multinationals.

Taebok Lee (pca5865@chollian.net) is President, Paradigm Consulting Associates Inc. in Seoul, Korea. with diversified experience in leadership development, change management and management innovation. Before starting his consultancy he worked for Samsung as part of the human resource development Team where he developed the organizational operating system and personnel system, prepared the wage and compensation system and planned human resource development He has a Bachelor of Arts in Public Administration from Sungkyunkwan University and an MBA from YeonSei University. His main clients include Hyundai Heavy Industry, Hyundai Motors, LG Chemicals, LG Industrial Systems, LG Electronics, LG Cables, LG Precisions, Samsung Heavy Industry, Samsung Electronics, Korea Telecom, Taepyungyang Group, POSCO, Kumho Group and others.

Shlomo Maital (smaital@techunix.technion.ac.il) is Academic Director of the Technion Institute of Management in Israel. He is also Visiting Professor at the MIT Sloan School of Management. He has taught MBA courses in Canada, Chile, France and the Netherlands, and received a Distinguished Teacher Award. Shlomo's latest book is *Managing New Product Development and Innovation: A Microeconomic Toolbox* (2001) (co-authored with Hariolf Grupp, Edward Elgar). His other publications include *Executive Economics: Ten Essential Tools For Management* (1994); and *Minds, Markets and Money: Psychological Foundations of Economic Behavior* (1982). His books have been translated into Spanish, Portuguese, Italian, Russian and Hebrew, and his articles have been published in several academic journals and numerous publications such as *Barrons* and the *New York Times*. Shlomo received his BA (with honours) and MA from Queen's University in Canada and his PhD in Economics from Princeton University. He was Director of the National and Economic Planning Authority for the Ministry of Economics and Planning in Israel. He is married to Sharone Levow Maital, a child-clinical psychologist. They have four children and five grandchildren.

Victoria Marsick (vmarsick@aol.com) is co-Director with Martha A. Gephart of the J.M. Huber Institute for Learning in Organizations at Teachers College, Columbia University, where she is a Professor of Adult and Organizational Learning, Department of Organization and Leadership. She holds a PhD in Adult Education from the University of California, Berkeley, and an MPA in International Public Administration from Syracuse University. Victoria consults with both the public and private sectors on learning organizations and on action learning. Some of her clients have included PSE&G,

AT&T, Coca Cola, EXXON, Travelers Companies, Arthur Andersen SC, the Canadian Imperial Bank of Commerce, and the Department of Defense. She has written many books and articles on informal learning, action learning, team learning and the learning organization. Her most recent books are *Facilitating the Learning Organization: Making Learning Count* (1999) (co-authored with Karen E. Watkins) and *Informal Learning on the Job* (1999) (co-edited with F. Marie Volpe).

Bonnie McIvor (Bonnie.Mcivor@unilever.com) is Head of Learning for Unilever Plc. Based in London, she is responsible for the implementation of leadership skills for the Unilever organization worldwide. Prior to joining Unilever, Bonnie managed General Electric's Asian Region Centre for Leadership Development (Crotonville) located in Hong Kong. It was during this time that CAP was introduced in Asia. She was previously a programme manager at Crotonville, after having spent several years in marketing roles in GE.

Mika Nakano Honjo (mika.honjo@dentsu.co.jp) is a Senior Fellow with The 21st Century Public Policy Institute, Tokyo, Japan. She is on secondment from the Dentsu Institute for Human Studies, where she has served as a researcher since 1987 after working for the Japan Center for Economic Research (JCER). Since 1995, Mika has also held the position of lecturer on modern Japanese lifestyles and values, in the Faculty of Literature, Keio University. She graduated from the University of Tokyo and in 1976 became Japanese Junior Chess Champion and participated in the World Junior Chess Championship as the youngest and only female player at that event. Among her major publications (in Japanese) are: 'The Working Style of Women at a Turning Point – Ten Years Since the Implementation of the Equal Employment Opportunity Act' (1996); 'The Psychology of Cross-Cultural Contact' (1995) (co-author, published by Kawashima Shoten,); 'Cross-Cultural Conflict Management in Corporations' (1993); 'Cross-Cultural Education in Executive Development' (1992); and 'Changing Sense of Values and Its Effects on Marriage and Families' (1992).

Judy O'Neil (jaoneil@aol.com) is President of the consulting firm Partners for the Learning Organization. She works with companies in the USA and internationally interested in development and change through action learning, and in becoming learning organizations. She has authored a number of journal articles and book chapters on her action learning work and research. Judy's doctoral research was on the role of learning coaches in action learning. Her most recent publications include co-editing the book *Action Learning: Successful Strategies for Individual, Team, and Organizational Development* (1999) and co-editing *What Works Online: Action Learning: Real Work, Real Learning* (2000). Judy is also an Assistant Professor and

Coordinator of the Organizational Management Masters Programme at Eastern Connecticut State University and has served as adjunct faculty at Teachers College, Columbia University.

Richard Pearson (rp@attglobal.net.) is an organizational change and development facilitator and executive coach working with CEOs and their teams to meet the challenges of the new team-based global economy. His company, LIM Asia, is the representative in Hong Kong for Leadership in International Management which develops global leaders through action reflection learning. His clients in Asia include Merck, Motorola, Mandarin Oriental Hotels, CLP Holdings, Schick, Korn/Ferry, Merrill Lynch, ING Barings, ON Seminconductor, Pepsi and SWIFT, as well as individual CEOs and entrepreneurs. He is also a guest lecturer at the Queen's University Executive MBA programme in Canada. Having lived and worked in 12 countries in Asia since 1988, Richard is passionate about assisting organizations develop a learning culture especially in a cross-cultural context.

Konrad Raiser is General Secretary of the World Council of Churches since 1993. He earned a doctorate in theology from the Protestant Theological Faculty in Tübingen, and before assuming his role in the WCC he was Professor of Systematic Theology/Ecumenics at the Protestant Theological Faculty of the University of the Ruhr, Bochum, and Director of the Faculty's Ecumenical Institute. Among other academic, church and ecumenical committee assignments during these years, he served on the commission of the German Protestant Kirchentag and as chair of the editorial board of the quarterly Ökumenische Rundschau. He is the author of four books (*Identität und Sozialität* [1971]; *Ökumene im Übergang* [1989] – English translation, Ecumenism in Transition (1991); *Wir stehen noch am Anfang* [1994]; and *To Be the Church* [1997]) and the editor of four others, with more than 200 articles and essays on theological and ecumenical subjects, including four entries in the *Dictionary of the Ecumenical Movement* (WCC Publications) for which he was also a member of the editorial board.

Tali Ramon is Marketing and Outreach Director of TIM, responsible for market research and communications, client development and public relations. Her previous experience includes coaching and management training for Israeli companies.

Åke Reinholdsson (ake@aru.se), since the fall of 1995, runs his own consulting firm in Stockholm, AR Utveckling AB, specializing in human strategies. He is a partner of the Global Executive Learning Network (GEL) and has assisted leading companies in their business driven action learning approaches and programmes in Europe. Åke studied at the University of Upsala and graduated in 1970, after which he joined the Swedish subsidiary of Philips Electronics where he worked for 17 years mainly in people development, including coordination of projects for the Nordic national organizations. From 1975 to 1986 he was the vice-President (VF) Human Resources for the major industrial units. In 1987 he joined Caliper, a human resource consultancy in Princeton, USA. He became VP Human Resources in KF Industri AB, Stockholm in 1990. During the years 1992–95 he was the Human Resources Director of the City of Stockholm.

Isabel Rimanoczy (ISABEL.RIMANOCZY@LIMGLOBAL.NET) is a partner of and LIM's Regional Manager for Latin America. She has worked in North America, Latin America, Europe and Asia with multinational corporations in the areas of organizational analysis and diagnosis, change and transition management, recruitment, coaching and executive development. Her writings have appeared in North American, South American and European business magazines. Isabel has an MA in Psychology from the University of Buenos Aires and an MBA from the University of Palermo. Isabel is the author of the *Handbook for Mergers and Acquisitions* (2000) and co-author of the LIM *Learning Coach Handbook* (2000) and the *Leader Coach Handbook* (2001). She has been editor of a monthly newsletter on management issues (*IRNews*) and co-editor of the *ARL News* and is presently working on the first book on Action Reflection Learning.

Nicolas Rolland (nico.rolland@free.fr) recently completed his PhD at the University of Grenoble. He has conducted a research project on Knowledge Management through Strategic Alliances with the Institute for Knowledge Management (Cambridge, USA). His current research concentrates on organizational learning and change, knowledge management and strategic alliances. Nicolas has authored a chapter 'Knowledge Transfer in Strategic Alliances' (2000) and has spoken at numerous conferences on knowledge management and action learning. He is also an academic partner of the European Centre for Knowledge Management (e^CKM, Marseille, France). Nicolas worked as a research fellow in an international management institute before joining M&N e-Intelligence where he supervises the research department.

Raymond Saner (saner@OrganisationalConsultants.com) is President and Partner of Organizational Consultants Ltd., a consulting firm specializing in change management. He is also a Director of the Centre for Socio-Eco-Nomic Development in Geneva, Switzerland. Nineteen years of experience in training and consulting in the fields of globalization, leadership development and international negotiations with multinational companies, governments and training institutions. He has worked extensively in Europe, North America, Asia, Africa and Latin America. He has also been consultant to the United Nations and its institutions and other intergovernmental organizations. Raymond also teaches at the Economic Science Centre of Basle University in Switzerland, and he has published extensively on the topics of international negotiations, human resource development and training and global leadership.

Peg Tourloukis (ptourloukis@attbi.com) is President of the Leadership Development Network, a company that specializes in helping clients around the globe achieve corporate goals through focused management training, executive coaching and action learning. Since 1984 she has served as an external consultant to General Electric as a member of the design and teaching faculty at Crotonville, GE's Management Development Institute, and as action learning coach for executives in GE's diverse businesses. Besides GE, her clients include Ford Motor Company, J.P.Morgan and General Mills. Recalling her former career as a public school teacher, Peg also consults with schools and community service organizations. She lives with her husband and two sons in Amherst, Massachusetts.

Krystyna Weinstein (krystyna.weinstein@virgin.net) is an independent consultant working in the UK who applies the action learning philosophy, values and processes in all her work. She has been involved in action learning programmes for many years in both the private and voluntary sectors, and is the author of *Action Learning: A Practical Guide* (2nd edn, 1999).

Lichia Yiu (saneryiu@csend.org), Chinese born in Taiwan with roots on both sides of the Taiwan Strait, received her doctorate from Indiana University and did postdoctoral studies in organizational psychology at Columbia University. Together with her husband and partner, Raymond Saner, she founded the Centre for Socio-Economic Development (CSEND) in Geneva in 1993, a non governmental research and development organization. Lichia has published books and articles on human resource development and training, leadership, and large system change.

Lyle Yorks (yorks@exchange.tc.columbia.edu) is Associate Professor of Adult and Organizational Learning, Teachers College, Columbia University, where he teaches courses in human resource development, strategy and leadership. He has researched and consulted on action learning, performance management, and staff and executive development issues with companies around the world. His recent books include (co-edited with Judy O'Neil and Victoria Marisck) *Action Learning: Successful Strategies for Individual, Team, and Organizational Learning*, in the Advances in Developing Human Resources monograph series sponsored by the Academy of Human Resource Development (1999), and *Collaborative Inquiry in Practice* (2000) (co-authored with John Bray, Joyce Lee and Linda Smith). Articles authored and co-authored by Lyle have appeared in the *Academy of Management Review, California Management Review, Human Resource Development Quarterly, Performance Improvement Quarterly, Sloan Management Review* and other professional journals. He holds Master of Arts degrees from Vanderbilt University and Columbia University and earned his doctorate at Columbia University.

Part I

What is Action Learning?
Context and Approaches

1
Action Learning: The Classic Approach
Krystyna Weinstein

In the past ten years or so, action learning has become 'fashionable'. Organizations of all kinds – private, public, voluntary – claim to be 'doing it'. Many are. But many are not!

How can I justify making such a bold statement? Well, easily, actually, if I look at what Professor Reg Revans, the founder of the notion of the educational process he called 'action learning' (those are his words) first used in print in 1945, based on his experiences in hospitals and nursing in the late 1930s, and the coal pits during the Second World War – and what he is still advocating. Yet it is, he points out, not a new idea. Learning from what we do by reflecting on it and talking about it is an ancient idea. In a recent interview, he remarked that all he wants people to do is to keep pausing to ask themselves – after being told something by someone, maybe an expert – 'Do I agree with this? Do I understand it? Have I got any suggestions of my own?' – and then to act on these questions. He concluded by saying 'I think it's only by bartering our own misunderstandings that we learn better how to understand.'

What Revans actually says

Probably the best way to begin a piece on action learning is to quote from Reg Revans himself, in his own inimitable style. All that he says is based on fundamental beliefs that he holds, of which probably two of the main ones are that managerial learning is a social exchange, and that taking action is fundamental to any learning. I have extracted the following pieces from his book *The ABC of Action Learning* (1983):

> In any epoch of rapid change those organizations unable to adapt are soon in trouble, and adaptation is achieved only by learning, namely by being able to do tomorrow that which might have been unnecessary today, or to be able to do today what was unnecessary last week...training systems intended to develop our young may do little more than to make them proficient in yesterday's techniques. Thus learning cannot be

solely the acquisition of new programmed knowledge... When none can say what the morrow shall bring forth, none can tell what stock of programmed propositions is most economically applicable... So it is that the subjective aspects of searching the unfamiliar, or of learning to pose useful and discriminating questions in conditions of ignorance, risk and confusion, must become as well understood, and as effectively employed, by managers as are all the syllabuses of programmed instruction... We may structure our argument from the outset by identifying the acquisition of programmed knowledge as P, and of questioning insight as Q, so writing the learning equation as $L = P + Q$.[1] (p. 11)

... This does not imply that action learning rejects all formal instruction (P); it merely recognises that such instruction, aimed at imparting what is normally known to others... cannot of itself stimulate the posing of insightful questions (Q)... P may be necessary but in the absence of Q cannot be sufficient. (p. 12)

Traditional instruction (P) prepares for the treatment of puzzles, or difficulties from which escapes are thought to be known, even although the escape or solution may be hard to discover, and call for the skill of experts; action learning, on the other hand, deals with the resolution of problems (and the acceptance of opportunities) about which no single course of action is to be justified by any code of programmed knowledge, so that different managers, all reasonable, experienced, and sober, might set out by treating them in markedly different ways; problems and opportunities are treated by leaders who must be aware of their own value systems, differing between individuals, and of the influences of their past personal experiences; these will strongly influence their subjective judgements and, hence, their predisposing willingness to take risks; such risks are diminished to the extent that further discriminating questions are posed and answered; this demands exploratory insight (Q). (p. 12)

Revans is stating that P – 'that which is deployed by experts' – is insufficient when tackling real-time work-focused problems or opportunities. Q he defines as 'an ability to pose useful questions when there can be no certainty as to what next might happen'. And his use of the term 'exploratory insight' is important, for it implies more than merely asking questions; he is stating something about the quality of those questions, which must be a full exploration of everything that impinges on an action – or inaction. As he puts it, 'all will constantly be required to expose for the most exacting scrutiny just what they think they are up to – and why'.

Revans is adamant that fundamental to action learning – and to an action learning programme – is that... 'each participant attacks a real-life task for which no course of treatment has yet been suggested... [He] is there to observe himself in managerial action.'[2]

The primary occupation of managers is to treat their problems (or to seize their opportunities) and these may be defined as the conditions that either obstruct or advance the attainment of their goals; managers, in other words, must make up their minds about what to do and settle for doing it. All secondary activity should be linked as closely as possible to this every-day task. For this simple reason, action learning is cradled in the very task itself, asking whether that task can be done so that, merely by reflecting upon how it currently seems to be done, the very doing of it supplies the learning generally offered far from the scenes of managerial activity. (p. 12)

...After reports about all the facts have reached their desks, after all the advice has been offered, all the opinions listened to, after everything has been listed for the final plan and the most talkative of the experts is on his way back to the airport deciding in advance what he is going to tell his next client, the manager still remain alone with his responsibilities: he is the man who has to get something done. Specialists have uttered their warnings, research consultants have thrown doubt upon the accuracy of the data...the public relations officer sees certain weakness if the affair has to be reported on the international network, and the eco-nomic adviser, while voicing no views about the cash flow, still shakes his head, knits his brow and purses his lips about the 'cash flow situation'...One mission of action learning is to help him bear his spe-cial burden...Managers are not employed to describe, to analyse nor to recommend: they are engaged to act. (p. 50)

Revans here offers four notions for action learners: firstly, that of the task, and being very clear what it is; secondly, reflecting upon how actions are carried out, and not only on what is to be done. For, as he points out, 'so much of managerial action is necessarily an exchange of words (issues of instructions, agreement to pay, approval of measure, and so forth) that the distinctions between getting something done and talking about getting it done may be simply overlooked...'.

Thirdly, the word 'reflecting' takes us into the realm that Revans consid-ers vital to action learning:

Every participant will, from time to time, find himself down another blind alley...if he is out of ideas, or needs to face mounting opposition on the job, the [participants] will help him more clearly to perceive where he must look, for in doing so and discussing why they are doing so, they will also be strengthening themselves. The mind gone blank can do little with itself save panic, but a few supportive minds aware that they them-selves might, too, go blank at any moment can provide the most refresh-ing tonic...By needing to crawl along [the project's] subterranean labyrinths, each participant will come to respect the subtleties and the contradictions that compose his project; all these he will seek to balance and to record, constantly stopping and turning to ask what is still unseen. In this exploration he will put aside instant response and turn to considerate reflection... (p. 39)

Lasting behavioural change is more likely to follow the re-interpretation of past experiences than the acquisition of fresh knowledge; among senior managers in particular, it is in re-reading what is already scribbled on the cortical slate that leads to changes in behaviour, rather than in copying out new messages upon it... such re-interpretations of past experience, being necessarily subjective, complex and ill-structured, are more likely to be intelligible through exchanges with other managers themselves anxious to learn by re-ordering their own perceptions than through discussions with non-managers (including teachers of management subjects) not exposed to real risk in responsible action... (p. 14)

So, fourthly, Revans focuses us on his meaning of learning – which amounts to self-knowledge. However,

...Any person, whether manager or not, changes his/her observable behaviour, or learns in the sense in which that word is used here, only if he/she wishes to do so; one learns, or changes, one's own behaviour of one's own volition and not at the will of others (unless under duress, bribery or other influences...); moreover one may be cognitively aware of a need to behave differently and yet remain determined not to do so in practice... (p. 14)

In learning such new behaviour, persons must attack real problems, preferable ill-defined, or fertile opportunities, howsoever remote, in such a manner as to remain continuously aware of their progress and of the influences determining that progress; in 'scientific' jargon, any system that is to learn, whether an individual manager or a national cabinet, must regularly receive and interpret inputs about is own outputs. (p. 13)

So, action learning is about learning about oneself by resolving a work-focused project, and reflecting on that action – and on oneself – in the company of others similarly engaged. To achieve this, Revans suggests four programme design options: (1) where participants work on a familiar problem in a familiar setting – within their own role in their own organization; (2) where participants work on a familiar problem in an unfamiliar setting – within their own role but in another organization; (3) where participants work on an unfamiliar problem in a familiar setting – tackling an issue outside their own work role in their own organization; and (4) where participants work on an unfamiliar problem in an unfamiliar setting – tackling an unfamiliar problem in another organization. Sets made up of people from different functions and from different organizations fulfil an element of option four, for they will be helping others in roles unfamiliar to them. Similarly, sets made up of participants from the same organization but from different functions fulfil an element of option two. The least challenging is a set where participants are all within the same job function and from the same organization. As Jean Lawrence points out (see below) it is diversity that leads to the greatest learning.

The other crucial ingredient of action learning is the 'set' – the group of like-minded people all engaged in learning from their actions. Revans calls this group a set to distinguish it from other working groups.

> The set [a group of four to six people] has been deliberately contrived so that managerial reflection can play upon the action of yesterday and anticipate the action of tomorrow... Action learning obliges participants to interpret all they are doing through the looking glasses of reflective argument; it obliges them constantly to polish the glasses so as to ensure its images are clearly seen. Whether he wipes clean his own mirror, or whether this is done for him by another member of the set, cannot be foretold... (p. 52)

Once into the programme, Revans suggests, sets should also meet to discuss how each participant's glasses are most effectively used, that is, to recognize their own individual learning, what is leading them to change their minds – whether by the action he or she is being forced to take, or whether from new interpretations forced by comments, or whether because he or she now has a new skill of holding his or her own looking-glass in a new way. By encouraging such open discussion – often between sets – Revans is in effect creating the beginning of a learning community.

As he again vividly puts it, those who... 'turn on at will their fountains of purest rhetoric uncontaminated by passing doubt have little to gain from action learning' (or, rather, they have much to learn, but will they chose to do so?). He continues: 'The learning dynamic is the recognition of a common ignorance rather than some collective superfluity of tradable knowledge... Action learning requires questions to be posed in conditions of ignorance, risk and confusion when nobody knows what to do next'. Thus, a prime idea of action learning is: 'Those unable to change themselves cannot change what goes on around them.'

The set is also intended... 'to make the participants in some degree curious about the impact they make on other persons, since they are about to start in a most unfamiliar fashion each upon their own substantial enquiry.' The set is 'the mirror in which the real-life action is reflected, not only from one participant to the next, just as are the empty containers pushed around the "case discussion", but also between the mind of the participant and the real world to which he will shortly return with his container freshly charged.'

A set – 'the cutting edge of every action learning program' – is thus a different sort of beast from any other group or meeting. And the actions that result from it may be about tasks to be carried out, but equally about belief or behavioural change. However, Revans is adamant that they are a far cry from the 'so-called sets that meet to exchange feelings and opinions not immediately derived from a current undertaking to change some reality, such as sensitivity training, or encounter groups.'

To achieve personal change with the help of the set – 'at which each gives to the others an account of his progress and his setbacks' – it is important, Revans underlines, that 'nothing must be allowed to stand in the way of the [participants'] regular appearances at it'. And because of the Q nature of the participants' interactions,

> [they] will ensure that no member of their set is allowed to coast along on the presentations of the others. All, with inexorable certitude, will be called upon to disclose much that they had for many years successfully hidden from themselves, such as what (if anything) they really believe in … or why they say the things they say, and do the things they do. (p. 52)

There is little doubt that inspiration for Revans' strong belief in the importance of such honesty sprang from a statement by Sir Ernest Rutherford, the physicist at the Cavendish Laboratory in Cambridge in the 1920s where Revans was himself a PhD student. After a meeting with fellow Nobel prizewinners, Rutherford exclaimed: 'Gentlemen, today I have become aware of the depth of my own ignorance. What does yours look like to you?'

To ensure that all this takes place, Revans says that it is important that each programme has a sponsor 'to act on behalf of the participants' and an individual client for each participant's project 'to ensure that something is done'. They in particular (though also the participants themselves) need to try and identify three key 'allies' for any undertaking: those who know about and understand the task or problem being tackled, who care about it and want something done, and who can have the power to do something about it.

Thus Revans' main thrust throughout his book, and in his other writing, is that action learning's main purpose is 'to develop the capacity to ask fresh questions rather than to communicate technical knowledge', all with a view to improving future actions. A well-designed action learning programme, he tells us,

> must engender within each participant the self-confidence that enables him to convince others that his advice is worth following simply because it is he himself who offers it. So it is that each participant must find out, in the course of the program, a lot of things about himself that he did not know when he joined.

Revans enjoys quoting what participants in a Belgian set responded when asked what was the most important question they had learnt to ask; it was 'What is an honest man, and what need I do to become one?' (p. 50)

Variations on a theme

Revans has acknowledged that recently the 'elements of action learning are offered under a great variety of ingenious brand names, from management action groups to executive exchange enrichment experience', but says he is pleased that there is 'scope for experimenting with the substance of action learning'. [3]

This is what is happening in many parts of the world, for action learning has taken hold in places as diverse as South Africa and Nepal, Colombia, Mexico and the USA, the Czech Republic, the UK, Scandinavia, the Netherlands, and many more places. It has also, as Revans predicted, moved out from the field of industrial and commercial management and permeated 'into many other forms of human development, including patient care, job creation, schools, labour relations.' Maybe, he ponders, the real challenge for action learning will be in its promise for industrial democracy, to bring the trade unions and the shop floor into raising the quality of life all round, not in productivity alone. The ills of society, too – violence, urban decay or unemployment – offer their own challenges which action learning is well able to help tackle.

There is, of course, a valid argument that any idea has to move with the times, has to adapt to be usable by people in a different time frame and context to when the idea was first mooted. But: where do we draw the line? What is it OK to change and adapt, and what needs to remain, for the original idea to be recognized, and for any such programme to still be called 'action learning'?

A debate about this took place a few years ago in the pages of a leading management development journal between two UK advocates of action learning.[4] Ian Cunningham posed the question:

Why should we care about keeping to definitions already established? One view is that it does not matter and that we should not be purist about these things. The problem with this 'anything goes stance' is that we end up in an Alice in Wonderland world which is fine for fairy stories but creates a mess in our world. The non-purist position is the equivalent of a chemist saying that sodium chloride and potassium fluoride are pretty similar and that, as sodium chloride is the more commonly known compound, we will call both NcCl and KF by the term 'sodium chloride'. Doing this in chemistry could harm some people, so making distinctions is important.

In our field, people may not be physically harmed as a result of these definition errors but they can end up wasting a great deal of money and hindering people's development. Therefore it is serious and we cannot ask to be treated as real professionals unless we take definitions seriously. Reg Revans has been quite right to criticise those who use the term 'action learning' in ways which are contrary to his definition of it. He invented the term, developed the ideas and provided us with rich material to take these ideas further. If any tired old course puts a bit of project work in it and calls itself 'action learning', and we don't challenge that, we are colluding with unacceptable practice.

In his rejoinder, Mark Easterby-Smith wrote:

The labels we use are based on agreed meanings; they are always subject to challenge and redefinition. No-one has the right to impose meaning on others – this is a liberal and relativistic position that I hold with some passion! Attempts to restrict usage of terms such as . . . action learning are dangerous because they inhibit experimentation and learning; they privilege the ideas of the past and downgrade experience.

Maybe because action learning's origins are in the UK, many programmes here adhere closely to Revans' original thesis. Thus substantial Revans elements can be found in most UK action learning programmes:

- a set, with up to six participants, which meets regularly, approximately once a month, for a day, over a six-month period;
- real-time work projects to be worked on (in a field familiar or unfamiliar to the participants, depending on the purpose of the programme): projects may be individual ones, or there may be a 'group' issue but where each individual works on a part of that task that is relevant and important for them;
- a sponsor for the programme, and clients for each participant's project;
- an emphasis on Q, that is the asking of helpful and explorative questions and the related skill of listening, and hence becoming more able to 'peel back the onion layers';
- a constant reminder to reflect – and become aware of insights and learning – by creating space at the end of the day when participants reflect on how they have been working together, the impact of this new way of working, and what they are learning;
- the presence – at least initially – of what Revans called a 'combiner' (more commonly known as a set adviser or facilitator), who models helpful interventions in the set, ensuring that the values and philosophy of action learning are followed. Most set advisers aim to work themselves out of a job as participants themselves become skilled at facilitating their

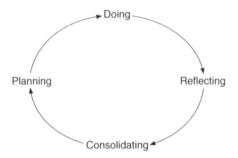

Figure 1.1   Learning cycle

own work (a skill not many miles removed from that of an effective manager or work colleague).

The Kolb learning cycle (Figure 1.1) is often used as a way of explaining – somewhat simplistically, inevitably – the steps needed for learning to take place: an action which is reflected on and from which some insights are drawn, followed by an undertaking to act on these in the future. In fact it is more of a learning spiral, for hopefully participants do not return to the same place they were at with their initial action! Of course, once participants become accustomed to reflecting, they will ideally be able to do so at any stage of a so-called learning cycle – including reflecting on their reflections! It is this need to go around a cycle a few times for the habit of recall, reflection and new actions to become an embedded new way of being that lies behind the usual length of six months for a programme.[5]

Elsewhere, Revans has written: 'Action learning takes so long to describe, so much longer to find interesting, and so much longer still to get started, because it is so simple.' And it is to help with this complex simplicity that many action learners have added their own tools, often extrapolating from Revans' writings and adding dimensions to help participants leap across the hurdle and begin to reflect on their own strengths and gaps, to become more aware of the processes they are using, focusing on this difficult concept called learning; that is, developing a self-awareness, an awareness of others, building insights, becoming more thoughtful.

Tampering with the learning equation

Inevitably, maybe, Revans' learning equation of $L = P + Q$ has been rewritten in several forms. Among some of the variations are:

- $Q1 + P + Q2 = L$, where Q begins at the reflection stage of the learning cycle, to which is added some P before further Q emerges. This equation has relevance for more academically-based programmes;

- $P + Q + A + R = L$, where the notions of action and the new (for many) skill of reflection are included;
- $P + Q + Sk = L$, which recognizes the skill needed to ask helpful Q: what Marilee Goldberg (1998) has called 'learner questions' as opposed to 'judger questions'.

Others point out that P – programmed knowledge – is not just what is read about in books, articles (or chapters!) but is all the programmed beliefs, assumptions and hence behaviours that each of us carries around without thinking (our personal baggage!), and which needs to be addressed if we are to learn and change.

And what is the task of the programme?

Before embarking on designing an action learning programme, it is vital to be clear – as Jean Lawrence (see also below) points out – about the purpose of the programme. By definition all programmes will require each participant to work on a project or task, but in service of what? Is the aim primarily to develop participants, or is it to develop the organization they work for? Whichever it is will change, somewhat, the emphasis of what participants work and focus on, whether in the set or outside it, although both will occur in any well-designed action learning programme.

It would be easy to list many people in the UK who have nudged the notion of action learning forward from Revans' original idea, or extrapolated from it. I have chosen just six.

The learning cycle and learning styles

Professor Alan Mumford with Peter Honey, both independent consultants, have always had a keen interest in the learning process, and the need for participants to 'recognise learning as a specific discrete activity, because otherwise it will get lost in the task'. As they rightly point out 'Many participants will have had no previous acquaintance with the idea that learning is a process which can be looked at and which individuals can understand and develop for themselves.'

They recognized the association of four preferred learning styles which correspond to different parts of the learning cycle (Figure 1.2). This has helped both participants and facilitators to better understand why different people have greater or less ease with learning at different stages of an action/learning cycle.

Activists, who enjoy tackling problems, 'are not likely to favour what they would regard as too frequent or too lengthy attempts to review what has been done and what has been learned.' In other words, they will be impatient – maybe even uncooperative – when asked to reflect and 'theorize'. Yet this is crucial for learning to take place. Reflectors, by contrast, will feel quite at

Figure 1.2   Learning cycle and learning styles

home at the reflective stage of a learning cycle – and hence with the whole concept of action learning – but may sometimes need to be pushed into action. Theoretists will like the opportunity of being stretched by a complex problem, and are the most likely to want inputs of *P*. Again they may also need to be encouraged to be more active, and may feel unhappy when faced with uncertainties and risks. Pragmatists tend to enjoy action learning programmes because the whole basis for them is to undertake and implement something practical at their place of work! The ideal set is made up of people who reflect these four preferences. In their book *Manual of Learning Styles*, Honey and Mumford (1992) offer a questionnaire to elicit each person's preferred learning style, with hints on how to enhance those least developed. An effective learner, they feel, is someone who has a balance of styles.

An action learning community

At the Corporation of London, Ray Mahoney, while Learning and Development manager, created – with participants – what they called an Action Learning Community. The idea emerged when Mahoney became puzzled by why it was difficult to encourage organizations to use action learning on a wider basis. As he put it:

> One day during the process review at the end of an action learning day, a suggestion emerged that we should stop trying to fit people into permanent sets. Workloads and priorities changing at short notice seemed the main reason for non-attendance at meetings. Having discarded the closed set – this most sacred of institutions – how could we work? (personal communication to author).

Someone suggested that the 50 or so people already involved in action learning call themselves the Action Learning Community. They decided on six community days a year for 'old hands', two months apart, coupled with three 'What is action learning?' introductory days for newcomers. The agenda for each community day was – typically – working on work issues. People attended all day, or for half a day. They formed sets around an issue brought by one or two people, or explored a topic in a set. Throughout they maintained the confidentiality crucial for any real work to be achieved in a set.

This model of action learning departs from Revans' precept that every set member presents his or her issue at each meeting. Only one or two people have such an opportunity at each meeting, set members vying with each other for the time-space at the outset of a meeting. Purists might argue that waiting maybe for up to three meetings – and hence in this instance possibly six months – to present the issue they are working on is not fulfilling Revans' original notion. But participants commented that this was more than made up for by learning to help others, and creating this network of relationships and experience.

Another set of five action learners, mostly independent consultants, also decided to see 'just how robust and flexible is the methodology?' They invited five new people to be interviewed to join them. Then, at each meeting, the group of ten divided into two self-selected – and rotating – sets depending either on choice of issues to be worked on, or around 'pragmatics', with no more than five people in either set, but ensuring that initially each set had a mix of 'old' and 'new' members. And they nominated one of the set to act as facilitator until, as one of them put it 'we were all more versed in the black arts of crowd control, equity of voice and understanding of action learning'. This experiment, said participants, gave them 'constant freshness, revitalised energy and a wholly different sense of challenge and support'.

Action learning and collaborative enquiry

Mike Pedler, currently associated with the Revans Institute for Action Learning and Research at Salford University (see also below) has focused on developing the – now obvious to many action learners – link between action learning and collaborative learning. His definition of the latter is 'learning to achieve things together', suggesting that 'learning can also take place in relationships'. He talks of team learning, the learning community (again) and the learning organization, which 'involve collective learning, co-operating in understanding, and acting to do things together on behalf of the whole. Here learning outcomes are not fully measured in terms of what individuals achieve, but by what is jointly created'. As he puts it 'the entity which is action learning is a flow of consciousness, of action and learning, between the inner (person) and outer (organizational problem) and vice versa, a continuous, iterative process.'

In a challenging chapter 'What do We Mean by Action Learning?' in *Action Learning in Practice*, Pedler (1997) explains the three-pronged nature of action learning, which are not mutually excluding – and is particularly drawn to the third:

- changing the external world;
- self-development;
- collaborative enquiry.

In collaborative enquiry,

> the focus is on the relationship of people in the set, and by extension with the wider context, rather than upon the individual actors and their organizational problems...The focus is on collective processes which may have a greater potential to transform the whole. Instead of individuals trying to change things on their own, this perspective has the person participating in a shared process of meaning-making, creating frameworks of understanding within which all may act.

Thus, 'where members share a common interpretation or a common way of making sense, a change in this can only come about through a dialogue which involves them all'.

Here Pedler is using the word 'dialogue' as David Bohm understood it: stemming from the Greek *dia* (through) and *logos* (word), a dialogue emphasizes the idea of a meaning that flows between people from which emerges a greater understanding – possibly even a shared meaning.

So, as Pedler stresses, there is a link between action learning, collaborative learning and organizational learning, and action learning is one way of understanding the organizational learning process. Revans himself saw this link which Nancy Dixon (1999) has graphically illustrated in her book *The Organizational Learning Cycle*.

Thus, one could claim that the processes of collaborating and communicating which action learning instils into set members become a model to be transferred to back-at-work encounters. The set – 'a community of practice of shared work, knowledge and ways of knowing' – is in essence a learning organization in miniature, where action learning, as Pedler points out, is 'an idea rather than a method'.

Working with differences

If collaboration is the key to the future success of organizations, Jean Lawrence, one of the original action learners in the UK with over 30 years experience of using its principles in all her work, brings to action learning a crucial dimension. From her experience of working with groups at the London-based Tavistock Institute, much of her focus is on helping participants understand the influence of the unconscious and how it affects not only relationships in the set, but also each individual as he or she struggles with the issue they have brought to work on. How does the set help or hinder each person with their working and their learning? As set members become conscious of what their underlying motives or fears are, and feel able to express and explore them, so they are also better able to understand colleagues back at work, with their unconscious motives and feelings.

Working mostly with senior managers and running intercompany programmes, she sees the bringing together of people from different roles in different walks of life as the main value of intercompany sets. This means that participants will be focusing on each others' 'unfamiliar' problems in 'unfamiliar' settings. The difference which each brings adds tremendously to the learning opportunities. For differences create more surprises, challenges and what Revans calls 'fresh questions about unconscious assumptions' – and result in greater exploration. Criticism and advice suddenly become redundant. Participants have only their common experiences as managers to draw on, and cannot fall back on shared organizational culture or professional know-how when supporting or challenging each other. Working in an intercompany set also avoids the likelihood of politics, rivalries or career concerns motivating the exchanges between set members. Thus the whole person, and not just the role person, is present to work with in the set.

Focusing on the values of action learning

Professor Tom Bourner, with Sue O'Hara and other colleagues at Brighton University's Management Development Research Unit, have been investigating how to help sets become self-facilitating. Revans suggests using facilitators to begin the process, but warns against the dependence created by continued reliance on them. Many have tried to let sets run on their own, with mixed results. At best the sets end up as project discussion groups and at worst they cease to meet. So what is the key to enabling them to self-facilitate their action learning set? Obviously, knowledge of the processes of action learning with its focus on questioning and the allocation of air space to each participant, with equal time being given to talking about action and learning.

But for Bourner and his colleagues the difference that makes the difference is whether or not participants subscribe to the values and beliefs underpinning action learning, and these need to be made explicit at the outset. Revans is very clear about the beliefs about learning on which action learning is based (as already outlined). According to Bourner and his colleagues, the core values underpinning action learning include:

- Learning for the purpose of making a difference (rather than learning for its own sake or for the sake of intellectual curiosity);
- Feedback (rather than protecting current own knowledge from the challenge of action or from the responses of other set members);
- Support and challenge of peers (rather than solitary learning);
- Self-responsibility and proactivity (rather than passivity or reactivity);

- Learning from action and action informed by learning (rather than action and learning being separate domains with learning as the passive one);
- Giving and receiving (the commitment to an action learning set is based on this).

The result is a programme of action learning without 'external' facilitators preceded by a workshop focused on (1) facilitation skills, (2) the beliefs of action learning, and (3) the values underlying action learning. These three elements of the workshop address the three familiar questions: who knows, who cares and who can? When problems occur in the process of an action learning set, as described in Cunningham (1987), participants who subscribe to the values and beliefs of action learning and have developed facilitation skills have what is necessary to find or create their own solutions.

The Revans Institute for Action Learning and Research

One of the more innovative uses of action learning is currently taking place at the Salford University-based Revans Institute for Action Learning and Research, where Revans is himself a Professorial Fellow. There are four research programmes where participants gain either a diploma, an MSc, an M.Phil or a PhD. Although called research programmes, the 'research' is in fact about each participant's work and practical actions: either their current job, or their role, or the issues they are facing at work, or the changes they need to bring about. They work on what is important to them, what matters to them, what risks they need to be taking.

Current participants come from 33 different professional groups and include managers from the medical and teaching professions; from local government; and owners of small or medium-sized businesses. Their backgrounds are as varied as their current jobs and roles, and their acceptance on the programme, as well as their decision of a 'project' are the result of numerous conversations with the staff of the Institute.

David Botham, Director of the Institute, talks of participants 'researching themselves doing their jobs'. There is no set syllabus (or 'silly-bus' as Revans might say!), although participants create their own massive reading lists. They meet frequently and regularly in sets with others, to share their actions, together with their progress, their thoughts and their doubts. Staff are on hand seven days a week, 24 hours a day, to help participants who might be stuck on some real-time work issue.

Evaluation takes into account what participants have achieved and a description of what they've learnt, an explanation of what, and how, they've learnt from others – in their sets or from written material, and a clear indication of how they intend to move forward in the future.

Action learning's future

Over the past few years there has been growing interest in the United Kingdom – as elsewhere – in large systems methodologies such as search conferencing, collaborative enquiry, open space and other approaches aimed at involving large groups of people in resolving their organization's needs and quests. They all have in common a recognition that everyone has something to offer. The trick has been to collect and harness these collective insights and energies. Action learning's deeply democratic philosophy and processes are totally in tune with these developments and, integrated with them, enable decisions – once taken – to be acted upon collaboratively.

Notes

1 His other equation, $L \geq C$, implies that learning must take place at a rate equal to or faster than the rate of change if organizations and those within them are to survive.
2 Revans uses the terms his/her and he/she in many places, though not always in the texts I have quoted. It is plain, however, that he means both. He also uses the word 'manager' throughout; but this has no bearing on the variety of programmes involving non-managers that both he and others have since run.
3 The focus on real-life work-based projects as a vehicle for learning, and on a group approach to resolving problems (though not always working as a set, with its characteristics), as well as some focus on learning (though often in a narrower sense than Revans envisaged) have meant that the term 'action learning' is applied to many programmes. However, I have chosen to omit these in this chapter.
4 *Organisations and People* (1996), vol. 3(2).
5 Being a scientist, Revans himself suggested a five-step scientific approach: of observation, hypothesis, testing, reviewing and controlling; that is, empirically testing managerial actions!

References

Dixon, N. (1994) *The Learning Organization*. New York: McGraw Hill.
Dixon, N. (1999) *The Organizational Learning Cycle*, 2nd edn. Aldershot: Gower.
Goldberg, M. C. (1997) *The Art of the Question*. Chichester, UK: John Wiley.
Heney, P. and Mumford, A. (1992) *Manual of Learning Styles*. Maidenhead: Peter Honey.
Cunningham, I. (1987) 'Structuring Set Advisor Training using Simulated Analysis'. *Training and Management Development Methods*, vol. 1(1).
Cunningham, I. and Easterby-Smith, M. (1996) Debate. *Organisations and People*, vol. 3(2); pp. 41–7.
Pedler, M. (ed). (1997) *Action Learning in Practice*. 3rd edn. Aldershot: Gower.
Revans, R. (1983) *The ABC of Action Learning*, republished 1998. London: Lemos & Crane.

2

Action Reflection Learning™ and Critical Reflection Approaches

Lyle Yorks, Judy O'Neil and Victoria Marsick

Yury Boshyk (2000) has noted that 'The house of action learning has many doors.' One of those doors is represented by an approach to action learning that emphasizes critical reflection and transformative learning and change. A prominent room that this critically reflective door leads to is the Action Reflection Learning™ or ARL™ model of action learning.[1] In this chapter we differentiate the critical reflection approach from other varieties of action learning, examine the history of the ARL™ model as an exemplar of this approach, look at some examples of ARL™ and other critical reflection action learning programmes, and discuss the strengths and limitations of ARL™.

Action learning

All of the varieties of action learning (AL) have in common a focus on helping people to learn through using work on an actual project or problem as the vehicle for learning (Yorks, O'Neil and Marsick, 1999). People work in small groups in order to help one another learn from the action they take to resolve their problem. They also learn how to learn from their actions, a process often facilitated by a learning coach who helps the participants to balance their work on the project or problem with the learning from doing that work. This is the key distinction between action learning and case study or other forms of experiential programmes such as outdoor adventure experiences that seek to elicit principles for later application in work settings. Action learning focuses on an actual or real work problem in real time. A fundamental assumption underlying AL is that people are most likely to experience significant learning when working on issues of real relevance to their lives.

Varieties of AL practice

During her research into various approaches to working with participants described by experienced action learning coaches, O'Neil (1999) identified four distinct approaches or 'schools' of AL practice – (1) the tacit school, (2) the scientific school, (3) the experiential school, and (4) the critical reflection school. It is beyond the scope of this chapter to describe each of the four variations. Elsewhere in this volume in the chapter by Steven Hicks, and in Yorks *et al.* (1999) these are described in detail. We have hypothesized a hierarchical-like relationship among the schools from tacit, through scientific, experiential and critical reflective approaches, with each level involving a deeper focus around questioning insight that is increasingly more critical and complex. Which approach is most appropriate for a particular situation is highly contingent on learning goals and context.

Critical reflection school of action learning

The defining characteristic of the critical reflection school of action learning is found in the type of reflection focused on by learning coaches. In the critical reflection approach, emphasis is placed on taking reflection to a level of challenging the premises underlying the thinking of participants, along with taken-for-granted norms of their organization. As such, this approach is a useful tool for examining the deep culture of an organization and creating space for transformative development on the part of participants. The goal is personal and organizational transformation by effecting a change in the processes of learning so as to affect a change in one's whole assumptive frame of reference. This is accomplished by learning coaches through the use of reflection to generate what Edward Cell (1984) has called trans-situational learning: learning how to change one's acts of interpretation through critical reflection on one's own learning processes. In other words, learning to learn generatively.

   Whether or not critical reflection is appropriate for a particular situation depends on the initial tolerance of participants, the organizational culture in which they function, and the learning intentions of the leadership group that symbolically shapes that culture. These issues will be explored in more depth later in this chapter. First, we will examine the history of the critical reflection school of action learning.

The emergence of the action reflection learning™ model

Many practitioners discuss the use of critical thinking and reflection in action learning. In the UK, Weinstein (1995) and Pedler (1996) discuss examining norms and values; taking action and critically reflecting on that action; and reframing and transforming problems in the action learning process. In the

United States, Dilworth (1996) discusses asking fresh questions for unfreezing underlying assumptions and creating new mental models, while Raelin (1993) advocates reflecting on the way in which the problem is formulated, tested and solved.

The critical reflection school finds one of its earliest full programmatic expressions in the approach of the Management in Lund (MiL) Institute, based in Sweden; and in both Leadership in International Management (LIM) and Cross Cultural Training (CCT), both based in the United States but working globally. MiL is a non-profit foundation established in 1977 by a network of companies, members of the staff at Lund University, various free agents, consultants and people from other universities at the initiative of Lennart Rohlin. The Institute describes its goal as contributing to strategic renewal, organizational development and effective management. Its core competence is designing and implementing learning processes that provide for both individual development and profitable results to participating companies:

> MiL is an idea and value based organisation with a humanistic perspective on people, a process oriented outlook on development and, to a large extent, a self developed learning philosophy and perspective on leadership. These perspectives constitute important departure points for how MiL runs, develops and organises [its] business. (MiL website, 2000).

Organized as a not-for-profit network of staff members and participating companies, personal development and face-to-face interaction are continuing hallmarks of MiL's work.

LIM is a private consulting organization based in the United States that shares many of MiL's principles. Like MiL, LIM also places a strong emphasis on personal development through intensive face-to-face interaction spread over time while working on important projects. Lars Cederholm, a former founding partner of LIM who works through his own long time firm CCT and as a MiL staff member also uses the ARL™ principles he helped to pioneer in his work. MiL developed ideas akin to, but separate from, the action learning practices championed by Reg Revans in Great Britain. Different from Revans, MiL developed a focus on learning coaches, working with participants in a co-learner relationship, but taking accountability for assertively catalyzing learning in the process.

The MiL focus on reflection places emphasis on participants developing their own theories of action through reflection on their own experience contrasted with the traditional business-school approach of teaching expert-based models. MiL extends this distinction, setting its approach apart from 'classical' action learning by emphasizing the synthesis of an action reflection theory through developing a learning community among researchers and managers who are seeking to understand the world through the interaction between theory and practice. We suspect this orientation was culturally influenced by the strong emergence of participatory action research models in the Scandinavian countries during this period. Rohlin, Skarvad and Nilsson (1994) developed MiL's learning principles and extended them to the concept of leadership in a learning society.

In 1985 an old friend of Lars Cederholm who was working with MiL visited the United States and renewed his acquaintance with Lars and his colleagues. Subsequently, Lars and his partner Ernie Turner participated as faculty in the personal development week of an MiL programme, and were impressed by the extent to which personal development grew out of action leading to actual business development. Lennart Rohlin and his colleagues were visiting the United States during the 1980s seeking alternative ways of diffusing MiL principles, and series of conversations ensued the outcome of which was the emergence in 1986 of LIM (a name suggested by MiL) with Lars and Ernie as its co-leaders. LIM became the American-based representative of the MiL approach and its co-leaders participated as staff members in MiL programmes. The alliance between the two groups represented MiL's interest in stimulating different ways of supporting the ideas and principles of this approach.

Lars and Ernie began discussing the MiL approach among interested members of the New York area Organizational Development network, including Tony Pearson, now a LIM partner, and Victoria Marsick, a professor of adult education at Teachers College, Columbia University.

Cultural differences between North American companies and those in Sweden soon emerged. Firms in the United States were not open to the kind of consortium or partnership programmes that were the foundation of the MiL model. LIM proposed in-house programmes because companies were not open to the multi-company model in which several companies sent executives to a programme, each with a project that would potentially be selected. Each participant would be assigned to a project team composed of members from other firms. No executive would work on a project team assigned a project from his or her company – part of the design for maximizing learning by immersing participants in a setting outside of their personal experience base.

During this time Victoria Marsick brought an emphasis on critical reflection to the LIM model (Marsick and Cederholm, 1988). Her research (Marsick, 1990) linked the transformative learning theory of Jack Mezirow (1981, 1985, 1991), with its focus on premise reflection for personal transformative learning, to workplace learning and by extension to action learning (O'Neil and Marsick, 1994). It was during this period that LIM suggested the term Action Reflection Learning to MiL in order to give increased focus to the role of reflection in their programmes. Both organizations subsequently registered the term.

LIM continued to develop and utilize the basic MiL design of programmes consisting of four weeks, spread over a four to six-month period, emphasizing personal development and business development through repeated cycles of action and reflection on projects within teams. Each programme also became a learning community.

Victoria Marsick subsequently left LIM to form 'Partners for the Learning Organization' with University of Georgia Professor Karen Watkins and Judy O'Neil to develop more fully the linkages between ARL™ practices and learning organizations. They emphasize critical reflection in the practices they use to foster individual, group, and organizational learning. All continue collegially to share experiences in critical reflective practice to further develop methods and designs.

Below we describe two of the early ARL™ programmes, which in many ways have provided the foundation for the realization that ARL™ is really a set of principle + values + elements, not a hard and fast design. This set includes question-driven, business and work-focused interventions; co-design with the client organization; just-in-time learning support; learning coach support; reflection as an important part of the programme, and action and follow-up on results. LIM has used these this set of practices in many different 'learning in action' situations including learning coach development programmes with Coca-Cola, Motorola and the Inter-American Bank, and in an MBA setting. CCT has applied these same principles in helping to jump-start the After School Programme in New York City and with a major European defense contractor. Interventions incorporating ARL™ principles and practices can last from a couple days to an academic semester.

Two early programmes

To further illustrate the ARL™ model, we next describe two early programmes – one headed by MiL, in which LIM associates worked, and one headed by LIM.

Volvo Truck Corporation

In the late 1980s, Volvo Truck Corporation (VTC) faced a number of external and internal challenges. The changing global environment was creating the need for VTC to reconsider its abilities in facing new competition and a focus on the customer. Internally, VTC was going through a rapid global expansion through acquisitions and mergers, while at the same time reorganizing into a more decentralized structure. These changes set the stage for the need for a change and development programme that would address both individual and organizational needs (O'Neil, Arnell and Turner, 1996).

At the time, VTC had been a member of the MiL network for about 10 years and had sent a few of their executives each year to participate in programmes. The need here, however, was for a much more significant development effort. Working with VTC, MiL developed an ARL™ programme to meet these specific needs. VTC ran one programme a year from 1990 through 1999 with 16–20 participants per programme. Programmes ran for a total of 25 days, divided into four weeks, and were split between residential seminars and project work. Participants were divided into four project teams that addressed strategic VTC issues that were outside the normal scope of their work areas. A high-level executive sponsored these issues. Each team worked with a learning coach drawn from MiL and LIM staff.

These staff worked to create situations that would enable critical reflection and personal transformative learning and organizational change. Lamm (2000) studied graduates from the VTC programme to understand what conditions enabled personal transformative learning. She found several conditions that enabled the participants to question their underlying assumptions and premises resulting in critical reflection. For example, participants cited having little or no experience in a learning area – the projects that were outside of their work area – led to transformative learning. 'I had a limited cross-function view...during the program, I realized other people looked upon things differently'. In another example, participants stressed the need for an open and trusting environment where they felt safe to be honest and vulnerable and supported in their learning. The conditions the participants described mirror many of the conditions Mezirow (1991) describes as needed for critical reflection.

Organizational change and transformation from critical reflection in the programme often came about as a result of a reframing of the original project. For example, one team was given a project to look at how an engineering process was being managed and to make some recommendations to improve it. Through the questioning and critical reflection that is a part of ARL™, participants realized that rather than focusing on improving the existing process, they needed to think about what the concept of engineering needed to look like in the future. They saw the strength of their own cross-functional team, and the assumptions that drove their work together, and ended up recommending a completely different engineering concept. After the CEO saw the results of their work he began to promote the use of cross-functional teams throughout the company. The output of this team ended up transforming not only the engineering function, but work overall in the company (O'Neil *et al.*, 1996).

Grace Cocoa

A second programme, headed up by Lars Cederholm and Ernie Turner of LIM, was with Grace Cocoa. At the time of the programme Grace Cocoa was 79 per cent owned by W. R. Grace and Co. and was the world's largest manufacturer of industrial chocolate, selling to food companies worldwide. Having been built through a series of acquisitions of prestigious companies, beginning with W. R. Grace and Co.'s purchase of Ambrosia Chocolate in the United States and Cacao DeZaan in Holland in 1964, Grace Cocoa was a multinational corporation with three divisions – World Press, Chocolate Europe and Chocolate America – that exhibited little cooperation between themselves (Dennis, Cederholm and Yorks, 1996). For a variety of reasons the CEO, Pedro Mata, believed that creating a truly integrated global organization with a single profit-and-loss statement mentality was critical to the future success of the company. These reasons included a trend towards globalization among the company's industrial customers, loss of potential business through lack of referral opportunities across division lines, missed potential efficiencies from global operations, and the decision of W. R. Grace to sell-off any non-core businesses that were not chemical or healthcare-based. The latter decision by the parent company exposed Grace Cocoa to the possibility of being broken up as part of a sale, something that would not make sense if the business was truly integrated.

A number of initial organizational development interventions, including a search conference and a company-wide culture survey, laid the groundwork for the ARL™ programme. These activities demonstrated that middle management believed in the potential for building a global organization, but did not believe that senior management, especially the division presidents, were committed to doing it. They believed that the skills and processes necessary for a global organization were not resident in the organization and needed to be developed. The ARL™ programme was initiated to meet these needs.

Three ARL™ programmes were conducted over a period of a little more than two years. Each had 20 participants drawn from upper management ranks and representative of the worldwide organization (Asia, Europe, Latin America and North America). Each programme consisted of four six-day meetings, spaced approximately five to six weeks apart, each meeting being held in a different part of the world where Grace Cocoa had an operation. This allowed for visits to the local Grace Cocoa facility and for the programme's design to incorporate experiences in which participants had assignments requiring them to get involved with the local culture and reflect on this experience. In each programme participants formed into four teams, with each team having a strategic project sponsored by a member of the Executive Committee to work on. Learning coaches, called project team advisers, observed the teams and periodically led periods of reflection. A learning community was built, in part through reflection and dialogue sessions that took place among the 20-participant group as a whole. Additionally, community wide learning experiences in the form of speakers and experiential activities were spaced throughout each week of the programme.

Some of the returns from the projects were tangible and immediate. For example, a logistics project was able to make recommendations that represented a 100 per cent return on the investment in the programme. Returns on other projects, such as the establishment of an ongoing taskforce on customer value, or the establishment of a structure for transitioning to a global senior management structure, were less immediately tangible but set the stage for the restructuring to a global profit-and-loss statement organization.

A primary purpose of the programme was to develop a global mindset and competencies for leadership in this kind of organization. An extensive assessment of the programme revealed that it was a success in terms of transformative learning among most of the participants, both in terms of their thinking about business challenges facing a globalized organization and in terms of the leadership culture the company needed to create (Yorks, Lamm and O'Neil, 1999). A global network of close personal working relationships was established, breaking down the barriers that existed among the three divisions.

A key supportive characteristic of the process was the openness of the senior team to learning through dialogue with the programme participants. Programme participants were not simply reporting to senior executive committee sponsors, but learning with them when executive committee members recognized that they too needed to learn how to function in the new organization. The ARL™ programme served a catalytic function in translating the support for globalization identified through the search conference and corporate culture survey into specific actions that were subsequently implemented. Yorks *et al.* (1997) suggest this framework creates a liberating structure in which all those involved, participants and sponsors alike, could learn their way into becoming a global organization.

Other critical reflection school programmes

There are many other programme designs, in addition to the ARL™ models described above, in which practitioners create situations from which critical thinking and transformative learning can emerge. As mentioned previously, the learning from these and other implementations has led to many designs derived from early ARL™ practices, emphasizing critical reflective practice.

For example, the Public Service Electric and Gas of New Jersey programme was developed in 1996 to help the company's distribution department learn how to be successful in the new competitive environment that was quickly replacing their former regulated and hierarchical world. Each programme session averaged 28 participants formed into four teams. Team projects were sponsored by senior leaders in the organization in order to make some progress on challenges in the division's new business plan. Each team met for a minimum of six and a half days over a six-week period with a learning coach, and additional days on their own (Marsick and Watkins, 1999).

This programme used a number of elements to enable critical reflection; for example, participants worked with one another on personal learning goals. This work took the structure of asking one another 'fresh' questions

(Dilworth, 1996), a kind of questioning process which often leads to critical reflection and personal insights. A typical comment from one person in an in-house programme evaluation suggested: 'One of my teammates asked me a question about my personal learning goal that made me rethink the action I was taking. I'd never thought about it from that perspective' (O'Nell, 1998).

Another exercise, called Challenging Personal Assumptions, involves participants working individually and in teams to go through a series of questions that leads them to some of their most basic assumptions. Participants come to the realization that they hold assumptions that are in fact contradictory, an insight which provided participants with new views of how they might interact with and influence the company: 'I found out this is about who we *are* – the problem then became miniscule. I'm going to take it back and learn who the guys are that I work with and then there'll be no problem that's too big' (O'Neil, 1998).

Critically reflective programmes continue to experiment with alternative programme designs and incorporate practices that help enable critical reflection. Partners for the Learning Organization often uses the creation of cases in the style pioneered in the work of Chris Argyris and his associates (Argyris, Putnam and Smith, 1985) as part of a programme design. Participants create individual cases that are a part of the problem on which they are working, and through the analysis of the case participants are able to develop a deeper understanding of their own behaviour and how it may be contributing to the problem. This understanding can then be used to help in learning from and solving the problem (Marsick and Sauquet, 2000).

Strengths, limitations and future prospects

Critically reflective programme designs vary in many ways, including differences in their length and frequency of meetings. Regardless of length and other design characteristics, all such programmes focus equally on both personal development and business development. Learning coaches look for opportunities to help participants engage in periodic critical reflection, and learning at both the participant and senior management level is a central objective with programmes typically spaced in a way to allow reflective learning over time.

The strength of critically reflective designs is their focus on personal development and transformative learning. They are most successful when a need for change is recognized and various levels of the organization are open to learning. Elsewhere we have presented a series of questions that can help people to assess the appropriateness of selecting a critically reflective approach (Yorks, Marsick and O'Neil, 1999). Among the most important questions are those regarding the extent to which senior management is prepared to be supportive in the face of the organizational 'noise' that is often produced in the early stages of this kind of programme. Participants are taken out of their comfort zone when they reflect critically on their own practices and deeply-held cultural assumptions in the organization. This is in contrast to more problem-solving objectives or programmes designed to reinforce or drive existing organizational cultures characterized by very individualistic senior leaders.

The strength of critically reflective action learning initiatives, therefore, can also be seen as a limitation in that managers begin to question the status quo. When the organization is prepared for such challenges, and links are developed to systematic organizational change, these outcomes are appropriate and helpful. When this is not the case, managers may not be rewarded for their new behaviours and their challenges cannot be used as leverage for culture change.

We conclude that critically reflective action learning programmes are likely to be increasingly useful to organizations that are caught up in the need for deep change because of today's turbulent environment. When these programmes are part of a larger change initiative, they can be a powerful tool in the arsenal of business and organizational development.

Note

1 Action Reflection Learning™ and ARL™ used throughout this chapter are registered trademarks of Leadership in International Management, Ltd (LIM) and the MiL Institute in Europe and are used with permission.

References

Argyris, C., Putnam, R. and Smith, D. M. (1985) *Action Science: Concepts, Methods, and Skills for Research and Intervention*. San Francisco: Jossey-Bass.

Boshyk, Y. (ed.) (2000) 'Introduction: Business Driven Action Learning: The Key Elements', in Y. Boshyk (ed.), *Business Driven Action Learning: Global Best Practices*, pp. xi–xvii. New York: St Martin's Press. Also presented as 'Diversity in Action Learning: Differing Theories, Varying Practices', at the annual Global Forum on Business Driven Action Learning and Executive Development, 30 May to 2 June. Boeing Leadership Centre, St Louis, USA.

Cell, E. (1984) *Learning to Learn from Experience*. Albany, NY: State University of New York Press.

Dennis, C., Cederholm, L. and Yorks, L. (1996) 'Learning Your Way to a Global Organization: Grace Cocoa', in K. E. Watkins and V. J. Marsick (eds), *In Action: Creating the Learning Organization*, pp. 165–77. Alexandria, VA: American Society for Training and Development.

Dilworth, R. L. (1996) 'Action Learning: Bridging Academic and Workplace Domains'. *Employee Counselling Today*, vol. 8(6), pp. 48–56.

Lamm, S. (2000) 'The Connection between Action Reflection Learning™ and Transformative Learning: An Awakening of Human Qualities in Leadership'. Unpublished doctoral dissertation, Teachers College, Columbia University, New York.

Marsick, V. J. (1990) 'Action Learning and Reflection in the Workplace', in J. Mezirow *et al.* (eds), *Fostering Critical Reflection in Adulthood*, pp. 23–46. San Francisco: Jossey-Bass.

Marsick, V. J. and Cederholm, L. (1988) 'Developing Leadership in International Managers – An Urgent Challenge!' *The Columbia Journal of World Business*, vol. 23(4) pp. 3–11.

Marsick, V. J. and Sauquet, A. (2000) 'Learning through Reflection', in M. Deutsch and P. Coleman (eds), *Handbook of Conflict Resolution: Theory and Practice*, pp. 382–99. San Francisco: Jossey-Bass.

Marsick, V. J. and Watkins, K. W. (1999) *Facilitating Learning Organizations*. Aldershot: Gower.

Mezirow, J. (1991) *Transformative Dimensions of Adult Learning*. San Francisco: Jossey-Bass.

O'Neil, J. (1998) 'Partners for the Learning Organization, Inc.' Presentation for the PSE&G OD group, unpublished paper.

O'Neil, J. Arnell, E. and Turner, E. (1996) 'Earning while Learning', in K. E. Watkins and V. J. Marsick (eds), *In Action: Creating the Learning Organization*, pp. 153–64. Alexandria, VA: American Society for Training and Development.

Pedler, M. (1996) *Action Learning for Managers*. London: Lemos & Crane.

Raelin, J. A. (1993) 'The Persean Ethic: Consistency of Belief and Actions in Managerial Practice'. *Human Relations*, vol. 46(5), pp. 575–621.

Rohlin, L., Skarvad, P. and Nilsson, S. (1994) *Strategic Leadership in the Learning Society*. Vasbyholm, Sweden: MiL Publishers.

Weinstein, K. (1995) *Action Learning: A Journey in Discovery and Development*. London: HarperCollins.

Yorks, L., Lamm, S. and O'Neil, J. (1999) 'Transfer of Learning from Action Learning Programmes to the Organizational Setting', in L. Yorks, J. O'Neil and V. J. Marsick (eds), *Action Learning: Successful Strategies for Individual, Team, and Organizational Development*. Advances in Developing Human Resources series, 2, pp. 56–74. Baton Rouge, LA: Academy of Human Resource Development, and San Francisco: Berrett-Koehler Communications.Sponsored by the Academy of Human Resource Development, Berrett-Koehler Publishers.

Yorks, L., O'Neil, J. and Marsick, V. J. (1999a) 'Action Learning: Theoretical Bases and Varieties of Practice', in L. Yorks, J. O'Neil and V. J. Marsick (eds), *Action Learning: Successful Strategies for Individual, Team, and Organizational Development*. Advances in Developing Human Resources series 2, pp. 1–18. Baton Rouge, LA: Academy of Human Resource Development, and San Francisco: Berrett-Koehler Communications.

Yorks, L., Marsick, V. J. and O'Neil, J. (1999) 'Lessons for Implementing Action Learning', in L. Yorks, J. O'Neil and V. J. Marsick (eds), *Action Learning: Successful Strategies for Individual, Team, and Organizational Development*. Advances in Developing Human Resources Series 2, pp. 96–113. Baton Rouge, LA: Academy of Human Resource Development, and San Francisco: Berrett-Koehler Communications.

3
Why Business Driven Action Learning?

Yury Boshyk

Business driven action learning is a term used to describe a results-focused orientation to individual leadership development and organizational learning and change. It can be summarized as integrating individual development and organizational strategy with business results. Although presently utilized by companies and organizations primarily in executive leadership development programmes, it can be adopted for 'just-in-time' learning and for just about any process or context where learning is tied to producing results and behavioural change. It can involve many different levels within the organization, from Chairman and CEO to supervisor and shopfloor personnel, and also include those formally outside the company – suppliers, customers and stakeholders such as government regulators. And it is not just for multinationals or large companies; it can be used very effectively by small and medium-sized businesses, and in the public and not-for-profit sectors. Figure 3.1 gives some indication of how and in what context business driven action learning can be used in an organization.

As this volume demonstrates most effectively, business driven action learning is quickly catching on around the world. In the public sector we clearly see a renewed emphasis on results-focused learning and development, and in the business world several attitudes and perspectives have also changed to favour more of what action learning stands for and advocates. This chapter will look at some reasons *why* companies have come to adopt approaches and values that are more aligned with the fundamental assumptions of action learning. We shall then explore *how* companies worldwide implement business driven action learning, with particular emphasis on executive leadership programmes and approaches.

The changing nature of the competitive landscape

To be sure, business was in general and in the past not particularly interested in fostering learning and the self-development of its people. At best, many

Figure 3.1   Business driven action learning: some examples of learning applications

in this community were skeptical of approaches that seemed far removed from skill and business-focused training. We can recall past experiences in several companies where even the word 'learning' was not acceptable to senior management, or senior management who rejected 'classical' action learning as a methodology only to wholeheartedly adopt some part of it in another guise. Although this tendency was much more pronounced in the past, sadly there are still occasions where senior executives think 'learning' is either too 'soft' or too 'negative' a term to be used in their organization. Arie de Geus described a similar way of thinking among Shell executives:

> Even the phrase 'I learned' was inadmissible in many Shell circles – which made it very difficult for people to enter into the kind of colloquy that would help us improve our decisions. To have to 'learn' something meant you didn't know it in the first place, and (particularly for those of us who came of age in the 1950s), it was considered much better to lie and give an answer – any answer – than to admit you don't know. This attitude is deeply ingrained in many companies – sometimes deeply ingrained.[1]

The positive side of the story is that Shell executives managed to break out of this counterproductive thinking and realized that decision-making could also be a positive learning activity, as de Greus says.

In this regard, there has been a sea-change recently that has served to refocus the nature of the discussion and the values associated with the role of learning, the value of people to an enterprise, and the need for an enlightened organization and leadership. The business world, and especially multinational companies, now share a common view that is quite different from that held in the past. One has only to think of the example of General Electric under Jack Welch; a decade ago it would have been very surprising to hear him extol the virtues and merits of General Electric as a 'learning organization', which is what he in fact started to do in the late 1990s shortly before his retirement.[2] No doubt he, like many other senior executives, went through a common experience summarized by Chris Argyris in his most recent book:

> [Those at the top of the organization] realized the importance of learning as a competency. They also realized that it would be unlikely that they could provide quality advice *and* add value to their clients without becoming a learning organization. In addition, they understood that building these generic competencies had to begin with the leaders of the firm.[3]

Perhaps a more convincing reason for this new acceptance was the changing nature of the competitive landscape. Product life-cycles, globalization, and indeed the entire pace of business life and decision-making took on a new meaning in the 1990s. The new business mantra included the key words speed, flexibility, shareholder value and customer focus and, hence, the necessity for change. On the minds of most senior executives was the need to align the organization and behaviours to these new objectives. Many surveys of executives during this time showed that they believed the greatest obstacle to the success of their company was the cultural 'baggage' of the past, and old ways of thinking. Almost all agreed that one of their top priorities was to change their corporate culture.

In the course of this corporate reassessment, the role of education and, hence, the learning organization were 'discovered' by chief executives. Indeed, one of the foremost specialists on corporate culture has remarked that many organizations 'learned that the only way to convince employees and managers of the need to do things differently is by educational interventions'. Many employees and even fellow executives 'do not believe what their leaders tell them unless they are educated to the economic realities of their business'. In the end, 'change programs...often have to begin with educational efforts, which may take time and energy'.[4]

At the same time, it was becoming clearer that even competitors were adopting this way of thinking and so the realities of business helped focus the minds of senior executives on the importance of learning quickly and, certainly, more quickly than competitors. One of the founders of action learning, Reg Revans, used to say that for competitive reasons 'learning must be equal to or greater than the rate of change'. But in the 1990s it became clear than competitive advantage was to be gained by those individuals and organizations that learned *faster* than the rate of change. For a variety of reasons, therefore, executives began to realize the importance of integrating education or learning with their organization's strategy and critical change processes.

The link to business issues and 'actionable knowledge'

The pressures on executives for business results and greater gains in efficiency also led them to scrutinize the investment in management education and its relationship to improved performance. This is understandable given the context: more than US $60 billion are spent on management training and executive development by corporations annually, more than the $43 billion spent annually on management consultants in the United States alone.[5]

In several companies, the human resource and organizational development departments were told by senior executives that while they supported education, the executive education being provided for the company was not being translated efficiently into business results. In the case of Johnson & Johnson and General Electric, for example, what was requested were programmes that provided 'a demonstrable, action-oriented link to current business issues' and addressed the 'leadership needs of the Corporation'.[6] Action learning in this context seemed the most appropriate approach to take.

In essence, about this time a change occurred in perception among senior executives on two dimensions that made action learning more relevant to new emerging needs. One was the realization that knowledge, with an emphasis on 'actionable knowledge', was a corporate asset and therefore had to be developed for competitive advantage. This was epitomized by a Hewlett-Packard executive who said that 'if Hewlett-Packard knew what Hewlett-Packard knows, we would be three times more profitable'.[7] But the more profound reality was that a power shift had occurred, and was seen to have occurred – power and competitiveness were to be based increasingly not on the traditional factors of violence and wealth, but on knowledge. The 'knowledge era' had arrived.[8]

Second, the past emphasis on individual development and education was being replaced with a view that individual learning should be tied more directly and clearly to organizational objectives as well. In other words, strategy and execution were being tied to people and executive development.[9] These trends were well-summarized over a decade ago:

There has been a shift in the *purpose* of executive development. Traditionally it was viewed as a way of developing *individuals* by preparing them for future assignments and broadening their perspectives. In its strategic role, executive development is seen as a vehicle to help the *organization* achieve its strategic objectives; the individual is developed in support of organizational goals.[10]

As a result, executive education, particularly in multinational companies and for at least a decade, has according to Jim Bolt taken on many of the following objectives:

- Establish organizational identity;
- Develop a shared vision and unity of purpose;
- Communicate and implement corporate strategy;
- Shape, manage, and if necessary, modify a culture;
- Develop critical attitudes, knowledge and skills;
- Identify and address key business issues;
- Build teamwork and networks;
- Provide a forum for management and communication;
- Enable a management team to understand the need for careful planning before action; and,
- Improve leadership.[11]

Efforts were also made in corporations to ensure that human resource personnel understood the business and integrated the human resource function to the strategic intent and specific business objectives. As with business driven action learning, so too with human capital – the connectivity to strategy and performance has increased and will continue to do so.[12] Publications and studies with titles like 'Measuring Learning and Performance' testify to the enormous change in perception and the new reality of the acceptance of learning in the corporate sector. In a deeper sense, the traditional divide between line managers and human resource professionals is very much counterproductive and out of kilter with the needs of the modern organization. For just as line managers now realize the importance of the so-called 'softer' issues like people skills and 'emotional intelligence', so too human resource professionals understand that they also must have a better understanding of the business issues and implementation dilemmas faced by line managers. In order to remain relevant to the twenty-first century organization, states Warner Burke, human resource professionals will have to understand at least nine critical concepts: performance improvement, restructuring, organizational change, globalization, groups and teams, time shifts, power shifts, interrelationships and action learning.[13]

Work-based learning

Another trend that has helped to influence the positive acceptance of business driven action learning is the increasing use of what Joe Raelin has recently called 'work-based learning'.[14] Some aspects of this, such as 'learning on the job' have been with us since the days of the guild system, and to this day this way of learning is also the preferred approach by organizations in such countries as Germany, Switzerland and Japan to name but a few.[15] Today, however, a difference exists for two main reasons. One is that we have now come to better understand how adults learn most effectively; there are better and measurable results when learning involves the active participation of adults. There is also strong evidence to suggest that adults learn best in teams and/or in the interaction between teams and the individual, rather than in solitary reflection.[16]

Secondly, in the lives of managers and executives we see greater and greater emphasis on tying learning to and with work. Some of this has to do with the pace of life and the emphasis on cost-cutting coupled with an ever-increasing number of new initiatives to maintain and increase growth. This places ever-greater demands on some individuals to do more and more with less and less, with less time for self-education and personal enhancement through learning in the traditional way. As a consequence, organizations are turning to eLearning – internet and intranet-based training programmes. Some companies, like Cisco, have the vast majority of their training programmes already available to employees in this way and others are following suit. This may be fine for training purposes, but for executives a different type of learning is required. We are seeing exciting new developments in such areas as 'just-in-time' learning and 'learning on the fly' by providing learning and information as it is required, quickly and efficiently (and not just electronically), especially to board members of the corporation.[17] This learning orientation will no doubt continue to expand due to the pace of business activities, the need for quick decision-making, and the revolution in communications technology.

Not surprisingly, governments are in the forefront of building appropriate technical and educational infrastructures to ensure the further development of this spread of information and education. Many have strategies to help provide their citizens with very fast access to the internet through wide bandwidth. Some even have entire strategic plans to catch up with more advanced countries, in particular the United States. Japan has been the most recent country to unveil its 'eJapan' strategy, and the Europeans before them announced their 'eEurope' initiatives. The President of the European Commission, Romano Prodi, in the early days of his Presidency, announced to the European Parliament that it was his dream and vision to make sure than within five years every graduate from secondary school in Europe would be as proficient and knowledgeable about software and internet applications as his or her US counterpart. At the heart of this vision is the reality that all the wealthier countries, with their ageing populations and declining birthrates, must 'work smarter' in order to maintain their quality of life: knowledge-based industries and the application of advanced technology will help preserve the present situation. Some analysts have also called for the need for 'learning societies' and not just learning organizations. One company, Skandia, uses what it refers to as the 'Country Navigator' to analyse countries and their future development on the basis of whether they have the capacities to learn and renew their human resources.[18]

Shareholder value, growth and leadership development

The value of a company's stock price is influenced by analysts who evaluate a company's earnings potential, and one of the criteria they use is whether there is sufficient 'leadership' throughout the crucial areas of the business, not only as regards CEO succession, but also whether there is demonstrable leadership development in the high-potential middle and upper-middle levels of management. This has led to a greater acceptance of the need for leadership and organizational development inside companies even though some boards are sometimes reluctant due to the expense and time needed to develop new leadership modes.[19] Nevertheless, most companies proceed with leadership development in order to demonstrate to the market and to analysts that the company has the leadership cadre at all crucial levels of the organization to implement a growth strategy.[20] Some companies, for example Philips, even categorize their high-potential young managers and upper-level managers into talent pools to emphasize the point that they are focused on leadership development. Besides, it makes good business sense and enhances the company's reputation considerably. In a recent study, the world's most admired companies were those that focus on leadership development programmes for staff and planned career assignments, and those that 'see improving human capital as a high priority'.[21]

At the same time, there is an interesting irony involved in this emphasis on shareholder value. Some critics say that this orientation has undermined the notion and reality of long-term employment and loyalty to a company, but has also led to demands in the managerial levels for more education and self-improvement. Ironically, individuals want these opportunities inside the company, as well as interesting work, in order to make themselves more marketable for other companies as they advance in their careers. Since they are seen to be 'expendable' they must take responsibility for developing their skills and education but at the company's expense. The deeper reality is that the drive for growth demanded by the shareholder-value philosophy has also made it obvious that there are not that many excellent managers available to sustain this orientation. Consequently, a so-called 'war for talent' has developed and one of the strategies to retain the best managers is to offer them educational opportunities and work on real company challenges – combining learning and working through action learning.[22]

Generational factors

As we have just suggested, there is a generational dimension or reason why companies are adopting business driven action learning. This is based on two factors – the focus on growth, and the demographic realities of ageing populations common in wealthier nations. Many companies, of course, mirror these demographic realities and so find themselves with an executive cadre of people mostly over 50 and too few younger excellent managers. Again, not a very positive message to shareholders and analysts.

In Japan, the CEO of a major multinational electronics firm is wrestling with these demographic realities in a nation where the ageing population makes it the second oldest country in the world – after Italy – and a harbinger of change for the wealthier countries of the world. In a recent interview, it was made clear that the new CEO wants to make sure that his company does not become the Japanese equivalent of IBM in the early 1990s. His organization has grown rapidly and he wishes to change it substantially by focusing on service and customer satisfaction rather than on finely engineered products. In order to do so, he needs a critical mass of younger executives very quickly, but because they lack experience he instituted business driven action learning in the company in order to develop a new generation of leaders to bring about this change.[23] Experts tell us that all the richer countries of the world and, of course, the companies in these countries will undergo a major problem within their executive ranks. In the United States, for example, 'the growth of the economy and of management jobs is outstripping the number of people developing in the right age range...[because] the demand for executives will increase by a third, while the number of those 33 to 44 will decline by 15 per cent'. As a result, states one recruiter, 'Some companies will wake up one day and say, "Lord, we don't have the right people anymore."'[24]

This generational challenge is to be found in the pubic sector as well. For example, a few years ago the Canadian public service embarked on an accelerated development programme for 'high potentials'. One of the most important reasons for doing so was the need to develop a larger pool of younger executives to replace the large numbers of older executives heading into retirement within the near future. Action learning was chosen as the methodology and philosophy of education and development.[25]

In summary, we have discussed some of the reasons why business driven action learning is being used more often by organizations throughout the world for individual development and organizational learning – two aspects of modern management that are not only recent in formulation but also in practice. We have argued that the reason for this state of affairs is to be found in the external realities of business. These include the emergence of a new competitive landscape that stresses shareholder value, globalization, strategic and cultural reorientation, and generational changes in the wealthier countries. Not the least of the changes that have occurred has been the growing appreciation and use of 'systems thinking' and the influence of what can be termed the 'new business paradigm' movement in the USA. Both challenged traditional business behaviour and thinking especially in the post-Cold War era. Systems thinking did this by pointing out short-sighted linear strategic thinking whose origins lay in engineering and the 'exact' sciences and was applied with vigour to the world of business, whereas the interconnectedness of things and actions and unintended consequences were infrequently considered due to a lack of a more holistic approach. The 'new paradigm' school questioned the values of traditional business emphasizing cooperation and win–win approaches, and the need for reflecting on a company's values. It also focused attention on the balance between individual performance and other relationships outside of business – family and society. It appealed to senior executives who well-understood the price of success, and one of the most influential books in this area was well-entitled *The Paradox of Success: When Winning at Work Means Losing at Life*, written by John O'Neill (1994), a former executive himself. The result of these and other intellectual and cultural movements was a greater realization on the part of senior executives in the corporate world that reflection and introspection were not to be shunned or considered unworthy of pursuit by business executives. They began to see value in this and, in turn, this realization helped them better appreciate the values of learning, self-awareness and reflection – all features of action learning.[26]

Internally, companies and organizations have realized the potential and importance of intellectual capital, the learning organization and the development of its leading cadres as a necessary and positive response to these challenges. While breakthrough and transformational results have been achieved through this methodology and approach, it is not for everyone and it is not so easy to implement and sustain.

* * *

We would now like to discuss the experiences of some companies with business driven action learning, especially in leadership programmes for executives and 'high potentials'. These programmes have involved a wide variety of learning methodologies and in terms of duration lasted anywhere from three days to a year, and were held in many locations throughout the world. Naturally, we will be making some generalizations with the hope of providing a point of reference for other practitioners as well as putting forward some observations or lessons learned. We shall also address a few questions often asked when companies start, or continue on their journey, with business driven action learning. Given the limitations of space in this volume, we shall focus on the critical role of senior executives and their responsibility in helping to choose the type and duration of programme and the right business issue(s) for action learning exploration.

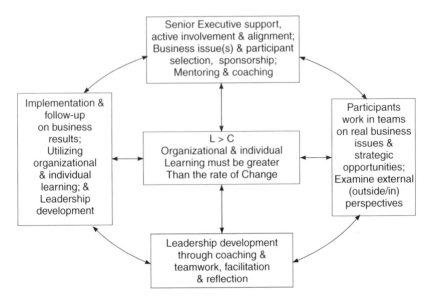

Figure 3.2   Business driven action learning executive programmes: the key elements

The four fundamental parts of business driven action learning executive programmes are outlined in Figure 3.2. They include the active support and involvement of senior executives, participants working in teams on real business issues and strategic opportunities, leadership development, and follow-up on the business issues and leadership development issues explored in an action learning programme. In the end, the programme must contribute to the company's business success and the personal development of its people, while ensuring that organizational and individual learning is always *greater* than the rate of change.

The starting point for considering business driven action learning as an approach to executive education is usually with human resource or organizational development (OD) professionals who want to ensure that their company's strategy is integrated with organizational and leadership development. We often find that these individuals have undertaken considerable research and thinking in exploring the latest best practices in executive education, and action learning in particular. Some do a careful and systematic comparison and analysis of various schools of thought and approaches within the broad field of action learning because they want to be certain that there is a good match between their organization's culture and business challenges, and the culture and approach used by practitioners in other companies and by consultancies.

A few words should also be said about the type of OD or Human Resource professional who embarks on implementing business driven action learning in his or her organization. They are not in general averse to risk-taking because they realize that implementing business driven action learning is a far more challenging and demanding initiative than the usual, and safer, route for executive education followed by most OD professionals. We are not being critical here. There is a need and place for these traditional approaches. For example, a representative of a recently denationalized energy company wanted an executive action learning programme to help his top team of about 200 people learn the basics of privatization and entrepreneurial behaviour – all in a programme of not more than five days in duration. In our view, this could not have been done in this time period using business driven action learning, and therefore a more traditional approach was recommended and a business school was found for this purpose. The point here is that it is important to have the courage to say 'no' to executives who want executive development and business driven action learning but who have no idea about the complexity of the task or about the commitment required.

Programme type and programme duration

While action learning can be and is indeed today being used in educational, healthcare and business activities and processes, business driven executive development programmes are a different matter. They are usually no less than 10 days in length and no longer than four weeks in duration. Some companies prefer to have these as consecutive days and weeks (sometimes referred to as 'compact' or concentrated programmes) while others prefer to have their participants involved in 'stretched' or longer-term programmes during which time participants return to their usual work in their respective businesses for a few weeks at a time, while at the same time continuing to work in 'virtual' teams on their business and project issues. These programmes are usually longer in duration, ranging in general from three to 12 months. Among the companies who practice or who have practiced the compact approach we could include, for example, Boeing, DuPont, General Electric, IBM and Johnson & Johnson. Among those who prefer the stretched version are Fujitsu, Philips, Siemens, Eli Lilly and Company, Samsung and Volvo Car Corp. to name a few. We are here excluding the examples of intact teams working on business issues but using action learning approaches, and what can be called 'mission critical action learning' processes.[27]

In general, every executive programme has at least five parts to it: the preparation or pre-programme phase; content and teamwork including 'virtual' teaming and work; outside/in activities such as interviews and benchmarking; analysis, presentation preparation and the actual presentation of recommendations; and, finally, implementation of the recommendations. The latter is not always carried out by all companies, at least not within the parameters of the actual executive programme.

Whether a compact or stretched version is used depends a great deal on the learning objectives of the programme and the culture of the organization. We can, nevertheless, observe a tendency that North American and especially US companies are more inclined to use the compact approach and not have their participants implement their recommendations within the time frame of the actual programmes, while other companies in Europe and Asia prefer the stretched version. We often hear companies who use the compact approach mention the following comments about their experience and orientation. They say that participants in such programmes are more focused and have a higher energy level than participants in stretched programmes; with little or no distraction from their usual business responsibilities; that there is deeper teambuilding and personal learning in the more stressful environment of compact programmes; and, finally, that all can more easily see the immediate business impact of recommendations on the business issues given to the participants by senior executive sponsors.

Companies that prefer to use the stretched version view the compact approaches in a more critical light. They argue that the time away from the business and from family is too long at one time; that compact programmes are not programmes at all but just another form of internal business consulting because they do not focus extensively on individual learning and leadership development as well; and, that there is little time for reflection in such programmes, and, by definition in their view, little time for deeper analysis of the business issues.

Whatever the decision on the duration best for a company and its participants, careful consideration should be given to choosing a date or dates for the programme in order to allow senior executives to attend the final presentation of recommendations. Usually this means avoiding holding programmes during such activities as the budgeting process and shareholder meetings. It is also important to avoid scheduling programmes during holidays in international locations that may be less familiar.

Sometimes at the pre-programme stage companies select an external adviser to work closely with the company programme director and assist in all or many aspects of the programme from its design, the selection of subject experts, implementation, even to post-programme implementation. The outside adviser's role proves particularly important in helping to define the business issue with executives and in other diagnostic activities that assess the organization's needs. On that basis, the external adviser is able to help facilitate and maximize organizational learning, leadership development and, of course, the impact on business results. This role should not be confused with the role played by subject experts or behavioural specialists who are more specialized and visible in their approach. There is no ideal profile but the experienced external adviser is someone who can integrate content and process, learning facilitation and strategic exploration, personal development and business results. At the same time, there must be respect and empathy between the programme director, the organization's senior executives and the external adviser.

Senior executive involvement, support and alignment

The OD professionals embarking on business driven action learning align their direction with the most senior executives in the organization because they well know that without senior executive support and involvement, the chances of realizing their intentions will be greatly diminished. In many instances, they already have a very good and direct relationship with senior line executives. On rare occasions, it is the CEO or a very senior executive who initiates the effort to introduce business driven action learning into the organization but this is an exception.

The second success factor is closely tied to the above-mentioned reality because business driven action learning must involve line managers and executives in a serious way to ensure the integrity and focus of the process and the implementation of results. The executives and managers should view these programmes as *their* programmes – that the results will help them in leading the organization and producing the results for which they will be judged and rewarded. One of the best ways of making sure this happens is to involve executives in the original pre-programme discussion about how best OD and executive education and development can serve the businesses' needs. Too often we see the OD or HR department assuming that it is their task to create a programme or approach for their company without the prior involvement of other key stakeholders in the company. This is a sure recipe for disaster in business driven action learning programmes.

There are many components to a business driven action learning executive programme and this is another reason for close collaboration with all stakeholders. Everyone involved should appreciate the complexity of these programmes, their own role and the amount of work and expenses involved. Aligning the expectations of all stakeholders, and keeping them aligned, is not an easy task. The programme director must always ensure that transparency and cooperation remain the norm.

What type of senior executive sponsor?

Ideally, the most senior executives in a company are not only sponsors but also participate actively in the various stages of these executive programmes. In our experience it also takes a very special type of executive to quickly understand the significance and the contribution business driven action learning can play in their businesses or organization. Perhaps no more than three out of ten senior executives grasp the benefits of business driven action learning on first discussion. Even in the celebrated case of General Electric, it should be remembered that Jack Welch did not immediately subscribe to action learning or participate in action learning executive programmes until after they were launched and sponsored by other senior executives in the company. In the case of Johnson & Johnson, the first sponsoring executive, Dr Tom Gorrie, was known as an innovator and from the beginning he not only understood the challenge but also that business driven executive programmes are both a business and educational opportunity for the company and for participants. Programmes of this nature flourish and accomplish their objectives best when such executives actively sponsor business driven action learning.

In some rare cases, the senior executives also want to experience business driven action learning themselves before committing their people to a fully developed executive programme. Some do this out of genuine interest and belief in the approach and others to test the concept. Usually this involves a scaled-down version, about three days in most cases, and can either be a series of vignettes on the subject inputs that would be covered in an executive programme or, in fact, an action learning real-time experience.

One company executive team in Europe did exactly this. The top team of Baxter Europe spent three days examining a proposal on making a major investment in several countries of Central and Eastern Europe, and the leadership and business issues that would be elaborated in the proposed executive programme. As part of the process they were briefed by internal and external subject experts and then traveled to these countries to conduct pre-arranged interviews with stakeholders (government leaders and specialists), customers and best-practice companies. On their return they spent the last day reflecting on the process, their own learning and examining the business proposal. Their comments on the process were enthusiastic and thoughtful. They appreciated the time spent on 'thinking rather than just doing'; they found it to be 'fun'; they thought it really helped the senior executive team to become 'more aligned'; and they saw how their learning was transformed into direct business results. In terms of the next steps for the executive programme, they readily understood the process and approach and volunteered to be sponsors for an upcoming business driven action learning programme.

To be avoided are those executives who see only the benefit to their own business or who see programme participants as only a task force to help them explore new business opportunities. One of the least rewarding programmes we have observed was when the senior executive sponsor delegated his responsibilities to a more junior executive who in turn passed the programme over to his Information Technology task force that wanted only a corroboration of their own thinking and plans for a new customer relationship management (CRM) system. In this case, responsibility for the business issue was not only delegated to more junior levels but the business issue was also tactical – and not strategic in nature – two recipes for failure in the broader understanding of learning and organizational objectives.

In some cases, an executive sponsor may tend to be regarded in the organization as the executive most critical of previous executive education efforts. At first he might strike terror in the hearts of OD people but in time these executives can also become the strongest supporters when they see the obvious direct benefit to the business and to participants. Naturally these executives become a very good reference point for other skeptical executives who mistrust what they do not understand at first.

The pre-programme role of senior executive sponsors: selecting the business issues

In general, senior executive sponsors have several responsibilities before, during and after the formal programme. These should be clearly stated so that there is alignment and agreement not only of expectations but also an understanding of the degree of involvement. As can be seen in Figure 3.3, the focal point or anchor point of any business driven action learning programme is the strategic business issue(s) or project(s) that are sponsored by senior executives.

In the pre-programme stage, senior executives play the most critical role in selecting and defining the business issues and then mobilizing the internal resources and support to assist in solving the business issues and hence in assisting the executive programme. Their role is to help involve all the

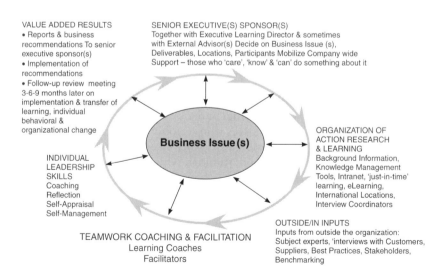

Figure 3.3   Components of business driven action learning executive programmes

people in the organization who know, care and can do something about the business issue or issues. Sometimes this could involve an external adviser in a series of interviews and meetings with top executives and the CEO to make sure the key issues are aired and discussed, with a view to selecting the most relevant issue for the programme participants and the organization. In other cases, executives are left on their own to come up with relevant business issues, what are referred to as 'issues that keep them awake at night'.

Executives can be assisted in the selection of business issues in a number of ways. In some organizations, a systematic set of guidelines is provided, as in the case of DuPont.[28]

DUPONT LEADERSHIP FOR GROWTH:
Questions for Project Sponsors

What is the background for this project?

What piece of information can the project team provide that would be of most value to you? Why don't you have this information now?

What questions do you have that you'd like the team to answer? What are the challenges in getting these answers? In making subsequent decisions? How will you measure the success of the project team?
– immediately following the teams recommendations
– 6 months from now
– one year from now

What is the critical information you can provide to the team? What critical information will the team need to identify/generate? Examples:
– business/strategic plans
– marketing plans
– competitive information
– financial results and plans
– benchmarking data

Who are the key people within the business/function that the team should meet with?
– marketing
– financial
– manufacturing
– legal
– sourcing
– other

Since developing solutions that meet all of our stakeholder needs is a critical aspect of Leadership for Growth, how can you help the project team gain access to these stakeholders?

What key people /organizations outside DuPont should the team engage? Examples:

– customers
– suppliers
– competitors
– trade associations
– government agencies

In the case of General Electric, Stephen Mercer who directed the senior executive action learning programmes for over a decade always made sure that all the business issues were strategic; involved cross-functional issues; were externally and market-focused; required interaction with customers/suppliers; were real business issues, requiring early resolution and a decision to be made.[29]

It is sometimes very worthwhile to have someone from outside the organization work with the executive programme director to assist the latter and the company to clarify the business issues with the executive sponsor or sponsors. Outsiders can usually ask more straightforward questions of senior executives to help them clarify their thinking and understand their role in an executive programme.

In general it has been our experience that about three to five iterations are necessary to clarify a business issue(s) and to come to an agreement on what is expected from the programme and from programme participants. This process can take time for a variety of reasons. These can range from a lack of clarity or agreement on critical business issues to even a lack of agreement on the definition of words and concepts. For example, one senior executive team had difficulties agreeing on the term 'alternative healthcare'. They wanted to explore some business opportunities in this area but realized that there were different operational definitions. The Europeans thought this referred to non-traditional medicine and healthcare, whereas the North American executives were thinking of all healthcare provided outside hospitals. This was clarified, of course, and also illustrates that the learning involved in business driven action learning executive programmes is not only restricted to those below the executive committees or even boards, but that learning takes place on all levels and by all.

After this iterative process a *business issue statement* is then drawn up that outlines why the topic was selected, gives some background information of present thinking on the topic inside the company, provides competitor or industry thinking, and clarifies what are sometimes called the 'deliverables' or expectations from the senior executive sponsor of the business issue. These are usually in the form of questions they would like answered and on which recommendations can be made. This document helps the sponsor and the participants, as well as all involved, to better align their understanding of objectives and expectations for the executive programme.

For executive and leadership development programmes most advice would stress the importance of choosing strategically interesting business issues. These can be new initiatives not tackled yet in the company; issues that 'keep the executives up at night', and even those that have already been discussed or studied (by outside consultants for example) but which need, perhaps, an outsider-like reality-check by an independent group of people. We have seen variations of all the above, and even business issues defined by the action learning teams themselves. In the end, the most impact and learning is gained when the top executive and his team formulate and assign the business issue(s). It is because at this level they can mobilize all within the company (and outside of it) who know, care and can do something about the business issue.

Some concrete examples of business issues assigned to action learning teams and for executive development programmes from a variety of companies are the following. Many are in what we would call the 'growth area', as for example:

- Doubling the business in Latin America by 2002;
- Going for 30% or more growth in Asia;
- Creating a $1billion service/solutions-based business for the company;
- Overcoming regulatory barriers to global growth;
- Identifying alliance partners and acquisitions;
- How can we better leverage our technology capability to create value for our customers?;
- How can we better capitalize on the network computing phenomenon to reassert leadership and growth?

And the business issues can also be very specific, both in terms of focus and geography, as the following examples indicate:

- If this were your business, how would you turn around customer perception, fix the product quality issues, return to market dominance, and develop a winning team attitude in your unit?;
- Identify sourcing opportunities in former Eastern Europe;
- How do we build a global solution brand business?
- If a low market share competitor broke all the rules (destroyyour company.com) how would we compete?
- Develop a global strategy for the XYZ division of the company.

It is at this stage that executives should be briefed on how they can best utilize the learning from these executive programmes and how best to deal with the recommendations on the business issue that will be made by participants. For example, will there be any follow up by the senior executive team and will participants be asked to implement the recommendations they make? And how will the learning from the executive programme be shared with the rest of the organization and how will participants' leadership development be further encouraged and nurtured?

Likewise at this pre-programme stage, the programme director should be thinking of ways to use information technology tools and techniques to capture and enhance the learning results through the use of a programme website and other means of communication to assist 'virtual teaming' and knowledge creation for the organization and the individuals involved.[30] Similarly, in some companies, the mentoring of participants by senior executives is also assigned in this period, as these executives are also briefed on their roles and responsibilities regarding mentoring or coaching.

The role of senior executives during the programme

During the executive programme senior executives introduce the objectives of the programme and the action learning business issues. Apart from explaining these in detail, the role of senior executives during this phase is to ensure that company experts on the business issues and all internal stakeholders take part in the briefing of participants, and that they 'open doors' for the participants by facilitating access to internal and external resources. They should also, of course, be present during the presentation of the recommendations. In some companies, senior executives also mentor or coach participants. But during the programme most executives do not become too deeply involved in order to allow participants to freely explore various options and solutions to the business issues. Unfettered by rank and senior interference, participants are usually given a wide berth for exploration and discovery.

The role of senior executives after the programme

It is the role of the senior executives after the programme to respond to the recommendations on the business issues made by participants. Usually this is done on the spot, so to speak, after the presentation, however more and more company executives have realized that greater benefit could be derived from this process. This example from a memo written by a very senior executive after such a presentation in a business driven action learning executive programme summarizes very well how some of the best executives take full advantage of the business driven action learning process and executive programmes:

Ever since Thursday, I have been reflecting on the presentations in Singapore. I was really energized by the reports – not only the content and the delivery, but the new learning that was achieved by these teams...Further, it was obvious that all the participants were also energized, learned a great deal and had a lot of fun. All in all, it was a great programme with 'wins' for all concerned.

The challenge that we, as line managers, now confront is how to take the output of the teams and put it to proper use in driving our business and achieving our goals. I believe we have a responsibility to stay connected with this exercise and to drive it to maximize the value form it.

Somewhere over the Pacific, I reviewed, again, each one of the presentations. I have concluded that if we are to gain value from this programme, we need to address the Issues and Recommendations BEFORE the next Business Plan Review...What I would like each of you to do is to go through the reports and prepare a presentation, which addresses EACH of the Issues and Recommendations presented by the teams.

This is one way in which senior executives and their teams have utilized business driven action learning executive programmes to deepen results and think about their planning and future challenges. There are many other ways ranging from asking teams to create a business based on their recommendations, to asking participants to be advisers to intact teams and senior executives who are setting up new opportunities within the company, based on their knowledge and expertise developed during these executive programmes. Not all senior executives who are also sponsors of these programmes fully understand how best to utilize the information and enthusiasm of the participants for business opportunities. It is advisable, therefore, that the programme director and the outside adviser assist these executives to think about how best to do so. In keeping with the objectives of integrating business results and individual leadership learning and development, good executive sponsorship of these programmes also acknowledges the value of deep personal learning that is very much part of the process and learning associated with this type of executive development programme.

On the other hand, ways of sharing the learning captured by participants in these programmes could be better explored in order to ensure communication among senior executives as well as throughout the company. The intranet or the programme website can go a long way to improving the capture and sharing of knowledge and encouraging the organization to be a learning organization. There is considerable room for improvement in this area as the technology evolves and as we tailor software to the participants' and organization's needs, and ways of working.

In this chapter we have focused on exploring the reasons why business driven action learning is being utilized so widely by organizations around the world, and we have also discussed some critical success factors for implementing business driven action learning – most importantly, the active involvement and role of senior executives. We have not, however, touched upon many other dimensions such as the selection of participants, post-programme reviews and follow-up, and the type of learning that takes place in such programmes. This could well prove the subject of another volume. At this point, mention should be made about the benefits of business driven action learning, to both the organization and the individual participant, and some lessons learned. Some companies feel that these results should be measured and tabulated, and there is, in fact, a variety of approaches to doing so.[31] Other organizations such as General Electric and Boeing believe that the business and developmental results are so positive and obvious that they feel no need to go through a formal process of evaluation. The following statement from Bill Weldon, recently appointed Chairman and CEO at Johnson & Johnson is just such an illustration: 'Business driven action learning has significantly enhanced [our] leadership development and has assisted us in improving our business by exploring new and exciting business opportunities'.[32] Whatever the approach, the success criteria is rooted in the artful and consequential integration of individual leadership development with organizational strategy for positive business results.

Notes

1   Arie de Geus, *The Living Company*. Boston: Harvard Business School Press, 1997, p. 74.
2   See the General Electric website for the values and the annual reports discussing the 'learning organization'.
3   Chrys Argyris, *Flawed Advice and the Management Trap: How Managers Can Know When They're Getting Good Advice and When They're Not*. New York: Oxford University Press, 2000, p. 222. 'Actionable knowledge' is the term used by Argyris.
4   Edgar H. Schein, *The Corporate Culture Survival Guide: Sense and Nonsense About Culture Change*. San Francisco: Jossey-Bass, 1999, pp. 120–1.
5   Jeffrey Pfeffer and Robert I. Sutton, *The Knowing–Doing Gap: How Smart Companies Turn Knowledge into Action*. Boston: Harvard Business School Press, 2000, pp. 1–2; see also the studies done by the American Society for Training and Development, most recently by Mark E. Van Buren, 2001, *ASTD State of the Industry Report*.
6   Ron Bossert, 'Johnson & Johnson: Executive Development and Strategic Business Solutions through Action Learning', in Yury Boshyk (ed.), *Business Driven Action Learning: Global Best Practices*. New York: St Martin's, p. 93; see also the chapter by Peg Tourloukis in this volume.
7   See, for example, Yury Boshyk, 'Beyond Knowledge Management: How Companies Mobilize Experience', in Donald A. Marchand, Thomas H. Davenport and Tim Dickson (eds), *Mastering Information Management*. London: *Financial Times*, 2000, pp. 51–8; Thomas H. Davenport and Laurence Prusak, *How Organizations Manage What They Know*. Boston: Harvard Business School Press, 1998; Jac Fitz-enz, *The E-Aligned Enterprise: How to Map and Measure Your Company's Course in the New Economy*. New York: American Management Association, 2001, pp. 192–3 on action learning.

8 Ernest Gellner, *Plough, Sword and Book: The Structure of Human History*. Chicago: University of Chicago, 1991; Alvin Toffler, *Powershift: Knowledge, Wealth and Violence at the Edge of the 21st Century*. New York: Bantam, 1991 (reprint); and the work of Manuel Castells, for example *The Power of Identity: The Information Age – Economy, Society and Culture*. Oxford: Blackwell, 1997.

9 Argyris, *op. cit.*, p. 238.

10 James F. Bolt, *Executive Development: A Strategy for Corporate Competitiveness*. Rancho Sante Fe, 1997 (1st edn 1989), p. 197, emphasis in the original.

11 Bolt, *ibid.*, pp. 194–7.

12 Jac Fitz-enz, *The ROI of Human Capital: Measuring the Economic Value of Employee Performance*. New York: American Management Association, 2000; see also, Toni Krucky Hodges (ed.), *In Action: Measuring Learning and Performance*. Alexandria, VA: American Society for Training and Development, 1999.

13 Warner Burke, 'What Human Resource Practitioners Need to Know for the Twenty-first Century', *Human Resource Management* (spring, 1997), pp. 71–9.

14 Joseph A. Raelin, *Work-Based Learning: The New Frontier of Management Development*. Upper Saddle, New Jersey: Prentice Hall, 2000.

15 See, for example, Peter A. Hall and David Soskice (eds), *Varieties of Capitalism: The Institutional Foundations of Comparative Advantage*. New York Oxford: Oxford University Press, 2001.

16 See for example, Malcolm S. Knowles, Elwood F. Holton III and Richard A. Swanson, *The Adult Learner*. Houston: Gulf Publishing Company, 1998 (reprint).

17 Among those exploring these new frontiers are Executive Development Associates, a consultancy based primarily in the USA (and it is their term 'learning on the fly', we have used here), and Senior Executive Learning Systems based in London, UK.

18 Philip Brown and Hugh Lauder, *Capitalism and Social Progress: The Future of Society in a Global Economy*. London: Palgrave, 2001. The Skandia Country Navigator is a variation of the Skandia Navigator that can be found on the Skandia website. See also Lennart Rohlin *et al.*, *Strategic Leadership in the Learning Society*. Vasbyholm, Sweden: MiL Publishers,1998.

19 'Chief Executives: Churning at the Top', in *The Economist*, 17 March 2001, p. 77.

20 See Ram Charan and Noel Tichy, *Every Business is a Growth Business*. New York: Wiley, 1998, pp. 62–4.

21 'Most "Admired Companies" Look to Leadership', in *Financial Times*, 8 October 1999, p. 13. The study was carried out by Hay Management Consultants.

22 See for example, Nigel Barrett, 'Learning the Hard Way: Creating an Executive Development Opportunity for Learning and Reflection', in Yury Boshyk (ed.), *Business Driven Action Learning: Global Best Practices*, *op. cit.*, pp. 227–8.

23 Interview, 28 February 2001 in Tokyo.

24 Claudia H. Deutsch, 'Management: Companies Sramble to Fill the Shoes at the Top', *New York Times* (1 November 2000), web version.

25 See Charles Brassard's chapter in this volume.

26 On the 'new paradigm' in business approach see for example, Alan Rinzler and Michael Ray (eds), *The New Paradigm in Business: Emerging Strategies for Leadership and Organizational Change*. New York: J.P. Tarcher, 1993; and John O'Neill, *The Paradox of Success: When Winning at Work Means Losing at Life – A Book of Renewal for Leaders*. New York: J.P. Tarcher, 1994. On systems thinking and its evolution see Peter Checkland, *Systems Thinking, Systems Practice*. Chichester: Wiley, 1999.

27 For the details on how these companies implement action learning see this volume and Yury Boshyk (ed.), *Business Driven Action Learning: Global Best Practices*, *op. cit.*

28   Victoria M. LeGros and Paula S. Topolosky, 'DuPont: Business Driven Action Learning to Shift Company Direction', in Yury Boshyk (ed.), *Business Driven Action Learning: Global Best Practices, op. cit.*, p. 40.

29   Stephen Mercer, 'General Electric's Executive Action Learning Programmes', in Yury Boshyk (ed.), *Business Driven Action Learning: Global Best Practices, op. cit.*, pp. 47–8.

30   See the presentation by Konrad Fassnacht, e-Learning Manager, Siemens Management Learning Centre on this subject from the 6th Annual Global Forum on Business Driven Action Learning and Executive Development, hosted by BHP Billiton, Melbourne, 22–25 May 2001, available on CD Rom and at <www.globalexecutivelearning.com.>

31   See for example the exhibits in William J. Rothwell, *The Action Learning Guidebook: A Real-Time Strategy for Problem Solving, Training Design, and Employee Development.* San Francisco: Jossey-Bass, 1999.

32   Communication to this author. William C. Weldon is now Chairman and CEO of Johnson & Johnson.

Part II

Action Learning in North and South America

4

How Companies Plan and Design Action Learning Management Development Programmes in the United States: Lessons from Practice

Steven Hicks

Corporations are demanding more from their management development programmes as the demands increase for greater management knowledge and skills due to the complexity of the global marketplace and rapid technological change. Though traditional educational and development programmes have utilized classroom-based, expert-led content delivery methods, today particularly in business education the traditional educational methods are being questioned and new forms of learning and development are emerging. In corporate management development programmes traditional methods are being replaced or supplemented by methods that are learner-centred, team-based and action-oriented. As a result, many US corporations are using action learning and finding it to be a dramatic improvement over their traditional methods for management development. They are embracing this experiential approach to learning and development through action and experience to build their management talent.

Over the last two decades action learning has emerged as a powerful tool for increasing individual and organizational effectiveness through learning and change. 'Action learning has recently become an effective method of executive development in large multinational companies in the United States' (Dixon, 1996). When used as a vehicle for learning in management development programmes, action learning creates opportunities for learners to transfer learning and to create new knowledge from structured experiences while simultaneously solving real problems. In management development programmes action learning can act as a catalyst to translate new knowledge into effective action.

Action learning is a flexible method of learning and problem-solving that has been applied successfully in different corporate environments in a variety of ways. It is a relatively simple concept to understand, but a difficult method to design and implement due to the organizational context, the number of design elements, the number and variety of people involved, and the risk and resistance it can generate. Currently there is no one best formula for success when applying action learning, and perhaps there cannot be due to the nature of action learning, but there are several variations in use by many practitioners around the world. The value and power of the approach appears to be derived from the combination of all elements within its design and how these elements are applied and managed in an organizational context. Because of the number of action learning variations, it is difficult for human resource development professionals to make choices about which variation to use and how to apply it so that it will achieve its intended outcomes. Only recently have expert practitioners offered us a framework with which to view, apply and study this powerful concept (O'Neil, 1999; Yorks, O'Neil and Marsick, 1999).

This chapter draws upon the wisdom of some expert practitioners of action learning and provides guidance and tools for human resource development professionals. This experience-driven wisdom was synthesized from recent doctoral dissertation research that included interviews with 16 human resource development professionals who have applied action learning in either the role of expert practitioner or corporate programme co-designer. The focus of this research project was to examine how action learning is designed and applied in practice to discover the critical design elements and their relationships. From this research, frameworks have emerged that can help programme planners understand the action learning planning and design process so they can make better decisions. Our goal is to describe the critical relationships, elements and activities in the planning and design process that lead to successful action learning interventions.

Programme planning for action learning

The programme planning process plays a significant role in the success of action learning. In the corporate management development context, the programme planning process is typically driven by two co-designers – a human resource development professional and an expert practitioner of action learning.

There are several important activities that programme co-designers must complete before undertaking action learning. The outcomes influence planning decisions and thus programme results. The planning process generally involves uncovering the needs, articulating the outcomes, designing and developing the process, implementing the activities and evaluating the results. With action learning, planning complexity arises from the external

pressures of the business context, the political context inside the organization, the involvement of multiple people at different levels with different
bases of power, and the incorporation of a relatively new learning and problem-solving method. To further complicate matters, action learning must be
implemented with people who have little or no experience with the process.
Although rarely stated directly, the clear warning that emerges from expert
practitioners and co-designers is that action learning should not be undertaken by the fainthearted.

In a recent research project focused on the programme planning and
design process for action learning, the findings revealed that experienced
field practitioners viewed the following activities as critical to the initial
planning stages:

- performing an organizational analysis to better understand the organization's performance gaps and readiness for change;
- clarifying the goals and gaining stakeholder commitment;
- developing and articulating a compelling case for using action learning;
- managing the process, working relationships and expectations of all key
  stakeholders; and
- managing risk and resistance to action learning.

Surprisingly, these activities do not necessarily represent a linear process; in
fact, they may need to be accomplished concurrently within a systematic
approach to planning. This idea will be explored in greater detail later in the
chapter.

Understanding the organizational context

The organizational context becomes the stage for action learning and has a
significant impact on the planning process. When planning for action learning, co-designers must understand the connection of action learning to the
larger system in which it will be used. Education experts suggest that planners should have a thorough understanding of the organization's mission,
resources, priorities, trends and constraints. This information helps provide
a better understanding of the context which can significantly influence the
decision-making process and the perceived success of action learning programmes.

In order to gain this understanding, action learning programme planners
must uncover the gaps in performance that drive the need to use action
learning. This needs-assessment or gap analysis can help discover the
opportunities for applying action learning. The analysis process should
include key stakeholders and senior managers who have power and influence inside the organization and are capable of supporting the initiative. It
is critical to gauge the organization's performance gaps, its readiness for

change, and potential sources of resistance that may become barriers to implementation. These gaps can be translated into programme outcomes or goals from the perspectives of key stakeholders. The organization's culture, structure or previous responses to organizational change initiatives may influence its readiness for change. Signals of readiness and resistance can give the co-designers insights about potential planning activities and design elements to use in the design.

With the results of an organizational analysis, programme planners achieve a thorough understanding of the business context, the organizational context and the key stakeholders, which provides them with a firm foundation for making initial decisions. This activity helps the co-designers begin to build a solid case for using action learning in an organizational intervention as opposed to using more traditional methods.

Gaining goal clarity and stakeholder commitment

Action learning is a goal-driven process and has achieved planned outcomes even though the process has varied among organizations that have used it. Clear goals, which take into consideration the views of all key stakeholders, must be established and communicated early in the planning process. Action learning has achieved significant outcomes including: generating solutions for problems, facilitating learning within the groups and sponsors, initiating behaviour changes through learning, and providing a catalyst for organizational change. Other less-publicized outcomes that have been documented are providing leadership development opportunities, enhancing networking relationships, providing an opportunity to assess managers, and providing results equivalent to that of a consulting project.

Goals and stakeholder commitment provide the direction and energy necessary to initiate action learning. When establishing goals in the management development context, stakeholder commitment is more likely if they are involved in goal formulation. The co-designers must manage relationships with all stakeholders and influence the key decision-makers within the organization. Stakeholder involvement and commitment can be achieved either by consultation or through the use of committees or advisery groups.

Commitment from the top of the organization is crucial for organization-focused action learning (Zuber-Skerritt, 1993; Lawrence, 1994; Marquardt, 1999). Expert practitioners agree that action learning initiatives need to be sanctioned and supported from the top of the organization to gain the necessary resources, reduce resistance to the initiative and insure the alignment of programme goals with the organization's business strategies. Senior management support can be exhibited in the sponsorship of a key business challenge and participation in the programme. Participation includes involvement in programme planning, working with a group of participants or attending the final programme session to hear the results and give participants feedback. An important part of managing the design process includes establishing relationships with these key stakeholders in the organization and continually managing their expectations about outcomes. It is important to note that this is an unfamiliar activity for senior management and, therefore, selection is important and sponsors need to be coached on how to function in their role.

The US Postal Service, the second largest organization in the USA, has successfully implemented action learning in its highest-level leadership development programme. In the early planning process it was difficult to engage sponsors with complex issues for the participants to tackle. After the several sponsors gained experience with the process and began to discover the benefits of involvement, word spread quickly and executives began to volunteer to bring their most complex issues to the action learning process. Executives have realized the benefits of gaining solutions to complex issues, learning from the dialogue with their best leaders around the country, and being able to influence these future organization leaders efficiently and effectively in a neutral environment. Early programme successes are helpful in gaining momentum with both sponsors and learners.

Developing a compelling case for action learning

Initially, the co-designers must make a case for using action learning versus other more familiar types of management development activities. With goals and a clear rationale, co-designers can influence others in the organization and gain their approval and commitment. Without a clear rationale, co-designers may not secure the necessary resources, management involvement and commitment from key stakeholders.

The co-designers must also promote a wide understanding of the direction and purpose of this organizational change activity for all stakeholders and the organization as a whole. The typical cases for using action learning centre around solving important complex problems while developing managers' capabilities, facilitating organizational change, or gaining measurable returns on investments in human capital. The dual capability of problem-solving and development is probably the most prevalent rationale for using action learning in the management development context. In the case of a statewide utility, they chose to use action learning because no other intervention had been successful in the past. The case for action learning must convince decision-makers that the investments of manager's time away from the job, the sponsor's time, and the programme budget used will yield positive outcomes for the organization. Co-designers may experience resistance to any corporate-driven initiative for these reasons. Given the relatively young history of action learning in the United States, there is still little proof that action learning will work with certainty.

Managing the project, process and people

The effort behind the planning process involves many people at all levels of the organization and requires resources and the ability to manage the project, processes and people to achieve programme success. Project management includes managing logistics, resources and learning activities. Process management includes managing the programme time and format, monitoring delivery, and re-designing as necessary. People management includes managing the involvement, role execution and expectations of all the key stakeholders.

Most importantly, co-designers must manage the temporary relationships with all stakeholders across organizational boundaries and management levels to implement a successful programme. The key stakeholders who are crucial are the business challenge sponsors, the expert practitioners, the participants, and the participants' managers. All stakeholders are intimately connected by the business challenge, which is the main vehicle for learning and development.

Managing involvement of several people in the process is a challenging task, especially when the various stakeholders hold different positions and levels within the organization. Relationships and, more importantly, stakeholder expectations need to be managed to successfully gain their involvement, commitment, motivation and support. Several tactics can be used to effectively manage stakeholders' expectations, including having a dialogue with senior management to gain clarity and selecting the business challenges, creating orientation sessions for participants and their managers, and managing the involvement and boundaries among all stakeholders.

Managing barriers and resistance

Several aspects of the action learning process can create barriers to success when using action learning. Barriers tend to centre around the lack of resources or stakeholder commitment and risk. The necessary resources include financial support, action learning expertise, intellectual resources (for example appropriate participants), space and time.

While the benefits can be great, experts warn that action learning is a risky proposition for all stakeholders and can generate significant resistance resulting in a lack of commitment to the process. Action learning is used to change something, and with change there is usually resistance from people in organizations. Expert practitioners suggest that if organizations are unwilling to tolerate the risk that action learning creates, it will undermine the action learning process (O'Neil and Dilworth, 1999). There is perceived risk for all key stakeholders involved in action learning, including senior managers, sponsors, participants and the co-designers. For the learner, the most common source of resistance comes from a lack of familiarity or discomfort with ambiguity in the action learning process, time pressure for group meetings, increased workloads and risk of failure. Participants and co-designers both run the risk of failure by not generating potential solutions to business challenges or meeting the expectations of sponsors and senior management. Sponsors risk implementing a bad solution and wasting resources. Perceived risk increases with problem complexity and scope, the involvement level of senior managers, lack of resources, lack of action learning expertise, and general unfamiliarity with a new change intervention tool.

Co-designers must pay close attention to the origins of risk and resistance to the action learning process and manage resistance effectively to optimize the effect of risk on the process. All significant learning involves risk-taking, and the peer support that is offered by action learning groups may support risk-taking behaviour. Practitioners acknowledge the elements of risk and resistance in action learning and suggest that high-level support can reduce anxiety due to ambiguity and possibly offset some of the risk for the learner (O'Neil, 1999; Raelin, 1997).

Though risk can be reduced, it does not always have a negative influence on programme success and it should not necessarily be eliminated. Some practitioners feel that risk increases the participant's energy and motivation and facilitates their engagement with the process. For example, it may be important for learners to experience risk, uncertainty and the chaos of group dynamics in order to have innovative ideas and solutions. Risk also mimics the realities of the business environment and thus provides a realistic experience for developing managers.

A United States-based financial institution recently introduced individually-focused action learning as part of a leadership development programme for high-potential leaders. The participants were initially interested in the action learning process but resisted it strongly when faced with the reality of presenting potential solutions to their top-level managers. Other complaints centred on the ambiguity of the process, lack of success parameters, lack of time to meet as a group, competition for their time with other company initiatives, and lack of direct supervisor support for the process. The resistance increased until the programme sponsors cancelled the action learning activity because they thought it would poison the management development initiative and reduce the organizational support.

Risk and organizational resistance are generated by the action learning process and must be expected and managed. If possible, the planners need to uncover the sources of risk, recognize its inevitable presence, plan for it, and reduce it or increase it depending on the purpose and design. Tactics for managing and reducing risks include gaining top management support and commitment, setting clear goals and expectations for the process and outcomes, communicating the business case, holding orientation sessions for stakeholders, increasing the time and resources available, ensuring early successes and closely monitoring the process.

Planning using a systems approach

Planning for action learning is more complex and fundamentally different than traditional methods of education and development, and therefore the planner's approach is important. A systems approach can help co-designers to recognize the patterns and interrelationships among the issues, structures and stakeholders that must be considered in the design process. This type of approach will inform the programme planning process and yield a strategic framework to guide decision-making so that action learning can be adapted to fit the organization and enable success.

Due to the complexity of programme planning with action learning, a framework such as the one depicted in Figure 4.1, can be used to help all stakeholders consider the dynamics of the planning process. Implied in this framework is the notion that action learning is a dynamic intervention that is notably different from traditional training models and therefore needs to be planned with a systems or non-linear approach. This planning model shows the action learning programme as a temporary system residing inside the context of the organization. It highlights the important factors and relationships that designers and practitioners need to consider.

The outer oval in the model depicted in Figure 4.1 indicates the general forces or pressures affecting most corporations today and constitutes a strategic contextual view for implementing an action learning programme. The next oval denotes the internal organizational dynamics including the strategy, structure, culture and politics. At the core of this model is the

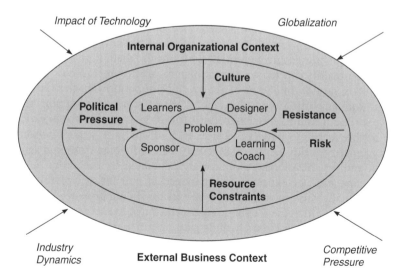

Figure 4.1 A planning model for action learning

temporary project organization created by key stakeholders. The key stakeholders are the sponsors, learners, co-designers and learning coaches. The business challenges serve as the main vehicle for learning in action learning and they link the key stakeholders to one another. Because of this linkage, the key stakeholders play critical roles in the planning and implementation process.

The innermost oval shows these roles temporarily connected by the business challenges. The co-designer's successful management of the relationships between stakeholders in the learning system is a major determinant of the system's success. The co-designers' ability to understand this context, achieve goal clarity, gain stakeholder commitment and manage the expectations and relationships are key factors in programme success in the management development context. By using this planning model, co-designers can approach this complex task holistically and take into consideration the many contextual variables that influence successful outcomes.

Designing action learning

Once the stage is set by the initial planning process in the organization, the co-designers are challenged to design an action learning process and activities to fit the organization and its goals. The design structure becomes the blueprint for turning the programme's goals into reality. The design structure also helps frame important programme decisions and therefore has a significant impact on intended and untended outcomes.

When co-designers consult the literature they are inundated by a variety of case examples and models that are applied in different organizational contexts. There is a general consensus among action learning experts about the two basic models of action learning: the individually focused model and the organizationally focused model (Marquardt, 1999); the basic difference lies in who is responsible for the business challenge. Beyond the basic models there is significant variation. In fact, models presently in the literature vary anywhere from containing three to 13 identifiable elements. Co-designers quite often copy a model from a well-respected company and experiment without a clear understanding of the interactions between the people, structure and process and action learning's potential risks. Recently, expert practitioners and researchers have suggested several new categories of action learning models (Yorks, O'Neil and Marsick, 1999; Boshyk, 2000); these basic models can be adapted by adding design elements to address contextually related or programmatic sub-goals. Co-designers can chose a basic action learning model and then adapt it to fit their context by adding a variety of design elements to meet the programme goals.

A framework for helping practitioners and co-designers conceptualize and make decisions on a design model for their context and goals is offered in Figure 4.2. This model builds on the pyramid model recently developed by

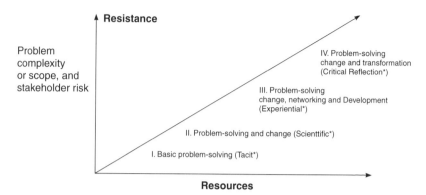

Figure 4.2 Program design variables and relationships
Source: Adapted from Yorks, O'Neil and Marsick (1999) Action Learning Pyramid.

expert practitioners and researchers (Yorks, O'Neil and Marsick; 1999), and can also be useful in the planning process to help the design team engage in a productive conversation about the design structure and process.

This design framework suggests that there are relationships and dependencies among several variables in the design of action learning. On the vertical axis, co-designers must consider factors that increase complexity: (1) the number of stakeholders, (2) the levels of the stakeholders, (3) the scope of the projects or problems, (4) the complexity of the problem (e.g. number of boundaries crossed), and (5) the expected resistance due to risk and other factors. Resistance increases with complexity and the amount or rate of change that is expected.

On the horizontal axis, co-designers must consider resources available such as: (1) time available, (2) expertise and experience with action learning, (3) administrative support, (4) experience with change interventions, and (5) participants' knowledge with respect to the problems. For example, if the co-designer plans for action learning to achieve high-level goals (I, II, III, IV) and greater change, he or she can expect greater problem complexity and scope, a larger number of stakeholders involved, and increased risk and resistance. As these variables increase, the demands on the action learning design rise and require more time, resources, expertise and additional design elements. Additionally, these elements have the potential to reduce resistance.

Designing action learning for corporate management development

There are several key design elements that are critical for the success of an action learning initiative. Co-designers must select the appropriate model considering their goals, participant capabilities, sponsor commitment level, and resources available. There are many action learning variations in the literature and the number of critical design elements ranges from three to 13. The findings from this research project suggest a model for the management development context with a minimum of nine elements.

First and most importantly, action learning involves real workplace problems that are important to individuals and the organization. There is a consensus in decades of literature that action learning is anchored in real, complex, workplace problems and that it uses a unique group process to gain greater insights into the problem. The choice of the appropriate complex challenge and its size and scope is critical to the success of the initiative. Strategic business problems that represent important strategic organizational challenges are the main focus for action learning activities in the management development context. These complex problems or challenges are capable of providing significant developmental stretches for participants.

Learning coaches are also critical for success in the management development context or learning gets lost in the shadow of the task. The learning coach provides necessary design expertise, process leadership and learner support, and he or she challenges the learners to generate innovative solutions to problems while learning throughout the process. Learning coaches are necessary to manage the conditions for learning by providing structure, group process guidance, and individual and group support. Learning coaches may also reduce the risk and resulting anxiety for learners and co-designers by providing expertise that can engender trust and confidence in the process. Learning coaches are not included in all models of action learning, but in the management development context they emerge as having an important role to guide the process, reduce risk and support learning. Learning coaches are typically external consultants who have experience and expertise in action learning.

Sponsors, who are sometimes called clients, play a pivotal role in the success of action learning programmes. They are the individuals who are ultimately responsible for the problem being addressed by an action learning group. The sponsor often selects the problem, helps the participants frame the problem, sets the problem scope, participates in a dialogue about an issue, provides appropriate resources, listens to the group's report at the end of the process and provides feedback.

Additionally, the sponsor provides motivation for the learners to generate viable solutions. The sponsor's level in the organization's hierarchy sends a strong signal to the learners about the relevance and importance of the projects or challenges for the corporation and increases their motivation and reduces their resistance. By being available for the presentation of results, the sponsor creates an additional learning opportunity when he or she engages learners in a dialogue about a complex problem and gives feedback. The interaction between participants and the sponsor provides an opportunity for insightful conversations that are highly relevant and contextual and provides rich opportunities for learning about the company and its challenges for change. It is important to recognize that the sponsor also learns in the action learning process, which can foster further commitment to the process. In the case of the US Postal Service, sponsors are finding that participating in the presentations can be a highly efficient way to influence the emerging leaders in the organization with feedback and key messages. They also highly value the learning and idea-generation benefits from these sessions. Sponsors are typically included in all basic designs of action learning but there is little guidance available on the roles and behaviours of sponsors and their impact on success. It is interesting to note that a sponsor is generally distant from the programme and has limited involvement, yet he or she has a significant amount of influence over the perceived success of a programme in the management development context.

Programme content and format are important elements for the design of an action learning programme. Action learning often serves as an integrator of programme content, a culminating experience or a fundamental activity supported by just-in-time learning activities. Action learning is typically embedded in the context of a management development programme and, therefore, the programme context influences the design of the action learning experience. A wide variety of content can be included in action learning programmes to accelerate or support problem solving and learning to meet the programme's goals. Co-designers must consider the content and format and their influence on creating optimal conditions and motivation for learning when planning action learning activities in a management development programme.

Action learning groups should consist of a diverse mix of people for the programme to be successful. Diversity can include the learners' backgrounds, work experience, gender, nationality or formal education. Diverse groups are a hallmark of action learning design models and an important factor in the success of action learning programmes examined in this study. Diversity enables the attainment of innovative problem solutions, cross-functional networking, and informal learning about the context by creating a place to share multiple perspectives. A global oil company emphasizes this design element in its action learning process because it allows participants to experience working in a high-performance multicultural global team. They manage participant selection for this leadership programme to take advantage of this design feature.

The inability to invest time may derail action learning. According to expert practitioners, time allocation varies widely in action learning depending on the model used, the organizational goals, programme format, and the amount of time the organization is willing to invest (O'Neil and Dilworth, 1999). Investing time is critical because groups need time to establish relationships, achieve open communication so they can challenge each other's thinking, and maintain the continuous communication to make progress on their task. Time is an important resource that is required for the action learning process to unfold and it includes time for action, reflection and transferring learning for development. Time for the groups to meet within the programme and between sessions is an important element in management development programmes. As organizations flatten and market responsiveness becomes more important, time as a resource becomes more difficult, especially with key corporate executives. Time will continue to be a great challenge when designing action learning.

Additional design factors may play important roles in the success of action learning in a particular context. Expert practitioners suggest group sizes of five to seven are appropriate, and they also suggest using a questioning-focused group process and the creation of opportunities for reflection as important activities to insure that learners are developmentally stretched. Participant selection is an important factor in some action learning models and may vary in its importance according to the goals of the programme. While most action learning groups are formed with peers, some companies have used multi-level participants in their groups to achieve specific programme goals.

A design model for management development

According to expert practitioners and co-designers in this study, there are nine essential design elements for organizationally-focused action learning in the management development context. The following structural design elements are critical for success: a real workplace problem, a learning coach, a sponsor, senior management involvement, programme content, diverse groups of learners, time, clear goals, and presentation of results. This model for management development emphasizes the involvement of top management in the planning process and at the end of the process for the presentation of results. As previously mentioned, senior management involvement in the action learning planning process is necessary for sanctioning the process, insuring its strategic nature, and providing appropriate problems and adequate resources. The model most closely resembles a model proposed by Dotlich and Noel (1998) that includes a sponsor, a strategic mandate, a learning process, a participant selection process, a coach, a learning team mix, an orientation, data gathering, data analysis, a draft presentation, a presentation and reflection. This model also resembles what has been described by researchers as the tacit action learning model in which problem outcomes are often emphasized over learning (O'Neil, 1999). The major difference is the inclusion of a learning coach and a plan for learning outcomes versus assuming incidental learning. The tacit model of action learning has been used successfully at companies to develop strategic thinking skills in corporate leadership development programmes. This management development model emphasizes a greater involvement of key stakeholders, before and during the implementation process. It also emphasizes the importance of the roles, responsibilities and activities of the learning coach, sponsor, senior management and the co-designers in the success of action learning in the management development context.

Summary and conclusions

Designing and implementing organizationally-focused action learning is a highly variable and complex activity. Planning action learning is not a linear process; in fact, a systematic approach is needed. In this chapter two planning frameworks have been suggested to assist human resource professionals as they approach decision-making in both programme planning and design phases. The first framework can help co-designers to determine the feasibility of implementing action learning in their organization; the second can help them consider the design elements that need to be incorporated to create the appropriate participant experience.

This research uncovered the critical elements of action learning that are effective in the management development context. These include: real problems, learning coaches, sponsors, top management involvement and support, programme content, diverse participant mix, time, clear goals, and a presentation of results. Action learning can be a flexible intervention and these elements can be designed and adapted to create variations for serving different goals in different contexts. There is no one best recipe for applying action learning in all organizations. The power of the approach is derived from the combination of these elements and the management of these elements of processes within its design.

The process must be planned and designed with careful judgment and managed effectively to insure its success. Action learning involves many people and requires change, and therefore it must be both led and managed inside of the organizational context. The co-designers need to be skilled leaders and managers to lead a change process inside an organization in order to implement action learning. Co-designers can increase the chances for the programme's success by establishing clear goals, engaging key stakeholders in planning and execution, gaining their commitment and support, and managing their relationships and expectations. These stakeholders must be fully engaged and execute their roles effectively. The importance of the sponsor's role must not be underestimated, especially given his or her limited time invested.

Co-designers must recognize that action learning creates risk for stakeholders and generates organizational resistance. It is essential for designers and practitioners to uncover the sources of risk and resistance early in the process, recognize their presence, and plan to reduce or increase their effects depending on the purpose and design of the programme.

There are several facets of the action learning planning process that are still not well-understood and represent potential challenges for human resource development professionals. These include assessing risk and dealing with resistance, the role of power and influence in planning, learner motivation, evaluating learning and results, compressing time in the process, and coaching stakeholders, especially sponsors, about how to implement their roles effectively.

Appendix A Theoretical schools of action learning

	Scientific	*Experiential*	*Critical reflection*	*Tacit*
Theory	Alpha, beta, gamma; $L = P\&Q$	Learning from experience (Kolb)	Learning through critical reflection (Mezirow & Schon)	Incidental learning (Marsick & Watkins)
Practitioners; some examples	Revans	McGill & Beaty; Mumford	Marsick; Pedler Weinstein	Noel Tichy
Role for learning adviser	(1)	X	X	
Reflection	X	X	X	
Groups/teams	X	X	X	X
Project/problem based on *real* work	X	X	X	X
Focus on group/team process	(2)	X	X	X
Questioning insight	X	X	X	
P knowledge or teaching	(3)	X	X	X
Just-in-time learning	X	X	X	
Individual problem	X	X	(4)	
Group/team problem/project		X	X	X

Notes:
(1) '. . . there is a role for a supernumerary (set adviser) in the early days of the set, to help the five or so fellows find their feet in this somewhat artificial venture, by encouraging them to

Appendix A   continued

exchange their experiences at the periodic meetings in accordance with an intelligible programme' (Revans, 1978).

(2) Revans (1978) explicitly says that action learning 'is not group dynamics', but also refers to a need for participants to be involved in the 'collective social process of the set'.

(3)'. . . this does not imply that action learning rejects all formal instruction; it merely recognizes that, however necessary such instruction may be, it is by no means sufficient . . .' (Revans, 1978).

(4) Participants may have individual projects, but group or team projects are the norm (O'Neil and Marsick, 1994; Pedler, 1996).

Source: O'Neil (1999).

Appendix B   Action learning pyramid

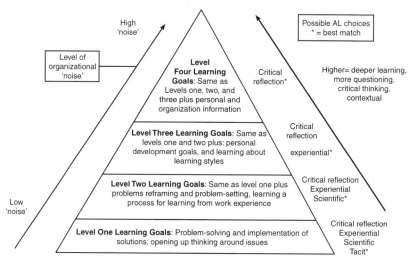

Source: Yorks, O'Neil and Marsick (1999, p. 14).

Appendix C   Typology of action learning, some examples

Example	*Prudential Assurance*	*AT&T* *Gap Group Process*
Source	Lewis and Marsh (1987); Keys (1990)	Vicere and Fulmer (1996); Froiland (1994)
Practitioner or co-designers	Wyndam Marsh, Ed Moorby	Sethi at AT&T and consultant Joe Galerneau
Purpose	Leadership development	To better frame personal issues; generate innovative solutions to problems; increase awareness of general mgmt issues; identify and overcome gaps in performance

Participants	400 district managers	Managers
Problem model multiple/single	(over 3 yrs)Single	Multiple
Project/problem based on *real* work	Real; 'owned' by the participant	Yes
Advisor/coach facilitator	Facilitated throughout life of group	Yes; Sethi and consultant
Sponsor	Client for problem	
Group structure	Group (6)	Multiple business units; High diversity
Group mix	Diverse: age, experience and geography	6–7
Focus on questioning insight		Possibly
Programme format	1.5 days in class; group meetings	7 days continuous; 30 mins per day on their problem
P knowledge or teaching	None (unless requested); 2-day orientation	Discussion of industry trends; financial topics; global business development; learning circles for application
Reflection	Reflection	Yes; in learning circles
Time in process	6 months with meetings spaced 1 month apart	7 days
Outcomes	Actions taken; increased: initiative, confidence, listening skills, informal relationships	Skills in problem-solving; increased self-confidence and managerial competence; progress towards problem resolution
Senior executive support	Yes	Yes
School or type (O'Neil, 1999)	Scientific	Scientific
Theoretical bases	Scientific (Revans) or critical reflection (Mezirow)	Scientific (Revans); or critical reflection (Mezirow)
Notes of interest	Note: failed at tacit model; moved to scientific model	Uses executives as instructors; often maintained network

Source: Adapted from Judy O'Neil's Typology (1999).
Note: Blank spaces represent unknowns or lack of clarity with respect to this element.

Example	*GE's 'Work-out' Programme*	*TRW 'Business Leadership Programme'*
Source	Meister (1998); Vicere and Fulmer (1996); Marquardt (1999); Davids *et al.,* in Boshyk (2002)	Clover (1991); Keys (1990); Downham, Noel & Prendergast (1992); Marsick and Watkins (1990)
Practitioner or co-designers	Jim Baughman*assisted by Steve Kerr, Dave Ulrich, Bob Miles, Todd Jick, Len Schlesinger, Noel Tichy and others	William Clover
Purpose	To eliminate unnecessary work; reduce bureaucracy and costs, break vertical and horizontal organizational barriers; solve system-wide problems	To develop senior execs; link strategy; to improve customer satisfaction; increase networking
Participants	Managers	High-potential managers (2×35)
Problem model multiple/single	Single	Multiple
Project/problem based on *real* work	Yes; linked to key business initiatives	Yes; participants chose
Advisor/coach facilitator	Facilitated; university faculty & consultants	
Sponsor	Senior leaders; defined the issues & championed selected managers	
Group structure	Range: 40–120	Teams
Group mix	7–9 person teams; multi-level & multi-function w/option customer and supplier	Peers from different business units
Focus on questioning insight	No	
Programme format	Senior sponsors had to act: agree with recommendations, say no, or ask for more information	2 one-week sessions spaced 3 months apart
P knowledge or teaching		Content delivered by experts
Reflection		
Time in process	2.5–3.0 days	
Outcomes	Teams empowered to take actions and were held account-	Shared vision and motivation; new business initiatives; operating

	able for results; solved organ-ization-wide problems, improved performance; transformed the climate at GE; improved competitiveness	results improved; programme ratings improved
Senior executive support	Yes	Yes
School or type (O'Neil, 1999)	Tacit	Tacit
Theoretical bases	Incidental learning (Marsick and Watkins) or Experiential (Kolb)	Incidental learning (Marsick and Watkins) or Experiential (Kolb)
Notes of interest	Note: presentation ground rules: senior manager either accepts/rejects/gets info	Conducted research between sessions

Source: Adapted from Judy O'Neil's Typology (1999).
Note: Blank spaces represent unknowns or lack of clarity with respect to this element.

Example	*Pacific Gas & Electric Action Forums*	*Aramark ExecutiveLeadership Institute*
Source	*Personnel Journal* 1990	Vicere and Fulmer (1996)
Practitioner or co-designers	HR	Penn State Executive Programmes; Ginny Tucker
Purpose	Solve internal and external organizational problems and challenges	To address core strategic imperatives; apply concepts; share practices; gain perspectives
Participants	Voluntary; multi-level managers	150 senior executives; cascaded down Multi-year process
Problem model multiple/single	Single	Single
Project/problem based on *real* work	Yes	Yes; Strategic issue for company; CEO selects
Advisor/coach facilitator	Yes; experts then HR trained facilitators	Facilitators used as resources between sessions
Sponsor	Yes: 'accountability manager'	Yes
Group structure	Multi-level; with knowledge about the issue; size 5–70	6 peers in executive development programme
Group mix	Diverse functions	Diverse; from multiple divisions
Focus on questioning insight	No	No

Appendix C   continued

Programme format	2–3 days forum	1 week plus 3 multi-day modules
P knowledge or teaching		Critical issues discussion led by experts; experiential activities
Reflection	No	
Time in process	6–8 weeks total	9 months total
Outcomes	Action taken; 90 follow-up on results; documented 273 million savings in 80 forums	Impact from projects; Increased networking; increase in organizational and self-awareness, collaborative leadership styles, creative thinking, development and risk-taking
Senior executive support	Yes	Yes
School or type (O'Neil, 1999)	Tacit	Tacit
Theoretical bases	Incidental (Marsick and Watkins) or Experiential (Kolb)	Incidental (Marsick and Watkins) or Experiential (Kolb)
Notes of interest		Attempt to measure results

Source: Adapted from Judy O'Neil's Typology (1999).
Note: Blank spaces represent unknowns or lack of clarity with respect to this element.

References

Boshyk, Y. (ed.) (2000) 'Business Driven Action Learning: The Key Elements', in Y. Boshyk (ed.), *Business Driven Action Learning: Global Best Practices*. London: Macmillan Business and New York: St Martin's Press, pp. xi–xvii.

Clover, W. H. (1991) 'At TRW, Executive Training Contributes to Quality', *Human Resources Professional*, vol. 3(2), pp. 16–20.

Dixon, N. (1996) 'Action Learning: More Than Just a Taskforce', in M. Pedlar (ed.), *Action Learning in Practice*. Aldershot: Gower, pp. 329–38.

Dotlich, D. L. and Noel, J. L. (1998) *Action Learning: How the World's Top Companies are Re-Creating Their Leaders and Themselves*. San Francisco: Jossey-Bass.

Downham, T. A., Noel, J. L. and Prendergast, A. E. (1992) 'Executive Development', *Human Resource Management*, vol. 31(1and 2), pp. 95–107.

Flynn, G. (1996) 'Think Tanks Power Up Employees', *Personnel Journal*, 75(6), pp.100–8.

Froiland, P. (1994) 'Action Learning: Taming Real Problems in Real Life', *Training*, vol. 31(1), pp. 27–32, 34.

Keys, L. (1994) 'Action Learning: Executive Development of Choice for the 1990s'. *Journal of Management Development*, 13(8), pp. 50–6.

Lawrence, J. (1994) 'Action Learning – a Questioning Approach', in A. Mumford (ed.), *Gower Handbook of Management Development*, 4th edn. Aldershot: Gower.

Lewis, A. and Marsh, W. (1987) 'Action Learning: The Development of Field Managers in Prudential Assurance', *Journal of Management Development*, vol. 6(2), pp. 45–56.

Marquardt, M. J. (1999) *Action Learning in Action. Transforming Problems and People for World Class Organizational Learning*. Palo Alto, California: Davies-Black Publishing.

Meister, J. C. (1998) *Corporate Universities: Lessons on Building a World-class Workforce*. New York: McGraw-Hill.

O'Neil, J. (1999) 'Facilitating Action Learning: The Role of the Learning Coach', in L. Yorks, J. O'Neil and V. Marsick (eds), *Action Learning: Successful Strategies for the Individual, Team, and Organizational Development*. Advances in Developing Human Resources, Academy of Human Resource Development, Series 2, 1999. San Francisco: Berrett-Koehler.

O'Neil, J. and Dilworth, R. L. (1999) 'Issues in the Design and Implementation of an Action Learning Initiative', in L. Yorks, J. O'Neil and V. Marsick (eds), *Action Learning: Successful Strategies for Individual, Team and Organizational Development*. Advances in Developing Human Resources, Academy of Human Resource Development, Series 2, 1999. San Francisco: Berret-Koehler.

Raelin, J. A. (1997) 'Action Learning and Action Science: Are They Different?' *Organization Dynamics*, summer.

Vicere, A. A. and Fulmer, R. M. (1996) *Crafting Competitiveness: Developing Leaders in the Shadow Pyramid*. Oxford: Captsone.

Yorks, L., O'Neil, J. and Marsick, V. J. (eds) (1999) 'Action Learning. Theoretical Bases and Varieties of Practice', in L. Yorks, J. O'Neil and V. Marsick (eds), *Action Learning: Successful Strategies for the Individual, Team, and Organizational Development*. Advances in Developing Human Resources, Academy of Human Resource Development, Series 2, 1999. San Francisco, Berrett-Koehler.

Zuber-Skerritt, O. (1993) 'Improving Learning and Teaching through Action Learning and Action Research', *Higher Education Research and Development*, vol. 12(1), pp. 45–58.

5

General Electric's Action Learning Change Initiatives: Work-Out™ and the Change Acceleration Process

Bev Davids, Carl Aspler and Bonnie McIvor*

The context

For some time, organizations have been looking for formulae for 'culture change'. Different companies have chosen a variety of tactics, from selecting new leaders who embody the new culture, to using education, to reengineering. General Electric has used several of these initiatives. The culture change at GE started with the appointment of Jack Welch as CEO in 1982, who started by selling non-core business units and buying new businesses that were a strategic fit. The remaining businesses were reorganized into 13 business units (at the time), with a goal for each of being number one or number two in any business sector that GE was in. A number of management levels were eliminated and the total workforce was reduced by one-third.

In addition to the structural and strategic changes (referred to by Welch as the 'hardware'), the company started to look not only on *what* was done, but *how* it was done, the 'software'. The vision was to be a big company moving with the speed of a small company. Over time, a vision evolved that is still in place today. Leadership started talking about the '3 Ss' – Speed, Simplicity and Self-Confidence.[1] Everything that GE did had to be speedy and simple;

---

* This article deals with two of the many change initiatives that have been used successfully by the General Electric Company (GE) since 1989 – Work-Out™, and the Change Acceleration Process (referred to in this article as CAP and introduced in 1992), were both the results of initiatives by Jack Welch, Chairman and CEO. The three authors of this article were all employees of GE during this time, and were involved in various aspects of introducing these processes in the company.

and it was to be managed in a way that saw the employees involved in a very empowered way. Over time, these values would be joined by 'Stretch', 'Integrity' and 'Boundarylessness', and would become the foundation of the changes made in GE and an integral part of the Work-Out™ and CAP processes.

Work-Out™: an enabler for culture change

GE is an old company, and despite all the restructuring much of the work was still tied to obsolete and inefficient processes. How was it possible to live out the three Ss when old habits persisted? To address the issue of bureaucracy, GE developed the Work-Out™ process, whose intent was to assemble groups of employees who would meet for several days and use a problem-solving process to identify ways of reducing or eliminating anything that violated the 'three Ss'. The basic flow of a Work-Out™ session is illustrated in Figure 5.1.

Work-Out™ differed from other organization improvement methods in a number of important ways. First, the GE business leaders were the owners of the Work-Out™ process. It was the operational leaders, not the human

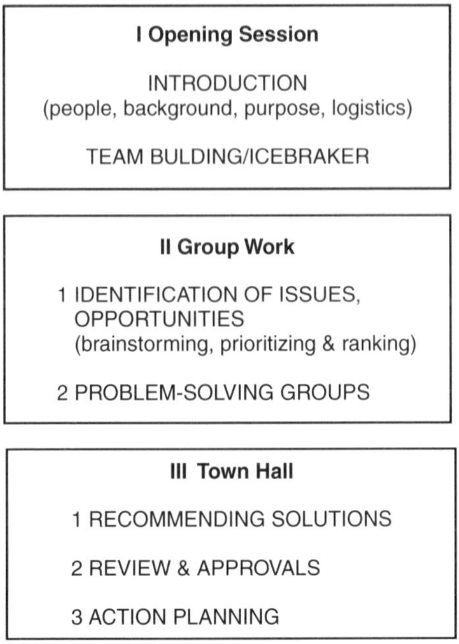

```
┌─────────────────────────────────────┐
│          I Opening Session           │
│                                      │
│            INTRODUCTION              │
│  (people, background, purpose,       │
│           logistics)                 │
│                                      │
│      TEAM BULDING/ICEBRAKER          │
└─────────────────────────────────────┘

┌─────────────────────────────────────┐
│            II Group Work             │
│                                      │
│   1 IDENTIFICATION OF ISSUES,        │
│     OPPORTUNITIES                    │
│     (brainstorming, prioritizing     │
│      & ranking)                      │
│                                      │
│   2 PROBLEM-SOLVING GROUPS           │
└─────────────────────────────────────┘

┌─────────────────────────────────────┐
│           III  Town Hall             │
│                                      │
│   1 RECOMMENDING SOLUTIONS           │
│                                      │
│   2 REVIEW & APPROVALS               │
│                                      │
│   3 ACTION PLANNING                  │
└─────────────────────────────────────┘
```

Figure 5.1 A Work-Out™ session

resources department that were charged with implementing the process in GE. Secondly, the off-site problem-solving activities excluded the senior managers. The managers were responsible for identifying the scope and vision for the Work-Out™, supplying the resources, introducing the session, making decisions about recommendations at the end and providing the support required to implement the decisions. Their role in Work-Out™ was to get out of the way of the employee groups, who were deemed to be the best experts in finding ways to 'fix' or improve the work, a core value of the process. Thirdly, Work-Out™ used an action learning focus: there were real employees working on real issues. At the same time, there was team-building as the participants were cross-functional and cross-level. The participants also learned to problem-solve, prioritize issues, express their opinions, resolve differences, and prepare and present recommendations.

Work-Out™ was meant to be more than just another productivity improvement exercise. Its larger intent was to get all employees to feel a greater ownership in their business, to empower them to take responsibility, and to develop a different mindset among the managers, many of whom remained overcontrolling and remote. This mindset was to trust employees who do the work to do what is right, to make decisions with speed and less reliance on having all the facts and information. This was a learning experience about a different leadership style for many managers, which they had to use when they returned to the session for the final 'Town Hall' meeting. It was at this meeting that employee teams presented their recommendations – on how to address the issues that they identified early in the Work-Out™.

The learning for the senior management group came not only from empowering employees to solve problems, but from a unique aspect of Work-Out™ which is that the senior management group was expected to come into a Town Hall session ready to approve the final recommendations. This expectation, communicated by Welch, came from the key value of the process – that committed employees could develop realistic and creative solutions. While the management group could reject or defer the recommendations, this was only done if there was a business reason that wasn't known to the group. The management group was coached to listen to every recommendation and think about how the recommendation needed to be modified so that they could accept it. The facilitators would work with the decision panel managers and the employee teams to modify the recommendations so that the managers were comfortable accepting them. Often managers pushed the employees to make their recommendations even more challenging (raising approval levels even higher than employees had suggested). This decision-making process forced managers to make decisions quickly, and in many cases on trust (not the usual way of making decisions). Recognizing that this process was uncomfortable for many managers, a briefing session was held just prior to the Town Hall meeting. Managers were

informed of the issues the teams had worked on, and for any recommendations that could be contentious a high level overview was given. This gave
managers a few minutes to collect their thoughts and make the process a
'win–win' situation for everyone.

Key to success of Work-Out™ was the implementation of the recommendations. Participants were expected to volunteer for tasks during the action-
planning process which would be completed after the Work-Out™. Some of
the participants also volunteered to be team leaders – responsible for ensuring the action plans were implemented. This helped them to learn project
management and communication skills. A follow-up process was implemented after the Work-Out™ which included regular conference calls to
determine if there were any problems with the implementation, and to take
care of the issues. Part of this success was the clear determination of roles.

Problem-solving process and key learnings

Depending on the topic of the Work-Out™, 30 to 50 issues were often identified, which required a mechanism to filter out the more critical issues. Once
all the issues were presented, the participants would allocate their priorities
within a payoff or priority matrix (Figure 5.2). Using the matrix as a guide, the
participants would identify the priority of the issue and vote (using coloured
stickers) for the issues that they thought should be problem-solved in the next
stage of the Work-Out™. This learning to reach agreement was important
throughout the process as participants problem-solved the selected issues. The

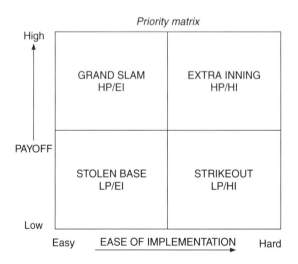

Figure 5.2 The payoff matrix

small groups were led through the problem-solving process by a facilitator, with participants taking leadership roles at various times.

During these stages of Work-Out™, participants learned how to write an issue/problem statement, how to prioritize, how to make a decision, how to reach agreement, how to solve a problem, how to resolve differences of opinion, how to write a concrete action plan, and how to present recommendations – all this while working on a real business issue.

As time passed, participants of Work-Out™ began to make changes in how they managed problems in their own work units. On a local level, the use of the process was more unplanned. White boards and meeting areas started appearing, and employee groups felt they had license to meet and brainstorm solutions and share ideas. If senior managers at Work-Outs™ were reconfiguring their role as enablers to Work-Out™ project teams, then why not managers and supervisors at other levels? In the words of one of the process consultants, the process was evolving from one that reflected 'unnatural acts in unnatural places' to one where the key elements of Work-Out™ – the challenging of the status quo, the development of innovative ideas and communicating across boundaries – were becoming part of the mindset of daily work life.

The evolution of Work-Out™ designs

Over time, the size and shape of Work-Outs™ have changed. Many of the early Work-Outs™ were large affairs – usually about 30 to 50 people working off-site over a two to three-day period. This has evolved into smaller, shorter and more focused events dealing with clearly-defined problems such as lowering inventory, reducing cycle time, eliminating downtime, improving recruitment practices, developing sales strategies, improving communication and job satisfaction, developing strategies for managing diversity and designing new organizations.

Examples of Work-Out™ topics

The following are topics that have been addressed in Work-Outs™:

- Reducing inventory levels;
- Removing bureaucracy (less approvals, simplify a process);
- Shortening cycle times (order process, billing process, sales process);
- Determining more customer-friendly packing options;
- Getting employees faster access to systems;
- Improving the level of safety in the workplace;
- Changing the role of the front-line leader;
- Simplifying the corporate budgeting process.

Internal facilitators developed

When Work-Out™ began in 1989, it was a cadre of external consultants working with the business executives who planned and facilitated the Work-Outs™. By 1990 it was felt that the process should be internalized and that the ownership of Work-Out™ should fall to the employees. At GE Canada (and other GE locations), high-potential employees were selected and trained as Work-Out™ facilitators (known as 'process leaders'), who were seen as more than small-group facilitators. They were designated as change agents who would not only manage the Town Hall sessions, but would also be actively involved in the planning of Work-Out™ strategies. They were trained in consulting skills as well as facilitation skills.

In Canada, GE was able to develop facilitators with a cross-business perspective. Process leaders from the Lighting business would facilitate in the Motors business and an Appliance employee would facilitate in the Aircraft Engines group, and so on. This 'external' assignment would also give them exposure within GE and enable them to push the host business to think 'outside-of-the-box'. The process leader role was seen as a leadership development activity – since it built excellent skills. Many of the original process leaders received promotions as a result of the new skills they developed, and the visibility they were given, and have gone on to use Work-Outs™ in their own departments. Many people were trained to be facilitators and are now taking an active role in planning and facilitating meetings of all types. They continue to use their skills with the major change initiatives in GE such as Six Sigma.

Work-Out's™ relationship with other change efforts

Work-Out™ was started in 1989 as an empowering, anti-bureaucratic and problem-solving process. It originally referred to the type of sessions outlined throughout this chapter, but the name was later used in GE to identify the company-wide change initiatives that followed. These initiatives are described in Figure 5.3.

The majority of these change initiatives continue to use the action learning process. Best-practice sessions were based on a study conducted of ten global businesses. GE business leadership teams would come to a session as an intact group; the best-practice learnings were presented and the teams then discussed the relevance of these learnings to their business and developed action plans to transfer the appropriate ideas.

Process Improvement was a result of realizing the need to start to look at processes instead of discreet activities – which was mostly the focus of the early Work-Out™ sessions. Again, the employees involved in the process were brought together and taught how to process map. They then went on to develop process maps and identify improvement areas.

Notes: *Quick Market Intelligence, New Product Introduction, Order to Remittance, Supplier Management, Globalization, Productivity Improvement.

Figure 5.3 Work-Out™ activities

The Change Acceleration Process (CAP) was taught to project teams of senior leaders who came to a CAP session with a specific change initiative they were trying to implement. They applied the CAP concepts directly to their project (this will be described in more detail in the section on the Change Acceleration Process). All of the key strategic initiatives were action-based. Quick Market Intelligence, a concept 'borrowed' from WalMart, involved employees on weekly conference calls sharing market knowledge and information in general, while New Product Introduction had teams of cross-functional and sometimes cross-business employees working together (and located together) in order to bring products to market quicker.

Making Customers Winners involved GE employees using the Work-Out™ initiatives to help customers with their business issues – in return for more sales, or a concession on price. Six-Sigma utilizes project teams who receive statistical analysis training, facilitation skills, project management skills and change-management skills. They apply all these skills to real issues where there is a gap in quality or in meeting customers' expectations.

Change acceleration process (CAP)

In the early 1990s (and continuing today), change was happening rapidly at GE. The company had been re-organized (fewer businesses, fewer layers), Work-Out™ sessions had initiated many changes as to how work was done, and best-practice studies were causing people to consider new ways of doing things. With speed, simplicity, self-confidence and boundarylessness as the goals, processes were constantly being analysed and redesigned, leading to changes in how tasks were approached.

Senior people in GE started to ask how successfully these changes were being implemented – based on a feeling that change wasn't happening fast enough. If changes were implemented, at what speed and what were the results? If they weren't implemented, why not and what were the lessons to be learned from this? A group of experts, that included Dave Ulrich from the University of Michigan, Steve Kerr, until recently GE's Chief Learning Officer, several outside consultants and several Crotonville employees, were charged with completing a study of how successful change happened. This study considered business, social, economic and personal changes. The group looked at what made some changes successful, and why others failed and the results of their study formed the content of the change acceleration process referred to in this chapter as 'CAP'. CAP is a simple framework for implementing change successfully.

Results of the research/basis of CAP

Organizations focus the majority of their efforts on the 'technical' aspects of creating change, including reengineering the processes, redesigning the organizations, establishing quality standards and so on. Most organizations are good at these technical aspects; they do an expert job at identifying an issue, completing the technical analysis and making recommendations for new methods and approaches. These are the types of things that project teams are measured on, and that leaders ask about in project reviews.

What is forgotten is the fact that for change to be implemented successfully, it is people that have to do things differently. People have the power to accept or reject a change, and the research showed that organizations spend little time on this 'cultural' aspect of change. They didn't focus on assessing how to help people understand and accept the change and to own the implementation. It is the attention paid to these cultural/human aspects of change that makes the difference between successful or unsuccessful changes.

CAP model: the seven levers

The CAP model outlines seven levers that are key to accelerating the implementation of change. It is not a linear process, and activities related to each lever happen simultaneously. The six levers, described below, are shown as arrows – indicative of moving change forward.

- *Leading change* – change requires a leader who guides the change effort, making it a personal priority, ensuring that it has the required resources, publicly supporting the change and helping in overcoming organizational resistance.

- *Creating a shared need* – It is necessary to get people throughout the organization to understand the justification for change, and to stimulate a sense of urgency. Is the change due to a threat or opportunity? How does it impact individuals? What are the current realities facing the organization?
- *Shaping a vision* – the desired result of the change needs to be clearly stated, shared by those affected, and communicated to and understood by the organization. The vision needs to be specific and translated into actionable behaviours so that people know what to do differently.
- *Mobilizing commitment* – this is a critical step, requiring commitment and support from the 'stakeholders'. This step focuses on identifying resistance and interests, and developing influence strategies to obtain buy-in.
- *Making change last* – the focus is on making the change visible, credible, integrated with other business activities, and that appropriate resources are committed to the change to enable it to be implemented along with celebrating early successes.
- *Monitoring progress* – this step ensures that there are measurements established for the change, that milestones are identified, that reviews are held to check progress, and that there is a process for mid-stream modification.

Each of these levers has a series of simple tools associated with it to help teams and individuals implement CAP into change activities and daily actions.

Implementing CAP using action learning

GE has a history of using action learning, and, as previously described, Work-Out™ was based on the action learning methodology. The majority of GE corporate leadership programmes also have action learning components[2] so it was natural that action learning would be used in the implementation of CAP.

The target audience for the introduction of CAP was the top 500 managers in GE. The feeling was that change started with this group, and if they didn't know how to make changes effectively it would impact the work of their employees. The senior managers would attend CAP training in business-related project teams, and each team, usually with eight to 12 members, would determine a change that they were trying to make in the business and use that change as the foundation for learning CAP. At the same time, they would make progress on a real business issue.

Each CAP workshop was comprised of three working sessions, each two days in length, scheduled six weeks apart. The timing was intended to allow for project work between sessions. The first and third sessions focused on applying different levers of the CAP model to the changes the teams were working on. The first session included several team start-up activities intended to help form the teams and clarify the changes the teams were going to work on. Each session was a combination of short lectures followed by long break-out application meetings.

The second session was a site visit to a location of a change best-practice operation. These best-practice locations were mainly GE plants or businesses, but other sites were chosen based on the change the group was working on. While the teams were at the site visits, they used the CAP model to diagnose the changes they saw. The teams met with the host management team, toured the site, and met with plant and office employees. At the end of the visit the teams would assess what they saw (using the CAP model) and make a presentation of learnings and suggestions to the host management team. The benefit to the organization hosting the visit was the feedback on business issues and processes from very senior GE executives. During the visit, the team would also apply the learnings to their projects.

At the end of 12 weeks the teams had a good understanding of CAP, had made progress on their changes, and had learned to work together as a team. An important part of these CAP workshops was the support the teams were given. Each team was assigned a 'CAP coach' to assist them through the duration of the workshop. At the early stages these coaches were external consultants but the skills were quickly migrated to internal GE employees that had been trained in CAP and were identified to be excellent facilitators. Once again the action learning methodology was being used. The internal coaches learned by shadowing an external coach in their first workshop – later internals shadowed internals. The coaches learned by working with the various teams and they helped the teams learn by coaching them through the application of the CAP tools to the change initiatives. It was an excellent way to learn by doing.

CAP today

At the time of writing, eight years have passed since the introduction of CAP in GE. It is still a key methodology in use and is still implemented using the action learning methodology. CAP workshops today are usually three days in length, and the teams that attend now are often joint customer/supplier-/GE teams. The change that they are working on is one that impacts the group members – introduction of a new product to a customer, a customer restructuring that requires GE to interface with them in a new way, and so on.

GE often runs customer CAP sessions, where customers are invited to attend by a GE business. The customer teams have a GE member(s) on them at the sessions, and are assigned a coach to work with them during the workshop. During the break-outs, they work on their initiatives – for example on mergers, acquisitions and new processes. Customers find these workshops

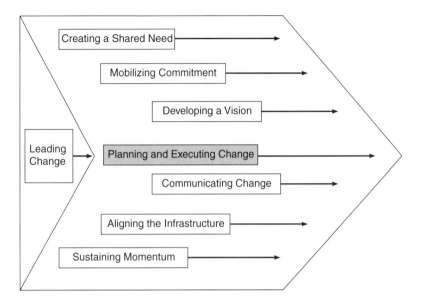

Figure 5.4 A change model

very helpful. GE uses CAP in this way to get closer to the customer, to transfer knowledge, and to strengthen its standing with customers. When CAP is run as a general skills course, the participants select a real change that one of them is leading, and this project is used for the break-out discussions.

CAP has been used in the implementation of Six Sigma, a quality improvement training which originally was all technically focused. At early reviews with team leaders, they identified that the teams could determine excellent strategies for change, but they were having trouble implementing the changes. As a result, in many of the GE businesses the Master Black Belts, Black Belts and teams received CAP training. In GE Capital, a full week of training on CAP and facilitation was a requirement of becoming a qualified Black Belt. This training was again designed on the basis of action learning principles. All the participants would be put in teams for the week; the team would select someone's Six Sigma project to use as the central focus of the break-out discussions – where they applied both the CAP tools and the facilitation skills that they were being taught. (The person whose project was being used left with very good ideas that the team had come up with.) The business leadership teams also received two days of CAP during their Six Sigma training. Again, they followed the training methodology used in other sessions – applying the CAP tools to an actual business change.

Modifications to CAP

Experience with using the CAP model within GE for many years, helping other clients deal with change, and further research into change has led to different models being developed, one of which is shown in Figure 5.4. This model includes reference to the actual technical change that is being implemented – 'planning and executing change'. Shown in the centre, it is surrounded by the elements of managing change. Another change is the addition of a lever called 'communicating change'. Since this is such a key success factor of change, it was worthy of being shown separately. This model also refers to 'aligning the infrastructure', which refers to a broader view of what needs to be modified in the company's procedures, systems and structures in order to sustain the change. 'Sustaining momentum' incorporates measurements, resources and other activities that are required in order to keep the change going – as long as required. 'Leading change' is shown driving the change – which is key for change to be successful.

Application of Work-Out™ and CAP outside of GE

Companies globally have implemented their versions of Work-Out™ and CAP with varying degrees of success. They have all continued to use the action learning methodology during implementation – learning while working on real issues. The action learning methodology helps the transfer of the processes since people can see the practicality of the process in the case of Work-Out™ or the framework and tools in the case of CAP. It is often leadership commitment and action, as well as the culture of the company where these change processes are to be implemented, that determines the degree of success or failure.

Work-Out™ requires stronger leadership and is a more difficult process to implement than CAP. This is due to a number of factors. Work-Out™ is more than a problem-solving process, but is targeted at changing the culture of an organization to one that is more empowered and values asking employees for their input. The nature of resources required is important. Although Work-Out™ is a simple process, it requires careful design and strong facilitation – both of which take time and skilled resources. Success with Work-Out™ requires a follow-up strategy and resources to do the follow-up. These involved need to work with the teams to ensure that their action items are being followed-up, and if they need support then the sponsor needs to be informed and involved. Sometimes there is resistance from people who have been through 'similar activities' before: these include quality circles or problem-solving teams. It is not clear to them how this is different – it is hard to understand the speed of problem-solving and decision-making not having participated in this type of session before.

Since CAP is a framework for change, one would think it would be easier to transfer. However, for the same reasons that the CAP model was developed – the focus on the technical side of change and lack of emphasis on the human side – it is difficult for organizations to see the need for a change framework. They often don't commit the time to focus on the human side since this aspect is less tangible, harder to formulate, and involves emotions and possibly conflict; nor are planning teams asked to report about their human strategies – usually just their business strategies.

Lessons learned from implementing Work-Out™

- There needs to be a clearly-defined and scoped business problem or opportunity.
- Work-Out™ needs strong sponsorship – throughout the process.
- Follow-up is critical. Employees must be part of the implementation of the ideas, and there needs to be an established process with check points and timelines. Leaders need to ensure that employees have the support needed to implement the action plans.
- It is important that the topics being worked on in the Work-Out™ do not duplicate other ongoing work in another department.
- There need to be clear boundaries on what is open to change and what is not. These boundaries, if respected, help make it easier for the decision panel to accept the recommendations.
- Work-Out™ requires strong facilitators that don't have vested interests. These can be trained internal people – usually facilitating in an area they don't normally work in.
- Management (sponsors) needs coaching on how Work-Out™ can assist in reaching business objectives as well as expectations of them during the opening session, the Town Hall Session, and during the follow-up process.
- The design of the process should be customized and flexible; what works in one company (or department) may not work in another.

Lessons learned from implementing CAP

- There has to be a willingness to consider the 'people issues' – it takes additional time at the beginning but saves time in the implementation. Senior executives and others need to understand that people issues are essential to examine from a results point-of-view.
- Questions about the 'people impacts' of change need to be built into the company's project review process.
- Change management should be recognized as a key competency of leaders.

- People need to see the value of applying the CAP framework to everyday changes as well as strategic business changes.
- Other tools used by the organization can be linked into CAP.
- CAP is best taught by applying it to real business issues – since it is very practical.
- CAP has a global impact because some concerns about change may be widely spread throughout the organization.

Conclusion

The intent of this chapter has been to show how action learning has played a major role in implementing Work-Out™ and the Change Acceleration Process in General Electric and in the many organizations that have introduced similar processes and programmes. In the CAP terminology, applying these processes to real work situations (a premise of action learning), helps to 'create the shared need' and 'mobilize the commitment' of participants and show the usefulness of the methodologies. Work-Out™ and CAP can be successful in any organization – if implemented with the right support and with a well-developed action plan.

Notes

1 'Speed, Simplicity, Self-confidence: An Interview with Jack Welch', *Harvard Business Review*, September–October 1989.
2 Mercer, S. (2000) 'General Electric's Executive Action Learning Programs', in Y. Boshyk (ed.), *Business Driven Action Learning: Global Best Practices*. London: Macmillan Business and New York: St Martin's Press, pp. 42–54.

6

Using Action Learning to Develop Human Resource Executives at General Electric

Peg Tourloukis

Beginning in the mid-1980s, Jack Welch, company Chairman and Chief Executive Officer at General Electric publicly blamed staff functions, especially Human Resources (HR), for creating, encouraging and sustaining self-serving, bureaucratic policies and procedures throughout the company. He claimed that these functions discouraged change and got in the way of managers managing their people and their businesses. He maintained that human resource managers in particular often seemed ignorant of how their businesses worked – what drove profitability, what opportunities and challenges their businesses faced in the marketplace. As a result, Welch fervently believed that many HR managers made decisions that worked against the best interests of the company. He pushed for radical downsizing of the function and retention, development and promotion of only those employees whose work made a significant and demonstrable contribution to business results. Human resource managers would have to 'earn their place at the table' by delivering financial results in partnership with line managers. Action learning as a human resource executive development initiative began to incubate at this time and in this context; the impetus for HR development through action learning projects at General Electric Co. (GE) came not from training and development managers, but from Jack Welch.

In response to Welch's criticism, and to develop the business acumen of HR executives, Noel Tichy, who at the time headed Crotonville – GE's management development centre – designed the Advanced Human Resource Development Course (AHRDC). In 1986, Crotonville conducted its first two-week executive development programme for high potential human resource managers slated for promotion to executive management jobs in

GE. A key component of the original course was analysis and problem-solving of company problems or issues identified by company officers. By 1991, programme managers who succeeded Tichy added a 'best-practices' component to the programme: given problems or questions by company leaders, course participants would visit sites external to GE, collect ideas about how other companies solved similar problems, and report back to the business leadership, all during the two-week course. These projects broadened the business perspective of participants, many of whom had not worked outside of GE or outside of the HR function.

One example of projects during this time period was a visit by some course participants to Walmart, a customer of several GE businesses. Participants studied Walmart's QMI (Quick Market Intelligence) process for immediately identifying challenges and opportunities in the marketplace by conducting weekly, structured conference calls with all key players so problems could be solved and opportunities addressed quickly by decision-makers at every level of the business. Leadership of GE Supply asked participants to find out how the QMI process worked, and how HR managers were involved in its implementation. The project significantly developed participants' knowledge and credibility as business leaders, and brought in useful ideas to several company businesses.

But not all of the projects were successful. Some sites were so different from GE in both culture and business focus that they yielded very little useful data. Usually, this was the result of poorly researched sites, uncertainty about what criteria to use in selecting a site, failure to really understand what problem or issue was being addressed by the project, a shortage of sites willing to host the teams, or a lack of knowledge about which companies were practicing and which individuals were capable of describing innovative practices that were applicable outside of their own company. Even when sites and informants were well chosen, projects themselves were often shallow – requiring participants simply to collect and regurgitate raw data, and adding little to their own development of business decision-making skills. Ineffective team dynamics led some teams to produce only minimal results.

In 1993, we created an action learning component to the AHRDC programme that dealt with these shortcomings. With annual refinements and modifications, it represents the fundamental structure of the programme we conduct today. The following is a description of our current demographics, our goals, our roles in making the projects work, our course design, and lessons we have learned along the way.

Demographics

AHRDC participants are high-potential senior professionals or managers who have worked in generalist roles and/or one or more HR functional area such as compensation, union relations, organization and staffing, or training and development. About 60 per cent are US citizens and 40 per cent are citizens of European or Asian countries, Canada or Latin America. All are employees of GE businesses, and many have completed university graduate programmes in business or law. All have participated in on-the job training via assignments in more than one GE business such as power systems, aircraft engines, broadcasting (NBC), medical systems, household appliances or financial services. Like all professional employees at GE, they have taken skill-based training in Six-Sigma (quality improvement) methodology and have applied their skills to implementing a quality-focused project within the company. Some have the job title 'Black Belt' or 'Master Black Belt', indicating their proficiency in using the methodology, their responsibility to teach and oversee the Six Sigma projects of other employees, and their designation as high-potential employees destined for promotion in the near term. About 35 participants from around the world are selected to attend AHRDC each year.

Course goals

The programme aims to enhance the pool of human resource people capable of taking on significant human resource leadership roles in GE. Specifically, participants are expected to (1) increase their understanding of GE specific business initiatives (for example Six Sigma, Supplier Management, Electronic Business Transition), (2) learn about innovative relevant human resource practices from university faculty or business leaders of companies external to GE, (3) share best practices regarding successful implementation of these practices, and (4) assess and develop their leadership skills in general business and in human resource functions.

Action learning projects in AHRDC address each of these goals to some degree, but focus primarily on skill development and application of participants' knowledge, skills and experiences to real business problems.

Roles

Each year, we redefine roles and responsibilities to ensure that we use time and other resources effectively. Key roles in our current programme are as follows:

Programme manager

The program manager decides what key company initiatives will be addressed in the course at large and in the action learning projects, specifically. She creates the agenda for the AHRDC course, selects speakers and topics, approves designs of course modules, and with senior human resource managers selects course participants. For action learning projects, the programme manager solicits proposals from senior human resource managers, screens proposals, selects participant teams (with input from faculty and participants themselves), and provides advice and feedback to teams and individuals when asked. We defined these responsibilities for GE's manager of corporate human resource development, a senior manager in the GE company who has an extensive network and whose credibility and expertise are recognized in the GE HR community. In past years, when the AHRDC programme manager role was designated as a developmental position for a less-experienced manager, the role was split into two parts, with the senior manager retaining ultimate decision-making authority in the responsibilities described.

Project sponsors/clients

Our clients are senior human resource managers and senior line managers of project-related departments in their businesses. They select issues or problems to be solved by AHRDC project teams, ensure cooperation of key stakeholders in their business, negotiate and approve written contracts (regarding project deliverables) with course faculty, create briefing materials for the team, participate in contracting and interview sessions before and during the course, attend the AHRDC presentation and feedback session at Crotonville, communicate results, decisions and agreed-upon actions to business stakeholders (see Appendix A for an example of a business-issue project).

Project teams

AHRDC teams are a cross-functional, cross-business, cross-cultural mix of participants who bring their knowledge and experience to business problems. They learn and implement a common consulting method, confirm contracts with clients, collect new data during site visits and phone interviews in clients' businesses, analyse and interpret data, create and deliver presentations of their findings, and manage feedback sessions with their clients to facilitate understanding and implementation of project recommendations.

Administrator

The project administrator manages all materials and logistics involving the projects. The administrator arranges transportation and lodging for multiple sites, oversees site administrators' arrangements, security passes, meals and schedules. The administrator also hires, supervises and coaches temporary employees who type and prepare graphics for teams' data analysis and data display.

Course faculty

Faculty serve as advisers and resources to project teams. In particular, an action learning faculty member teaches a consulting method which teams use as a basis for their work on AHRDC projects. She leads discussions on team effectiveness, learning styles, giving and receiving feedback, presentation and facilitation skills, as these relate to individual projects. He or she also approves and scopes projects and coaches clients as they define and plan their projects, serving as senior consultant on all four action learning teams.

Procedures: in general

Action learning is interwoven throughout AHRDC. Before the course, four projects are selected and developed by the AHRDC programme manager, action learning faculty and project sponsors/clients from GE businesses. The process takes one or two days of the programme manager's time, four or five days of the action learning faculty member's time, and about five days of each sponsor/client's time – spread over a six to eight-week period.

During the course, AHRDC participants receive team assignments and briefing binders on the first night of their two-week course at Crotonville, the GE management development centre that is their home base for the duration of the course (see Appendix B for the AHRDC programme schedule). They read and study these materials in their own time during the first four days of the course. During class time they participate in lectures, discussions and project work related to their work as HR managers at GE. They also consult with each other on projects they define and develop in teams during the early part of the course.

On Friday of their first week, they work with their action learning project team for the first time, under the direction of action learning faculty. During the day they prepare for phone meetings with clients to clarify expectations and reconfirm their contract. They also create work plans and contracts for their own teams, and get approval for their plans from action learning faculty. On Sunday evening, the beginning of week 2, most participants travel to hotels near the GE sites they will visit on Monday. They spend all day Monday collecting data according to the work plan they previously devised, returning to Crotonville late on Monday evening. On Tuesday morning they share their data and begin their analyses. Working largely to their own schedule, they identify findings and recommendations appropriate for their clients' organizations, and frame focused presentations. On Wednesday they finish their presentations and plan feedback sessions which they will conduct privately with their clients. Thursday morning they practice their presentations, get feedback from faculty and the programme manager, and make revisions. On Thursday afternoon presentations and feedback sessions with clients are held, and afterwards clients and teams exchange written feedback. Later that evening, team members review and assess their own and each other's work on the projects in a private team meeting.

After the course, programme manager and action learning faculty review the programme, consider participant and client feedback and determine 'lessons learned' to carry over to the following year.

Procedures: pre-course

We begin to develop action learning projects at least three months before the course is scheduled to occur. The AHRDC programme manager studies and reviews materials produced at the annual operating managers meeting of GE's top 500 managers held each year in Boca Raton, Florida. She identifies the four or five key initiatives that the company CEO has chosen to focus on in that year. (In 2000, these initiatives included: integrating Six Sigma quality methodology to achieve faster designs and higher quality products and services, reinventing and restructuring traditional businesses as 'E-businesses', globalizing operations, and continuing to grow earnings through mergers and acquisitions).

We talk about which business initiatives could be impacted by our work, and then e-mail a request for proposals to all senior human resource managers (HRMs) in the company asking them to propose projects that meet the following criteria:

1　Are related to key corporate initiatives identified by the company chairman.
2　Do not have a known solution.
3　Have quantifiable business consequences (that is, If the problem or issue is not solved or addressed, the business will suffer financially or will miss a clearly quantifiable opportunity).
4　Require an integrated human resources and line-management approach.
5　Have clearly defined sponsorship from senior line management and senior human resources management.

We ask that proposals (one or two-paragraph summaries of the project) be submitted within six weeks. We still have to promote the idea of sponsoring projects each year, announcing them at meetings and discussing possibilities in phone conversations. We do not promise that we will accept projects at this stage, but we do promise to consider any project that meets our criteria.

Within a week of our deadline, we discuss all proposals that meet our criteria. We move forward on all projects that (1) have potential to provide substantial benefit to the sponsoring business, (2) will develop and challenge the knowledge and skills of participants, and (3) are feasible within the time frame we have available in the course. In conference calls with senior HRMs, we clarify the importance of the project, the commitment of key individuals, and overarching goals of the project. At this point we decide on which projects we will move forward, which we will enhance and which we will reject. The following projects were accepted for AHRDC programmes in 1999 and 2000:

1 Enhancing the talent pipeline for branch managers at GE supply.
2 Integrating multiple sales operations with different compensation plans while substantially growing net income at GE Capital Commercial Equipment Finance.
3 Creating a high-quality, high-tech, Aircraft Engines global engineering group, balancing lower labour costs against business risks (focused on operations in Mexico and India).
4 Improving performance of a New Product Introduction design and launch team with members located in seven countries and responsible for a highly-visible, highly-integrated and, potentially, very profitable new product at GE Industrial Systems.
5 Improving sales force effectiveness at GE Capital Commercial Finance (see Appendix A for details).
6 Aligning compensation with strategic needs to attract, retain and promote talented employees at NBC.
7 Increasing the success of mergers and acquisitions at GE Industrial Systems via the 'right' decisions and processes for benefits plan selection.
8 Enhancing business results at GE Capital Fleet Services via the application of sound e-business processes.

Once we've decided to move forward on a project, an AHRDC action learning coach works with the client/sponsor to create and confirm a project description (a three to five-page definition of the business issues, business context and deliverables that meet the criteria for the course). Some clients decide to amend or even drop their projects at this stage, usually because they have underestimated the time, complexity or risks involved. The contracting process clarifies these factors for them. After the project description and deliverables are accepted by all business clients, AHRDC faculty and programme managers, the document becomes a contract to guide everyone's efforts.

Then, clients create a briefing binder for the AHRDC team assigned to work with their business. The purpose of this binder is three-fold. First, it provides an executive-level summary for the AHRDC team to get acquainted with the business and the problem or issue under investigation before they visit in-person. Second, it reassures the client that the team has received adequate information to be credible and useful as consultants in the business. Clients are advised that binders should include written copies of any presentations, reports or financial data that participants need to know, since their site visit schedule does not allow time for them to listen to presentations – they only have time to collect and interpret new data in accordance with their contracts. Finally, and perhaps most importantly, the briefing binder helps key individuals in the client organization better understand their own problem or issue: as they make decisions about what is and is not important for others to know, they clarify what is important for themselves. They determine to which locations they want to send AHRDC team members; who in their organizations should be interviewed; and after consulting with the action learning coach they set up and confirm a schedule of interviews. The role of the action learning coach at this stage is to challenge clients' choices by asking 'Why?' or 'Why not?' to further clarify their understanding of the issues at hand.

Procedures: during course

On Sunday, the first day of AHRDC, participants arrive at Crotonville from their home locations around the world (see Appendix B for details). Many are very tired after long plane trips, but, in spite of this, we have decided to introduce action learning projects on the evening that they arrive so that they have adequate time to prepare themselves to participate in action learning teams at the end of the first week. Participants are also typically anxious to know what project they will be working on. They receive briefing binders and team assignments and are reminded to complete or review pre-course reading assignments (we assign readings in Peter Block's (1999) *Flawless Consulting* text – in general, we use Block's simple consulting model as a framework for project work in the course).

An action learning coach briefly provides a context for the projects. Participants are provided with overarching goals of the projects for them and for the GE businesses, the roles of key players (as described above), and a schedule of consulting activities already completed as well as those which will occur during the class. They are asked to read the binders to determine what they can contribute to the project: where they can provide leadership and where they can provide support. They are asked to work individually and within the confines of the AHRDC community for the first week of the course; that is, they are asked not to contact clients' organizations or any potential advisers or informants outside of the classroom during the first week. We created this rule after participants in some of the early team projects, in an effort to demonstrate their initiative, approached a client organization during the first few days of the course and began asking unplanned, 'off-the-cuff' questions in the client's organization, confusing employees and embarrassing the client. So, we ask them to discuss their projects only with AHRDC participants and faculty during the first week, and ask them to use action learning faculty as their intermediary if they need additional information during the first week. We also decided to focus teams on making purposeful decisions about their data collection methods, and on reviewing their decisions with colleagues, later in the week, after everyone is prepared to make informed decisions. Finally, we assure client organizations that our teams will 'do no harm', and our context-setting discussion on Sunday evening helps ensure that we keep our promise. Knowing that some participants are suffering from jet lag, we reinforce our assignments and 'rules' in a written handout. An action learning faculty member spends Sunday evening and Monday morning at breakfast meeting privately with teams, answering questions and providing relevant data about client organizations and concerns. Participants are encouraged to call or e-mail questions during the week, but reminded not to call their clients' organizations.

On Friday morning, a full day of project-centred work takes place. Generally, after four days of concentrated classroom work, participants are anxious to start solving problems and it is the role of action learning faculty to slow them down and bring a more thoughtful perspective to their efforts. So, the day begins with reflections about their other project work during the week, considering what lessons they have learned. Given their training and functional expertise, participants are usually disconcerted that they often did not practice the basics of good teamwork in many of their class project efforts. Sometimes, they neglected to clarify their goals, or to stay focused on their deliverables, choosing to focus on what they knew how to do rather than on what was needed. Sometimes they failed to give useful feedback to colleagues during exercises, and experienced inefficient teamwork or poor quality team products as a result. Whatever they learned, we use their experiences as a starting place for discussions about how to create effective action learning project teams for the intense teamwork to come.

Learning from our own experiences, we have recently added a session early on Friday morning in which we focus on individual needs and differences among team members. Previously, we considered cultural differences as our starting point for that discussion, but found that many participants felt stereotyped or that, in their efforts to be 'culturally sensitive', participants sometimes failed to confront each other regarding unproductive behaviours. We have now learned that by focusing on learning styles we can uncover many individual and cultural differences and begin to view these as assets for the team. We use the *Learning Style Inventory* published by Hay/McBer Training Resources Group as a starting point for our discussion. This instrument ranks participants on two dimensions: their preference for collecting data using active experimentation or reflective observation, and their preference for processing and evaluating data through conceptual, logical models, or on the basis of their own concrete experience. Participants are asked to describe what helps them learn and what gets in the way when they attempt to learn new material, to identify when their style might be an asset to the team, and to predict what results might occur if action learning teams underused or overused their style. They work in same-style teams for this exercise, and playful arguments between teams help illustrate the importance of negotiating agreements, as well as honouring and taking advantage of differences to increase the energy and focus of team members.

In terms of consulting-skills development, participants review the consulting process they will use with illustrations from Peter Block, participant experiences, faculty experience, and examples from previous AHRDC projects. Focus is on the importance of contracting, especially how to manage a contracting meeting with clients, and data collection and analysis methodology. Again, participant and faculty experiences as well as text references illustrate the content.

Then, in their first team exercise with their action learning teams, participants create the skeleton of their working agreement. They are asked to define and state goals of their action learning projects, roles each team member will play insofar as they can anticipate these roles, procedures they will use for conducting their meetings, making decisions, using their differing styles and skills, collecting and analysing data, and requests for information or support from other members of the class and from faculty. This framework is completed by each action learning team, and is then reviewed by the entire class. We build a community of support for each team in this manner.

Later in the day teams work independently to refine their work plans using advice they have heard from their colleagues and their own experiences in effective project management, and to plan a contracting meeting with their sponsors. They are encouraged to develop Role-Responsibility grids in which they map out each step of their process and assign a responsible team member for each step. While contracts have already been negotiated between clients and action learning faculty members (in their capacity as senior consultants on each team), AHRDC teams are required to clarify their understanding of the deliverables, the content of the briefing binders, and any logistical details that are unclear to them in a phone meeting with clients. (This meeting is scheduled by action learning faculty in advance of the course and may occur on Friday evening or during the day on Saturday. All AHRDC team members are required to attend this meeting and to adjust their team's work plans to reflect whatever changes were discussed in the contract meeting.) Team members are also required to develop a standard script (protocol) for introducing themselves to all interviewees in their client business and a written list of questions they will ask during their site visits.

All protocols, interview questions and contract meeting plans must be approved by action learning faculty before they are used in client organizations. If participants do not finish their work on Friday, they are expected to use whatever time they need to finish their work during the weekend. Faculty is available during the weekend to review their materials via phone or e-mail. While intense faculty involvement at this stage may appear overbearing, it has proved absolutely necessary to the success of the projects and the development of participants. Teams often stray away from their purposes early in these projects, and this tendency shows up first in questions that are 'interesting' rather than those that collect data the clients need. Also, participants unfamiliar with this kind of data collection often ask questions that have easily misunderstood answers, or are unnecessarily confusing or complex. Faculty reviews prevent many of these problems. In reviewing their protocol and contract meeting plans, faculty give feedback regarding content, tone and time management of the meeting plans to help participants present themselves confidently and credibly to client organizations.

On Sunday evening of the second week of AHRDC, participants fly or drive to clients' business sites unless the sites are within a very short drive from Crotonville as is sometimes the case with GE Capital sites. Many teams are split into two or three subgroups, each collecting data at a different site selected by the client and approved by action learning faculty in advance of the course. Sometimes, when interviewees are at sites far distant from Crotonville, interviews are conducted by telephone or teleconference. Sometimes, interviewees travel to a central location. Sometimes, action learning team members travel long distances because the site itself provides data critical to their understanding a problem and making credible recommendations to their clients. We make tradeoffs.

On Monday, the teams work at business sites collecting data according to their plans. Generally, their days begin with a brief stage-setting session with their key clients. Clients and site administrators are designated as hosts for the teams. Interviews have all been prescheduled and confirmed for them. Teams sometimes request additional interviews, but they never cancel interviews out of respect for clients and their employees. Conference rooms, meals and transportation to and from the airport are arranged for them by site administrators and confirmed with our AHRDC programme administrator. We have learned to appoint only very competent people for these administrative roles and to put very specific logistical processes in place to guarantee that no time is wasted during site visits.

On Tuesday, we conduct an 'all-hands' meeting to share stories, answer questions and ask for support from each other. We review expectations for participants' presentations to clients on Thursday afternoon, and we schedule project status reviews for each team with faculty late on Tuesday afternoon. During these 45-minute reviews, participants are asked what they've accomplished, what's going well, and what challenges they face. Each team member is asked individually to comment on the team's process and his satisfaction with results to date. Each is asked to recommend improvements. Faculty review results and offer suggestions, information or coaching on participants' work or process. We have learned that it is important to schedule these interventions; otherwise, participants view them as an intrusion. Faculty are available to help or to answer questions during the day, but only make one unscheduled, unrequested visit to team meetings during the day. Faculty make themselves available at meal times, coffee breaks and during social hours to ensure that individual questions or concerns of participants can be addressed. Typists and graphics specialists are available for eight hours as resources to create the teams' data displays, for data analysis, and to create text or graphics for teams' presentations.

On Wednesday morning we hold another all-hands meeting, this time to gauge progress on project work and to discuss the feedback session teams will hold on Thursday with their clients. We discourage teams from inventing a process for this meeting, and instead ask them to follow an agenda proposed in Block's *Flawless Consulting*, with some modifications. We suggest that they clarify roles for this meeting and create an agenda that allows clients to get their needs met. We ask them to consider how they will share confidential information and how they will handle resistance – specifically, we ask them to separate what their data revealed from what they believe to be true based on their own experience and to clarify this difference in their discussions with clients. Faculty schedule a review of each team's plans for the feedback meeting with clients. Because this kind of meeting is new for many participants, some assume it can be handled as a casual social conversation. Faculty review ensures that teams create at least the rudiments of a plan for this very important meeting. Typists and graphics specialists are available for 10 hours during the day and evening.

Participants practice their presentations before faculty on Thursday morning. After self-appraisal, team feedback and faculty feedback, presenters and their teams revise presentations and prepare themselves for Thursday afternoon presentations for clients. Beginning at one o'clock, each team presents to all assembled clients for 20 minutes followed by 10 minutes of questions and answers. At three o'clock, after all four teams have presented, individual teams break away from the two-hour feedback meetings which include discussions of specific, sometimes confidential data, and recommendations regarding their business problem. The sessions are private; faculty members do not participate in these meetings. Afterwards, clients evaluate AHRDC teams and teams evaluate clients' efforts via short questionnaires. Both groups are asked what was done well, what could have been done better, and what improvements are recommended. At the end of the day on Thursday, AHRDC teams use comments from the questionnaires to evaluate themselves and their teams.

With few exceptions, clients have been pleased with the results of these projects. One general manager at GE Capital stated that the team's work had moved the business leaders six months ahead in their decision-making. Presidents of GE Supply and CNBC have credited AHRDC action learning teams with helping them move forward on critical business initiatives in recruiting talented managers and increasing advertising revenues. We are proud of these accomplishments. However, we view our greatest accomplishment as the development of people in GE businesses and in the AHRDC classroom.

Lessons learned: summary

We have learned two important lessons during the eight years we have conducted action learning projects at GE in AHRDC. The first is that we need to work on excellent projects with excellent people. This may sound simplistic, but we struggled to achieve success on any measure in our early attempts largely because our projects didn't deal with issues that mattered to the business or the people. Good projects and high expectations for results attract interested, influential sponsors and clients. They, in turn, drive extraordinary motivation and high-quality effort and results from teams. We cannot create this kind of motivation in action learning teams; it must come from the projects themselves.

The second important lesson we have learned is that high-energy activity, even if it produces intended business results, does not equate with learning. If learning and development are to be achieved, programme faculty, management and staff must give priority to reflection, direction, coaching, discussion, peer and faculty reviews, feedback and community building. These activities take time, but without them only minimal incidental learning occurs for individuals and organizations, and the benefits of action learning projects are diminished significantly.

References

Block, P. (1999) *Flawless Consulting: A Guide to Getting Your Expertise Used*, 2nd edn. San Francisco: Jossey-Bass.
Learning Style Inventory. Developed by David A. Kolb. Boston- London: Hay/McBer (now Hay Group) Training Resources Group.

Appendix A   Example of a business issue for action learning projects: GE Commercial Finance – sales force effectiveness project

GE Capital Commercial Finance (CF) is a leading global provider of innovative financing solutions primarily for leveraged companies. Our expertise in providing customized business financing solutions enables our customers to maximize the value of their assets and provides them flexibility crucial to success in a competitive market. In seven years CF has grown from the smallest business in GE Capital Services to one of the top 20 businesses in GE Company.

Commercial Finance has over $13 billion in assets with over 1500 employees worldwide. It has eight business segments operating in 10 countries with regional offices in over 40 cities. The business segments are: Small Enterprise Services, Middle Market, Specialty Markets, Merchant Banking, Capital Markets, Bank Loan Group, GE Capital Finance – Europe, and GE Capital Commercial Finance International. CF is headquartered in Stamford, Connecticut.

CF is a growing business that is uniquely positioned to:

- provide fast, customized solutions to customers' needs;
- approach business as corporate finance professionals, not as bankers;
- be able to take a broader view of risk and asset valuation;
- have sales force and underwriters work together in the field as a team; and
- allow our empowered team of sales people and underwriters to make rapid decisions.

CF products and service/market and customers

CF customers include owners, managers and buyers of both public and private companies principally manufacturers, distributors, retailers and diversified service providers.

Products include senior secured debt to US middle market companies: working capital revolving facilities and long-term debt financing, letter of credit facilities, acquisition financing, growth capital/business expansion, accounts receivable securitization and factoring, equity distributions, and recapitalizations: stock and debt repurchases.

Middle market segment overview

The middle market focus is on below-investment grade companies. Customers are primarily in manufacturing, retail, wholesale and service segments. As a result of significant growth and increasing complexity, CF made the decision to appoint a middle market segment leader. Prior to a June 2000 reorganization, four regional managing directors reported directly to Michael Gaudino, President and General Manager of Commercial Finance.

Commercial Finance's middle market is now led by Willie Brasser, Managing Director. The middle market is comprised of our geographic regions covering US and Canada: Northeast Region HQ - Norwalk, CT, Midwest Region HQ - Chicago, IL, South Region HQ - Atlanta, GA, West Region HQ - Los Angeles, CA. Also, a fifth region was formed, the Restructuring Group, to focus primarily on bankruptcy lending and restructuring.

Each region is headed by a managing director with senior risk managers and senior sales leaders comprising their management team. Under these managers are the sales representatives; underwriters/portfolio managers; collateral analysts and administrative resources. Prior to the segment leader appointment, each of the four regional MDs determine their sales and 'go-to-market' strategy, compensation, staffing plans, and measurement processes/criteria. At CF headquarters (M. Gaudino, GM; CFO; MD Human Resources) reviewed all these in order to provide some level of consistency. The year 2000 showed that the middle market segment had one compensation plan for the entire sales force.

Key issues and challenges

There are significant recruiting and staffing challenges. Are we hiring the right people? The current profile is strong technical versus sales skills. There is no clearly defined sales competency model that clarifies skills and abilities at all levels. This impacts the ability to recruit, assimilate, develop, train and promote. The current rewards and compensation system is skewed toward financial metrics versus leadership skills and values.

There have been inconsistent operating standards and processes due to the prior organization structure. This decentralized approach resulted in the regions operating autonomously and independently of each other.

Currently there is no clearly articulated-shared vision and strategy for the middle market.

Deliverables

- Identify the critical skills, competencies and behaviours necessary to be an effective sales person at the Associate, Assistant Vice-President, Vice-President, Senior Vice-President and Managing Director levels. Develop a sales profile/model.
- What do our top performers bring to the table and how do they differentiate themselves in terms of experience and training?
- Are the most highly compensated sales people delivering what we want?
- Recommend key elements/criteria for sales-force training.
- What are the key variables and barriers impacting current levels of effectiveness of the sales force? Make recommendations.

- Develop and recommend sales strategies to increase transactions completed by originator.
- Identify the key stakeholders needed and their roles and responsibilities to successfully execute and implement the sales strategy.

Appendix B Programme Schedule – an example

AHRDC, 29 October–10 November 2000, Week 1 GE Crotonville (Education Building – Lyceum)

Sunday, 29 October	Monday, 30 October	Tuesday, 31 October	Wednesday, 1 November	Thursday, 2 November	Friday, 3 November	Saturday, 4 November
	7:00 a.m. Breakfast Main Dining Room (MDR)	7:00 a.m. Breakfast (MDR)	7:00 a.m. Breakfast (MDR)	7:00 a.m. Breakfast (MDR)	7:00 a.m. Breakfast (MDR)	7:00 a.m. Breakfast (MDR)
ARRIVAL	8:00–9:00 a.m. Intro/Housekeeping Jill Wannemacher	8:00–12:00 p.m. GEMS e-Business	8:00–12:00 p.m. Aircraft Engines Globalization: Sourcing Intellectual Capital	8:00–12:00 p.m. Quality – Customer Centricity Jerry Jacobs Jo Ann Rabitz	8:00–12:00 p.m. Consulting Skills Peg Tourloukis	8:00–12:00 p.m. Finance Essentials Bob Gannon
	9:00–12:00 p.m. John Boudreau Cornell Univ./ Pete Ramstad/ PDI — 10:00–10:15 a.m. BREAK	John Chiminsky/ Matthew Fairbairn — 10:00–10:15 a.m. BREAK	Rick Stanley Tom Quick — 10:00–10:15 a.m. BREAK	10:00–10:15 a.m. BREAK	10:00–10:15 a.m. BREAK	10:00–10:15 a.m. BREAK
	Enhancing the Human Capital Dividend at GE					
	12:00–1:00 p.m. Lunch – MDR	12:00–1:00 p.m. Lunch – MDR	12:00–1:15 p.m. Group Photo then Lunch – MDR	12:00–1:15 p.m. Working Lunch – (Lyc.) e-Tool Demo Alan Burke/ Anesa Chaibi	12:00–1:00 p.m. Lunch – MDR	12:00–1:00 p.m. Lunch – MDR

Sunday, 29 October	Monday, 30 October	Tuesday, 31 October	Wednesday, 1 November	Thursday, 2 November	Friday, 3 November	Saturday, 4 November
6:00 p.m. Dinner – Pavilion (Room off Main Dining area in Residence Building)	1:00–4:00 p.m. John Boudreau cont'd	1:00–4:00 p.m. GEPS Services Growth Ric Artigas Rob Powers	1:15–3:00 p.m. Work on Mini-Consulting Projects in Break-out Rooms	1:15–2:45 p.m. Bob Corcoran Digitization & e-HR	1:00–6:30 p.m. Business Project Planning Peg Tourloukis	FREE TIME
				3:00–4:00 p.m. Susan Beauregard e-HR Initiatives		
7:00 p.m. Welcome & Course Objectives Jill Wannemacher George Anderson	4:00–4:30 p.m. STRETCH BREAK	4:00–5:00 p.m. BREAK/FREE TIME	3:00–5:00 p.m. Project Report Outs	4:00–4:45 p.m. Tim McCleary GE.com		
					4.00–4.30 p.m. STRETCH BREAK	
	4:30–5:30 p.m. Bill Lane Effective Presentations	5:00–6:00 p.m. BILL CONATY	5:00–7:00 p.m. FREE TIME	4:45–5:45 p.m. Cynthia Tragge-Lakra e-EMS / e-Profile		
8:30 p.m. (Lyceum) Business Project Introductions Peg Tourloukis		6:00–7:00 p.m. RECEPTION – (Outside Auditorium)		5:45 p.m. e-Tools Cont'd. Lobby of Ed. Bldg..	6:30–7:30 p.m. Dinner (MDR)	
	6:00–7:30 p.m. Dinner (MDR) -and- Intro. to Mini-Consulting Project	7:00 p.m. – Dinner (MDR) -and- work on Mini-Consulting Projects in Break-out Rooms	7:00 p.m. Dinner (MDR)	7:00 p.m. Dinner (MDR)	7:30 p.m. Business Project Planning – Break-out Rooms	

AHRDC, 29 October–10 November 2000, Week 2 GE Crotonville (Education Building – Lyceum)

Http://web02.corporate.ge.com/forums/hrlp/dispatch.cgi/

Sunday, November 5	Monday, November 6	Tuesday, November 7	Wednesday, November 8	Thursday, November 9	Friday, November 10
7:00 a.m. Breakfast - Main Dining Room (MDR)	7:00 a.m. Breakfast - (MDR)	7:00 a.m. Breakfast - (MDR)	7:00 a.m. Breakfast - (MDR)	7:00 a.m. Breakfast - (MDR)	7:00 a.m. Breakfast - (MDR)
DEPART FOR SITE VISIT	SITE VISIT	8:00–12:00 p.m. *Lyceum* Data Analysis – *Peg Tourloukis*	8:00–12:00 noon- *Lyceum* Data Analysis/Prepare Recommendations- *Peg Tourloukis*	8:00–12:00 noon Finalize Presentations (Ed. Bldg.) Team 1-Room Den Team 2-Room 209 Team 3-Room 206 Team 4-Room 205	8:00–12:00 p.m. *Lyceum* *Jill Wannemacher* HR Career Development Wrap-Up
		12:00–1:00 p.m. *Lunch – MDR*	12:00–1:10p.m. *Lunch – MDR*	Admin/Temp Help Room Conf. B	12:00–1:00 p.m. *Lunch – MDR*
Business Projects • Improving Sales Force Effectiveness at GE Capital Commercial Finance				12:00–1:00 p.m. *Lunch – MDR*	

Sunday, November 5	Monday, November 6	Tuesday, November 7	Wednesday, November 8	Thursday, November 9	Friday, November 10
•Aligning Compensation with strategic Needs to Attract, Retain, and Promote Talented Employees at NBC		1:00 p.m. Work on Business Project (Ed. Bldg.) Team 1-Room Den Team 2-Room 209 Team 3-Room 206 Team 4-Room 205	1:00 p.m. Work on Project/Presentations (Ed. Bldg.) Team 1-Room Den Team 2-Room 209 Team 3-Room 206 Team 4-Room 205	1:00–3:00 p.m. Team Presentations to Sponsors - LEARNING CENTER GREAT ROOM 1&2	DEPART
•Increasing the Success of Mergers and Acquisitions at GE Industrial Systems via the 'right' decisions and processes regarding acquired employees' benefits packages		Admin/Temp Help Room Conf. B	Admin/Temp Help Room Conf. B	3:00–5:00 p.m. Individual Team Meetings with Sponsors Team 1-Great Room 1 & 2 Team 2-101/102 Team 3-103/104 Team 4-105/106	
•Enhancing Business Results at GE Capital Fleet Services via application of sound e-business processes and procedures	Return to Crotonville (Late)			5:00–6:00 p.m. Individual Project Team De-Briefs and Feedback	
		7.00 p.m. - DINNER (MDR)	7.00 p.m. - DINNER (MDR)	7:00 p.m. DINNER & CELEBRATION (MDR)	

7

Getting to the Future First and the e-Business Leadership Challenge: Business Driven Action Learning at Lilly

Scott Byrd and Laura Dorsey

Introduction

Eli Lilly and Company is a global research-based pharmaceutical corporation dedicated to creating and delivering innovative pharmaceutical-based healthcare solutions. Our products address previously unmet medical needs and often reduce the cost of disease, thereby providing significant health and economic benefits for patients, providers and payers. Lilly employs more than 30 000 people worldwide and markets its medicines in 179 countries. The company has major research and development facilities in nine countries and conducts clinical trials in more than 30. Since it was founded more than a century ago, Lilly has been at the forefront of many of the most significant breakthroughs in modern medicine. Lilly was among the first companies to develop a method to massproduce penicillin, the world's first antibiotic, and in 1982 introduce Humulin® – the first human insulin. Then in 1988, Lilly launched Prozac®, the first in a new class of drugs for treatment of clinical depression. Prozac remains the world's most widely prescribed antidepressant.

Throughout the past decade, Lilly has been a company in transition from its old culture, rooted in a business environment of relative stability, to a new culture, adapting to an environment of rapid, constant, and discontinuous change. Lilly's senior management team has voiced and demonstrated its interest in revitalizing leadership and the culture of Lilly to meet that challenge. With critical emphasis on action and creating change, the organization is moving and reinventing itself. This reinvention and change require behaviour change, new approaches and new thinking. But mastering leadership and change isn't achievable solely by deciding to behave and think differently. It also requires mechanisms for *building* leaders. Mastering leadership requires a 'masters' programme. Leadership V, a business-driven action learning programme, was developed to fill that critical need. It is intended to take Lilly's leaders to the next level, and does so by combining one-on-one leadership coaching and self-assessment with real-life problem-solving and reflection. Because leadership requires action and is relevant only in the context of ambiguity and change, the real-life issues addressed in Leadership V programmes are both difficult to resolve and of great importance to the company. They require true leadership. Few, if any development programmes have been so strongly sponsored. The CEO and key members of the senior management committee provide direct hands–on support, before, during and after the formal programme. Similarly, no programme has ever been charged with such an important and difficult task. In this pilot programme the CEO challenged the participants, 'to understand the new business realities being created by information technology, separate them from the hype and, given our strategy, culture, size, etc., identify how Lilly can leverage technology (i.e. e-business) to generate growth and create competitive advantage.'

That sounds like a tall order for a 'training' programme. Does it work? What actually happens? Is it fun, interesting, or exciting? Is it painful? Is the personal and organizational investment worthwhile? These are all valid questions. The following story is intended to answer them and many more. It is the true story of the inaugural Leadership V programme at Lilly: 'Getting to the Future First – The e-Business Challenge.' The story is told as seen through the eyes of a young marketing manager, not yet eligible to participate as a full member of the programme but invited to observe, learn and share that learning with others.

Prologue: the author's perspective

When originally asked if I would be interested in joining the Leadership V staff and participants on their odyssey, I wasn't exactly sure what my role would be. It was explained something like this. 'Think of yourself as a cross between a business analyst and anthropologist. We want to capture how the programme unfolds and the interrelationship between the process and the business topic.' The idea was to analyse the evolution of the programme and help identify learnings that could be incorporated to improve the programme both now and in the future. My initial interpretation, however, was slightly more rudimentary. 'Oh, you want someone like Jane Goodall!' While that interpretation was a bit off the mark, there were a few parallels. Reluctantly, I'll stay away from the most obvious parallel and spare the participants from any specific comparisons that might be drawn with Dr Goodall's 'gorillas in the midst'. One parallel I haven't been able to escape, however, is that I was affected by the Leadership V experience in a manner not all that unlike the way Dr Goodall was influenced by the environment she entered. Not only was it nearly impossible to keep from engaging in the programme itself, but it was also inevitable that the energy, emotion and learning generated by the team would have an irreversible impact on a close observer. Like the participants, I was and am excited about the opportunities ahead (especially in e-business), I recognize the criticality of leading change and am determined to carry it forward into my own 'day job'. The objective of this prologue is not to emphasize the personal impact Leadership V had on me, but rather to place an exclamation mark on the power of the experience – positive change, leadership, empowerment and action are infectious. This is the story of the Leadership V initiative and the events, emotions and experiences of the 17 leaders that participated in it.

The story

e-Xpectations

In April 2000, a small cadre of Lilly leaders came together for a five-week odyssey intended to literally change the company. As they prepared to depart for the first week of this inaugural Leadership V (action learning) programme, a survey of the participants would have revealed only one common characteristic – uncertainty about what to expect. Questions, both spoken and unspoken, were abundant. 'What exactly are we expected to deliver?' 'How will we go about it?' 'Do we have the expertise necessary to solve the problems posed to us?' Although a plethora of preparation materials (including two books, 30 articles, several cases, and hundreds of presentation slides) were made available, mostly via a Lotus Notes database, prior to departure, the uncertainty among the team was not surprising. A personal invitation from the CEO had underscored his high expectation of and for the group. He was seeking 'not only deep analysis but also bold, confident recommendations for creating strategic advantage' that would result in 'significant gains not only for the business but also for each participant as a developing leader'. The breadth and complexity of the business issue, e-business, only heightened the tension.

In addition to uncertainty, there were a few other themes. There was at least a moderate level of skepticism flavoured with a hint of dread or irritation. Some were concerned that this might be just another training programme or a black hole from which nothing escaped, especially their most valued commodity – time. A brief look at the programme timeline served only to increase the trepidation – over the next five weeks, the programme would require more than three *long* weeks away from family and jobs. They were being asked to engage in a programme where the personal and professional costs were high and the value doubtful.

The coming weeks would validate some initial feelings and concerns, but they would also prove others to be unwarranted in a dramatic fashion. The next five weeks would be filled with unprecedented levels of uncertainty, high rates of learning, strong convictions of purpose and strategic direction, and numerous surprises (and confirmations) about Lilly and the business environment. It would prove to be a wild ride that encompassed both exciting highs and frustrating lows. In the end, it certainly wouldn't be characterized as just another training programme or a sinkhole of time and value. In the words of one participant, 'It is the best development programme I have ever been on (and I'd rate many of the others highly). It has been enormously energizing, and I learned not only about the business topic but also gained much insight about myself.'

e-boot camp

Day 1.

Week one had all the trappings of boot camp; green recruits, exhausting days, obstacles, frustration, sweat, team-building, transformation, and the graduation of e-troops. On the flight to Palo Alto, where they would spend the next five days, two things were clear. First, few really understood what the programme was all about. Second, the level of e-business knowledge among recruits (a.k.a. programme participants) ranged from practically nil to expert and averaged somewhere about that of the standard teenager (which isn't really that low, just somewhat inexperienced). The participant diversity spanned all classifications including level, function, geography and demographics. (It is worth noting that all participants were carefully selected as having high potential within the corporation, so a more precise analogy may actually be OCS, Officer Candidate School.) With the exceptions of age, fashion and mode of transportation, it might have been difficult to tell apart the new Leadership V participants from a busload of new Army recruits. The emotions and sense of anticipation mixed with trepidation were probably not all that different. Even the arrival at the final destination carried similarities. Just as Army recruits look wide-eyed at their new desolate, stark home for the next 16 weeks, the participants looked incredulously at the 1950s-era hotel in the middle of Palo Alto identified by one observer as 'aging bungalows with grass growing from random roof shingles'. One could feel the question hanging in the air as everyone gathered his/her bags in the lobby, 'What in the world will the next week hold for us?'

The first day delivered both increased clarity of the task at hand and an emerging awareness of the magnitude and importance of the strategic problem to be addressed. The mood of the group on day one was low and grumbling with only occasional spurts of energetic engagement to balance the more pervasive sense of anxiousness. This was the beginning of the group's march towards the zone of terror. The zone of terror is the time in a project in which complexity peaks, divergence in thought dominates, and processes become unclear. It is a necessary and unavoidable stage for groups attacking difficult problems and is typically followed by ever-increasing clarity, alignment and strategic resolve. The group's first introduction to the business issue by the Vice-President of Global Marketing and Sales via video-conference, provided improved clarity of the challenge with which they were charged: 'What should Lilly's strategy for e-business be? What are the value propositions, tangible next steps, resource requirements, and measures we should employ?' With a stronger handle on the charge came the first inklings of the magnitude of the challenge. These feelings would continue to grow over the next few days.

The CEO's personal, face-to-face conversation with the group in the afternoon had several important effects. First, his presence and expressed support highlighted the strategic importance of the programme. With his discussion, the size of the problem was joined by the recognition of its corporate importance and priority among senior management. It was clear to everyone in the room that this was a complex problem, it was strategically important to the company, and it was a high priority for the chairman and the senior management team. Ultimately, this ensured a high level of focus and intensity and would prove vital to the morale of the team over the course of the programme. The second important aspect of the Chairman's discussion was that it tied together the business challenge and the leadership challenge. The seeds had been planted . . . cultural change is essential, external focus vital, and speed crucial.

Days 2–4

Boot camp came in full force on Tuesday. For the next three days the participants were inundated with information about their leadership styles, internet technology and vocabulary, e-commerce, global business and economic trends, and Lilly e-commerce initiatives. By Thursday, they had been through more than 36 hours of training, exercises and group discussions. As if the long days weren't strenuous enough, they also had to contend with slow Internet connections, stiff chairs, and flies the size of small birds.

Each day included several two-to-three hour e-business training sessions separated by plenary discussions, break-out group exercises and individual leadership coaching sessions. By Wednesday, day 3, the group was squarely in the zone of terror. Enormous amounts of technical content seemed to cloud the business issue. Few, if any, were comfortable with where they were or where they were going. While there didn't seem to be fear of the unknown, there was an observable level of uncertainty and frustration. The team increasingly focused on processes and frameworks in an effort to provide some structure to the discussions and methods to manage the data volume and complexity. With greater understanding of the Internet and its new business principles, even the clarity of the business problem became obscured. The following comments, made during a plenary discussion on Wednesday, are representative of the discussion:

- 'Is our role to optimize what we currently have in place or create something radically new?'
- 'How do we structure the problem?'
- 'At what level do we operate?'
- 'How do we organize ourselves?'
- 'What information do we need?'
- 'We don't know what we don't know.'

As in basic training, e-boot camp had its own (mental) endurance tests and obstacle courses.

By Thursday evening, long days, data overload, and the reemergence of uncertainty was pulling morale to its low point. A follow-up conference call with the CEO and other senior management sponsors provided a needed boost by reinforcing their willingness (or even eagerness) to consider *any* recommendation from the team, but it did not result in a more defined task/objective – something the team seemed to be craving. By Thursday afternoon, a mutiny had begun to take shape. The pressure of personal and professional obligations that, in reality, had not been left behind, coupled with the belief that little more could be accomplished in Palo Alto, led to a public outcry of 'who was the crazy person who designed this programme?' and an appeal to end the first week's session a day early. The response from programme staff, 'Its your choice to stay or leave – its your programme. You are the ones who must face the business sponsors and policy committee in five weeks', made it unavoidably clear that the participants were not only accountable they were in control. Participant ownership was expected from the beginning, but Thursday proved to be the day when the team not only accepted it but demanded it. From this point on, the agenda, resources and so forth were managed by the participants themselves. Late that evening (after 8 p.m.), a group of four participants reconvened to brainstorm a plan for the coming weeks. On Friday morning, they presented a framework for organizing, analysing data, conducting external interviews and sharing learnings. This marked the true beginning of the team as a unit and was the first example of leaders learning to follow. Next, the participants would take their first steps into the e-world by interviewing local e-business executives.

The 'e-piphany'

'We've crossed a line and we can't go back!' exclaimed one participant upon return from the first interview. Another asked, 'How do we do that (what the dot.coms are doing)?' While Thursday represented a necessary canyon in the mood and morale of the group, the Friday interviews rocketed participants to the top of the Himalayas. In preparation for the next phase, a week of in-depth interviews with leading technology and healthcare companies, teams of two were sent into 'the valley' to talk with some of the premiere technology firms—such as Yahoo, Versity.com, Cisco, Intel, and DoubleTwist, Inc. (see Box). They witnessed an energy level and drive that was completely foreign to these veterans of 'the establishment'. The energy level was so high, in fact, that it was infectious – the group was literally transformed. This culture of speed, drive, autonomy and risk that is so pervasive throughout the information technology industry was strong enough and positive enough to affect, or rather infect, the participants after only a few hours of exposure. So began the transformation and the 'e-Piphany'.

Unlike basic training, participants were able to return home for a week at their jobs at the conclusion of e-boot camp. The next phase in the project, the core of the e-piphany, was a week of extensive travel as teams of two covered the world to conduct more than 150 interviews of global thought

---

Box   A Day on the road

0630: Flight from L.A –S.Fran.
0900: Arrive at airport and call XXXX to verify schedule. One adjustment 4pm meeting with XXXX moved to 6pm. Flight to Seattle changed from 6pm to 8pm departure.
0920: Car pick-up for travel to 1st appt.
1000: Meet with Group VP-Seibel Systems.
1125: '1-hour' meeting with Seibel ends.
1130: Depart for noon meeting at Yahoo
1207: Arrive for meeting with VP-Bus. Dev., meeting starts at 12:20.
1330: Meeting w/ Yahoo ends
1340: Travel Mountain View
1400: Lunch
1500: Debrief morning interviews
1715: Call home.
1730: Call XXXXX. Interview on Thursday with XXXX canceled, but new interview with XXXXX set up for Friday morning.
1800: Meet with Ventro COO
1900: Travel to airport
2040: Still waiting for 8pm flight to board
2120: Flight finally leaves for Seattle, discuss the great conversations of the day
2330: Arrive in Seattle, stay at airport hotel cause it's closer
0010: Set alarm for 6:30am

leaders and senior executives of technology and healthcare firms. As with most other portions of the project, it was an exhausting but extremely rewarding week. With several flights per day and schedules changing continuously, the participants were probably as qualified for jobs as airport food critics, travel agents or beat reporters as they were for pharmaceutical executive positions. Nevertheless, this was an unprecedented opportunity to explore other organizations and extraordinary people. Thought leaders ranged from Esther Dyson, Chairman, Edventure Holdings and Internet prophet, to Gary Hamel, best-selling author of multiple corporate strategy bibles. Industry pundits included George Shaheen, CEO of Webvan; Guy Kawasaki, chief evangelist officer of Garage.com; Neal Thomison, chief technology officer of Sun Microsystems; Jeff Tangney, co-founder of Epocrates; and Fernando Alfaro, CEO of Bankinter in Madrid Spain. Referring to the interviews and the entire exercise, one executive commented, 'I was concerned that this would be an impediment to our daily work, but I'm beginning to think that my daily work is an impediment to this!'

The interview phase itself exemplified one critical element of the e-piphany – the importance of external focus. It couldn't have been stated more clearly than, 'there is another world out there!' More than one person commented on return from the initial interview, 'I'm beginning to learn what I don't know, where to look, and what to search for.' It was through these interviews that the real learning took place. While e-boot camp was absolutely essential for understanding the technical elements of the business issue, the interviews provided exposure to both environmental context and operational (strategic) content unavailable from external consultants or inside Lilly's walls. The externally-focused interviews and the intervening periods for reflection and discussion allowed the team to 'get it'. Indeed, there would have been no e-piphanies, no ah-has, or eurekas without these interviews. The next several paragraphs highlight a few of the key elements of the e-piphany from the inaugural Leadership V.

Some members of the group probably entered the project with the expectation of solving a technology problem. During e-boot camp, it became clearer that the concerns were broader than technology and the Internet. They understood that the task at hand was truly a business problem that spanned functions, the value-chain and geography. By the completion of the interviews, there was little question in anyone's mind that it's not about technology and it's not even about solving a business problem *per se*, it's about culture and cultural change. Moreover, it is a leadership challenge. Competing effectively in e-business, or more accurately competing effectively in the future, will require cultural change. E-business, given its expected role in transforming competition, is potentially the most significant business challenge requiring cultural change in traditional companies. When describing experiences with the most successful e-businesses, one participant suggests 'culture drives these companies. They have an inherently high level of trust and low level of bureaucracy'. Speed, urgency, ownership and willingness to take risks typify the cultures witnessed. One particularly colourful comparison between traditional firms and the successful revolutionaries was, 'we're like molasses in winter!' The leadership challenge associated with cultural change was certainly not lost on the group. Cultural change, they said, 'requires behaviour change in us, *now*, as well as from senior management. It won't happen overnight, but we must become agents of change immediately.' And because the change will be evolutionary in nature, many e-initiatives (the revolutionary ideas) will have to begin outside classic Lilly. They must eventually be incorporated into Lilly, but their survival in the embryonic stages will require a cultural environment radically different from that which currently exists.

An equally important element of the e-piphany was the elucidation that the Internet and associated technologies are about power to the people. While not radical news to many in the group, it was validation that we (the industry generally and Lilly specifically) will require a much better understanding of our customers, including consumers. Information availability will continue to increase exponentially. We must find ways to leverage both the information we have and the information available to us. The opportunities to do this are innumerable, yet the implications are clear – we must change how we think about our products and our relationships with our customers (and our employees). The power to the people is not relegated solely to our customers but also to employees as business partners. With increased information comes greater flexibility and a more frictionless environment. Access to and utilization of talent will and must change. The team probably knew much of this prior to the project, but rigorous external examination provided examples that made it inescapably real and urgent.

It would take far too many pages to describe everything the teams learned during their globetrotting, but at least one other topic deserves mention. In the future, e-business will play a significant role in the creation of competitive advantage and the achievement of growth and success across industries, specifically in healthcare and pharmaceuticals. Utilizing e-business to generate advantage will require culture change in established firms, it will require speed of action and decision-making, and it will require the adoption of discontinuous change. What isn't clear to anyone, however, is which business models will succeed and what discontinuous changes will be necessary. The implication, therefore, and this is one element of the e-piphany, is that firms must find a way to test new business models and new business processes that by their very nature are disruptive to the current business. Engaging in this testing will produce benefits in two fundamental ways: first, some tests will work and could position the pioneering firm as a leader; second, the act of engaging in these tests will in itself create learning and knowledge of the evolving environment and business processes that will allow faster identification and adoption of new (and potentially disruptive) business models.

Pulling it together – the final week

After a week of digesting the interviews and internalizing the e-piphanies, the group reconvened to prepare its recommendations for the CEO and senior management committee. The first half of the day was spent simply sharing stories of what was learned during everyone's journeys. This was no campfire chat, however, but a set of impassioned messages of what Lilly must do to both survive and win in the rapidly changing business environment. The task was enormous – distilling over 150 interviews and five weeks of thinking by 17 team members into a single set of coherent, actionable and relevant recommendations. What would follow on this first day back together couldn't have been predicted. The complexity and uneasiness that characterized large portions of the previous weeks somehow disappeared. Anyone that witnessed the debates, uncertainty and restlessness of earlier weeks could never have predicted the focus, excitement and sense of purpose the team displayed on its first day back together. The seeds of most, if not all, of the final recommendations were planted during this first day – participants were translating their e-piphanies into strategic decisions. The remaining challenge for the week was not content development but refining the recommendations and organizing them for relevance and communication. Having lived through the e-boot camp and e-piphany experiences, the team members understood very well the intricacies and importance of their core recommendations. Articulating them to an audience with comparatively little e-xperience would be another challenge altogether. Much of the discussion during the remaining days focused on the importance of communicating their experience and energy back into the broader organization. The message was not and should not be a senior management-only concern. Everyone repeatedly agreed on a common goal – infect the organization with the energy, empowerment and sense of urgency experienced during this programme. As stated by one team member, 'This is what leadership is! We must accept the challenge and put our own personal skin in the game!'

One might get the impression that the participants' focus on leadership and internalizing it was a natural outgrowth of solving the business problem, but that's only part of the story. Throughout the workshop, the participants operated at two levels. At one level, they attacked the business problem directly with a focus on what Lilly must do and how Lilly must change to succeed in the future. On another, they engaged in a continuous introspective assessment of their own leadership styles and what they must do personally to succeed as leaders. During the two weeks the full team was assembled, the participants engaged in multiple one-on-ones with professional external leadership coaches. These coaches worked closely with each participant to ensure understanding of personal style and 'derailer' assessments and incorporate their learnings real-time. Many of the participants actively tested new approaches and made specific efforts to build on their personal leadership styles. In the end, knowing what needs to be done is only half of the solution – learning how to do it makes it achievable. These leaders recognized this need and actively sought to personalize the overarching objective of driving change.

Day two was spent in small groups attacking segments of the overarching strategy (for example culture, commercialization, manufacturing/B2B, R&D and governance). Though the processes were at some points analogous to making sausage, that is you don't really want to see how it's done, they resulted in a refined set of recommendations with strategic alignment. Just as important as the recommendations themselves, the group began adopting their own principles of leadership – take risks, trust your teammates and accept responsibility. The underlying tendency for many of these leaders was to remain involved in all aspects of the initiative, be heard, and personally coordinate. Recognizing that acting on these tendencies was and would continue to be destructive, they took risks by empowering each other, trusting that the work would be executed, and delegating coordination/leadership responsibilities to one of their teammates. This could not have been an easy task for a group of executives who have excelled through their own roles as leaders. Whether consciously or subconsciously, these leaders recognized that it is sometimes necessary to follow. On the last day prior to the presentation, the team reconvened to coordinate, ensure alignment, and not practice. They wanted the presentation to be fresh. With no rehearsals, it would be fresh by definition. With confidence, optimism and hope, the team adjourned to a barbecue on the lake. (Note: to eliminate any fears the team might have of a 'shipwreck' the next morning with the policy committee, this author deliberately ran the boat aground during the trip across the lake. There were no casualties, with the exception of a propeller, and the team charged forward with confidence that even a shipwreck is survivable.)

Making it real

Clearly, much of the energy generated by the team throughout the programme was derived from the e-world they had entered, but there is no question that some of that energy came from the support and attention of the Chairman and senior management committee. The credibility of senior management and the long-term commitment of the participants would hinge on the presentation and the willingness of the committee to respond swiftly to the team's recommendations (either positively or negatively). The importance of decisiveness was emphasized not only by the participants' extensive commitment to the initiative, but also by the content of the business problem (e-speed) and the leadership context. On the morning of the presentation, there was palpable sense of confidence and optimism, but beneath the surface, questions remained. Would the committee rise to its own challenge?

The entire project was laden with an aura of excitement and sense of urgency. Without the ownership of decisions or the ability to allocate funding and human resources, however, the discussion to date was academic or even somewhat artificial. This is probably not the response one would have received by polling the participants, but with the benefit of hindsight, the observation is clear. The meeting began with stories of the team's experiences, providing a necessary and dynamic context for the eminent discussion of recommendations. These impassioned stories, told by each of the interview teams, provided rich examples of the dynamic changes that would be necessary to succeed. The first recommendation slide required about 10 minutes of presentation and discussion. Among the key recommendations were to name an e-exec (and create e-Lilly) and provide (specified) funding. The committee's response, the moment of truth, was one that few were really prepared for. The chairman's immediate response was 'agreed, we will name an e-exec within two weeks and she/he will report to me…appropriate funding will be made available.' One participant described the moment, 'when the chairman said yes and it will be implemented within two weeks, it took my breath away. I thought, "oh my gosh, this is real."' This one simple response set the tone for the remainder of the meeting (and future programmes). By no means did all recommendations meet with strong support and approval. Some decisions, while immediate and unwavering, were negative. Regardless of the outcome, the committee responses were clear, immediate and decisive. Five weeks of education, investigation, discussion and debate became reality in the span of three hours. As stated by one participant and a future leader of e-Lilly, 'I felt like the dog who finally caught the car.' Now it's time to implement.

Epilogue: e-Lilly

On Wednesday, 14 June 2000, Eli Lilly and Company announced the formation of e-Lilly, a new organization within the company that will define and implement use of Internet technology and new business models to radically speed up and improve the implementation of the company's strategy in the new economy. The Chairman of the Board, President and Chief Executive Officer of Lilly, explained:

> e-Lilly represents a new way for us to implement our growth strategy and further build our creativity, flexibility, customer focus, and risk taking. The new organization will deploy technology-enabled approaches that demand these values and place our customers at the center of our company.

Two Leadership V participants were named to lead the new organization reporting to the CEO. The charter for e-Lilly is derived from and involves numerous, diverse components of the Lilly organization, including pharmaceutical discovery research, clinical development, human resources, procurement, sales and marketing, and supply-chain management. Areas of opportunity for e-Lilly include:

- Web-based networking and enhanced information processing that will enable Lilly and its R&D partners to perform 'virtual discovery' and collaborate online in 'cyberlabs'.
- Participating in global electronic markets for alternative molecules that may be candidates for new drugs.
- The application of new technologies to significantly reduce the time it takes to develop new drugs, obtain regulatory approvals and move new treatments and cures to patients.
- Investments in IT capabilities to gain internal efficiencies in back-office areas such as procurement, where the pharmaceutical industry has lagged other industries, and in business-to-business transactions.
- Customer relationship management and the application of e-commerce in relationships with both physicians and consumers.

Coinciding with the announcement of e-Lilly, the CEO reiterated his commitment to Leadership V as a central tool for the development of leaders at Lilly. Leadership V 2001 would be implemented in the spring quarter of 2001.

8
Learning as an Adventure in a High-Growth Environment: The Cyberplex Story

Dean Hopkins

As I sat down to write this chapter I thought of ways I could convey the richness of our experience as a growing company struggling to learn at a pace in keeping with our expansion. It occurred to me that the best way is also the simplest: just tell the story. This is a journey through our trials and tribulations, successes and failures, experiments and insights. I hope by exploring Cyberplex's challenges you discover learning opportunities that apply to your own business's growth, making the journey of learning a more enjoyable, productive and enlightening experience.

Phase 1: starting up, 1994–96

In 1994, when there were only 20 commercial web sites in the entire world, my friend and soon-to-be partner Vernon Lobo and I had the 'brilliant' idea that we should go into business together. I would leave my prestigious position as a management consultant at McKinsey & Co. and we would each invest a substantial amount of our life savings in building an Internet business – a virtual 'mall' that stores would join to showcase their wares online. Despite being only 26 years old, having neither a background nor exposure to entrepreneurialism, and never having run a business, I leapt at the opportunity. Everyone thought I had finally lost my marbles. They could not fathom leaving a growing career at McKinsey to build a company in an industry that did not yet exist, and that no one really understood. For me, that was proof enough that I was on to something.

Eager, ambitious and ready to take on the world, we began facing the challenges that would shape our learning and make Cyberplex was it is today.

Challenge #1   Sounds great, but what's the Internet?

Our first mistake was a big one. We had chosen a business that had no customers. For three months we called everyone we could think of to sign them up to our Internet Mall, confident no one could pass up an amazing opportunity to do business in a virtual environment that would draw customers like flies. Wrong. Not only were businesses unwilling to invest money to put up a storefront, they didn't even understand what the Internet *was*. We were ahead of the times.

We faced two options: give up or restrategize. We obviously chose the latter – licking our wounds, we limped back to the drawing board.

Learning opportunity #1   Go with what you know

Instead of giving up, Cyberplex (still only consisting of Vernon and me) concentrated on what we could become to better serve the *existing* market. We decided to leverage our consulting experience to educate the novice market on this strange beast called the Internet. We would be the harbinger of its enormous potential and inevitable, dramatic effect on business, and in doing so shape the e-commerce industry. To build Cyberplex on a consultancy-focused foundation we became Internet evangelists. We still couldn't get anyone to pay us, but now people were listening to what we had to say and, more importantly, starting to believe it.

We provided our expertise on a *pro bono* basis to organizations such as the prestigious Shaw Festival and outdoor adventure company Outward Bound, clients that had no infrastructure but believed in our message. Although these projects contributed to our active portfolio, we were still bringing in no money. Eight months later, after much hard work and on the verge of bankruptcy, we signed a contract with our first paying client – MacLean Hunter. This client opened the door to more paying work and began our business of offering services that were aligned with the market's needs. Twelve months after that, we grew from one to 15 employees.

Learning synopsis

What did we learn from our first significant challenge? To be patient, adaptable, persistent, and to never stop pursuing our dream. Despite all the hardship we were convinced that our instincts were right. We knew that Cyberplex was more than just a company that could build an Internet mall. It was a company that understood the Internet and its strategic business applications. The trials and tribulations that came out of the early failure helped us understand who we were as a company and clarify our objectives and goals. Those objectives and goals became the foundation for today's Cyberplex.

Challenge #2   We've got clients, now we need employees!

Professional services firms are a function of their people – the better the team, the better the company. As a small firm unable to pay the huge salaries that top talent were being offered, we faced a conundrum: How could we build a world-class firm if we couldn't attract and retain the best people? We simply did not have the financial resources these people deserved.

Learning opportunity # 2   Learning by listening

To overcome this hiring obstacle we set out to understand why the incredible staff we did have had accepted lower pay for a role in our company. We interviewed both internal Cyberplex employees and prospective staff we were attempting to recruit. The results of those interviews helped us identify the main organizational ingredient that would stack the deck in our favour: Cyberplex's unique corporate culture. We discovered that we were building a company with a specific set of values that was highly attractive to top talent. Our magnetism for top talent allowed us to win the best contracts with top companies, which then in turn allowed us to attract even more high-achievers – the perfect cycle.

So what did Cyberplex offer that our competitors couldn't? From listening to our team, we learned that Cyberplex was a refuge from the corporate world. We were an organizational culture that was somewhere different, somewhere new and somewhere fresh. We broke all of the taboos of the existing corporate world. Remember, this was 1995/1996 and dot-com or new ventures companies were few and far between. Cyberplex's youthful, casual, hip-tech atmosphere was a novel one.

Learning synopsis

By engaging the high achievers we already had on staff, and future employees, we were able to build a working culture and the atmosphere that set us apart from our competitors and made us an employer of choice. It was an environment that encouraged creativity and off-the-wall ideas, hard work and harder play, friendship, technological ingenuity, independence and honesty.

With the root of a great culture in place we were poised for success. Or at least we thought we were...

Phase 2: scaling to critical mass, 1997–99

Through the latter half of 1996 it became clear that we were on to something big. Yet although we were winning business hand over fist, our brand was sailing to the top of the Canadian scene and we were recruiting the top people in the country to our team, we felt something was missing. We didn't have a handle on Cyberplex's future strategy and vision, and we suspected the business model we were putting in place wasn't structured to be the permanent platform for our success.

We analysed the present and the future state of Cyberplex and arrived at several conclusions. One, we had a culture that attracted great people but lacked the awards systems to retain them. We wanted our employees to have a stake in the value of what we were building; however, the compensation structure to offer this was absent.

Second, after analysing several marketplaces whose evolution mirrored the birth and growth of e-business, we realized that the Internet industry's early fragmentation would eventually give way to a series of strategic mergers, acquisitions and consolidations. Growing smaller companies would be bought out by the industry pioneers, and a second round of consolidations would involve medium-sized players being rolled up into bigger companies. We believed these examples of industry osmosis would be very much part of what would happen to businesses involved in the Internet. In 1997 we were seeing the early stages of the first round of consolidation and Cyberplex felt that being proactive rather than passive would be critical for long-term survival.

Third, after analysing our financial state it became clear that relatively easy access to capital would become an important factor to our aggressive growth. We needed a currency to reward our employees through an option plan, we needed a currency to acquire companies and we needed a form of liquidity and cash-raising potential. The one solution for all three of those problems was to become a public company. With only 20 people on staff and a million dollars in revenue we made the decision to go public. No professional services firms were going public, much less Canadian public professional services firms. People thought we were crazy. Thankfully, we were.

Challenge #3   Going for it – going public

Delving into market opportunities we realized that going public was critical to our long-term success. A public offering would give us the currency we needed for strategic mergers and acquisitions, the ability to retain our top-talent staff with stock options and the readily accessible cash needed for liquidity.

We sought out and talked to a lot of different bankers, all of whom told us we were insane. Unwavering in our determination, we ignored their advice and went public anyway, taking the only path that was available to us – a reverse takeover of a public company on a small almost unknown exchange called the Alberta Stock Exchange. By taking over this public company Cyberplex became public. At the same time we raised CDN$1.5 million from friends and family and emerged onto the market with a CDN$8 million market capitalization, trading at CDN$0.625. We had arrived.

Learning opportunity #3   Going public does not equal overnight success

We quickly learned the hardships of going public. Few investors knew our story; fewer still understood the Internet and were prepared to invest. This was 1997 and dot-com fever had yet to hit. We were lumped in with the high-risk companies typical of the exchange on which we traded, and many investors wanted to see a longer track record before they would be willing to invest. Despite our lofty plans we realized that building a currency and a public capability was not going to happen overnight.

Learning synopsis

By listening to our people and acting on our insights as to how the market was going to evolve we created the currency essential for our success. By choosing to ignore the bankers and go public, we were able to rapidly build the foundations for currency that went into place about a year later. Over the first eight or nine months of the public offering we built a following and generated some sense that we were a real company. The stock started to trade more than once every couple of days, three or four thousand shares at a time.

Our newfound success then led to us to consider how we would use this currency to raise money and acquire companies.

Challenge # 4   The first acquisition

Cyberplex was again on the rise and suddenly we had the currency to make deals. Our first major step was to comb Canada for companies that we could buy and use to build our expertise base.

We identified 40 companies across the country, interviewed 10 and chose three that we wanted to pursue. We selected Webworks, a Halifax-based production company with sales offices in Toronto. Webworks' business was complementary to Cyberplex, and its organizational culture was almost identical. Integrating Webworks into Cyberplex, however, posed new challenges for us. We had to learn how to modify our business model, integrate a new group of people into our existing organizational structure and culture, and work for the first time with a regional office.

Learning opportunity #4   A new organizational model for a new company

In overcoming those challenges we realized something very profound: production centres should be situated where there are pools of talent, and sales teams should be based where there are pools of clients. Thus, production and sales didn't necessary have to be in the same city. Following this approach we realized that we could create an agile and distinct organization. This first acquisition caused us to fundamentally rethink Cyberplex's organizational structure. We began to reorganize the company while simultaneously addressing both market and talent needs. This process, which started with the acquisition of Webworks, ultimately affected our future growth and success.

Learning synopsis

Facing adversity also gave us great insight into our own company, and start-lingly simple ways of making it run more efficiently based on established talent pools. We now have five production centres and eight sales centres across North America, and only a few of the sales centres share space with the production centres. The production centres are located in Halifax, San Francisco Bay area, Toronto and Waterloo, Ontario. The sales centres are in Austin, Boston, Charlotte, San Diego, San Francisco and Toronto.

Challenge #5   Selling Canadian 'success stories' to the US market

Following our distributed production and sales approach, we decided to expand into the USA. Cyberplex had many advantages over US firms, including the abundance of talented technology and business professionals, the attractive Canadian dollar and the lower cost of living – all providing us with the potential to earn a higher margin than our competitors.

We began our US penetration by opening a remote sales office in Raleigh Durham, North Carolina, an area ripe with opportunity yet not saturated with service providers similar to Cyberplex. We recruited and trained a Canadian to staff it with the intention of selling our Canadian offering to the US market. However, after eight months with no solid results we realized that the American audience simply wasn't interested in hearing Canadian success stories. We had to change our tactics – fast.

Learning opportunity #5   Telling them what they want to hear

Our first foray into the USA demonstrated we didn't know as much as we thought we did about the American market. Despite using some very suc-cessful and high-profile Canadian success stories, Americans weren't biting. Cyberplex needed to have US stories and US client successes to be able to attract US customers. This realization led us to our first US acquisition. We searched throughout the USA and purchased Saper Media Group in Austin, Texas. Saper Media group consisted of only 20 people, but its clientele included Dell, 3M, Tivoli and Southwestern Bell. We acquired Saper for its impressive credentials and well-earned reputation in e-business. Immediately following this acquisition we opened offices in San Francisco and Boston. Within a year, Cyberplex's overall revenue from sources outside of Canada went from zero to over 75 per cent. We jumped from a gross mar-gin of 51 per cent to 59 per cent.

Learning synopsis

Our initial failure in the USA awakened us to the fact that we needed to tailor our client successes to the market we were pursuing. American companies weren't interested in what a Canadian operation had done for Canadian clients, they wanted to see what we could accomplish in the larger more competitive US market. To build those persuasive US clients, we needed to build an American presence through the acquisition of American companies. Once we had this insight in our heads, we struck quickly and turned the situation to our favour. The moral of this challenge? Know your audience. Assuming you have all of the answers usually means you haven't understood the question.

Phase 3: leveraging success, 1999–

At the end of 1999 we were building serious momentum in the USA with five American offices and 12 American clients on our roster. Our accession through the e-business industry was steady and impressive, and our attention turned to igniting the organization for accelerated, aggressive growth. Up to this point we were operating as a centralized management team of seven people each responsible for different departments within Cyberplex. However, the acquisitions process had begun to change the dynamics, confronting the management team with new, unexpected challenges.

Challenge #6   Growing pains and regional empowerment

The management team was experiencing Cyberplex's first real growing pains and we simply weren't dealing with those issues fast enough. Webworks and Saper Media Group, who prior to joining Cyberplex had led their own businesses independently, were looking for that freedom again. The managers in the regional offices had lost power and authority and felt micro-managed by the head office in Toronto. Cracks were beginning to show in our supposedly seamless integration. To save Cyberplex from self-destruction we needed to repair the damage and make progressive, sweeping changes to our management structure.

Learning opportunity #6   Sharing the reins, sharing the success

We recognized that the distribution of management responsibilities within the organization was essential for our long-term survival. In late 1999/early 2000 we redistributed the power within Cyberplex. Each regional office became responsible for its own budget, hiring, profit & loss and, most important, its own internal management and leadership. Very clear milestones were established for each office to meet, including precise structures and metrics to hit.

   The transformation was deep. The positive effect of distributed power became unmistakable when we started running quarterly management meetings. In this forum the leader of each regional office would represent their quarterly targeted performance and budget. We immediately noticed that the remarkable improvement in economic performance from each office was directly related to this return of power. The regional offices wanted not just to succeed but outperform on the targets that were established by corporate office.

Learning synopsis

Distributing power to Cyberplex's regional offices reinvigorated the sense of spirited entrepreneurialism that had slowly evaporated from the company. Now responsible for their own successes and failures, regional offices became more creative with their solutions, more motivated, and generated more excitement among their teams. People were thinking more broadly about the organization rather than just in their local office. All of this came from just giving people the tools and support that they needed. The redistribution also resulted in Cyberplex's management team taking on a different role, instead of managers we became strategic leaders. To borrow from the popular analogy, we stopped doing the fishing for regional offices and instead taught them to fish. Our role became that of a coach – encouraging better execution, setting strategies and setting goals. We focused on the stewardship of the organization, rather than the daily management.

Discovering our learning philosophy and putting it into practice

After six years of making some colossal mistakes and even larger insights, we have crystallized a learning philosophy in the company that is imparted to every employee throughout the organization. We realized that Cyberplex is made up of very motivated leaders that were looking for a chance to lead, and self-starters who were hungry for opportunities. We need to feed these high-achievers with something we have in abundance: challenge.

We know our learning agenda should be one that celebrates and utilizes this capability rather than circumventing it. We realized through some early training programmes that the whole concept of academic classroom-style learning is very contrary to how Cyberplexers think and work. The rapid-fire pace of technology, and Cyberplex's challenge to keep ahead of it, meant time was precious for employees; learning schedules and training programmes became almost impossible to attend. Balancing the need for learning and the realities of a daily workload dictated a change to the model.

What we constructed was a learning environment that puts the responsibility for learning on the employee, rather than the organization. For this approach to be successful, proactive learning had to become a core value of Cyberplex, one embraced by all current and future employees.

The second phase of our philosophy was creating an environment that taught people *how* to be good learners. We began searching for an exceptional teaching model that not only complemented our intense growth, yet was both organic and oriented to our employees autonomous nature. McMaster University in Canada applied a reputable learning methodology that mirrored Cyberplex's own learning philosophies and fit Cyberplex's corporate strategy perfectly. And so after studying McMaster University's positive results, we implemented their model into our organizational structure.

To ensure the scope of this innovative learning methodology permeated through the entire organization, Cyberplex hired a Learning Specialist. This learning professional is responsible for facilitating our processes from the top down. It is imperative that managers are committed to the intrinsic value of learning and impart that belief to the employees they mentor. Everyone at Cyberplex is an active and participative learner, as well as a resource to other learners. Our programme makes up-to-date learning resources such as contextual formats, online materials and videos available throughout the organization. Employees are expected to ask themselves learning-related questions that will advance their careers: 'What do I want to learn to catalyze my career?' 'What don't I know or what could I know better?' 'How can I advance myself professionally and personally?' Employees then need to identify where the resources that can best answer those questions are and how to maximize them. As a final stage, employees must self-evaluate and explore the quality of the learning that has been achieved.

As a result of this employee-centred learning agenda, we have structured an organic learning process that empowers people to take responsibility for their own learning. Employees learn at their own rate and according to their own schedules. Our approach to autonomic learning has been developed as a response to the needs of the confident self-starters that comprise Cyberplex.

The results of self-directed learning: two examples of employee response

Cyberplex's self-empowered learning structure puts into practice our belief that ideal Cyberplex employees need to be entrepreneurial and self-directed. The following two examples demonstrate how our fluid learning methodology can catalyze or cripple an employee's professional advancement at Cyberplex.

The first example involves an interface developer who had a serious interest in wireless technology. Believing this new technology could have a very positive impact on Cyberplex, he asked for support from Cyberplex to pursue additional training and education. Once he was confidently trained in wireless technology he began marketing himself within Cyberplex as a valuable internal resource. Eventually client-need matched the interface developer's recently acquired wireless skill-set and he was brought into the project to pitch the concept. The result was profitable for Cyberplex and has led to more wireless technology work. One employee's grassroots learning initiative has imparted incredible value to the entire company.

However, self-motivated learning has proven too fluid for some employees who came to Cyberplex as top performers. One such employee, who came from a military background, simply could not adapt to an environment that required him to define and actualize his own learning agenda. Without the learning structure laid out for him to follow, he lacked the self-awareness and initiative to formalize and achieve concrete learning objectives. Cyberplex's organic structure proved anti-productive for this type of performer.

Cyberplex's future learning initiatives

While the fluidity and organic nature of our learning methodology has proved immensely successful for Cyberplex, our future initiatives involve imbedding these processes in a more formal employee-orientation framework. Promoting the concept of continuous learning right from the recruitment stage will help channel top performers into achievement-oriented careers at Cyberplex. Also on our prospective agenda is making the concerted effort to orient employees in new learning roles; supporting employees in their transition through ascending leadership levels and ensuring they continue to foster learning in others throughout their career advancement.

Afterword

Business is about trial and error, with some vision, smarts and luck thrown into the mix. Obviously for us, the learning isn't over, nor will it ever be. Once we stop facing challenges, we stop learning and growing. End of story.

9

Learning in Action: Accelerating the Development of High-Potential Executives in the Canadian Public Service

Charles Brassard

Action learning is a powerful concept and application for meeting the development needs of individuals and supporting the priorities of organizations. It provides the foundation for an innovative programme established within the federal public service of Canada designed to help address the leadership gap created by rapidly retiring senior executives. In the spirit of action learning, this chapter describes the various components of the Accelerated Executive Development Programme in light of the lessons learned from its implementation over the past two to three years. It will hopefully serve as a useful point of reference for practitioners with an interest in action learning, both from an overall programme design perspective, and from its specific applications 'on the ground'. The article concludes by high-lighting key success factors associated with action learning programmes based on this experience and related future developments.

Why this programme?

The public service of Canada, like that in many other countries, has undergone a significant transformation during the past decade, a period of increasing interdependence between economies, organizations and people. The expansion of the knowledge-based economy and its implications on the nature of work, the radical pace of adaptation to science and technology innovations, and the increasing relevance of 'multinational' governance to domestic policy-making are just a few example of the forces challenging the traditional role of government within society and that of its public service. The 1990s are also known in Canada for the sustained effort by governments (federal and provincial) to regain control over long-standing budget deficits. Comprehensive programme reviews at the federal level led

133

to substantial job cuts, the merging of government departments, new initiatives and mechanisms to deliver programmes and services, and a new accountability framework for people and organizations.

The demographic backdrop to these combined forces is significant for the public service, which began to face at the same time a major people crisis with the ageing of the postwar 'baby boomers' which dominated its ranks and their accelerated exodus. The persistent lack of significant recruitment to renew the public service at its base over a 20-year period brought the generation gap into sharp focus and urgently called attention to the human element of public service renewal. Multifaceted initiatives under 'La Releve' were launched later in the decade to sustain efforts to make the public service a modern and dynamic institution and to ensure the recruitment, retention and development of skilled and committed people capable to meet the challenges of their time. The Accelerated Executive Development Programme was born in this context as one of the means to address the need for leadership renewal in the federal public service.

The generation gap

The following key demographic indicators illustrate the challenge of renewing the executive cadre of the public service.

- 90 per cent of Assistant Deputy Ministers* (275 in total) are in a position to retire by 2005.
- Over two-thirds of public service executives (3000 in total) are between the ages of 45 and 54.
- Over 70 per cent of these executives could retire within 10 years.
- 56 per cent of people in the executive feeder groups are in the 45–54 age category.

(*Assistant Deputy Ministers report to Deputy Ministers who are the highest ranking public servants and normally responsible for running a government department.)

What is this programme about?

The objective of the Accelerated Executive Development Programme (AEXDP) is to identify a representative group of executives demonstrating the potential to become Assistant Deputy Ministers and accelerate their development and career advancement. The major components of the programme can be drawn from its objective:

- A selection process is used to identify a representative group of high-potential executives;

- A learning and development component supports individuals in reaching that potential; and
- An assessment and promotion process provides a vehicle for their accelerated career advancement.

Individuals join the programme for a period of one to three years depending on their current level in the executive hierarchy (that is, EX 1, 2 or 3). They complete the programme sometime after reaching executive level three (EX 3 is the level just below that of an ADM) and meeting their development goals, or after successfully competing for a position at the ADM level (EX 4/5); that is, the programme does not guarantee their appointment at the ADM level.

This article discusses all three components of the AEXDP but focuses principally on the learning and development dimension given its greater relevance to the underlying theme of action learning.

Selecting participants

Candidates to the AEXDP self-identify and their leadership competencies are assessed through a variety of tools (for example track record assessment, reference checks, interview). The results of these assessments form the basis for recommending acceptance to the AEXDP. The leadership competency profile (see Figure 9.1) used as a basis for the selection assessment is also used to guide the personal learning and development goals of participants as well as a standard for promotion reviews within the programme.

Two selection rounds (74 participants enrolled) have been held between the inception of the programme in mid-1997 and early 2000, and the

Cognitive capacity	Creativity	Visioning
Action management	Organizational awareness	Team work
Partnering	Interpersonal relations	Communications
Stamina/stress resistance	Ethics and values	Personality
Behavioural flexibility	Self-confidence	

Figure 9.1   Public service leadership competencies

programme is still experimenting with finding the best combination of selection tools, that is one that balances objective standards for identifying high-potential candidates with human judgment. In support of this goal, considerable effort has been devoted to training people responsible for conducting assessments, interviews and other related reviews (often representing major time commitments from the most senior executives) in order to ensure the highest standards of objectivity and fairness. However, some degree of subjectivity is unavoidable and perhaps even desirable in such a context. Human intuition or judgment (reflecting one's values, experiences, organizational awareness and so forth) plays a role in the AEXDP selection process because it is offset by opportunities for challenge and debate and by consideration of a range of 'objective' indicators (that is, observable and comparable).

While indicators can be established for every competency under review, it is obvious that not every one of them can be measured with the same degree of objectivity. Similarly, while it is important to establish an individual's level of competence for all attributes of public service leadership for differentiation and selection purposes, it is important to recognize that not all competencies are equally responsive to learning and development stimuli. Increasing attention is being given in selection assessments to the relative importance of competencies that are innate (for example stamina, personality) versus those that are susceptible to development (for example action management, partnership).

One of the other issues being addressed in the selection process is the unintended bias towards people already possessing a deep and diversified experience in core government functions (usually older people) which favours their ability to reach the ADM level within the three years or less period targeted when they join the programme. This has meant that a number of younger people with high-potential attributes but less experience may not have been able to participate in the programme to date. The possibility of lengthening the targeted development period could be one option to qualify younger people in the pool of participants, a measure which could also make a contribution towards addressing the generation gap illustrated before. Key points to note are that:

- It is important to keep experimenting with assessment tools until the right balance and mix is found.
- Room should be left in selection decisions for judgments which reflect more subjective organizational criteria.
- Selection criteria should reflect the importance and weight given to competencies amenable to development as compared to those that are largely innate.
- Selection criteria should be aligned with the broader corporate and human resources priorities.

Making the most of learning

The learning and development component of the programme provides participants with innovative tools that help to enhance their leadership competencies and their experience in core government functions. Action learning is a primary objective of all elements of the programme and is expressed in the following programme design criteria:

• Skills should be developed in real time through practical experiences;
• Learning should lead to individual and collective action;
• A continuous action-reflection cycle should be nurtured;
• Learning outcomes should meet both individual and corporate needs;
• The development of lifelong learning behaviours should be supported; and,
• Opportunities to build learning partnerships should be maximized.

Action learning is a powerful vehicle because it is grounded in the reality and the commitments of individuals and organizations. For individuals, the workplace provides a unique field of observation and practice from which, reflection, learning and action can be generated. For organizations, action learning can provide the synergy required to meet a corporate challenge while improving the leadership competencies of its people. In both cases, the challenge lies in carefully balancing efforts and investments in all aspects of this powerful equation (Figure 9.2).

Focusing primarily on the learning aspects provides people with worthwhile knowledge and experiences but few incentives to correct their own practices and behaviours in the real world. Focusing mainly on action can lead to great business results but leaves little residual capacity for people to learn and self-generate changes in their behaviours for the long term. Balancing the individual and the collective approach is also important. Individuals require the freedom to reflect and learn on their own terms but

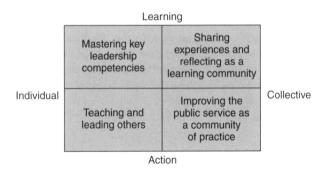

Figure 9.2   AEXDP objectives in an action learning context

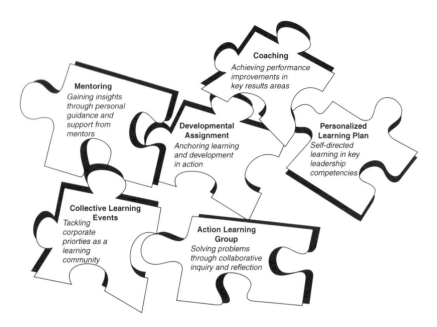

Figure 9.3   Accelerated executive development programme learning approach

can lose perspective on their progress and forego rich insights without interaction and feedback from others. On the other hand, learning and working with others can be incredibly stimulating but can leave room for people to free-ride on the action learning commitments of their peers. The objectives and desired outcome of any development programme dictate where that balance lies and how to connect the programme components together. AEXDP is designed to work on all fronts simultaneously and in a complementary fashion.

The learning components of AEXDP (Figure 9.3) are designed to mutually support and reinforce each other in meeting the objectives of the programme. They provide opportunities for cross fertilization among people within and outside the programme, and for debate and reflection about leadership and public service issues shaping the lives of participants and their organizations.

Developmental assignments

Government departments provide developmental assignments that ensure intense and meaningful work experiences for participants. These assignments are carefully chosen with participants to enable them to gain a breadth and depth of experience in core government functions they have not been exposed to before and to home-in on specific competencies. An Executive Advisor is assigned to each participant at the beginning of the programme to provide advice and guidance on all matters related to developmental assignments (for example identification, negotiation of terms and conditions) and learning.

Developmental assignments are the participants' anchor for action, reflection and learning. This means that participants are practicing the skills they need in real time. They reflect to derive meaning from these experiences and to focus their actions and commitments. In this way, their work experiences are a source of continuous learning.

An important consideration for the success of developmental assignments is their duration. At the outset of the programme, assignments were planned to be of shorter duration (12–15 months) to enable more rapid movement between unfamiliar work experiences. It quickly became apparent that while shorter assignments are quite valid for meeting certain developmental goals, longer assignment periods allow for the experience to be more complete in terms of how achievements, breakdowns and challenges contribute to learning and development. It is also apparent that longer assignments create more stability in the host organization.

Managers of participants are key to making developmental assignments work and to maximizing the learning potential and value for the participant, his team and beyond. As managers, they help set and meet performance objectives. As learning partners, they are important sources of support and feedback in all phases of the assignment: the *transition* into the organization and the adjustments that follow in terms of building self-confidence, relationships and so on (this is the phase during which the learning curve is the steepest); the stage at which *performance* is rapidly increasing and peaking (that is, a track record is being set); and *completion*, when the participant moves on to another assignment. As learning partners, managers can also be ideal conduits for imparting new ideas and practices into the organization.

Quality of assignments and leadership role models are both crucial to the success of the programme. While one doesn't necessarily follow the other, the screening associated with the ultimate selection of developmental assignments (and by extension the choice of managers) helps to set clear expectations and to minimize setbacks for participants as well as the host organization. Still, communicating and raising awareness to the programme's objectives and the role of developmental assignments and managers are crucial at the front end of the programme (even before assignments are proposed). Once a participant and his host organization agree to pursue an assignment, Executive Advisors ensure that the term and conditions of the formal agreement are aligned with the objectives of the programme and relevant to the learning and development goals of the individual. They use this and other opportunities to set or clarify expectations and commitments associated with participation in the programme (that is, in relation to performance objectives and commitment to learning). Workshops (that is, structured discussion sessions) are also held throughout the year to help new and experienced managers in the programme to be more effective in their coaching role.

Despite this supporting environment, participants routinely find they must make trade-offs between meeting their performance goals (which is relevant to the promotion process) and investing in their learning and development. The fact that both spheres complement each other and that 'performance' in learning is also a key determinant of leadership potential is now being communicated and acknowledged more clearly at all phases of the programme. Key points to note are that:

- The choice and duration of developmental assignments must balance the need to achieve the desired learning and development outcomes against the need to compress experiences in time in order to accelerate careers.
- The managers of participants are invaluable learning partners and must be supported in their role and acknowledged for their contribution. The involvement of managers in the design and/or review of such a programme is also highly recommended.
- Expectations and goals related to performance, learning and development must be set and distinguished clearly to allow the participant and the organization to tap the full potential from the assignment experience.

Personalized learning plans

The personalized learning plan, developed with the support of Executive Advisors, provides participants with a learning road map to enhance their competency in key areas. The results from the selection process and those emerging from additional self-assessment work done following acceptance to the programme are used initially to focus learning needs. The plan, however, evolves continuously in response to challenges, opportunities or feedback from managers, peers, staff and other observers. In the long term, the plan provides a broad learning framework that focuses on core government functions and leadership competencies. In the short term, it focuses on enhancing certain facets of competencies and diversifying practical experiences in very specific areas through relevant learning endeavours, tasks and other job-related activities. The participation of a coach or a mentor, or the involvement of the action learning group, for example, is sometimes identified as a useful avenue to meet particular learning objectives in the plan. Time lines and results indicators are established to help participants mark progress towards their development objectives. The personalized learning plan is a way for them to chart and reflect upon their progress as lifelong learners.

Developing learning plans require considerable research, analysis and reflection on the part of both participants and their learning partners (in particular executive advisers). Once competency needs have been identified, one of the most challenging tasks is to translate those needs into compelling learning objectives and activities that are integrated into the overall scope of work of the participant. The knowledge, experience and creativity of advisers and partners are most highly valued during that phase of the planning process. When necessary, special expertise brought in at this stage can bring enormous dividends.

Learning is a personal journey in the sense that learning styles, approaches and outcomes can be different for everyone. Therefore, the extent to which one should be accountable for meeting his/her anticipated learning goals can be a sensitive issue, particularly when the learning plan is personal in name and nature. Even so, third-party involvement (for example manager, peer, coach) in designing learning exercises, observing, providing feedback and so on has proved to be crucial in ensuring that the various goals of the plan are met according to objective standards (that is, other than one's own impression of improvement). The challenge in planning and implementing learning plans throughout the programme has been to balance individuals' desire for confidentiality and the need to mark progress and assess results in a deliberate fashion. This is where linking the learning plan to the performance appraisal process can provide one of the means to reinforce accountability and commitment. Key points to note are that:

- Within a broad set of learning objectives, personal learning plans are more effective when they are used to pursue only a limited number of time-bound, results-oriented learning commitments.
- Experienced learning advisers can make the difference between using the plan as a highly powerful learning tool and as a useful reference document.
- Making the learning plan 'public' (that is, to relevant learning partners) can provide a useful form of accountability for achieving intended results.

Coaching

Within the context of the programme, coaching is defined as a confidential, results-oriented and highly personal learning process which aims to build on talents and enhance professional effectiveness. A coach works with individual participants as a thinking and learning partner. He helps them to gain the ability to observe the world in a different way such that different actions are available to produce a different future. He observes participants in action and engages in conversations to help them uncover new possibilities and reframe their relationships and commitments to achieve breakthroughs in their performance. Coaching is a voluntary but formal process structured around specific intended results and time frames. The coaching relationship is based on mutual trust, mutual respect and freedom of expression.

In this context, coaches are selected for AEXDP following a rigorous process to ensure that their experience and approach are congruent with the needs and objectives of the programme. The need for a coach normally flows out of the personalized learning plan process. During the first 18 months of the programme (to Spring 1999), approximately 60 per cent of the participants had worked at least with one coach to help improve their performance or enhance their personal or professional competencies in a specific domain.

In addition to one-on-one coaching, the programme also helps participants to develop their own skills as manager-coaches as part of a collective learning event. This event has a powerful impact on the behaviours, actions and commitments of many participants, individually and collectively, and their ability to play a greater leadership role within their own spheres of influence and the public service at large. Other collective events complement this approach through their focus on current public service priorities. In our experience, however, the impacts and benefits of coaching (one-on-one or in a group) vary according to individuals and their openness or readiness to be coached and to become coaches.

A great coaching programme requires a substantial investment in people and learning resources. Other important aspects of implementing such a programme include the need to assess the performance of coaches on an ongoing basis, the need to monitor the progress of participants in meeting desired results, and the need to ensure financial accountability. While the need for confidentiality is axiomatic in the process of coaching, feedback mechanisms have their place in supporting these activities. In the same vein, and at the initiation of the participant, a coach could potentially co-operate with other learning partners (for example manager, executive adviser, mentor) as a way to create synergy for learning and development. Key points to note are that:

- Approaches to executive coaching can vary greatly. A sound philosophical and practical foundation for coaching is essential to recruiting the right coaches and supporting the goals of the coaching programme.
- A rigorous selection process for coaches can be time-consuming but is well worth the effort to ensure that participants have access to the best resources in the field as they cope with their developmental assignments.
- Coaching is a powerful vehicle for leadership development. It can be reinforced through cross-fertilization in the design and delivery of other programme components and links among relevant learning partners.

Mentoring

Mentoring is a learning relationship between a mature, experienced, caring senior executive and a less-experienced executive who seeks guidance and support to enrich his or her professional journey. Mentors help participants to reflect and learn from their experiences in the public service. They also share their own experiences and insights about the intricacies of the organization and help participants navigate through the challenges and opportunities they may face. Mentors are role models. They help participants to develop a greater sense of self-awareness and competence while enhancing their recognition in the organization and outside.

Participants who do not already have a mentor can select one from a pool of volunteer senior executives who work inside the federal public service and who are familiar with the mentoring approach. In this context, they receive an orientation and support in developing skills related to mentoring. Mentoring relationships evolve over time as commitments change and can come to closure once the relationship has fulfilled its purpose. Informal agreements are used to define expectations, developmental needs and goals and the frequency of meetings.

The mentoring component adds a psychosocial and professional development dimension to the other elements of the programme. This is the aspect of mentoring which distinguishes it the most from coaching (even though some form of coaching is most often present in a mentoring relationship). The differences and similarities between mentoring and coaching are important to clarify at the outset of the programme, however, because they inform the choices participants make and the investments they dedicate to learning throughout their involvement in the programme.

The potential role of mentors in connection with other learning partners, as well as the possibility of involving mentors from outside the public service, both merit further consideration in the evolution of the mentoring component. One significant impact of the increased awareness of participants to mentoring (lived or infused) is their openness and commitment to assume the role of mentor with younger executives and managers. In doing so they contribute to spreading the benefits of mentoring and extend their leadership beyond their immediate sphere of influence. Key points to note are that:

- Mentoring relationships can provide a strong foundation to address many of the learning and development needs of participants. Mentors are in a unique position to support their psychosocial and professional development.
- Building on their own experience, participants are well-positioned to extend the reach of the programme by supporting others through mentoring relationships.

Action learning groups

Action learning and its expression in small learning groups within the AEXDP follows the pioneering work of Dr Reg Revans in this area. In this context of the programme, action learning is defined as a process of collaborative inquiry among a group of committed and competent people who are diverse in their background, experience and perspectives. Action learning groups are composed of five or six AEXDP participants, which meet every six to eight weeks for full-day sessions. Participants come to meetings to reflect on and address real work situations or challenges that are important to them and their organization. They use the process of questioning and reflection to help each other learn from their experiences, to challenge their beliefs and their assumptions, and to open up new possibilities for action. The development of listening and questioning skills are critical to the group's success as well as to individuals' competence as public service leaders.

Facilitators (executive advisers in most cases) initiate, guide and stimulate the process, helping participants to maximize reflection, action and learning during and between meetings. They also challenge the group's effectiveness and the contribution and commitment of individuals. They model their facilitation skills to the group and, over time, gradually relinquish their role as learning groups become autonomous. A total of 11 action learning groups have been created since the inception of the programme, many of which have been active for over two years and some of which operate independently (that is without the support of a facilitator). Participants generally rate learning groups as the most powerful learning tool they have at their disposal. It provides a focus for learning and dialogue with their peers. The groups have been resilient. Some participants that have graduated from the programme have remained members of their original group; others have created action learning groups within their own organization, thereby extending the reach and impact of this approach.

Launching action learning groups is a very important step to their early success. Members need to share an understanding of the basic tenets of the approach and to practice together the discipline of listening, questioning and reflection. Each group, however, needs to find its own stride, that is build the trust and skills that support a performing team. The facilitator plays a key role at this stage and beyond by ensuring that the group respects their commitment to the action learning process. But as the group matures, its ground rules and meeting routine can be adapted to reflect its own dynamic. At the same time, the facilitator and the group must remain alert to ensure that the group remains productive as it reaches a certain 'comfort zone'; that is, members get set in their ways or their interpretations and miss opportunities to challenge each other in a more diversified fashion. This is where the group must remain in balance with respect to maintaining an environment of trust and openness and remaining productive and performing.

Group members are accountable to themselves and to the group for their learning and the actions they take as a result of group interaction. They best express their commitment to each other by protecting their participation in learning group meetings from demanding jobs and by investing adequate time in preparing and following-up between meetings. When participants use learning groups as a means to enhance their effectiveness and performance on the job, they are more likely to commit their time and energy to the process. Moreover, when they choose to make their action learning goals public by involving colleagues, staff or their manager, they increase their accountability towards meeting these goals and the potential benefits to their organization. Key points to note are that:

- The adoption of sound principles and practices to support the work of action learning groups is important to their success but flexibility is required in their application to maximize their effectiveness, that is let the theory adapt to the practice.
- Action learning groups demonstrate the high impact of peer learning. Within that context, the groups not only provide a focal point for dialogue, learning and action around work challenges, but also a continuing network to address emerging leadership issues from other learning events and the public service at large.
- To be successful over time, groups must continuously assess their performance in creating a climate conducive to action, reflection and learning. Members must also constantly challenge their commitment and accountability to each other.

Collective learning events

Collective learning events are opportunities for AEXDP participants to learn together. Participants explore topics that reflect the priorities and emerging challenges in the federal public service. The events include a mix of experiential learning and structured discussions that maximize peer exchanges and interactions with leaders from within and outside the public service. They help participants to make distinctions and gain new insights in terms of their own leadership role (present and future), and to commit, as individuals and together, to actions that will help to improve the federal public service.

Four learning events are held over an 18-month period:

- An orientation session is held soon after participants join the programme. This session facilitates the emergence of a learning community and enrolls participants in the action learning framework offered by the programme.
- A leadership development event is held once participants have gained some experience in their new assignments. The session challenges

participants to consider what breakthrough results they wish to achieve in the future, and how they can enhance their performance, the performance of their organizations and of the public service.

- A third learning event supports the goal to modernize service delivery in the public sector. It challenges participants to reflect on their role and contribution as leaders of a public service that is committed to citizen-centred service delivery.
- The fourth learning event supports the goal of building effective policy capacity within the public service of Canada. It challenges participants to define and assume leadership in an increasingly complex and interdependent policy environment and to explore the decision-making structures and relationships at play in shaping policy.

In these events, action learning is pursued through a combination of strategies. One key element is ensuring the relevance of issues or challenges addressed, both for the participant, the organization and the public service. For participants, 'back-home scenarios' are an important aspect of their preparation, their reflection during learning events, and their follow-up actions. Back-home scenarios are the connection between the participant's real world and what he observes on the outside. They help to translate the knowledge, skills and insights gained during events into practical commitments and actions inside their organization.

For the public service, relevance means that the objectives and lines of inquiry of the learning event produce an outcome that helps to advance some of its goals or priorities. This requires effective consultation with relevant stakeholders within and outside the public service, to design an event which has a potential to make such a contribution. It also requires that a senior client (or group of clients) within the public service, demands an outcome from the learning event (one that will focus the collective resolve of participants). Clients of individual participants (such as a boss, management team, and so on) can also play a useful role in helping to define potential outcomes and to follow through on their implementation within the organization.

This type of 'action learning' accountability has been difficult to establish within the programme probably in part because the leadership focus of learning events leads to less tangible and measurable outcomes than recommendations of an operational nature (that is, often associated with business driven action learning), and consequently because clients are more diffuse. Making action learning more relevant in this context means, at a minimum, helping participants evolve from a community of learners to a community of practice, both during the programme and after, through enduring collaborative networks. The use of internet-based tools for ongoing communications, discussions and learning can facilitate the creation of these networks within the programme and beyond, as participants extend their own spheres of influence. Key points to note are that:

- In an action learning context, collective events have to strike a balance between meeting the learning needs of participants and making a contribution to achieving the priorities of the organization.
- Consultation with participants and stakeholders in the design of events is essential to achieving these objectives.
- Events generate more individual and collective commitments to 'action learning' when guided by clients that demand an outcome.

Supporting career advancement

The third major component of the AEXDP is the process supporting the career advancement of participants. It is briefly reviewed here to complement the description of the programme.

In order to be promoted, participants must be assessed against the competency profile for the targeted executive level. The assessment, which the supervisor is responsible to complete, consists in determining for each competency the ability of the participant to perform at the superior level based on a set of behaviour indicators. The participant's performance appraisal is also considered as part of the assessment. Managers are guided in this process by programme staff (executive advisers), who also ensure that the recommendation for promotion is addressed by the responsible authority (that is, the Public Service Commission).

This promotion process is unique to the AEXDP and leads to an appointment to level (that is, participants who receive a promotion normally complete their current developmental assignment) as opposed to the competitive process used throughout the public service, which is designed to fill specific jobs. Since AEXDP participants were deemed upon joining the programme to have ADM potential, their promotion review is simplified but still key in determining if and how their progress is sustained and where to focus future learning and development efforts. The potential for rapid career advancement is an attractive feature of the programme for participants, but also one which supports the public service in bridging the transition of promising executives to more senior positions. Key points to note are that:

- Managing communications in the executive community regarding the two-tier system of executive promotion should be an important part of raising awareness about the nature and scope of such a programme and the opportunities that exist outside the programme for development and career advancement.

- Balancing the urgent corporate need for senior executives and the time required for participants to reach their development goals is very important to their credibility in 'the marketplace' and that of the programme.

What does this experience mean for the future?

Three years into its implementation, the AEXDP is still experimenting with ways in which to improve the effectiveness and results of every dimension of the programme, from selection to graduation. Programme staff, participants and programme stakeholders have all played an important role in sharing their experiences and insights and helping to improve the programme. The success factors shown in Table 9.1 emerge from our experience to date and could serve as a point of reference in designing and implementing executive programmes based on action learning.

Results are difficult to gauge at this early stage in terms of real programme impacts. From a career development perspective, the relative success of the programme can be measured by the number of 'careers advanced' (most participants have been promoted to a higher executive level), including the number of programme graduates that eventually make it to the ADM level (about a dozen AEXDP participants have reached that level during the first three years of the programme). Such numbers can have a high communication impact but do not reveal anything about peoples' leadership abilities or how the organization has benefited from their participation in the programme. While surveys and assessments have provided useful feedback, it is tangible actions such as those highlighted below that demonstrate the extent to which participants are committed to assuming an increasing leadership role within the public. This is where the programme generates its greatest dividends and value added:

- Becoming mentors to younger executives and managers;
- Transferring their reflecting and learning skills within their team and their organization;
- Adapting the learning outcomes from the programme to the operational realities of their organization;
- Using their coaching skills to improve communication, relationships and performance within their work environment;
- Making specific commitments as a community of AEXDP participants to play a leadership role in improving services to the public.

A number of questions and challenges need to be explored as the programme continues to evolve to meet the need of the public service at large:

Table 9.1 Success factors

Success factors	What is needed to make action learning work
Relevance	Learning is grounded in real work challenges and in in the priorities of the organization
Leverage	Action learning outcomes support the development of individuals who also contribute to improving the organization
Outreach	Action learning outcomes support individuals in becoming lifelong learners, teachers and agents of change in their organization and beyond
Accountability	Action learning objectives are made public and clients expect an outcome
Partnership	Participants, learning partners and other stakeholders are actively involved in setting action learning goals and working collaboratively to achieve them
Balance	Learning and development goals and performance/action goals are pursued in a balanced and complementary fashion
Momentum	A sustained cycle of action, reflection and learning is integrated into all learning components of the programme
Flexibility	The principles and practices of action learning provide a benchmark from which to innovate in order to meet specific organizational needs
Commitment	The organization's most senior management is equally committed to the action learning programme as are the participants and their learning partners
Systemic	Relevant programme elements and initiatives are connected to the organization's management systems (decision-making, human resources, and so on)

- How can we best adapt such an action learning programme for managers and executives at a much broader scale? Efforts are underway to implement a learning architecture that will provide all managers and executives with opportunities to develop the knowledge and skills that are relevant to public service management excellence. The challenge will be to integrate action learning principles and practices throughout such a comprehensive initiative.

- How can we better link this and similar programmes to existing human resources systems (e.g. recognition, succession planning, performance management) so as to optimize investments in management and leadership development? While programmes such as AEXDP have 'systems' of their own, broader based 'decentralized' learning and development initiatives need to establish those systemic links up-front at the design stage.
- How can we bring more diversity and intensity in the learning experiences of participants? When 'accelerating' is a key objective, the challenge is to offer participants intense and diversified learning experiences that can be 'processed' quickly through their own reality. One possibility is to offer more possibilities for interchanges with private and other non-governmental organizations through assignments, projects or participation in certain components of the learning programme.
- How do we better support this new critical mass of modern senior executives as key public sector actors and leaders in the new knowledge economy? Sustaining the momentum of action learning, individually and collectively, beyond the boundaries of the programme is an important challenge. It can be met by better developing the meta-learning skills of participants during the programme and by nurturing enduring networks (e.g. action learning groups) which serve as channels for continuous learning, leadership dialogue and collaborative action beyond the programme.

The AEXDP is part of the public service effort to provide managers and their employees with opportunities for lifelong learning so that they can collectively contribute to serving Canadians better in the 'knowledge age'. In pursuing the broader goal of becoming a learning organization, the public service as a whole aims to ensure the ongoing relevance of government to citizens and to create the comparative advantages that Canada will need in the global competition for talent and investment.

A number of ideas and approaches to learning and development drawn from this experience will be helpful in addressing the issues and challenges facing the public service as a learning organization in this period of intense change, namely:

- Translating the corporate commitment to learning into strategic investments in learning and knowledge management;
- Providing people full and fair access to learning and development opportunities wherever they may be in serving Canadians;
- Creating tools and opportunities to help people take responsibility for developing the knowledge and skills that are relevant to public service management excellence;

- Aligning learning and development efforts to the strategic intent of the public service and its diversified organizations;
- Connecting learning and development effectively to the full range of human resources systems (e.g. performance management, recruitment, retention); and,
- Empowering people to learn and teach others through multiple channels and networks promoting continuous learning and collaborative action.

In this context, a learning organization is probably one which values learning in action because it helps to generate a capacity for continuous learning and knowledge-sharing. This form of 'generative' learning seems to be an essential ingredient to the development of modern, compassionate and competitive organizations. To enable generative learning, an organization must, however, create appropriate conditions for experimentation, risk-taking and innovation; invest sufficiently in its people; value diversity and the exchange of opinions and ideas; and support the development of competencies which enable people to contribute actively to organizational learning.

Each of these 'enablers' could form the basis of much further reflection. Since competencies are so linked to the model of executive development presented in this paper, it may be useful here to briefly conclude by highlighting some of the competencies that seem essential to leaders of learning organizations: anticipating and leading change; managing issues and challenges through horizontal networks; learning and teaching on the fly; harnessing diversity; and developing and nurturing relationships of mutual trust and respect. More work needs to be done to identify these competencies and to integrate them into our management and executive curricula so that executive development can be an effective channel for making the learning organization a reality.

10

Action Reflection Learning™ in Latin America

Isabel Rimanoczy

Some six or seven years ago, I had the chance to attend a Round Table at the University of Nijenrode, in Holland. The central discussion was on 'Innovative Organizations' and several academics, consultants and executives gathered to discuss some innovations made in two organizations, a Danish hearing-aid manufacturer and an electronics company from Rotterdam. I was delighted to see how traditional organizations had transformed themselves into participative, learning environments, where the 'way it has always been' had been courageously questioned, and dozens of processes had been replaced by new and creative ideas, all developed by the employees.

At that time I was living in Argentina, and as I left the Round Table I had a melancholy feeling 'This is so nice', I told myself, 'but it just wouldn't work in the Latin American culture.' I was therefore astonished when, weeks later, I discovered a book (*Maverick*, by Ricardo Semler) in which Semler, a Brazilian entrepreneur, described the turnaround in a traditional organization through the application of exactly those values I had seen in Europe, namely the people leading the change, learning and questioning how to develop new ways of getting things done. This opened a door for me: reality had defied my assumptions of what is and what is not possible.

Soon after, I began exploring the possibilities of bringing Action Reflection Learning™ (ARL™) (a differentiated approach based on action learning) to the Argentine corporate world, which clearly provided fertile ground for innovative change. The reasons were many:

- the country was going through economic upheaval and Argentine industries needed to become highly efficient in order to compete in global markets;
- in order to be more cost-effective, the companies were cutting down their training/development budgets because, they reasoned, there were other priorities with a better returns on their investment;

- after decades of military governments, with employees and processes both still imbued with an authoritarian mindset, organizations wanted to implement a more participative style of leadership;
- change in the world was getting faster and there was a growing awareness that if you don't learn fast, 'if you don't change fast, you are out of the picture'.

Interestingly, similar conditions were found in other Latin American countries, and so it was that, beginning in 1996, ARL™ was introduced by LIM (Leadership in International Management) into Argentina, Colombia, Brazil, Ecuador and, most recently, in Mexico and Honduras.

How has Action Reflection Learning™ fared in Latin America?

We have had a variety of experiences: with family-owned corporations, with private business schools, with multinationals and large national corporations, with independent consultants and with government. The scope of designs in which we used the ARL™ principles has also varied and has included Learning Coach Development Programmes, Executive Coaching, Team Development Programmes, and Leadership Development Programmes.

Examining these different applications and organizational types, we observed that the best results were achieved when two situations pertained.

1 The first centered on the *attitude* of the organization or person involved in the process. We found that success was easier and more likely when the organization or person had a positive attitude towards:

(a) participation of employees in the change effort,
(b) learning itself,
(c) questioning procedures, and
(d) creativity and innovation.

This was the case in the subsidiaries of multinational corporations, where they received messages from the HQ (Europe and USA) about the desired changes in leadership and management behaviours. We also found it in some organizational pockets inside a larger and traditional organization, where a certain sector or group of people worked in some kind of 'progressive subculture'. In the case of ARL™ used in one-on-one-coaching, the results were always successful, due to the fact that this kind of relation can only take place when the 'coachee' is interested in learning, questioning and reviewing his/her behaviours.

2 The second set of conditions that precipitated movement and change was the acceptance of the challenge that the organization or individual had to become more effective in order to grow and thrive. For some reason,

these organizations/individuals needed to experience some pain to engage in this process, and the pain we observed had different faces. In the organizations the factors that led to action included:

- significant losses of stock value,
- loss of market share,
- loss of people,
- loss of clients,
- new competitors in the global market,
- changes in local regulations (from protected markets to an open market),
- need to launch more and/or faster products and services, and
- reduction of operating capital.

In the case of individuals the factors we observed included:

- problems with others (superiors, employees, peers),
- conflict in balancing life/work,
- pressure of high expectations (one's own or those of others), and
- pressure of new challenges.

It is possible, of course, that these conditions may be also applicable to regions other than Latin America. Although both groups of conditions were present in all the cases with successful results, the weights varied in the corporate and in the individual clients.

While our philosophical equation is that Learning = Earning, our corporate clients have shown greater interest in the earning side. The ARL™ process is often seen as a means to an end, which is to solve the business problem. Perhaps this is inevitable, since the notion of learning as a competitive advantage is new in Latin America, and we have had to work hard to instill this mindset in the heads of senior executives. Old ways die hard, and in the case of employees receiving coaching inside the organization we observed a tendency to value an increased self-awareness as a means to be more efficient in their daily interactions.

On the other hand, when working with independent consultants and teachers, the weight has been on the learning and development side, and they considered the 'earning' as an interesting byproduct.

An illustration of the impact of the ARL™ process on one Latin American organization is told in the following case history of Siemens South America in Argentina.

A case history

In the last quarter of 1998, Siemens Argentina began the local implementation of an international management development programme which included a number of teams working on small projects with high economical impact, over a period of time. The aim of the programme was to 'enhance the management, entrepreneurial and leadership abilities through an integrated, global and results oriented approach'. The initial design included some outdoor team-building activities and workshops offered to the participants as support during their tasks.

Silvia Leon and Ana Dufour, partners and learning coaches from LIM Argentina, were invited into this programme to help the group of 32 participants (middle managers from across the organization) to extract learning from their team sessions, and also to link the leadership concepts and tools to their day-to-day reality back on the job. This support was offered through a one-on-one coaching process using action reflection learning (see Tables 10.1 to 10.3 and Figure 10.1).

Table 10.1   The key components of ARL™-based individual coaching

√ Question-driven	√ Action–Reflection sequence to extract the learning
√ Balance of task and learning	√ Determine the person's learning style and act upon it
√ Only Just-in-Time tools and concepts	√ Reflection
√ Exchange of learnings with others	√ Link between the present situation and other scenarios
√ Learning/change are sequential processes – thus several sessions are essential for the learning to 'take'	√ Use of a Personal Journal to capture learnings and to help develop personal theories of leadership
√ Systemic approach	√ Appreciative approach

Source: I. Rimanoczy, *Action Reflection Learning: Application for Individual Learning Process* (1999). Gajal Archives (www.irdc.com/journals/gajal/)

Table 10.2   What does a learning coach in ARL™-based coaching do?

√ Listening	√ Mirroring
√ Asking questions	√ Offering Just-in-Time tools and concepts to deepen awareness and insight
√ Linking past experience, present insight and future possibilities	√ No... • Telling • Taking charge • Leading, guiding • Judging • Problem-solving
√ Challenging perspectives and assumptions	√ Helping to set next steps and action plans

Table 10.3 What is ARL™-based individual coaching?

- Learning from reflecting on own behaviours and their impact
- A way of increasing self-awareness
- Understanding others' behaviours
- Improving 'people skills'

Source: The LIM *Learning Coach Handbook*, 2000.

Figure 10.1 The change cycle

We understand learning as a change of behaviours. The ARL™ approach uses the change cycle as the basis for individual or team designs. Each phase is supported by different interventions and tools to reach depth and efficiency of the cycle. A learning coach who is trained to see the 'just-in-time' learning opportunities guides the learner/s along the cycle and introduces tools and concepts to optimize the process of working on a task.
Source: I. Rimanoczy (1999) 'Serving as a Set Advisor/Learning Coach', in M. Marquardt, *Action Learning in Action* pp. 209–13. Palo Alto: Davies-Black.

The contracting phase

Since this type of intervention represented a new experience for the organization, the learning coaches deliberately made an open contract with the participants. They offered the 32 employees the option to take one or more coaching sessions, with a limit of two per month and for a maximum period of 10 months (the duration of the 'Basic Management Programme S4'). The learning coaches made a presentation of what coaching meant and how it could support the participants in their professional development (see Table 10.2) and indicated that the participants were free to try it.

Implementation

Surprisingly, 32 of 33 participants signed up. Not all of them took up the offer at the outset, but the word of mouth was swift and so even those who felt reluctant at the beginning signed up for the experience. Indeed, after a while even people outside this group of 32 participants were asking if the corporation would offer coaching support to employees not included in the programme! Ultimately, 90 per cent of the group ended up using all their authorized 20 sessions.

After the learning coaches and employees completed the process of contracting mutual expectations and roles, each employee was invited to find an issue or challenge on which he/she wanted to focus, and to frame the issue in the form of a question. In some cases people had difficulties choosing a meaningful issue, or to phrase it as a question. The learning coaches suggested that participants use their latest performance appraisal as a guide for determining the professional issue to work on. It was the experience of many participants that the question they formulated as the key question to answer underwent change and evolved into a different question altogether.

The learning coaches used the power-planning process to help coachees to frame their answers in the context of: exploring lessons from the past, generating assumptions, evaluating possible solutions, selecting one and then planning its implementation (see Figure 10.1). This process acknowledges that coachee have specific and far-reaching knowledge that they can bring to a situation. This was a key element of the process, since it validated the coachees' experiences as a significant part of the answer. The point is that the experience, the body of knowledge accumulated from work situations, from discussions and from seminars, all serve to provide the answer sought. The task of the coach was to help coachees access that information and to use it through a combination of active listening, an appreciative approach, and focused questions that generated insightful reflection.

Obstacles encountered

Even in organizations where practice of one-on-one coaching is fairly well-established, there can be resistance to the notion that managers need help. In a country where the practice is still growing, the learning coaches met resistance in several forms. According to Dufour and Leon's researches, the obstacles they encountered can be grouped into three categories:

- obstacles related to coaching itself;
- obstacles stemming from the national culture; and
- organizational obstacles.

Obstacles related to coaching itself

Although the Argentine population is very familiar with therapeutic sessions (Argentina has the highest ratio of psychologists in Latin America), coaching is a very new practice. Therefore the learning coaches encountered some reluctance to the notion of 'sharing problems', of 'speaking openly and frankly'. Coachees feared that they were being evaluated by the learning coaches, who would in turn give this information to participants' bosses. Further, they didn't believe real results could be achieved, partly due to their former experiences with training and development that had promised learning and change, but which in effect was rarely applicable to the daily work of the manager. These obstacles were soon solved by developing a trusting relationship between learning coaches and participants, by setting clear expectations, by establishing norms of behaviour, by clear contracting of the role of the learning coaches, and by ensuring confidentiality. The appreciative attitude of the learning coaches was key to developing the trust of coachees that they were not being judged.

Obstacles stemming from the national culture

Cultural obstacles proved to be a major problem throughout the process. Some of these issues were addressed in the beginning, and the act of bringing them to the coachees' awareness helped neutralize them, while others remained as a personal challenge for the coachees until the end.

The most frequent cultural obstacles that impeded progress were the:

- need to solve everything fast, without any reflection;
- a tendency to blame, and consider that 'things cannot be changed';
- a tendency to give negative feedback, highlighting the negative aspects and the problems met;
- the lack of a tradition of celebrating learning and success;
- the fact that participants were not used to sharing learning with the team, colleagues or superiors;
- a predisposition to frame the wish to learn as an acknowledgement that you don't know something; 'not knowing' equals weakness, ignorance, and should not be exposed publicly. There is a fear of punishment or negative consequences on one's image/career if this lack of knowledge is shown;
- a view that asking questions is only accepted if you ask 'intelligent' questions, showing how much you know or understand, or how brave you are to challenge others and so on;
- the fact that learning and the desire to learn are not widespread or valued concepts in adulthood. Learning is linked to schools and children/teenagers. Adults already 'know';
- a tendency not to value reflection. Reflection is viewed as inactivity, as philosophizing, as meditation;

- an expectation that Argentines have to be 'told' what and how to do things by experts. They are all too familiar with, and readily accept, the traditional teacher role of the manager. It is still a surprise to be pushed to seek their own answers and solutions;
- a predisposition to complain and to focus on difficulties, not seeing them as opportunities nor perceiving their own capability to influence circumstances;
- an initial distrust of the learning coaches because they were female (90 per cent of the participants were male) and the ensuing attitude – 'what can THEY teach us?';
- a lack of tradition in directing their own learning process, and in following their own interests and answering their own questions; and
- poor planning, both medium and long term, that is the result of a tendency to view improvization as more 'organic' than planning.

Organizational obstacles

There were not many organizational obstacles. The Human Resource Department had made the determination that coaching based on ARL™ principles would play a valuable role in developing the managers. The most significant problems centred on (a) getting enough support from participants' superiors in some cases, and (b) ensuring that there were sufficient opportunities to maintain the learning exchange after the programme ended.

Results of the coaching

The experience was rated highly successful by participants in their individual feedback to their coaches. The participants seemed to realize, and to value, the individual attention paid to their personal and professional development, and a typical remark from a participant stated: 'This has been the most caring demonstration of the organization towards my development'. They felt supported by the organization and cited the following items that they especially valued:

- the trusting relationship that permitted them to discuss their managerial challenges with the learning coaches;
- the chance to try out and implement new behaviours;
- the just-in-time tools to improve their teamwork and leadership skills;
- the just-in-time concepts that permitted a better understanding of human behaviour;
- increasing their people skills – giving feedback, communicating, managing conflicts;
- learning from reflecting on their daily actions, getting used to extracting learnings and to reflect further on new plans of action;

- being able to connect previous knowledge with current situations;
- increased self-awareness;
- improved performance that was the result of the coaching.

I often think back to my experience in Nijenrode and my prejudiced assumptions about the readiness of the Argentine culture to welcome new ways to lead, and creative ways to develop employees. I realize that attitudinal change will not occur without resistance – as I have discussed above – but this experience and the growth of action learning principles on the continent bodes well for the future.

Reference

Semler, R. (1995) *Maverick: The Success Story Behind the World's Most Unusual Workplace.* New York: Warner.

Part III

Action Learning in Europe, the Middle East and Africa

11

Northern Light: A Survey of Action Learning in the Nordic Region of Europe*

Åke Reinholdsson

This article is based on a survey carried out among leading Nordic companies in 1998 and then in 2000. The object was to collect some basic data about action learning and how it is used in executive development. Some 25 companies took part and the results of the surveys are briefly presented and discussed.

The environment at a glance

Within the Nordic countries of Denmark, Finland, Norway and Sweden, business life is dominated by a few companies that operate internationally and are based on technology and natural resources. The larger ones have two-thirds or more of their total business and employees outside the region. The consumer goods companies are, with few exceptions (that is, IKEA, H&M), comparably small and operate locally.

Nordic home markets are small and growing companies are consequently forced to enter foreign markets at an early stage in their development. This explains why expansion into new markets is a common theme for assignments in action learning programmes. Legislation, capital and infrastructure in this overall region have favoured size and growth, and, as a result, among the present Fortune 500 companies there are more of Nordic origin than would be estimated based on the size of the Nordic population. Another consideration is that the public sector within Nordic countries is comparatively large. Besides traditional functions, governments have considerable

---

* This chapter is based on information from the following corporations: ABB, Assi Domän, BT Industries, Cardo, Danisco, Ericsson, Finnair, ISS, Mil Institute, NCC, Neste Corp., Perstorp, Pharmacia & Upjohn, PLM, Rautaruukki, Sandvik, SAS, Scancem, Scania, SEB, Skanska, Svenska Handelsbanken, Trelleborg, Valmet and Volvo.

influence in a number of important companies. Medical care is organized, financed and managed by political institutions. A substantial part of power and water supply companies are owned and operated by the state or by larger communities.

With a total population of the Nordic countries exceeding 25 million, the labour force comprises slightly more than eight million people, with the private and public sectors employing equal numbers. Lacking a common definition of 'executive', we can assume that there is on average one executive per 200 employees. There are, therefore, some 40 000 individuals holding executive positions in the Nordic countries, although the number of persons with the potential for such positions is likely to be at least four times the number of present holders. Consequently the number of persons in executive careers is of the magnitude of 200 000.

Executive development

In the Nordic region, the general attitude towards executive development is quite positive. Companies spend considerable amounts for development of those holding senior positions and those rated as of high potential. The development programmes are based on real actual needs, but they are also used as ways of recognizing valuable, hard-working and successful performers.

Most leading companies also have in-house management development programmes. In some cases a few companies in non-competing businesses work together in consortium programmes run by leading management institutes. The IFL (the Swedish Institute of Management) and MiL in Lund have been, for a few years now, the leading executive development institutes in the region. IFL's annual turnover exceeds SEK 100 000 000 which means that it belongs to the group of larger European management institutes.

Another indication of interest in executive development is that Nordic executives, and Swedish in particular, are frequent participants in open or public international development programmes organized by business schools. The reason for this is that the region's companies constantly need to internationalize their management capacity. The Nordic market for international management institutes exceeds USD 15 000 000, meaning that Nordic executives on average spend more time in international programmes than their colleagues in most other countries.

The definition of action learning

There is no worldwide common definition of action learning. However, when representatives from leading companies describe their programmes there are some more or less common denominators. Action learning implies:

- learning by doing – working;
- working in groups or teams;
- working with real and prioritized business issues;
- working with and for real organizations; and
- working in real time – when there is a need for decision-making.

The participants are put in the role of the problem-solver. The result is expected to be innovative, profitable or add value to the organization – apart from being a first-class learning experience.

Action learning – an established method

In the Nordic countries, action learning has been used as one means of executive development for decades. MiL has been and still is an important stimulator and driving force in Sweden, as well as in the other Nordic countries – Denmark, Finland and Norway. Among the selected companies for this study more than half run programmes based on action learning. We assume that this figure is valid for the whole population of leading Nordic companies.

Most of the action learning programmes were designed during the 1990s. A few companies are not running programmes at present due to lack of participants, whilst a few others are redesigning and plan to start new programmes within the next couple of years. The study was made after a period of downsizing among major companies, which is the reason why there has been some discontinuity in the programmes. As can be seen below, there is no lack of ideas for the future. Like other methods, action learning is changing and being revised over time.

Levels

Given that the CEO represents level 1, the majority of companies use action learning programmes for levels 2 and 3. Two companies use action learning on all levels, in one case including blue-collar workers. Companies arrange action learning for trainees as well, and trainee programmes have become one of the most important ways to attract young talented people – such programmes are highly appreciated as a 'soft start' of the professional career. Action learning is considered an important part of trainee programmes since it provides a stronger confrontation with reality than other methods.

Geographical area

Since the Nordic leading companies have to work internationally, executive programmes are necessarily international as well and include input and participants from various parts of the world. Actually, two-thirds of the companies organize their action learning programmes internationally, with one-third of the really large ones organizing their programmes regionally or per country. The choice of assignments (see below) clearly demonstrates the international character of the programmes.

The fact that most groups are formed by people from various cultures adds an extra dimension to the learning process. They can use the asset of being multilingual or they have to overcome the differences and other cultural obstacles to get on with their assignments.

Duration

The duration of the programmes varies between three and 40 days. Short duration indicates that the action learning is an integrated, minor part of a more extensive programme. Longer duration indicates that the assignment is the entire programme or the major part of it.

Companies allow participants to spend varying resources; the percentage of working time invested to study, learn, draw conclusions and write reports varies between 15 and 100. Programmes of short duration are, as expected, more intense than those of long duration. The total time spent for the assignment varies between three and 32 days with an average of 12.

Who issues the assignment?

The assignments are normally determined by management. Other sources are 'the problem owner', business areas or even the board of directors. Thus, programmes are generally well-known and appreciated by top management, and, furthermore, they enjoy a considerable prestige among managers on all levels, especially among potential participants.

Top management is involved more or less deeply. One of the companies made the following statement:

> This programme is designed to develop in depth competence regarding all dimensions of leadership. The programme comprises a major project thesis. The subjects for these projects are of strategic importance for the company and are therefore determined in collaboration with top corporate executives.

Costs

There are several costs to be considered when organizing an extensive executive development programme. In this study we limited the question to total cost per participant, excluding salary. The cost interval measured in this way is US$ 4000–15 000 with an average of US$ 10 000 (at 1997 price levels).

Programmes are financed in traditional ways. Half of the companies have a general budget for executive development, with one-quarter financing the programme by internal invoicing and another quarter by separate budgets. Just one company of the sample raised money from a sponsor, in this actual case the director of marketing – 'the problem owner'.

The picture, however, is likely to change. When more of the programmes meet with all the criteria mentioned above, they will probably be funded by those who are using the results – the sponsors or problem owners.

Nomination and selection of participants

The most common start of the selection process is 'recommendation by superior manager'. Another is 'recommendation by HR manager'. A third is a response to the internal policy – the programme is 'compulsory' at a certain level of the organization. There are also combinations, and, naturally, initiatives can be taken jointly by the boss and the HR manager. In a few cases – one-fifth – the potential participants can or are expected to apply themselves.

Do the companies use more formal and/or scientific methods in the selection process? How do we know if the candidates have the potential the nomination implies? The best programme fails if the participants don't meet with the expected standards. Who decides what the standard shall be? Less than half use tests, 360-degree feedback or assessment centres to increase the objectiveness of the selection process. It seems that the question 'what' awakes much more interest than the question 'who'.

Additional resources

The majority of the companies use external resources for programme development, lecturing and for facilitating the planning and project work. With regard to the selection of participants, external sources are only used occasionally.

Support during the team work with assignments varies. Some teams are left more or less on their own to plan, administer, make contacts and so on, whilst in other cases there are more strict definitions of who's doing what for whom. In one company participants are selected from a special group of executives: the assignment is always issued by the CEO and the groups are supported by one coordinator, one facilitator and one documenter with well-defined roles in the development process.

Cooperation between companies

Executive development programmes can benefit from being organized in consortiums with a few non-competitive companies with similar values, interests and ambitions. In the small Nordic countries where 'everybody knows everybody', such consortiums are probably more common than in many other regions. Of this sample, one-third has experienced programmes beyond company borders. Just one of them, however, has carried out programmes together with customers and suppliers.

There are various arguments for consortiums: costs and number of participants are practical ones. But there are also training specialists who argue that the results are better when participants are forced to leave their

normal environment and cross institutional as well as professional bound-
eries. These programmes also add extra value to the participating companies, since they get talented people looking into their problems 'free of
charge'.

Assignments

The companies were asked to give typical examples of assignment headlines.
Here are some:

- Strategy for expansion of product X in the Far East
- Analysis of future markets in the Baltic area
- Examination of the possibilities for investments in real estate in
  Prague
- Identification of new markets and development of business concept for
  our daughter company Y.
- Customer base orientation
- Fundaments of TQM – what can they mean for our company?
- Supportive leadership
- Small-scale operation
- Our presence in Eastern Europe
- Eastern Europe strategy
- Logistics in the USA
- Resources for future development
- Internal recruitment policy
- Managing the chain – customer-driven product development
- Develop benchmarking tools for the company
- Euro currency impact on our prices
- Building a stronger presence in the US market
- Building a stronger presence in Benelux.
- Maintenance cost analysis
- Market segmentation
- Strategic management
- Learning organization
- Development of a new service concept for Z.
- Market research – preparation of the launch of a new product
- Environmental management
- Inter-company mobility
- Develop a service concept for business unit X

Notice the large number of market-oriented subjects; 12 out of 25
assignments have a market focus or deal with a market-related problem.
New organizational and or leadership ideas are requested in six cases,
method development is interesting, the same goes for general subjects like

strategic management, learning organization and inter-company mobility. One is quite specific: the real-estate situation in Prague. Financial and technological subjects are rare. The time orientation is the present in 11 cases, and the future in 14.

Comments from participants

The participants' motivation, reactions and opinions are of fundamental importance for learning effects and evaluation of any programme. The study did not touch on these aspects, but one of the companies did give some recent reactions from participants which seem to be typical:

'It was about us. We tried – it was reality.'
'The top management listened and believed in what we said.'
'We understood the connections – how the system is working.'
'The climate was open and supportive.'
'The task – a great challenge.'
'Risk taking was necessary.'
'The success was the prime reward.'
'Our superiors were very interested in the results, what we learned and how we could use the new experiences.'
'I learned about myself and how I react in complex situations.'

The participants seem to be somewhat surprised by the direct connection between their work and the programmes. Maybe most of them had expected more classroom education. Their answers certainly reveal their own enthusiasm as well as the involvement of top management.

Is it worth it?

The fact that most participants are enthusiastic is not the complete answer to the question of whether extensive action learning programmes are worth the cost. However, the VPs of human resources seem to be just as convinced that action learning is the right thing:

'We started our programmes on request from the business management itself.'
'Our limitless projects help management define new activities.'
'Business development and management development are two ways of dealing with the same challenge. Tomorrow they will be merged.'
'The most important thing we have done so far.'

Of course managers defend their previous decisions, but these statements go beyond defence, they show conviction and a drive to continue.

Plans for the years ahead

This was an open question. The following are examples of answers followed by short comments:

- *Focus even more on action learning.*
  In this case the traditional classroom sessions will be fewer and the team learning based on assignments will dominate during the years to come.
- *More tailor-made and individual programmes.*
  This means that the number of team activities will be fewer and the individuals themselves will have a more pronounced responsibility for their own development.
- *Support in the implementation of the corporate strategy.*
  This indicates that the company will start to use their programmes in an even more operative way. Where is the future borderline between executive development and day-to-day management?
- *Focus on 'action-reflection' learning.*
  Senge, MiL and others have stressed the importance of reflection in development programmes for executives and other groups. The company will include the time and the means for reflection in future programmes.
- *Training of teams.*
  Coaching and team development have so far had a low priority in Nordic companies. There is considerable room for initiatives that strengthen team spirit and efficiency.
- *Young-professionals programmes.*
  High-potential professionals are a key category for the future. The more we reduce the number of hierarchical levels and the more we specialize, the greater the importance of professionals. They will influence the decision-making much more in the future than they did in the past. This company plans to focus on professionals as the next target group for development.
- *Interactive development processes.*
  This answer indicates that modern technologies will be used to a greater extent in the future.
- *Action learning for top executives.*
  Action learning is perceived as an interesting, meaningful and efficient method even for the senior people at the top. No doubt the initiator has seen the possibility for his or her peers to deal with fundamental issues in another setting than the usual.
- *Go on with the same – more projects.*
- *Focus the business problem or issues being examined more than in past programmes.*
  Again, an example that indicates closer links between learning and the business reality.

- *Increase flexibility and individualization.*
  Again a small sign that individualization is on its way. Since action learning is normally based on team work, it will be interesting to learn more about how these new ideas will be realized .
- *Reintroduce action learning on a pan-European level.*
  This company did have action learning programmes in the past. Since it has grown, there is a need for a partly new concept.
- *A new nine-months programme with four modules and project work for 30 days.*
- *Build a learning organization via individual learning plans.*
  Individual plans again!
- *A mix of action learning, teaching and task forces.*
- *A greater emphasis on critical projects.*
- *Link the projects closer to the business.*
- *Extend the use of IT in the projects.*
- *Make international business communication more efficient.*
- *Help managers to know more about themselves. 'How does my behavior affect others? How do I create a good balance between the various duties in life?'*

Some comments are frequently made, and closer links between reality and learning is certainly one of them – expressed in various ways. Individualization is another, vaguely described so far. Just a few have mentioned IT and its potential impact. Practically all intend to go on, develop their ideas and make the learning even more efficient. They seem to be quite enthusiastic about the possibilities.

Additional comments

As mentioned previously, the purpose of the study was basic fact-finding. The results, however, also lead to further questions such as:

- What are the best methods for the selection of participants? This requires more sophisticated answers to the question 'who'? The selection process seems to be very traditional: nomination is so far the Nordic Way. There is no doubt that this part of the total development process is quite important; programmes are costly, and mistakes in the selection process are expensive socially as well as financially.
- How can action learning be even more integrated into the total executive development process?
- How can the short-term usefulness and value of the assignments be assured?
- How can the long-term value for the individual participant be measured?
- Are there interesting, international benchmarking possibilities?
- How can IT be utilized more in action learning?
- Why are assignments related to finance and technology unusual?

Several critical issues are well taken care of. Top management seems to be deeply involved, and HR managers are strongly motivated to go further. Creativity when it comes to assignments is impressive. Some companies have opened up and work in consortiums; most work internationally.

Follow-up in March 2000

The study from 1998 was completed with interviews in March 2000, and the intentions mentioned earlier were to a great extent fulfilled. Even more companies have started action learning. In some cases, the level of ambition has changed somewhat – more participants take part, but less individual time is spent on the programmes.

As foreseen, IT means a number of new opportunities. Obviously, communication among participants is facilitated, and the production and distribution of the programme report (when applicable) can be done far more efficiently then in the past. IT also means better possibilities to individualize the learning. However, IT can also lead to segregation: one company reports that future programmes will take the participants' IT skills into consideration: 'Maybe we will develop different, parallel programmes – one for those who can handle IT as a tool for learning, and one for those who can't'.

There is a tendency to leave more of the learning process to the individual: 'You see to it yourself that you have the competence necessary to build a successful career. We, your management, provide you with (some) resources and guidance.' To some extent, this has always been the case, but at the same time the managerial presence has been regarded as a key condition for success. Will lack of management development professionals, absence of line management and almost unlimited faith in the individual lead to better results?

The major developments are threefold. First, there is a rapid restructuring going on among Nordic companies. Major mergers and acquisitions are occurring frequently; new alliances are forged to gain competitive edge regionally and worldwide. This means that most if not all executive development is taking pace in a global context. The second major development is a stronger integration of real business issues into executive development. Factors stimulating this are time, speed and participants' motivation, as well as top management's interest and commitment. The third development is the profound impact of IT: it has developed very quickly in the Nordic countries, especially in Finland and Sweden. IT is changing the business landscape and will also change management and leadership in the large, leading organizations.

Nordic HR professionals are eager to go on and develop their concepts and programmes in response to changing needs. There is most certainly a Northern Light; maybe it is comparable with the light shining in other parts of the world.

12
Strategic Executive Learning and Development in French Multinationals*

Nicolas Rolland

This chapter is based on research conducted on thirty-five of the largest French multinationals. The purpose of the research was to determine the main characteristics of strategic executive learning and executive development approaches in French multinationals and to ascertain what learning methods and philosophies were being utilized and/or considered by these companies. In particular, we wanted to investigate whether action learning was widely used. This article is a synthesis of the interviews that we have carried out over a period of three months.

Motivations

French firms think that their executives need to learn the latest management tools and methods, and to understand the trends in their respective business environments. But they are also interested in assessing and utilizing the capabilities of their executives.

Mobilization of competencies

Today, some describe a corporation as a portfolio of core competencies (Hamel and Prahalad, 1990) whereby competence is defined as the capacity

---

* After a through search of printed and electronic sources, a questionnaire was sent out to 50 leading French firms. The following responded and most agreed to follow-up interviews that were conducted. We would like to thank the following firms for their cooperation: Air France, Air Liquide, Alcatel, Aventis, Axa GIE, B.N.P., Canal +, Cap Gémini, Carrefour, Casino, Companie St GOBAIN, Crédit Lyonnais , Damart, Danone, EDF-GDF, Elf, Eurotunel, FNAC, France Telecom, L'Oreal, La Poste , Lafarge, Renault, Société Générale, Somfy, Suez Lyonnaise, Thomson CSF, Usinor Solac, VALEO, VIVENDI UNIVERSAL and others.

of the firm to mobilize and implement knowledge, behaviours and experiences in a business environment. Multinationals have realized that creating value, an essential factor for achieving a competitive edge, now depends on the mobilization and realization of their competencies rather than their environmental positioning (Grant, 1996). These competencies have gained importance and are now viewed as being more strategic.

Developing executive competencies means sharing knowledge and experiences within an organization. The first French firm that adopted this approach was BSN (now Danone). According to Antoine Riboud (1987), managing director of BSN in the 1980s, 'continuous increase in competencies has beneficial effects on the quality of products and thus on the company's competitive edge'. But this implies radical changes, particularly in work organization and development.

Each firm that we interviewed has modified or is in the process of modifying, or has expressed the desire to modify, its organization in order to better coordinate the development of its competencies. Their strategic focus for the coming years is to create value through the sharing of knowledge and experience. The main resource is no longer so-called tangible assets, but human, individual and collective capabilities. Such an objective implies an organizational, structural and behavioural change. Firms must no longer be seen as a group of independent divisions, they must tackle managerial development with a global and lateral approach, creating global leadership capabilities. Not surprisingly, these firms also wish to globalize their competencies.

The main question for firms today is how to mobilize competencies and intellectual capital. Learning and work are being integrated in a way that changes the organization into a learning organization. But we also observed many different approaches to these issues and these in turn seemed to depend on a company's culture and history.

Global culture

All the firms interviewed stated that one of the main goals of their executive development programmes was the development of a global organizational culture. For example, the director of human resource development of one of the largest of the French multinationals interviewed, a leader in six different business sectors and active in 40 countries, told us that one of the most important changes in their organization in the past years was the desire to create a global company culture. He believes that a cohesive multinational corporate culture is essential to being a successful company.

It is also important to keep in mind that over 75 per cent of the firms interviewed have been nationalized for a considerable period of time – they used to be owned by the state. They have thus had very little exposure to global competition and have not experienced any particular culture allowing for strategic freedom, independent from the government or a purely national focus. This dimension is important for the evolution and change in executive development for French firms.

French executive development practices

Several characteristics of senior executive development programmes in firms that we interviewed are congruent with action learning. However, the major differences with French multinationals is their understanding and use of project work based on real business issues, teamwork, company-wide support for the programmes and top management involvement in these programmes. Their executive development programmes can be classified as shown in Table 12.1.

The main differences are not due to the industry's characteristics but to the firm's approach to strategy, its organizational structures and its corporate culture. For example, we noted that companies with strong hierarchical lines and weak interdivisional relationships do not have action learning executive development programmes.

Table 12.1 Executive/managerial development among French multinationals

A (12.5%)	B (52.5%)		C (35%)
Classical training	Business focus	Project	Business driven action learning
	Real business issue(s)	Developmental business issue(s)	
• Executive development through teaching	• Firm-based real business issue(s)	• Non-actual or non-firm-based business issue(s)	• Learning by doing
• Different courses at various stages of the career	• Involvement in business projects	• Involvement in personal managerial development	• Real business issues
• Use of business games	• Done irregularly throughout the year.	• Done often throughout the year	• Learning in teams
			• Top-executive involvement
			• Company-wide support
			• Individual leadership development and coaching/teamwork.
			• Responsible for recommendations

Note: The percentages refer to the percentage of the firms interviewed. Our definition of business driven action learning is the one to be found in Boshyk (2000).

Classical training

Classical or traditional training is used by French multinationals to explain their organizational structure and culture to senior executives – the 'look and feel' of the company. In this case, executive development is carried out through teaching. Several university professors and professionals explain, during various courses, how to manage a team or small-sized division and how to manage in a multinational and multicultural context. Executive decision-making and strategic involvement are taught using business games and simulations. At lower hierarchical levels, teaching is carried out through case studies related to the current situation of the company. This method includes several different varieties of training, including several seminars in which professors are responsible for the training, which may not necessarily be connected with the current strategic issues of the company. These executive development programmes consist of five to eight sessions with each session running between five to eight days and with participants selected on the basis of their business performance and motivation, but also mainly upon the recommendations of their direct reports. Many companies use their own management institute to develop their own managers (EDF-GDF, L'Oreal and others). The objectives of these institutes are to organize the firm's human development, to centralize information, and to further the understanding of concepts and managerial practices within organizations.

This choice of executive development is more relevant to inculcating the company culture and knowledge rather than exploring strategic opportunities. Seventy per cent of the firms interviewed are fully satisfied with this development method, and 35 per cent of them believe that this is the best method for strategic executive development.

Business projects

Many French multinationals use business projects to develop their executives. Of the companies interviewed, 91 per cent use business projects and 62.5 per cent use them for business *and* executive development purposes.

Business projects were originally designed to develop a product or an idea. Since the companies have reorganized their structures according to the principle of competencies, they believe that a project can allow executives to share their knowledge and competencies regarding the business issue, and consequently learn through action. The use of projects is traditional in French firms, and is considered useful in anticipating actions for the future. Ever since its creation in 1930 by the Paris Chambre de Commerce et d'Industrie, the Centre de Préparation aux Affaires (CPA group) has been known for its executive educational methods using projects. The main objective of business project development is to develop the executive's ability to translate the strategic vision of the company into concrete decision and actions. Participants have to work in teams and resolve a business issue chosen by top executives. During these group meetings, emphasis is placed on the exchange of knowledge and experience through solving business issues and far less, if any, emphasis given to the personal development of participants. Also, participants are not necessarily responsible for the implementation, and neither are participants exclusively or necessarily senior executives.

We tried to determine which companies really did give an executive development perspective to their business projects. We also noted that some project work also involves a somewhat different approach than a direct business focus. For example, in one company, once a year, participants are asked to develop an initiative in the company. In this case executives were asked to organize a fund-raiser to assist some charities. In the process, the effort became an action learning event: top executives defined the business approach, selected the participants and asked them to organize the process in a way which related to issues involved in new product development. Although participants in this project worked as team members, an individual effort was also required.

These two methods are obviously quite different. In the first case, companies take advantage of the strategic development being carried out to implement executive development and focus only on the business results, whereas in the second case executive development is the company's main goal. Business project development can be described as shown in Figure 12.1.

Many companies wish to develop their executives through work on business projects because they involve them in global corporate strategies, give them greater motivation, and the opportunity to present project reports and recommendations to management, even though they do not all work on real business issues. These companies use business projects because their

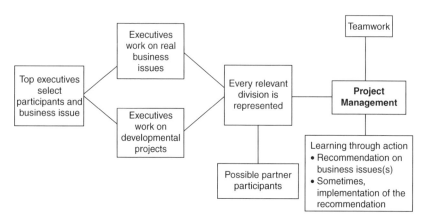

Figure 12.1 Business project development in French multinationals

business is very complex, and requires a broadly-based mobilization of competencies. In such a case, working with others who have a different body of knowledge implies sharing experiences, learning and involvement in a real project. An executive development manager told us that he believed in teamwork and the use of questions to create learning, rather than using existing knowledge to look at business issues. According to him, 'tomorrow is necessarily different from yesterday, and so new things need to be done; what new questions need to be asked before solutions are sought?'

Resolving a business project issue requires different competencies and knowledge throughout the various stages of the programme. This is why sharing knowledge and experiences is interesting and enriching for the participants. Business projects and action learning are in a way similar because both have the same programme philosophy: a social exchange in which managers learn with and from others during the diagnosis and handling of real issues. And, sometimes, the participants are responsible for implementing the recommendations. At the end of the project, if the executive is not responsible for the implementation the learning can be extended. When he returns to his regular job with additional knowledge and experience, he shares these with the rest of the staff.

Many levels – managers, junior managers and engineers – take part in business projects while doing their regular job. With these initiatives, they are given the opportunity to manage a team, knowledge, competencies and cultures. Programmes that are not related to real business issues last between 25 days to five months; programmes that are related to real business issues last between 30 days to three years.

Participants are selected according to their competence, knowledge and experience with the issue in question. Indeed, if an executive's competencies are essential, he may be appointed to more than one project. Therefore, according to this approach the project can be viewed not only as a developmental process but also as a way to develop business experience. These companies use external resources, including business-school instructors, suppliers and other professionals to help them with the business issue. Typical business issues deal with international market development, customer orientation, rapid growth, market segmentation, product development and sales. Information before, during and after the programme is generally centralized, but business project results are available on the company's Intranet.

Business project work is preferred to traditional training because companies believe that these programmes are based on current strategic needs. Business project development is similar to the notion of learning organizations and employee involvement in corporate life. Ninety per cent of the firms interviewed are satisfied with this executive development method and wish to continue in this way. Fifty per cent do not understand the difference between their executive development programme and business driven action learning.

Business project best practice

One of the firms interviewed (firm A) has used business projects in executive development for ten years, the projects being used to solve business issues. In this case the issue was: 'How to integrate Quality Management in all the levels of our production process?' An executive team was built with people with different competencies on the subject chosen from all the levels relating to production. The top management appointed the executives, preferring junior to senior managers: 'developing young capacities is more attractive for top management because they are the next generation of global managers'.

The project took seven months to complete, and the company used external resources to present the competitive environment involved in the business issue. Professors explained the characteristics of the general strategic options that could be implemented to solve the issue and apply the recommendations. The junior executives had to present solutions with all the organizational, financial and human aspects and the strategic processes in a project report. In this case, a cooperation agreement with a Japanese company was proposed, and many of these junior executives were later involved in implementing the recommendations.

Business driven action learning

Action learning is an Anglo-Saxon term; there is no true equivalent in the French language or French executives' lexicon. However, 35 per cent of the interviewed companies use action learning – as we have defined action learning in this article – as strategic organizational and executive development. This includes learning by doing, teamwork on current business issues, full involvement of the management and company learning, individual and teamwork skills and perhaps participants implementing recommendations.

In most French companies surveyed, participants involved in action learning processes come from heterogeneous hierarchical levels. Some firms only use action learning for top executives, some others for junior managers. The least frequent practice, and yet the most interesting, is using action learning at all levels. Senior managers can then share their competencies with the younger ones, who can in turn bring a new vision to the issue. Firms that are practising this kind of business driven action learning are service firms. French multinationals using only senior executives in their business driven action learning programmes practice an original brainstorming approach, allowing executives to develop some ideas and to share their managerial experiences on a new business issue or on a new activity. This approach was developed around the same time that benchmarking techniques and business intelligence practices were introduced in French companies.

The selection process and programme characteristics are usually as follows:

- election of the participants by the top management team;
- participants are never volunteers;
- selection is based on competencies and also experience;
- there are 20 to 30 participants per programme;
- firms try to have participants who have never worked together previously.

Top management defines the business issue, which is never disclosed before the programme begins. One of the main criteria for choosing a business issue is its impact on the growth of the firm and on the learning opportunities for participants. The main issues are related to international development (including strategic alliances), new market penetration, new product or service development (strategic diversification) and, recently, Internet development (B2B, B2C, and others). These issues are mainly related to the firm's international ventures because French multinationals think that an unfamiliar environment stimulates more reflection about the strategy. Programmes last from four weeks to 10 months, and some of these programmes are divided into different stages. For example, one of the most important French telecommunication companies has a total of 45 day-long sessions over 10 months. Most companies use external resources; they work with professionals in the strategic field, and in partnership with management institutes and business schools that help them to define concrete business issues.

During these courses, executives continue to work on projects with the assistance of the other participants as well as qualified professors and facilitators who help them through their project experiences. The second category of resource is the 'business partner and specialist' category, where suppliers and industrial experts can come and present their ideas on the subject. Business issues have covered the following areas: strategic alliances, international development, cultural integration problems, new market penetration and new product development.

One of the main characteristics of French business driven action learning practices is that when companies use this approach for the first time they were often than not do so outside of France; that is, in their foreign subsidiaries. We did not receive detailed explanations for this, but some companies explained that this practice allows them to spread new values and beliefs thereby developing a global corporate culture. At the same time, it appears that some French companies are using this approach to test this executive education method to see how executives respond. French firms usually implement these 'more experimental' learning programmes in northern Europe (Denmark, Norway, Sweden, UK), whilst their strategic programmes tend to be run in their US subsidiaries. The choice of northern Europe can be explained by the fact that many companies are using action learning in these countries, principally in the UK where 'classic' action learning practices are commonly used by firms (though not really according to a business driven action learning definition) – and in Sweden where some companies use action reflection learning™ to develop their executives. French firms in the USA are testing action learning methods there because they think action learning programmes in the USA (for example those by General Electric and other US companies) are well-known and that therefore their executives in the United States will be more receptive to this type of educational programme. Sometimes, their subsidiaries are frequently autonomous and use action learning even if the home-country group does not use it.

Business driven action learning best practice

Defining an action learning best practice in French firms is both easy and difficult. Easy because few firms use action learning, and the choice was not very large. However, the French multinational companies that we interviewed did not all use the same action learning process.

Firm B is one of the biggest French multinationals, present in more than 100 countries. Firm B's programme is not run in France but in the north of Europe. The duration of the programme is one year, divided into three sessions: preparation, advancement and presentation of the report. The programme's objective is to combine strategic and executive development, and the top executive chooses six business issues. In the first part some professors and business experts come to explain the country's culture, the market and some managerial tools. After this first step, the 24 participants are divided into teams of six, each team working separately on a business issue. All the groups have a sponsor who helps them, and many experts come to explain their ideas about the issue and the market. One of the business issues has been: 'how to reduce the time to market'; another, 'How to control the quality in the supply chain'. The third part is to present a report on the recommendations. Most of the executives on the programme have been made responsible for implementing their recommendations.

Action learning limitations in French multinationals

The first reason for limitation is related to organizational structure. Many French multinational companies clearly separate strategic development from executive development; they consider that executives enter the organization with their knowledge and competencies, and they then build up experience. They then only need to attend training seminars to share the spirit, culture and values of the company. The second reason is French organizational culture. In many multinational companies a formal hierarchy separates the divisions which prevents a global and lateral approach to executive development. Moreover, many French multinationals were, until recently, owned by the state. They were closely tied to economic and governmental policies and had little autonomy in decision-making. This foundation is not conducive with today's predominant desire to involve executives in strategic decisions.

Executive development: future perspectives

French multinationals that have adopted action learning have done so only recently. Over 50 per cent of them adopted the approach less than five years ago. As this is a new practice, companies are enthusiastic and wish to continue in this way. Executives are particularly responsive to action learning, believing that this method matches their personal development expectations and makes top management listen to their strategic opinions on current issues. For these companies, action learning is a way to built social relationships, commitment and engagement. Action learning thus corresponds to their executive learning principles: senior executives learn more efficiently when they work in teams and in real situations. Action learning also gives them the possibility of developing their competence base. As previously explained, French multinationals have, in general, begun to restructure their organizations and focus more on competencies than on professional functional skills. Action learning integrates this logic: it could be the answer to their needs and hence this process could further develop in French multinationals in the coming years. The current problem is that top management does not really believe in this type of development method because they do not in general see how executive development can go hand in hand with strategic development.

French firms that practice business driven action learning believe that, in this field, the role of human resources is strategic and can thus create and sustain organizational performance and a competitive edge. They argue that human resources must no longer be considered only as a cost or source of efficiency gains. Nevertheless, the past decade has revealed a certain desire from the authorities and top managers to integrate employee involvement, job restructuring and, in particular, teamwork. The contingency of all these changes necessarily implies enhanced organizational performance. Employees and managers must be motivated to share their experiences and competencies through work on a real business issue. Companies thinking in this way are, according to our survey, still in the minority but they nevertheless think they are on the right path in the new global business environment.

References

Andrews, K. R. (1987) *The Concept of Corporate Strategy*, 3rd edn. New York: Irwin.
Argyris, C. and Schön, D. (1978) *Organizational Learning: A Theory of Action Perspective*. Reading, MA: Addison-Wesley.

Becker, B. and Gerhart, B. (1996), 'The Impact of Human Resource Management on Organizational Performance: Progress and Prospects', *The Academy of Management Journal*, vol. 39(4).

Boshyk, Y. (1999) 'Knowledge Management and Beyond: How Companies Mobilize Experience', *Financial Times*, 8 February 1999, Mastering Management Series, pp. 12–13.

Boshyk, Y. (2000) 'Introduction: Business Driven Action Learning: The Key Elements', in Y. Boshyk (ed.), *Business Driven Action Learning: Global Best Practices*. London: Macmillan, and New York: St. Martin's Press, pp. xi–xvii.

Foss, N. J. (1997) *Resources, Firms and Strategies*. New York: Oxford University Press.

Grant, R. M. (1996) 'Prospering in Dynamically-Competitive Environments: Organizational Capability as Knowledge Integration', *Organization Science*, vol. 7, pp. 375–87.

Hamel, G. and Prahalad, C. K. (1990) 'The Core Competence of the Corporation', *Harvard Business Review*, vol. 68(3), pp. 79–81.

Hofstede, G. (1994) *Cultures and Organizations*. London: HarperCollins Business.

McGill, I. and Beaty, L. (1995). *Action Learning: A Guide for Professional, Management and Educational Development*, 2nd edn. London: Kogan Page.

Riboud, A. (1987) 'Modernisation, mode d'emploi. Rapport au premier ministre', Union Moderne d'édition, collection 10/18.

13
Changing the Rules at the World Council of Churches: Action Learning as Large-Scale System Change

Konrad Raiser and R. Morgan Gould

Introduction

Faced with increasing conflicts worldwide, religious pluralism and increased competition for resources among ecumenical bodies, the World Council of Churches (WCC) was compelled to take action. An institution celebrating its 50th year, the WCC sought to 'de-institutionalize' so as to become more flexible and responsive to the needs and concerns of its members. After 10 years of dialogue and close consultation with its 337 member churches, the WCC wished to implement a team-based structure and evolve a different work ethos in-house. The WCC knew 'what' it wished to do, and action learning became the vehicle for knowing 'how' to implement these changes.

What is ecumenism?

For those unfamiliar with church history and doctrine, ecumenism might best be understood as the desire to bring into harmony church differences and differing points of view. As many already know, these differences often evoke deep feeling and passionate if not furious antagonism. Ecumenism – the call for unity – first found expression in the earliest days of the Christian movement some 2000 years ago, but its modern antecedents extend to turn-of-the-century efforts for reconciliation and unity among an increasingly divided Christian church. As a movement, ecumenism has grown steadily since, and like the churches, competing points of view have emerged making common ecumenical ground a far-off challenge. The World Council of Churches, based in Geneva, Switzerland, was founded at its very first World Assembly in September 1948, and stands as the leading ecumenical body today.

Constitution and members

At present the WCC counts among its membership some 337 mostly national church bodies worldwide representing some 450 million individuals coming from over 100 countries in the world. The WCC exists for the principle purpose of 'fellowship' or relationship among these members and individuals; its constitutional charter makes this explicit:

> The World Council of Churches is a fellowship of churches which have committed themselves to make visible their unity in Christ and to call one another to a deeper expression of that unity through worship and common life, witness and service to the world.

Every seven years these members from over 100 nations gather in a World Assembly to decide as one body on overall policy, a programme and constitutional matters. The WCC takes as its highest authority this World Assembly, and its directives regarding policy and programme. The eighth World Assembly, commemorating the 50th year of the founding of the World Council of Churches, was held in December 1998 in Harare, Zimbabwe, just prior to the general elections there. Some 5000 participants from every corner of the world gathered, and among them 900 delegates who took collective decisions regarding the WCC's institutional directions for the next seven years.

Governance at the WCC

A complex governing structure

The governing structure of the World Council of Churches reflects the complexity and diversity it represents. The Central Committee, its members elected by the Assembly, is comprised of 150 members plus the eight Presidents of the World Council. It holds the constitutional power of the Assembly in the intervening seven years between World Assemblies, and convenes – together with its two standing sub-committees (Programme and Finance) – every 12 to 18 months. The Executive Committee, some 25 members, is the administrative body to oversee the work of the council; it meets every six months. There are five established Commissions and Boards holding separate advisory authority with tripartite relationships to the (a) member churches, (b) the Central Committee and (c) the WCC staff; in addition, there is a plethora of advisory bodies each reflecting programmatic areas of the WCC with similar tripartite relationships.

The World Council of Churches' past achievements

From its beginnings 52 years ago, the World Council of Churches has emerged as the leading ecumenical body in the world today, and an organization of renoun. The WCC's reputation is known globally as witnessed in Zimbabwe when then President of the Republic of South Africa, Nelson Mandela, made a surprise visit to the General Assembly. In his address, President Mandela held up the WCC for its help in the fight against apartheid; he asked the world to remember the WCC's role in educating black youth when no other means were then available.

This glowing tribute points to the WCC's acknowledged role in issues concerning peace, reconciliation and justice – a strong and vibrant history of global involvement in bringing an end to violence and hatred during the period of apartheid. The WCC gained similar prominence in its theological reflections concerning baptism, communion and ministry – divisive issues among churches – and its works on a common confession of the Christian faith; its Faith and Order Commission was one of the founding movements of the WCC and remains fully intact in the present structure. The WCC's role in international affairs similarly found prominence in its negotiations of a peace accord in Sudan, mediation efforts in Guatemala, and in opening initial contact between North and South Korea.

Emerging concerns

Ecumenical pluralism

Significantly, many countries now on every continent had formed national associations of churches with ecumenical aims, as had the major denominational groups (Christian World Communions like the Lutherans, Presbyterians, Baptists and others), and various other Christian communities and movements. The ecumenical playing field had grown and matured considerably. What had been, and continue to be, denominational differences dividing churches had found expression in an increasingly plural ecumenism. Ecumenical pluralism was only one of the trends now significantly affecting the WCC, and reflected the upsurge of religious pluralism in the world generally.

Declining resources

From the beginning of the 1990s, the WCC began to experience a steady but certain decline in financial support from its traditional funding partners. Two previous restructurings had led to significant downsizing of staff and programme activity, and now, less than seven years later, another layer of staff reductions were anticipated. The resources available to the World Council of Churches were increasingly having to be shared with a plethora of competing ecumenical organizations with similar mandates and programmes, and the funding agencies themselves were exerting greater pressure for transparency in reporting the use of those funds.

Globalization and cultural crises

The introduction of technologies to enable communication were seen to have quite the opposite effect: globalization, aided by instantaneous communication and accessibility, was yielding cultural crises and conflict worldwide, and the erosion of trust in 'institutions' generally, especially among the young. The explosion of information available to the world, far from bringing enlightenment, seemed on the contrary to bring escalating demands and possibilities of conflict. The WCC's historical role in peace and in seeking unity among the faithful lay precisely at the intersection of these trends of globalization, mass communication and increasing cultural conflict.

The change imperative

Consultation with WCC members

The changes within the ecumenical world and those in the global fields of finance, economy and politics generally clearly called for a response from the World Council of Churches. The need for a response had been anticipated for some time. Starting from 1989, the WCC had initiated a process of reflection with its member bodies entitled 'Towards a Common Understanding and Vision of the World Council of Churches.' This process was completed with a policy document adopted by the Central Committee in 1997; both the process and policies gave renewed emphasis to the following areas:

1 first and foremost, a call to a deeper expression of unity and common life among the churches;
2 to address a time of crisis in the world whose deepest dimensions can be perceived to be spiritual, most especially the erosion of the human community, and the need for greater mutual accountability and empowerment;
3 to affirm the Christian hope of life for all, the healing of the human community and the wholeness of God's entire creation through common witness and action by the churches, and through the life of the church as an inclusive community;
4 a new organizational structure that reflects the WCC's identity as a fellowship of churches by working in an integrated way on the full range of issues which members acknowledge;
5 to give priority to reflection and deliberation on key issues facing members rather those issues dominated by institutional concerns.

To this end, the World Council of Churches consciously undertook, under the leadership of its newly elected Secretary General, Konrad Raiser, its own 'de-institutionalization' in an effort to become more responsive to its members, and to revitalize its role within the broader ecumenical movement.

A proposed new structure

The previous WCC structure resembled that of most western corporations organized along divisional or business-unit lines, though in this instance the organizing principle was mostly thematic concerns or issues, programmatic emphases, or what could be characterized as the WCC's 'products'. The proposed new structure was to replace this divisional structure with a team-based approach to programme development and delivery. Thematic concerns and issues were represented by teams that were in turn grouped into two broad programme clusters. An additional two clusters were devoted to the more functional aspects of organizational life, such as finance and administration, and communication (including information technology).

The directors of these four clusters would together with the Secretary General and his Deputy comprise the Staff Leadership Group, or top-executive body. Each team would have its own coordinator, and these coordinators would also meet regularly for the purposes of communication and sharing of information. Finally, a consultative body comprised of all members of the organization (Staff Consultative Group, SCG) would also meet for input and review of programme and policy concerns.

The consultative process

The consultation mandate

The World Council of Churches decided early to seek consultation during an extended change process. Another staff reduction was anticipated, and the new team structure required implementation with a staff already weary of change. Most importantly, however, the World Assembly was less than 12 months away. Gould & Associates were engaged because of their past experience and knowledge in change management generally, and also because of their commitment to and practice in action learning. The WCC did not seek 'advice' but someone to 'accompany' the WCC in its change process. The mandates given to the consultants were two: January 1998–December 1998, to assist in the painful process of staff reductions and subsequently bring to life the new team-based structure. January 1999–December 1999, to help evolve a new work ethos within the WCC culture towards greater flexibility and responsiveness to member churches.

General description of the consultative process

While the mandate for consultation was broad, and the role of the consultant(s) loosely defined, the World Council of Churches did embrace action learning as an approach consistent with the value they give to consensus, most especially evident in their governance structure and among their members. Of immediate concern was the considerable work pressures on staff as they prepared for the World Assembly at the very same time that a change effort of some magnitude was being introduced.

In order to minimize disruption to the WCC's own ongoing activities, the consultation focused almost exclusively on the tasks at hand. Regular meetings of the Staff Leadership Group (SLG: the executive corps) were attended, and over the course of the consultation seven 'Learning Conferences' of one to two days duration were designed for the SLG on topics ranging from authority and decision-making of the SLG, and future scenario planning, to operational planning. Similarly, the WCC historically met as an entire organization twice annually, and these meetings were used as platforms for discussion of issues of concern, and for policy and programme planning following the World Assembly. Meetings with the team coordinators (equivalent to 'middle management') as a group were held less frequently during the first year, but accelerated during the second year as we began to address the issues of work ethos, integration of activities and coordination among the teams and between clusters. These meetings were nearly always long in discussion, but always productive, even when disagreement was the primary outcome. We later indicate those methodologies that were not successful.

The issues and activities that were addressed over the course of the consultation were broad, highly varied and emergent. They can be characterized as follows.

First year

- *Process and criteria for decisions regarding redundancies*
  Interviews of each and every administrative staff member were undertaken by the team coordinators, and review of the last two performance appraisals. The SLG took the final decision as a body. Where possible (and almost in every instance) senior staff close to retirement were offered generous severance packages with no adverse affect on their pensions. The planned timeline for announcement of redundancies was accelerated.
- *Position descriptions for the new teams*
  Generic role descriptions were written for every team member and forwarded to SLG for general review and approval.
- *Training*
  Training was provided for the teams to undertake a work load analysis of their current portfolios of activities, and in cross-cultural learning regarding management style and methods among the teams.
- *Staff re-allocation to new teams*
  The methods and processes for determining staff placements in the new team structures were jointly decided and executed, including the identification of new functions, areas of intentional overlap and coordination requirements.

- *Scenario planning*
  A two-day strategy retreat of SLG using Future Search methods resulted in identification of key areas of involvement for the future WCC role in the ecumenical movement

Second year

- *Interpreting the World Assembly*
  As preparation for a formal planning process, the entire organization gathered several times over a six-week period to 'interpret' the policies and programme guidelines issued by the World Assembly held in Harare. Differing group process methods were tried for the first time
- *Strategic planning*
  A strategic planning method and process was jointly defined and implemented resulting in an organization-wide strategic plan for a three-year period
- *Compensation and remuneration*
  An in-house survey was designed and distributed to clarify staff preferences regarding compensation and remuneration for the purpose of understanding staff motivation, and for designing a new staff classification and remuneration system

The role of consultant(s) was to catalyse, reflect and jointly design methods where necessary, and to otherwise support the change initiatives as they were introduced. Each and every meeting of the various administrative bodies – SLG, team coordinators, week of meetings, and so forth – were attended. Mostly, however, the consultant(s) spent countless hours, every week, coaching individuals on the change underway, listening to people's concerns, and attempting to relate the change initiatives to individuals' hopes and the WCC's future.

Life at the World Council of Churches

The importance of the constitution charter

The constitutional constraints, and the role of the World Assembly and Central Committee, cannot be given enough emphasis in understanding the unique life at the World Council of Churches. Time and time again, the consultant had to be reminded of these constraints. The WCC is a fellowship of churches, which implies a relationship of some duration, and as such any policy directives or programme emphases must initiate from within the WCC member bodies, and most specifically must be endorsed by the World Assembly or by their Central Committee. Decision-making and lead times on issues of some weight can be quite long; consensus is always sought, and the agreement of members is paramount.

Two values in tension

The World Council of Churches had been founded historically from the Faith and Order movement which had focused on issues of doctrine that divided the churches, and the Life and Work movement which promoted collaboration by the churches in social action. These two founding impulses of the WCC – between faith and social action – were still evident some 60 years later in the tensions and conflict within the member bodies. The activities of these movements remain reflected in WCC programme activity into the new and present structure, and the tension between social action and spiritual reflection remains.

A cross-cultural staff

The staff at the World Council of Churches are among the most multicultural of any organization. Staff members represent some 40 countries of the world, and staff teams themselves represent widely different nationalities, religious profession and professional backgrounds. The intercultural composition of the WCC reflects two quite distinct cultural world views – between the western practice and those more typically expressing community leadership and practice – that can never really be resolved unambiguously once and forever. The following staff values, then, reflect these multicultural perspectives:

Culture of autonomy

Among staff generally there was a quite vivid, unmistakable desire for autonomy. This was sometimes expressed through open resistance to active leadership, or in many instances a healthy skepticism of what might be called 'management'. Staff – administrative and executive – were quite accustomed to working and taking decisions quite independently; accountability for these decisions were less easily accepted, however, and a culture had emerged that too often engaged in scapegoating when things went wrong.

High-touch culture

Calls for increased communication have been frequent within the WCC, not only between divisional units, but both from the top-down and from the bottom-up. Staff sought and often expressed their need for more frequent communication, and the wish to be informed at quite high levels of detail concerning all aspects of life at the WCC. Briefings by the Secretary General were routinely held, but then the 'real' conversations would often occur in the hallways or offices behind closed doors about what was 'really' meant.

High involvement

Similarly, calls for greater transparency in decision-making were made by staff, as well as a desire for greater participation in those decisions directly affecting them. Staff with long tenure at the WCC worked with tremendous dedication, and nearly any issue of any note of the WCC was felt to be of concern to them. Similarly, staff wished for greater decisiveness and coherence in the decisions taken by the leadership of the WCC.

Anticipatory

All the change initiatives – whether of anticipated redundancies, decisions regarding team composition or planning – were received with a good deal of anxiety by staff, and demands for clarity, concreteness and specificity of decisions were called for even before a formal process had begun. As early as four months into the consultation, and some eight months before the new structure was to be implemented, staff were anxious to know: 'What will be the role of the Team Coordinator', 'when will the new teams begin to function', 'what will be the process for team formation', 'what will their names be', 'will it imply a move of offices', 'will all the teams be the same size?' This culture of anticipation was to accompany the change process from beginning to end.

Tight departmental boundaries

The World Council of Churches, like many institutions half-a-century old, had devolved into quite tight factional clans – the former divisions or units – with very little communication among them. Directors of these units conducted their own separate programme planning activities, and similarly sought and secured their own resources for these activities. A quite lively spirit of competition existed between these units, and there was strong identification among staff within them.

A community of service

Finally, the staff and employees of the World Council of Churches have enjoyed a quite long period of relative prosperity and high recognition for their many achievements. Life at the WCC has been cohesive, with an emphasis on community and fellowship within. To work at the WCC has been not simply employment, but a calling into a vocation of service. However, over the years this had begun to erode, with not all staff members declared Christians. Also, there has been a tremendous distrust of western management theories and approaches, a skepticism that remains to this day.

The interventions

Respect for values and history of the organization

The World Council of Churches is an organization that values consensus, community and deep respect for the individual. Since its founding, there have been only four Secretary Generals (Dr Raiser will retire in 2003); institutional memory is long, as two of the previous Secretary Generals (from the Caribbean and South America) are still very much involved in the ecumenical movement. Skepticism concerning western corporate practices derives from deeply held beliefs about community, what it means to be church, and, most importantly, values about the dignity of the human being.

Many of the early analytic tools – work-load analysis, process mapping, cross-cultural training – were flatly rejected or found to be irrelevant for supporting the change process. The consultant, in this instance, had no choice but to work within the existing values, beliefs and assumptions held by the World Council of Churches, and to jettison an approach that was more analytic, 'western' and felt to be dehumanizing. How, then, to meet the two consulting mandates?

Understanding the rules of the game

Act first

After some months of action, reflection and observation, a curious dynamic could be noted: immediately following a policy decision or directive, staff within the old unit structure would move with incredible speed towards implementation. Often, within a day or two, critical actions and decisions would be taken. This dynamic was quite opposite to notions of institutional lethargy and bureaucratic delay. Only after some weeks more did the reason for this behaviour become clear.

Secure a position of influence

In a resource-constrained environment, with the prospect of declining resources, a process of political negotiation had emerged to obtain and secure the resources for one's own programmes. If you were first in line, had secured the necessary commitments before others, then your work could proceed uninterrupted. Additionally, the greater the resource base you could obtain, the more your political influence within the larger ecumenical movement. A political model of organization had emerged with a decided bias against a management culture.

Designing interventions to change the rules of the game: conscious reflection not possible

Any intervention for cultural change within the operational practices of the WCC had to keep in mind these very deep rules. Conversations with executive staff gently probing this issue convinced us that most staff remained unaware of both the hidden assumption or the related behaviour. Invitations to bring this deep assumption into conscious awareness were not accepted, or deferred. How, then, to address this deeply embedded practice?

Interventions at the task level, using the existing structure: the task culture, not a change programme

A conscious effort was taken to not address 'behaviour' or 'attitude' or other behavioural approaches to culture change. Instead, our previous work in change management had convinced us that interventions at the level of task were the most effective. This approach has an additional advantage: the ongoing work or activities of the client system can be used, thus avoiding a costly 'change programme' that detracts from the ongoing responsibilities of management and staff.

Design the process to thwart the old rules

As the new team structure was installed, and following the 8th World Assembly, staff were expected to undertake programmatic planning to give expression to the directives of their executive body. How to do this planning? We were clear that the process should be designed in such a way as to make impossible the invoking of the old rules or 'political' model. The planning process, then, was designed to occur across the entire organization at the same time, using the same process, and culminating in complete transparency of each team's three-year programme plan. A subsequent process was also designed for the teams to revise their plans based on input from the other teams, and to define areas of joint activity. Just as important was defining the process with a defined end to make impossible separate negotiations between teams outside the planning window. This approach to planning was a marked departure from practice as usual. Would it work?

How is this action learning? Surfacing assumptions and reflecting on actions

Those who insist on cross-functionality of the action learning teams around an identified problem or issue, would argue our approach was simply 'business-as-usual'. The approach we chose exemplifies the fundamental principles of action learning, and extends those principles to effect a quite broad mandate of culture change. Action learning is:

1 consistent with the history and value of the company or organization;
2 identifies and surfaces hidden assumptions or deeply-held rules;
3 takes action in ways that challenge those assumptions;
4 reflects on the outcomes; and
5 revisits the starting point.

What did and didn't work

Action learning involves 'successive approximation' – that is, learning

The planning process, and other related processes, did have its intended outcome of greater sharing and transparency of information across the teams.

An earlier effort inviting teams to share their work had not met with success, but the second effort, and familiarity with the process, led in the desired direction. Not surprisingly, action learning requires learning, and as organization members gain experience and confidence, the learning accelerates.

Breaking the first principle

Several interventions were not successful, and give greater clarity to the importance of these action learning principles. Analytic methods and tools introduced for the purpose of process mapping were flatly rejected, and some consultants were not always accepted because of their management or corporate biases. Attempts at cross-functional teams in some areas simply did not succeed, though in one key area – compensation and remuneration – a group is still working today. In each instance, these were experienced as breaking the first principle.

Assumptions that changed

A learning agenda

The executive group – Staff Leadership Group – met at the end of the consultation to review their learning, and to anticipate priority issues in the following year. They were asked to reflect on what had been learned, and what changes had been accomplished. The following summarizes their discussion:

1 There is growing ownership of the WCC in its entirety, not just at team level;
2 The new structure is in place and working as intended;
3 The WCC works in a more coordinated way;
4 Programming, budgeting and resource allocation are more integrated;
5 A growing acceptance to take some risk that we can learn by doing; we can experiment and stop midway if it is not working;
6 There is a growing ethic of accepting where the problems are, we can admit failure, or at least talk about where we are;
7 Early defensiveness on the issue of organizational change is now gone;
8 The change was guided by institutional purpose, not simply financial concerns.

Need to involve external stakeholders

New working methods were required, and members of the SLG recognized at the time that much more was now required in engaging their external partners – funding agencies and member churches (their 'suppliers' and 'customers') – in their planning processes in order to have their inputs of concerns, issues and needs. Additionally, there was recognition that the

WCC needed greater learning of new working methods to replace their heavy emphasis on the traditional methods of conferences and consultations; this would probably imply the introduction of new technologies and viewing travel as an instrument or methodology in itself.

Confidence of external funding agencies restored

A final note concerns the relationship to the WCC's external partners. The above changes, most notably the emphasis on planning and budgeting, led to increased confidence among the WCC's traditional donors and contributors. While financial concerns do remain, the renewal of confidence among the external partner agencies is evidence that these internal changes to the WCC are significant. The many changes at the level of organizational processes are significant, and paradigmatic of what other member churches are now facing and must go through.

Similarities and differences to the private sector

Similarities

Those in the corporate world may wonder how the experience of action learning has any relevance to the private sector. What is the same, what is different? What might the corporate world learn? Can action learning at this broad, strategic level have any relevance to corporate practices today?

The World Council of Churches has a strong *bias towards action*, much like most companies today. While this action-orientation drives towards results, this often, however, results in attenuated learning. Are we being effective? What worked and why? The lack of reflection can be characteristic of many corporations today who compete under tremendous pressures of time.

Similarly, the WCC is *accountable to its stakeholders* – notably the World Assembly and the Central Committee representing 330 member churches or over 300 million people. The private sector has similar injunctions from shareholders for increasing value, and parallel demands from its customers and consumers similar to the WCC constituencies who request and receive its products and offers.

Finally, both the WCC and the corporate world are living in an age of *complexity and uncertainty*. Strategic change is imperative to both. The WCC's challenges in this respect have much to do with the plethora of religious traditions, most deeply felt and held beliefs, than with competitors or changes in the industry, and could arguably be said to experience greater complexity than that of the corporate sector.

Differences

The largest difference centres around *organizational mission and purpose*, and concerns the 'bottom line'. For the corporate sector this is clearly expressed in such things as margin (profit), return on investment, and other corporate financial goals. The World Council of Churches' main areas of emphasis have been on mediation, compromise and peace-building. These differences are reflected, of course, in the charter and articles of constitution of both, and dictate quite differing organizational purposes. But, the WCC differs greatly with respect to the relevance and meaning of its corporate charter; the charter informs their every decision, and anchors their daily actions. The WCC is a 'fellowship of churches' as stated in its constitution, and this charter remains foremost in the WCC's strategy, structure, programmes and resource commitments.

A second difference concerns *means–ends consonance*. Given the purposes of the World Council of Churches, not all means towards a given end are considered appropriate. Thus the WCC is acutely aware of the need for consonance between stated goals and objectives, and the means employed for achieving them. The historical emphasis on peace, on reconciliation, on education and formation, leads the WCC to eschew management practices that would compromise the dignity and worth of its members. As only one example, decisions regarding dismissal are painstakingly taken only after wide consultation and agreement, and always with the worth of the person in mind. All decisions are instinctively taken in view of their ethical implications.

Thirdly, the *meaning of employment* or membership within the fellowship and within the WCC is quite different from the private sector. Employment of the WCC is still viewed by most employees as a vocation, and, similarly, the WCC views its employees as more than workers, as members of a community of common interest and calling. While this may have been true for some corporations in the past – somewhat similar in quality to the Japanese corporation – there is increasing divergence on this key difference between the WCC and the private sector.

The final difference centres around *individual autonomy versus corporate loyalty*. There are historical and institutional values cross-cutting the WCC that place tremendous emphasis on individual autonomy, even to the exclusion of institutional purpose. Most professional staff are identified with a particular programme or issue – whether of conflict issues, racism, poverty, rights of indigenous people, and so on – and their first identity, in fact professional passion, derives from their area of specialization. Throughout the course of the consultation, as we develop below, the issue of authority as it relates to institutional mission and purpose was questioned and often held in some suspicion. This rather skeptical view of authority is distinctly different from corporate cultures where position-power and hierarchy are both ascendant.

Conclusion: change lessons

We reiterate that issues concerning management and governance in a value-based organization that is highly intercultural will never be fully and unambiguously resolved. There is a strong argument for the benefits to an organization that not only tolerates but invites and welcomes differing points of view; the WCC is one such, and its constitutional mandate demands it do so. There can be little surprise, then, at issues regarding authority and autonomy discussed below:

Strong leadership versus participation

The World Council of Churches espouses and practices values of participation and consensus building. From the beginning, a participatory and inclusive process of learning was designed consistent with the principles of action learning. Executive staff both promoted and expected WCC members to be involved, to contribute, and to be decisive in helping to evolve a different work ethos towards greater flexibility. Yet, organization members simultaneously called for strong, personalized leadership for opening the way to change, both by way of providing a role model for learning, and to overcome the fears and uncertainties of learning. This tension of expectations – between strong leadership, and active inclusion and participation – characterized the consultation from beginning to end.

Staff autonomy versus leadership

Members of the executive staff (Staff Leadership Group, SLG) were often called to account by staff, most frequently for greater decisiveness and forcefulness in leading the change. Yet, simultaneously, staff desires for autonomy often led to open rejection of such leadership or, more often, criticism. SLG would sense this irritation and conflicting signals coming from staff – often in the form of rumours and misinformation – and struggle to know what to do. Respond? Deny? Ignore? The role of consultant proved helpful to the SLG during such times of confusion. Neither a member of staff nor of SLG, he could provide much-needed objective reflection.

Meeting resistance

Resistance is a much-discussed topic in change management literature. Our observation was that many who resisted were the historical guardians of the WCC, and seasoned professionals. Only one approach made sense: accept the resistance and invite into the process those actively resisting.

An external point of view

The consulting role proved invaluable. The WCC leadership knew that engaging in a process of change of this magnitude would require an external point of view. As leaders of the change, they would themselves get 'caught' in the dynamics of the change situation, or become defensive and stuck in their own routines. The consultant helped 'supervise' the process management, and made it possible for them to not take personally the resistance at particular phases of the change process.

Intervention knowledge, practice and theory

Finally, the implementation of strategic change is little different whether in the corporate sector (the consultant's primary experience) or in a values-based organization like the World Council of Churches. There is increasing pressure in both sectors to get strategy 'right' the first time, because the cost of delay is simply too much for any company to pay. The interventions employed were many and varied, and knowledge and expertise in intervention theory and approaches – when to use which intervention for what purpose – is invaluable in undertaking strategic change. Such knowledge can make the difference between success and failure.

14

Developing Managerial Cadres in an Emerging Economy: The Case of Poland

Grażyna Leśniak-Łebkowska

Introduction

Poland at the beginning of the third millennium is at the crossroads of two entirely different systems. It is attempting to successfully pass the transition from a centrally-planned and politically-driven economy to an internationally-integrated, market-oriented economy, like other leading countries. For the present state of the system, financial experts forged a poetic name: an emerging market.

'The significant problems we face cannot be solved at the same level of thinking we were at when we created them' – these words of Albert Einstein could be the leitmotif for the *big change* we are determined to implement. The driving forces of change heavily depend on strategic executive development. There are three sources of the increased interest in new management education: the *must*, the high *aspirations* of individuals and new *opportunities* – nowadays in Poland they coincide more than ever.

The need for new managerial education

In the 1990s, Poland underwent changes of unprecedented scale and scope to meet new challenges stemming from its own systemic transformation and from the dramatically changing nature of business in the world marketplace. Lean yet powerful organizations, fast and flexible reactions, communication and integration across all former borders, cooperation and tough competition, high quality and low-cost manufacturing – these formed the new face of entrepreneurship of old giants and the array of small businesses. How to look for an orientation in this world of paradoxes? Who will survive? Who is our friend and who is the enemy? Who will win?

The most dynamic people always ask : Why not us? If so, let's pose new questions frequently asked in Poland: What is possible, what is desirable, how to get there? All individuals, organizations, regions, countries – despite their present resources – have to answer these questions on their way to success or failure. Emerging markets like China, South Africa or Poland are looking for positive answers with great enthusiasm and determination to create a better world for their populations, after years of being impoverished and deprived by political powers of access to a better life. New opportunities have inspired a very strong motivation to succeed, with a wave of expectations that have placed great pressure on politicians and all institutions to set up the right conditions for change. Thus, when facing the cascade of economic, social, political or environmental problems, an out-of-date education is not sufficient to find proper solutions.

The first stage of transition in Poland has been remarkably successful. The cumulative economic growth over the past few years has been very positive, far outpacing other countries in Central and Eastern Europe – inflation has decreased, so has unemployment. Poland has also entered into debt-reduction agreements with the Paris and London clubs, and has achieved membership of the OECD and NATO. The next milestone is membership of the European Union.

From a strategic point of view, however, the choices are even more complicated. The triadal leadership in world business development gives us at least three fast-moving trains to the future, with the US pattern proving its dominance. The market value of US corporations, high growth and the largest inflow of foreign direct investments to the most promising markets indicate long-term perspectives for growth. Over the recent period, US companies have dominated other foreign investors in Poland. At the same time, turbulence in the former Soviet Union with its depressed economy and political climate discourages us from relying on stable and mutually beneficial relationships with that part of the world.

For the strategic education of executives in Poland after the Cold War, this is certainly a new consideration: how and from whom to learn effective ways of management; and are they universal or culture-based? How to attain our goals, to adjust, without losing country-specific values? Now Poland again stands at a crossroads. It must continue its structural reforms to correct the remaining shortcomings inherited from the centrally-managed economy, while concurrently moving ahead to implement the next round of reforms.

Polish managers and their companies as the users of management education programmes

Poland has always sought to provide its citizens with a free education. Solid basic knowledge in many traditional disciplines of science was not, however, followed with practical skills and management techniques which could bring feasible solutions to new situations calling for entrepreneurial, but well-calculated moves. The profesional successes of numerous Polish emigrants who graduated from universities in the 1970s proved that a thorough knowledge of mathematics, physics, biology or chemistry, that could not be effectively used in Poland due to the limited absorption potential of obsolete industries, was nevertheless sufficient for personal careers abroad.

The shortage of resources, inertia of institutions, the time pressures for necessary improvement, social conflict and the need for deep and complex change (for example in the Polish healthcare system, coal mining, agriculture, water resources, energy) – in such circumstances the old-style managers could barely survive, and many of them have lost social credibility. Their vast experience, personal contacts and loyalty towards political elites – this rationale could no longer work as the sole prerequisite for success. The survival of such managers depends on the pace at which they can forget the past, learn new rules and win the trust of new owners, or start again with their own small businesses.

There is no doubt that the professional background and strategic skills of executives have a crucial impact on results in business; they are as important as new technologies, product innovations and financial resources. The desperate need for updated knowledge pushed those who survived the political turbulence to set up new businesses, to restructure the uncompetitive companies, and to try to understand more and build new skills. The pressure of everyday problems is so strong that no-one argues about what needs should be met or what actions should be taken. Instead, they discuss 'in what way' and 'at what cost': how to allocate scarce resources among competing applications, each one being important and urgent? The illusion that outside consultants can solve our problems quickly has disappeared. Book knowledge about decision trees, risk analysis, rates of return and capital asset pricing do not by themselves make decisions and carry them out. The knowledge should be personally assimilated, well-anchored in a business context and followed by a personal drive to succeed, to make decisions, to implement, to fight against innumerable obstacles, to assume responsibility, and even then live with the reality that the prize may be very uncertain.

The new boom in managerial education has strong roots in the entrepreneurial nature of young aspirants aggressively wanting better personal careers and ready to invest in their future. They are the driving force of change in their companies, and these companies in turn pay for their studies, to better prepare them for the future. All ambitious individuals are assessing prospects for their profession, their companies, and themselves in this context. Many of them want to test several opportunities, many want to gain wider knowledge to be flexible in case of necessity. All of them want to secure a better future for the long run. This orientation never existed before.

The uncertainty caused by the change in the system and the weak protection mechanisms were the best teachers of self-reliance. The expected privatization and transformation of subsequent business sectors and institutions make more and more people interested in playing an active role in this process, while their employers are slowly realizing the importance of financially supporting this education. People at companies already operating in a competitive environment have already managed to change their attitudes to business but they need effective instruments, entrepreneurship and navigation skills to function in a dynamic situation. How are the Polish managers – young, experienced or old – prepared to face these challenges?

Harvard Business School Professors F. Aguillar and G. Loveman, investigating the executive education challenges in Eastern Europe, have recommended training as the primary source of change, and have emphasized strategic management, finance, investment, marketing and human resources management as being the main fields. These quickly became the standard components of every executive programme.

The newspaper *Rzeczpospolita*, in cooperation with Coopers & Lybrand and the Sopot-based Social Research Centre, have been exploring the opinions and attitudes of Polish managers since 1992. In every questionnaire there were questions asking about professional background, the need for further education, and time and money spent on education and development. The research sample embraced all fields of the economy and business, and some results of these soundings are presented in Table 14.1.

Statistically, the majority of Polish managers are men, aged between 31 to 50 years of age, running a private company in a city of over 200 000 inhabitants, employed on contract, or as a shareholder or owner of a company. Comparing these figures with the strategic gap we face, and the amount of money being spent on management education, one can see that the management cadre is not prepared for what is required. They are lacking in higher education and only a very few have a general knowledge of business administration. Moreover, companies have reduced their budgets for managerial education. These figures reflect the heritage of the old system and the necessity of focusing on more urgent issues.

In 1993, 81 per cent of the managers interviewed had no possibility of participating in any management training, and even less, namely 97 per cent, from distribution or service companies. In 1994, 74 per cent still stated that their promotion was not conditional on completing any management training, while in 1997 not less than 61 per cent gave a positive answer to the same question. This may be perceived as an indication of a new trend. Bigger companies (in the Polish economy those employing over 500 people) report that 42 per cent of managers received some form of training, while in smaller private firms (5–20 persons employed) their share did not exceed 18 per cent. This may mean that they are still financially weak.

Table 14.1   Survey results on Polish managers

Polish managers by education (%)			Time spent on managerial education(%)	
Type of education	1995/1996	1997		
Primary	1.3	1.3	not even one day	29
Vocational	2.8	3.1	up to 10 days	26
Secondary	30.2	30.2	11–20 days	24
Higher (economic)	23.3	18.2	21–30 days	12
Higher (MBA)	0	0.2	over 30 days	9
Higher (law)	5.0	4.2		
Higher (engineering)	29.6	35.9		
higher (other)	7.8	6.9		

Source: Coopers & Lybrand, PBS,.
Rzeczpospolita

Source: As above, 1997.

The amount of money spent by Polish companies on managerial education (%, 1997)		Number of times on training within the past two years (%)	
0	46	None	26
1–3000 zl	23	1–2	31
3000–10 000 zl	18	3–4	24
over 10 000 zl	13	Over 4	19

(1 $US = apx.3 zl)
Source: As above.

Source: As above, 1995/1996.

In asking about the training needs of the biggest Polish, foreign and joint-venture companies, the Polish–American Centre of Management and Economics at the Warsaw School of Economics (in an incidental and not representative sounding) found that human resources managers in these companies are evaluating the performance of company leaders as satisfactory (in the middle of a 6-point scale), sometimes as mediocre (1–2 points) and rarely as high (5–6 points). Yet training was limited to one or two short courses outside the company, run by mixed teams of Polish and foreign experts representing university and business practice. The interest in foreign training was reduced because of high prices, separation from the job and a perceived uncertainty about how this training might fit in with the company's needs. Again, this survey confirmed the strange feeling of comfort with small training efforts and the preference for 'education-in-a-pill'.

But this could lead us to oversimplified conclusions since the survey does not take into account the context: the preference of good companies to employ young and 'ready-to-learn' people, the limited number of well-trained managers, the low mobility of top-ranking specialists, the limited career opportunities for well-qualified and skilled executives, the resistance of other managers to the top leadership's values, the weak financial situation of companies and low budgets for training, extensive learning-on-the-job, and the lack of fit between a company's real needs and educational offerings by outside providers.

Executive education programmes and their providers

Despite these constraints, the demand for management education is booming and has risen ten-fold within recent years, and the number of students has tripled over the same period. The market now accepts high tuition fees for good, standard programmes, and even higher fees for customized programmes. Some new programmes, such as the Master of Business Administration (MBA), are not that familiar and not yet in much demand. Growing competition and the pace of change and innovation is also affecting not only executives but also training providers. Wherever there is a market requirement, enterprising people will set out to meet customer needs and we now see a proliferation of programmes and training offerings. The traditional university-based programmes in management sciences or business administration are now in competition with specialized management development centres, private training companies, management consulting firms, independent consultants, and in-house training centres – compared to 'mature market economies', there are no corporate universities in Poland. The market impact on management education is remarkable. Numerous private tuition-dependent schools have been set up in order to attract candidates not accepted by public schools where education is free.

Academia-driven programmes for managers developed from the teaching programmes designed for day students are being strengthened by the research or consulting knowledge of individual faculty members, and new skills gained due to foreign scholarships. Yet, a radical shift to foreign standards, both in content and teaching methods, has not been possible due to the lack of high-quality teaching materials to fit the complex situation of the country, its industries and companies. Their preparation and validity is still not cost-effective. The poor knowledge of foreign languages by the generation over 40 is a barrier to the use of original materials. Younger people can learn in English but the preference is for knowledge that is useful now and maybe in the near future. Thus, teaching methods are not adequate for a variety of reasons.

Universities are still bureaucratic entities and to have autonomous status like most business schools is a dream. The education of managers is perceived by academic authorities predominantly as a source of cash and not an investment in the future. Some disciplines, even in the strong academic centres, have never been well-developed and even they are not flexible enough in their administrative responses to be attractive to potential foreign academic partners. Public universities suffer from obsolete and 'under-invested' facilities and the cost of adjustment is very high. There is no money for new investments and so the needs of more and more demanding business people cannot be met.

Only the strongest academic centres can offer full MBA programmes, one-year post-diploma studies and an array of short courses and workshops with topics that meet the diverse needs of business customers. Only they have the human resource potential to implement complex programmes and to create the right environment for research and the development of teaching staff. All other providers increasingly focus on 'cherry-picking' individual faculty members to contribute to their programmes, rather than building relationships with the schools.

Consulting companies started to offer training in an attempt to capitalize on their own market expertise and understanding of company needs in diverse industries. They have trained their own employees and want to make the best use of company potential. This training at a high professional level also helps them build the market for their services, their reputation and competitive advantage. Customers may be discouraged mainly because of the relatively high price of this training and the rather restricted offerings.

Private management training centres and individual consultants also usually offer a limited training portfolio. They try to be very flexible in finding topical niches and trainers, and most frequently use rented or leased facilities and part-time trainers. They differ widely in terms of price and effectiveness, and have to struggle to keep the quality of delivery at a reasonable level. They are usually very clever in attracting new customers through more aggressive marketing tactics, but cannot in general attract the best specialists as instructors.

With intra-company training or customized programmes, 'there is no better school than the company school' – a motto still very popular among many foreign investors who train their employees on their own according to their own needs, planned resources and criteria. More ambitious people find it difficult to accept this dependence, and try to test more employers and to plan their careers according to their ambitions and possibilities. Completing many company courses is their asset when looking for a new job. Big companies can afford to send their managers abroad to their own training centres or universities. They prefer, however, short workshops as more practical and less expensive (more people satisfied for the same budget) since there are fewer problems in replacing staff during longer abscences while training.

In Poland the institutions that give high priority to managerial training are mainly banks and financial institutions, national investment funds, companies that compete in the international arena or cooperate with companies from abroad.

Finally we should not forget the extremely intensive self-education that takes place, as can be witnessed by the vast number of business books sold and the everyday practice in companies operating in a turbulent environment. Real experience can never be simulated in any business school or management training, and such experience and education, supplementing a solid background in any field, is the one most frequently sought after in the labour market.

The market has just started to recognize the need and necessity for deeper and continuous management education at all levels of the organization. The most dynamic people search for the most valuable and expert programmes, and young people aspiring to top positions put a great deal of emphasis on personal development. Companies with better market positions are starting to invest more in management education and their human resources managers have created a professional association to foster progress in this area. Better infrastructure and more attractive compensation policies applied by leading companies make further management education more and more in demand. The management training and educational centres, from the leading ones such as the Warsaw School of Economics to the smallest training units, dream of the time when training will become an investment that may be deducted from taxes and lead to increased salaries and more efficient work.

All of these factors lead us to believe that Poland and its managers are now in a better position to take full advantage of the benefits of action learning and executive education. On the other hand, the acid test for the restructuring process will be its ability to absorb, retain and make the best use of high quality executive education graduates from Poland and abroad.

15

Action Learning and National Competitive Strategy: A Case Study on the Technion Institute of Management in Israel*

Shlomo Maital, Sherri Cizin, Galit Gilan and Tali Ramon

TIM's point of departure for its marketing efforts is this: The product we produce and market is not static, off-the-shelf. Rather, it is *dynamic*, living, breathing, customized, and evolves according to our clients' needs. TIM's programmes are tailored *by* executives *for* executives and integrate coaching, experiential education and the monitoring of individual progress. Our programmes are professional, fun, relevant, modern, and have heart and soul, and the team project is a key component. Let's be careful, though, not to oversell or over-promise what the team project can achieve. As we re-examine our methodology, I urge you all to think creatively – and positively.

Yoram Yahav, Executive Director, TIM

The Technion Institute of Management (TIM) is the executive education arm of Technion, Israel's science and technology university founded in 1924, and located in Haifa. Early in 2000, two years after launching its action learning-based Scott M. Black Senior Management Programme, TIM

* This case was written by TIM staff: Shlomo Maital, Academic Director; Sherri Cizin, Director of the Sheldon Solow Management Programme for Emerging Companies; Galit Gilan, TIM Programme Director; and Tail Ramon, Marketing and Outreach Director. It is unusual for an organization to write a case about itself. We found it a useful, though difficult, exercise for evaluating our action learning model and initiating a process of change. We are grateful to TIM participants, business coaches and alumni/ae for their assistance. An earlier version was presented by Sherri Cizin at the Global Forum on Business Driven Action Learning and Executive Development held in St. Louis at the Boeing Leadership Center, May 2000, organized and chaired by Yury Boshyk.

set out to evaluate its programmes and methodology. A few days after a particularly intense staff meeting led by Yahav, the staff of TIM reviewed the minutes of the meeting. Against a background of demonstrable success, TIM sought to resolve a series of paradoxes by adapting its existing programmes to the changing needs of Israel's new and established companies, creating new programmes and revising or fine-tuning its underlying methodology.

Summarizing a series of staff meetings, Tali Ramon, marketing and outreach director, listed six key questions that had emerged:

- How does TIM's SMP (Senior Management Programme) differ from the numerous other executive education programmes available in the marketplace? What unique value-added does it create?
- How will synergy be created optimally among the various elements of the SMP programme – in particular, the business coaches?
- How will TIM measure whether it has succeeded or failed? Over what period of time will TIM's performance be measured?
- Who is TIM's client: The CEO? Participants? The whole company?
- Is the team project the main goal? Or is it simply a means to an end? Or both? How important is the personal development of individual participants' skills and knowledge, apart from the team aspects?
- How can TIM's action learning programme become a catalyst for corporate change and learning?

Background

The State of Israel

Israel is a parliamentary democracy in the Middle East, with a population of slightly over six million, a GDP of $100 billion. and per capita GDP of about $17 000. Israel absorbed 1 million immigrants from the former USSR during the 10-year period between mid-1989 and 1999. These immigrants helped supply high-level personnel for Israel's burgeoning high-tech sector and fueled a startup boom that brought Israel the nickname 'Silicon Wadi'. According to IMD's *World Competitiveness Yearbook 2000* (see Box 15.1) Israel ranked 23rd (out of 47) in competitiveness, up from 25th in 1998 and 24th in 1999. Competitiveness is a weighted-average score of eight categories, including 'people' (human resources), 'science and technology' and management. Israel ranks 8th in 'people', and 11th in 'science and technology', but only 19th in 'management' and between 23rd and 32nd in the other five factors. Research shows there is a direct link between a country's competitiveness and its per capita GDP and growth rate. In order to increase its per capita GDP from current $17 000 levels to those of, say, Hong Kong or Singapore ($25 000), Israel needed to become more globally competitive. That, in turn, required a significant upgrade in Israel's management skills. This is why TIM was born.

Box 15.1   IMD World Competitiveness Index
Israel: selected strengths and weaknesses

Several hundred variables comprise IMD's overall competitiveness index for each of 47 countries. Below: some of the specific variables for which scores for Israel are much *higher* than the 47-country average (strengths), or much *lower* (weaknesses).

Strengths (Israel's rank out of 47 countries listed in brackets)
Science & Technology: Science and technology and youth (1); technological cooperation (2); availability of information technology skills (4); company–university cooperation (5); total expenditure on R&D % (7).
People: pupil–teacher ratio, secondary education (1); alcohol and drug abuse (2); university education (3); total and current public expenditure on education (4); working hours (12).

Weaknesses (Israel's rank out of 47 countries listed in brackets)
Management: industrial disputes (43); overall productivity growth (38); social responsibility (32); customer orientation (28); industrial relations (28).

Israel, overall competitiveness score and components rank (out of 47), 1996–2000

	1996	1997	1998	1999	2000
Overall:	**24th**	**26th**	**25th**	**24th**	**23rd**
Infrastructure	**20**	**24**	**22**	**25**	**24**
Management	**22**	**24**	**19**	**14**	**19**
Science & tech.	**15**	**13**	**10**	**15**	**11**
People	**17**	**16**	**16**	**19**	**8**
Domestic economy	**14**	**15**	**27**	**22**	**24**
Internationalization	**18**	**34**	**33**	**23**	**23**
Finance	**24**	**30**	**27**	**24**	**23**

Source: *World Competitiveness Yearbook 2000.* Lausanne, Switzerland: IMD.

TIM – origins

The Technion-Israel Institute of Technology was founded by a small group of German-Jewish engineers in Haifa in 1924, 24 years before the birth of the State itself. With nearly 12 000 students, Technion has matriculated some 40 000 engineers and scientists since its founding. Many of its graduates play key roles in both startup companies and established knowledge-based firms in Israel.

Technion has a strong organization of supporters in the USA, known as the American Technion Society (ATS). In the late 1980s, the then-President of ATS, Edward Goldberg, now a senior VP with Donaldson, Lufkin & Jenrette, observed:

> The elements required to become competitive in a global environment are starting to emerge in Israel, but have not yet coalesced in a way to insure sustainable growth. Truly wonderful businesses are not being created that are fast-growing, leverageable and with defensible barriers to entry.

Goldberg proposed establishing a Technion Institute of Management (TIM) whose programmes would help raise the quality of management in Israel to match the level of its technology. A Board of Advisors was assembled, located in Boston, that has accompanied TIM from its birth.

At a meeting of the Technion Senate (a body comprising all the full professors) in May 1992, TIM's Charter was approved. TIM's mission, as defined in the Charter, was:

> to significantly improve the performance of Israeli knowledge-based companies serving global markets, by providing uniquely appropriate management education, information and expertise. TIM's commitment is to achieve a competitive advantage for these companies.

A lengthy search process led to the appointment of Yoram Yahav as founding Executive Director in 1996. Yahav had international marketing and consulting experience with Fortune 500 companies and headed the US–Israel Commission on Science & Technology. Another key appointment was that of Lester Thurow as TIM Chairman. Thurow brought MIT Sloan School of Management to number one ranking among business schools during his tenure as Dean in 1987–93.

Thurow and Yahav initiated a design workshop attended by distinguished academics, CEOs and consultants from all over the world. Previously, an exhaustive survey of the leading management programmes in the USA and Europe had been undertaken, together with more than 600 interviews with Israeli executives, along with an availability study of all existing programmes in Israel. The design group addressed two key questions:

- What do Israeli high-tech managers need to do better?
- What is state-of-the-art in executive education?

From the workshop, a new action learning model was built.

According to Yahav:

Israel is a world-recognized center of innovative technology with a skilled, productive and cost-effective workforce. The country offers an advanced technology infrastructure, and transportation systems serving the world market.

Despite these significant advantages, Israel's potential is not being fully realized. Few Israeli companies have successfully realized a global scale of operations; while many have tried, few have succeeded – in many instances, because management did not have the tools and experience to cope with continuous change in multicultural business environments.

Consider Finland. Comparable in population to Israel, Finland has four companies in the Global 1000 list of companies – including Nokia, with market capitalization of $242 billion as of 31 May 2000 and a presence in 140 countries – Israel has none.[1] Thurow has observed that a large Israeli global company could act as Israel's 'eyes and ears' to the world and supply cadres of globally-experienced managers for fledgling startups.

Programmes

Senior management programme (SMP)

TIM's flagship programme is the Scott M. Black SMP – a learning by-doing alternative to conventional expert-based training. Each TIM Senior Management Programme is customized to a learning team selected by sponsoring companies and is assigned to a 'dual-track' learning process. Participant teams (five high-potential senior managers per company) attend six-monthly management workshops, together with teams from five other companies. In parallel, each team is assigned a strategic company project. A corporate mentor functions as their 'internal client' and manages the interface within the organization. TIM then integrates the knowledge content and learning process to the business and corporate environment and objectives of the sponsoring companies.

A three-way interaction of corporate mentor, business coach and faculty lies at the core of the TIM action learning model (see Figure 15-1). The centerpiece of this model is the team project, whose objective was to serve as an action framework for learning. The programme includes an intensive international management trip to a knowledge-based business centre abroad, where participants meet with CEOs and government leaders. Senior executives work and learn simultaneously, acquiring knowledge which they directly apply to their organization. The curriculum is built to address issues such as:

- Recognizing and acting upon emerging opportunities;
- Managing accelerated technological change;

Figure 15.1   Senior management programme: action learning model

- Developing strategic partnerships;
- Achieving a critical business mass in global markets;
- Integrating management activities: finance, R&D, marketing, production;
- Adapting to rapidly shifting multicultural markets;
- Creating and sustaining customer value.

The model is seen as a paradigm shift in Israeli executive education for two reasons: each participating company pays $100 000, an unprecedented fee for non-degree executive education programmes in Israel; and each participating company's CEO makes a personal commitment to leverage the TIM programme to generate a quantum leap in the level of management in the company. TIM is now completing its third SMP cycle (see Box 15.2).

Management programme for emerging companies (MPEC)

Launched in April 2000, the Sheldon Solow Foundation MPEC is the first programme of its kind in Israel to exclusively target the entrepreneurial market. TIM's MPEC programme was created by an international team of entrepreneurs, investors and educators from institutions such as MIT, Babson and IMD. Spread over the course of one year, the programme features strategic workshops and skills training programmes, as well as mentoring by experienced business professionals. The coaches serve as confidants, accompanying start-ups through a very critical year in their development. Programme participants learn essential business management skills that can be directly applied to their current and future challenges. TIM's MPEC begins with an in-depth assessment of each participating company's needs and goals. The programme is based on the principles of action learning – learning by doing rather than by study. TIM provides the framework to learn crucial business lessons in 'real time' through intensive, work-centred interventions. This minimizes participants' time away from work, while maximizing each lesson's immediate impact. MPEC's five-track learning process includes:

Box 15.2   SMP participating companies: first three cycles

First cycle, March 1998

1   *Check Point Software Technologies Ltd.* Check Point was founded in 1993 and is traded in NASDAQ. The company is a leading provider of policy-based enterprise security and traffic management solutions. Through its patented Stateful Inspection technology, the company is uniquely positioned to deliver Secure Enterprise Connectivity solutions that protect information assets and enhance the performance of enterprise networks. www.checkpoint.com

2   *Ormat Industries Ltd.* Ormat is a public company listed on the Tel-Aviv Stock Exchange. Established in 1965, Ormat brings more than 30 years experience in the use of its unique technology to the development, manufacturing and marketing of innovative power systems. Over 100 patents protect Ormat technology. (www.ormat.com)

3   *GE Ultrasound (Diasonics).* Founded as Diasonics and acquired by GE during the SMP programme, GE Ultrasound makes PC-based ultrasound devices for cardiology. (www.ge.com/medical/ultrasound/isc/)

4   *IDF (Israeli Defense Forces).* The Israel Defense Forces (IDF) is an organization established in 1948, and is subject to the Israeli government. The main activities of the IDF are to protect the country's territorial sovereignty, its people and citizens, and to guard the national interests against threats. The IDF is the biggest organization in Israel. (www.idf.il)

5   *Teva Pharmaceutical Company.* A global company with manufacturing facilities and marketing networks in Israel and abroad. Over 70% of Teva's sales are to overseas markets, primarily the United States and Europe. Teva is a public company traded on the Tel-Aviv, NASDAQ and SEAQ International Stock Exchanges. (www.tevapharm.com)

6   *Siemens* (now reorganized, under a different name). (www.siemens.de)

Second cycle, 1998/9

1   *Aladdin Knowledge Products.* Aladdin is a leading supplier of information security solutions for software developers. The company develops, manufactures and markets proprietary software security and smart-card products. The company is traded in NASDAQ. (www.aks.com)

Box 15.2 *continued*

2 *Elite Industries Ltd*. Elite is a major food group headquartered in Israel. The company markets and distributes a broad range of food products including chocolate, confectionary, coffee, salty snacks and bakery goods. The company was founded in 1933, and in 1973 became a public company and is traded on the Tel Aviv Stock Exchange. (www.elite.co.il)

3 *Haifa Chemicals Ltd*. Haifa Chemicals is the world's largest supplier of potassium nitrate, an essential fertilizer for modern agriculture. The company converts locally produced potash and phosphate rock into products of highadded value: potassium nitrate using an original process, and phosphoric acid and phosphate salts for use in agriculture, industry and food production. Established in 1966, Haifa Chemicals is wholly owned by USA-based Trans Resources Inc. (www.haifachem.co.il)

4 *Rafael*, the Armaments Development Authority (a government-owned organization), was founded in 1948. The company has researched, developed, produced and marketed advanced weapons systems for almost half a century. Drawing on the Israel Defense Forces combat experience, Rafael employs in-house know-how to provide cost-effective, state-of-the-art systems and components for military and commercial applications. (www.rafael.co.il)

5 *Teva Pharmaceutical Industries Ltd*. (see above)

Third cycle, 2000

1 *Rafael* (see above).

2 *Orbotech*. Orbotech designs, develops, manufactures, markets and services automated optical inspection (AOI) systems and imaging solutions for PCB production, and AOI systems and markets computer aided manufacturing (CAM) solutions for PCB production. Orbotech has developed a global presence through wholly owned subsidiaries and operations located in 20 countries spanning 3 continents and is traded on NASDAQ. (www.orbotech.com)

3 *Paradigm Geophysical*. This company provides software and geophysical services; they develop, market and support integrated computer-aided exploration software systems, and provide seismic data processing and interpretation services to companies engaging in oil and gas exploration and production (E&D) worldwide. The company is traded on NASDAQ. (www.geodepth.com)

4   *Sapiens*. Founded in 1986; a global e-business solutions provider offering large-scale end-to-end solutions that empower enterprises to meet their IT challenges. Sapiens' vertical market solutions and cross-industry offerings leverage mission-critical assets and incorporate new business models and processes for e-business, euro migration and reengineering. Sapiens is traded on NASDAQ. (www.sapiens.com)
5   *Teva* (see above).
6   *Israel Defense Force* (see above).
7   *Indigo*. Engages in the research, development, production, marketing, distribution, and servicing of electronic color printing products and is recognized as an innovator in digital color electronic printing systems. Today, Indigo markets digital color printing products, both directly and through its family of distributors, in more than 40 countries. Indigo is traded on NASDAQ. www.indigonet.com

Fourth cycle, 2001

1   *Bezeq International*. Bezeq is an arm of Israel's telecom company.
2   *Creo-Scitex*. Formed by a merger between the Canadian firm Creo and the Israeli firm Scitex, specializing in digital pre-print.
3   *IBM Research Laboratory*. one of several IBM R&D labs around the world, based in Haifa.
4   *MicroSuisse*. A supplier to the semi-conductor industry.
5   *Strauss*. Parent firm of Elite (see above); a food company with strengths in dairy products, ice cream, confections.
6   *Teva* (see above).

- Strategic workshops for the entire management team on topics like international marketing, governance and managing growth;
- Continuous mentoring by international business professionals;
- Skills training programmes on key issues like international negotiations, financial strategies, presentations, sales and project management;
- An international management trip focusing on customer service, quality assurance, product development and financial markets;
- The opportunity to network with seasoned CEOs and venture capitalists from around the globe.

By developing their cross-cultural management skills, MPEC participants seek to overcome one of Israel's most fundamental disadvantages – distance from the market, both physically and psychologically. MPEC enrolls six carefully-selected companies that have been in business no more than five years. Recommended by an investor, candidates are chosen based on their business model and management team potential. To qualify, companies must have between $50 000 to $10 million in revenue, be 'cash plus one year', have a favourable chance of success and a highly-motivated management team (see Box 15-3).

TIM's staff members also manage frequent programmes for alumni and have launched a web site (www.tim.co.il), a quarterly Newsletter and a case-

---

Box 15.3 MPEC programme participants (first cycle)

Allot Communications. Allot Communications delivers policy-based networking solutions that improve the performance and ensure the quality of mission critical and time-sensitive applications running on IP networks. Allot's products allow network managers to define relationships between organizational needs and network infrastructure in order to achieve maximum efficiency from network and server resources. (http://www.allot.com/)

Envision Advanced Medical Systems. Established in 1998, Envisions mission is to revolutionize the use and impact of minimally invasive surgery (MIS) worldwide by building new software-based endoscopic technologies. The current product is a generic sensor that replaces the old optical technology based, endoscopes and operating room microscopes. (http://www.envision.co.il)

Friendly Robotics. Founded in 1995, Friendly Robotics developed RoboScan, a patented technology for navigating and controlling robotic appliances. Their first product, the robotic lawnmower, is currently distributed around the world. Other products in development include self-guide vacuum cleaners, snow blowers and garbage removal systems. (http://www.friendlyrobotics.com)

I-Impact. Founded in 1998, I-Impact provides products and services that comprise comprehensive end-to-end business analysis and guidance solutions to suit the growing needs of dynamic e-businesses. (http://www.i-impact.com)

RTview. Founded in 1997, RTview has developed a breakthrough technology platform that provides the means to significantly shorten the development time and dramatically reduce customer support costs of embedded systems. (http://www.rtview.co.il)

Tdsoft. Tdsoft is a leading provider of Voice over Next Generation Access (VoNGA) solutions for the telecommunications industry. Tdsoft's open solutions enable service providers to increase their revenues by adding voice services over existing next generation access infrastructure (Cable, xDSL and Wireless). (http://www.tdsoft.com/)

writing project. In addition, a new programme for a consortium of biotechnology companies is at an advanced planning stage.

A mid-course correction

By the end of 1999, TIM had completed two full cycles of its SMP programme, graduating 30 participants in each, with six workshops culminating in an international trip to Singapore (first cycle) and Taiwan (second cycle). As the third SMP cycle unfolded early in 2000, everything was in place. Most of the companies and participants for TIM's third SMP programme had been chosen (see Box 15.3); faculty workshops were ready, and in just a few days the initial workshop on globalization led by TIM Chair Lester Thurow would begin. TIM was perceived as a success; its 'brand name' was becoming known. The first two cycles of SMP participants were well-satisfied. Yet all was not well.

Executive Director Yoram Yahav sensed unrest among TIM's participating companies. Two of the companies failed to select qualified teams with members sufficiently senior for the programme. Yahav knew that any business's chief asset was a winning business design – and TIM's business model, built around the team project and faculty/mentor/coach triangle, needed some adjustment and fine-tuning. The business coach aspect was at the centre of Yahav's – and TIM staffers' – concern.

Only days away from the opening workshop, Yahav called each of the participating companies and informed them he was redesigning the SMP programme. In place of the opening globalization workshop, he, Lester Thurow and TIM staffers visited each of the enrolled firms and listened to their needs and future directions. The visits often took the form of informal strategic audits. The companies reacted favourably. TIM's SMP programme was marketed through its focus on the bottom-line-oriented project, yet it emerged that it is the *process* of SMP and its team-building that added value, perhaps as much as or more so than the *product* – the high-impact team project facilitated by coaches. As a result, intense internal discussions began on what Yahav and other staff members perceived had become the core issue in TIM's action learning model – the role of the business coaches.

Action learning: the role of business coaches

Three different perspectives on the role of business coaches and the team projects were elicited: those of (a) TIM's staff, (b) SMP alumni, and (c) TIM's business coaches themselves.

SMP alumni: process or product?

Through a large number of informal conversations and formal interviews and debriefings, the following two views appeared to represent a broad consensus among SMP alumni. Observed Nurit Kalman, plant manager for Teva and a graduate of SMP II:

> Before the SMP (Senior Management Programme), I thought I knew a lot. Now I know how much I need to learn, and need to know more. I think you need a programme like SMP to get exposure to the world – the parts of it you don't get to see in your job. I learned from SMP that I need to try to see a bigger picture.
>
> Do we view the team project as a personal skill-building one, or a team bottom-line-building one? Both. Overall, we learned a lot about Teva that we did not know before; we made friends; everyone in our multidisciplinary team contributed, and we did achieve integration. The team project contributed to this. Our business coach added much value in encouraging us, in helping us define our project and get it going. He was always available when needed. As the project moved along, his value-added declined – perhaps, as it should have. In my view, the key function of the business coach is *to bring an external perspective*.
>
> I found that our project took an enormous number of hours. For this reason, the project must be one of *central importance* to the firm. I think that the corporate mentor should be able to dedicate significant chunks of time, especially to get the project rolling.

Jacob Vind, Senior VP at Aladdin Knowledge, like Nurit Kalman a graduate of SMP II, tended to agree:

> I see the team project *not* as a product, whose performance is measured by its contribution to the 'bottom line', but instead as a *process* whose performance is measured by its learning effect – enhancement of the skills of those involved in it, and to the company, and to initiation of change. You provided us with useful tools, with new ways of thinking. My goal in participating with my team in the TIM SMP programme was not the project, but to establish a strong management team. The key benefit of the TIM project is to upgrade individual skills of the participants. TIM was a 'catalyst' for this process.
>
> The business coach was really a mentor. He understood our key issues very rapidly. Coaches should be advisers, friends, role models – but should not press the project...TIM should have said that it was aiming at the *process*, not at the product.

TIM staff: how the role of business coaches evolved and changed

In TIM's model, the business coach, a seasoned senior executive from Israeli industry, plays three roles: manages the task issues as they related to the project itself; helps build the team project plan; and ensures that the recommendations and strategies emerging from the project were sound from a business perspective (see Box 15.4).

MPEC Director Sherri Cizin reviews some of the SMP programme's unfolding history:

Box 15.4   The role of the business coach

Purpose

The business coach has three primary roles: (a) to lead the project team in defining the project; (b) to create a project plan; and (c) to make sure the analysis, conclusions and recommendations are sound from a business standpoint.

Programme development

- The business coach participates in a pre-programme orientation meeting for business coaches, and project review meetings with all TIM's business coaches once a month. These meetings provide TIM's management with an ongoing assessment of the projects' status.
- The business coach meets with his/her team on a regular basis during the course of the programme and guides the team in project execution according to the project plan.

Project team coaching

The business coach:

- Provides team members with objective business management perspectives and insights, in order to assure the company team's recommendations derive reasonably from their findings; are feasible in light of market conditions, company culture and competitive conditions; and use appropriate methods and business insights, especially those provided by faculty workshops.
- Assists SMP participants to suitably apply workshop concepts to the project and identify consultants who may help do so.
- Attend workshops, to help build links between workshop-originating theory and project requirements for applications
- Offer feedback to workshop faculty, based on key issues arising within the company team, to enhance workshop relevance.
- Assist SMP workshop faculty by identifying local (Israeli) resources and relevant local examples and cases, to 'localize' workshop presentations by global authorities.

It was our belief that simply putting a cross-functional project team together without adequate support might not result in new learning, but rather, doing things the 'company way'. In order to manage the learning, TIM originally conceived of two 'coaches' who would be assigned to each team. One coach, called a 'learning facilitator' would manage process issues. The 'business coach', would manage the task issues as they related to the project itself.

During the first run of the SMP, we quickly found that the Learning Facilitators (those with expertise in organizational development and training professionals) could not work well with the Business Coaches (senior executives from Israeli industry). The Learning Facilitators were charged with week-by-week monitoring of the team's progress and internal team issues – the 'reflection' aspect of action learning – and were supposed to call in the Business Coaches as needed on specific business issues, i.e. the project plan, the proposal, budgets, etc. Because of differences in culture, there was an explicit lack of appreciation between these two groups about the value each could offer the other. The Learning Facilitators, not being business people *per se*, did not bring the business content of the workshops into the project work. Also, Israeli industry is highly task oriented, with little tolerance for process and self-reflection. The business coaches felt underutilized, and the participants felt they hadn't received the business expertise they were promised. In response, for the second SMP session the roles were flipped. Given the content of the workshops, the Learning Facilitator role was put on the back burner and each team was assigned a business coach, who was instructed to bring in a facilitator when and as needed.

Once again, the business coaches failed to utilize the process facilitation available. There was no *reflection* activity in the teams and the 'process' learning agenda was dropped. Furthermore, the business coaches relied on their own models for working with the team, rather than becoming coaches. For instance, one senior executive led the team as though he were the project leader, another became a mentor in one-on-one meetings, and a third led the team as he would a consulting project.

From the outset TIM had sought to implement an action-reflection learning model.[2] Now TIM staff observed that a cultural issue had emerged. Cizin noted:

It appears that the *reflection* part of the learning process may not be culturally viable in Israel. The native Israeli is called a 'sabra' – the desert fruit or prickly pear. The metaphor implies that, like the fruit, Israeli's are prickly on the outside and sweet on the inside. This image of the 'tough Israeli' has been mythologized through years of defending itself in a hostile Mideast neighbourhood. Even today, most Israeli men must still actively serve in the military reserves through age 45. So it's not a surprise that Israeli culture puts high value on strength. Reflection in this culture may very well be perceived as a sign of weakness, which may be exacerbated by the learning team setting. In my experience, participants are much more able to engage in reflection in one-on-one conversation, than they are in a group. Israeli style dictates that people voice their ideas and opinions openly and with directness (they have very low 'power-distance').[3] Nevertheless, this should not be confused with a willingness to expose oneself, as being unsure or in need of help.

Programme Director Galit Gilan interacts with the business coaches on a daily basis. She observed:

> Let me first say what the business coach is NOT. The coach is not an instructor, nor a behavioral facilitator. Rather the coach is an objective, focused, business-oriented 'sounding board' for the project team. This means that the coach should not assume responsibility for running the project (apart from ensuring it is realistic in scope and span).
>
> The coach's role is to guide the company team and offer them business perspectives on their ideas, analysis and findings. The coach should help find the right methods and techniques and provide constant feedback on the team's progress.
>
> I think it is crucial that the project team is *self-managed*. They bear full responsibility for the success of their project. Yet they can, and should, turn to any and all of three 'supporters': the corporate mentor (who may be the CEO or senior VP), for company-based issues such as resources, priority, etc.; the learning coach, for problems related to decision-making, problem solving or individual related issues; and their business coach, for all business-related topics.

Gilan observed, however, that in some cases the role of the business coach was transformed from a *supportive* one to an *instructive* one. This creates a paradox. The coach, who by definition has many years of management experience, often holds an answer or solution he or she thinks is best. So rather than suggesting possible alternatives for the team to consider and choose, the coach gives the point of view he or she favours and this is at once accepted by strength of his reputation and authority. *The coach thus becomes the dominating figure in the three-way triangle*. As a result, team members often turn to the business coach when in fact they should have consulted their corporate mentor or learning facilitator. The result: 'we often do not get the synergy we hoped for and expected', Gilan observes. She continues:

> The personality differences among our business coaches were so great, that often we could not find an integrative definition of their role, let alone implement it. So – we are left with an unanswered question, one

that is crucial for our action learning model: How do we enlist business expertise in the form of experienced coaches, without the coaches becoming dominant, and telling rather than supporting self managed teams? How do we resolve the internal conflict between the way coaches sometimes operate and the fundamental principles of action learning?

TIM staffers had identified a fundamental difficulty in TIM's business-coach-based action learning model. Academic Director Shlomo Maital summarized it:

John Dewey observed that learning is a shared activity. He argued that only if teachers and students work as partners will the true end of education – the ability to use knowledge and think creatively – be achieved. How can the wisdom of our business coaches, true and proven leaders, be enlisted in action learning programmes, without them engaging in the actions that leaders normally generate: 'Here is what should be done, let's tackle it now!'

TIM business coaches: unique competitive advantage

In the competitive world of executive education in Israel, TIM's team of business coaches provided a powerful competitive edge. Hand-picked by Executive Director Yoram Yahav, and often persuaded to join TIM on the basis of personal friendship with Yahav, TIM's 10 coaches represented long years of experience in entrepreneurship, R&D, venture capital, major companies and government. They all shared a deep personal commitment to TIM's vision and goals and in particular felt the pressing need to address Israel's severe shortage of experienced managerial leadership. Each allocated large amounts of time to TIM, despite already-full schedules.

In March 2000, a meeting attended by four of the coaches – Dagan, Boas, Mlavsky and Meltzer – was convened, together with Yahav and the TIM staff. The purpose of the meeting was to explore and define TIM's action learning model in general, and the role of the business coaches in particular. Prior to the meeting, a memo was circulated that defined some of the issues for discussion (see Box 15–5).

A.I. (Ed) Mlavsky, former founding director of the US–Israel Binational R&D Foundation (BIRD-F) and head of Gemini, a successful venture capital fund, began the discussion. As a new business coach, he noted, he had asked: 'What is my job? What shall I do?' He had not received clear answers and lacked a written formal coaching methodology. The project he helped direct as business coach did not impact the company, and was, he felt, predetermined. Moreover, observed Mlvasky, for a five-person team to impact a whole company with a single project is unrealistic.

Avi Dagan said that the team project need not impact the entire company, but only a part of it. His consulting company had developed expertise in

Box 15.5   Memo to TIM staff and coaches

Issues for discussion

Boundaries: At what point does TIM's (and its business coaches') role step beyond that of executive education (skill enhancement, etc.) and cross into the territory of consulting? How can coaches facilitate learning, yet not actually teach?

Corporate mentor: Resistance on the part of the corporate mentor to projects that initiate major change is to be expected. So far, the conservative nature of project proposals probably reflect, in part, the tendency of mentors to resist significant change. How can this resistance be channeled without mortally wounding the team project methodology, or losing TIM a client?

Confidentiality: Few companies like to exhibit their laundry in public. To the extent that the projects grapple with serious issues, there will be decreasing ability to expose them to public view, thus impairing the synergy arising from group thinking and discussion. How can truthtelling – an essential component of learning – be made compatible with loyalty and discretion?

Expertise: Can business coaches effectively guide a team project, without exhaustive detailed knowledge of the company's technology and markets? If not, is an industry-specific business coach model feasible?

Criteria: Should there be clear, specific criteria for team projects? Should companies be selected for TIM programmes according, in part, to how well their project proposals meet those criteria? And should TIM cancel participation of teams who do not live up to their project proposals?

'auditing' a company, its strengths and weaknesses. Based on such an audit, they had once turned down a major job because he felt they could not succeed at it. He volunteered his expertise should TIM choose to implement a SWOT (strengths–weaknesses–opportunities– threats) strategic audit process as part of its action learning model.

David Boas, formerly Budget Director for the Israel Ministry of Finance, asked that TIM screen participating companies more carefully. We must ask, he said, four questions: (1) are they serious? (2) do they have insights into their company's shortcomings? (3) is the company sufficiently mature to benefit from TIM's programme? and (4) is there effective communication within the company? He cited one company, for which he served as coach, where none of these conditions were fulfilled. He repeatedly alerted TIM that the team project at this company was not going well – but felt his warnings were insufficiently heeded. In contrast to this unsuccessful example, he cited a successful one: Working with the Israel Defense Force (IDF) team. The team was hard working and disciplined, the work flow was good, and the project had high impact. The group noted how acceptance of an army team into a business programme had been hotly debated, but turned out to be highly positive.

Gurion Meltzer challenged the group by arguing that they in fact were not business coaches. The standard definition of business coach, he noted, is someone who comes from inside the company. As outsiders, we are overseers, or guides, he claimed. He noted that there was a major difference between small and big companies, and in general, argued that each company required its own coaching methodology, tailored to its own needs and personality. Part of the methodology could be the same for each company; but part had to be different, varying with the individuals involved and with the company. As for the team project, Gurion noted that perhaps the biggest impact TIM had on a participating company was that on Diasonics (later acquired by General Electric and became GE Ultrasound); the impact was not directly related to the team project but rather to the participants themselves, and ultimately contributed to development of a radically new product (PC-based ultrasound cardiology) now finding success worldwide.

A time for decisions

In the course of reevaluating their models and methods, TIM staff and business coaches noted a chain of paradoxes centering around TIM's approach to business driven action learning.

- In just two years, TIM had become a market leader in executive education in Israel and a candidate for a Ministry of Education award for innovation in education; yet it was clear that major changes were needed in TIM's action learning model.
- Programme evaluations supplied by TIM alumni revealed a high level of customer satisfaction; yet the main reason given was the personal skills and knowledge acquired through TIM's programmes, rather than the team project on which TIM's marketing efforts focused.
- TIM's business coaches were a vital element in the overall learning model; yet they comprised a scarce resource constraint that hindered TIM from scaling up its programmes.
- TIM's success led to demand for new and expanded programmes, and it was clear that TIM could and should grow; yet growth could seriously strain TIM's financial and human resources and threatened to dilute the quality of TIM's customized programmes.
- TIM's source of competitive advantage was its customer-driven design featuring practical bottom-line-oriented programmes; yet TIM staff, fac-

ulty and coaches often diagnosed participating companies' needs quite differently than the companies themselves.

- TIM's team projects aimed at creating significant measurable improvement in companies' profitability; yet corporate mentors often favoured conservative projects whose degree of risk was below the high-impact results TIM sought.

As TIM geared up for the fourth cyle of the SMP programme, major Israel companies continued to enroll: among them, Creo-Scitex and Strauss. TIM's six key action learning principles were redefined (see Box 15.6), and a growing literature on business coaching was carefully reviewed (see Box 15.7).

Box 15.6   Six principles of action learning at TIM

1   All learning is contextual. Knowledge becomes usable when it is acquired in situations that entail applications to concrete problem-solving. (Elmore, 1991)

2   Acquisition and application of knowledge are fundamentally social acts. Formal learning often discourages interaction, and hence is self-defeating. (Elmore, 1991)

3   The basis of 'active learning' is to create a community of interest in which students think of themselves as enabling each other's learning. (Garvin,1991)

4   Action learning seeks to use, in a positive direction, the 'pygmalion effect' – the fact that instructors tend to get from students performance at the level they expect.

5   Action learning can itself be learned, and in fact it must be, by all practitioners on an ongoing basis.

6   Business people must be able to meet in action the problems arising out of new situations in an ever-changing environment. Education consists of acquiring facility to act in the presence of new experience. [Action learning] asks not how a person may be trained to *know*, but how a person may be trained to *act*. (A.S. Dewing, in Christensen, 1994)

Sources: R. F. Elmore (1991), in C. R. Christensen, D. A. Garvin and A. Sweet (eds), *Education for Judgment. The Artistry of Discussion Leadership* (Boston: Harvard Business School): C. R. Christensen (1994) 'Teaching with Cases at Harvard Business School', in: C. R. Christensen (ed.), Teaching and the Case Method (Boston: Harvard Business School): A. Garvin in R. F. Elmore (1991).

Box 15.7   References on business coaching

The Corporate Coach by James B. Miller, Paul B. Brown and Ron Zemke. New York: HarperBusiness, 1994.

Coaching: Evoking Excellence in Others by James Flaherty. Butterworth-Heinemann, 1998.

The Heart of Coaching: Using Transformational Coaching to Create a High-Performance Culture by Thomas G. Crane. FTA Publishers, 1998.

The Handbook of Coaching: A Comprehensive Resource Guide for Managers, Executives, Consultants, and HR ed. by Frederic M. Hudson. Jossey-Bass, 1999.

Executive Coaching with Backbone and Heart: A Systems Approach to Engaging Leaders with Their Challenges by Mary Beth O'Neill. Jossey-Bass, 2000.

Action Coaching: How to Leverage Individual Performance for Company Success by David L. Dotlich and Peter C. Cairo. Jossey-Bass, 1999.

The time had come to make some hard choices, to resolve the basic paradoxes identified in TIM's action learning model and in particular to deal with ways for integrating team projects more tightly with workshops, and to resolve the fundamental conflict between the leadership of seasoned business coaches and the need to allow project teams to learn and think on their own. TIM had to face a growth issue: its success enabled it to grow its programmes, yet the basic action learning model using business coaches was not easily scalable, in part owing to the limited supply of high-quality business coaches who met TIM's standards. Because of all this, the Managing Newly-Emerging Companies programme utilized a network of business mentors. Mentors are invited to all workshops, where it is up to participants to initiate a mentoring relationship with them. This new model, while appropriate for startups, involves much less formal commitment from both sides and has so far resulted in some measure of success.

Maital cited the Church of England's definition of progress: 'Why cannot the status quo be the way forward?'[4] What *was* the way forward for TIM and its action learning programmes? How could the six paradoxes be resolved? What were the answers to the six questions the staff meeting had posed? And what was the right response to Yahav's challenge?

Whatever direction TIM took, it would not be the status quo. Or would it?

Notes

1 *Business Week*, 27 July 2000. 'The Global 1000: The World's Most Valuable Companies', p. 107.
2 Action Reflection Learning™ has been trademarked by Columbia University Professor Victoria Marsick. See her chapter in this volume.
3 Power distance is a measure of organizational democracy. Low power distance means that even low-ranking individuals feel they have the right and the obligations to express their views to higher ranking ones. See G. Hofstede (1984), *Cultures Consequences: International Differences in Work-Related Values*. London: Sage.
4 Quoted in C. Handy (1998), *The Age of Unreason*. Boston: Harvard Business School Press.

16
Action Learning Beyond Survival: A South African Journey

Brian Isaacson

> This is the finest training programme that I've ever participated in.
> It's certainly the best that we've ever done at MBSA.*
> The results are absolutely outstanding!'
>> Christoph Köpke, Chairman, Mercedes-Benz South Africa

Ten years ago, in San Francisco, I was introduced to the concepts and results associated with action learning. While discussing South Africa's challenges with Columbia University's Victoria Marsick, she mentioned that action learning, or her specific approach, Action Reflection Learning™ might be worth some further consideration.

Behaviour and results

The essence of action learning involves simultaneously impacting behaviour *and* results. South Africa, after years of isolation, protectionism and the distortions related to the apartheid policies and practices, has to simultaneously 'transform and perform'.

We South Africans are stumbling and blundering through this fundamental change process. We move from exhilaration to despair. The change is profound in that we have changed our political system and are simultaneously changing the workplace, the church, new neighbours on our streets and different pupils at our schools. In the business environment the excitement and fears associated with these changes is interwoven with the intense pressures brought about by global competitiveness. Jobs continue to be shed

---

* Mercedes-Benz South Africa. Note that since the DaimlerChrysler merger, Honda products are no longer part of the South African product range.

at a faster rate than new employment opportunities are being created: South Africa's unemployment figures are approximately 40 per cent. The *World Competitiveness Report* ranks South Africa at the bottom of the second league in terms of human resources development. South Africa, too, is at the south-ernmost tip of Africa, a continent associated with losing, disease, grants and aid, and horrific wars. Kissinger's comment at a conference in Johannesburg (1995) epitomized the pessimists' views of the continent's future. When commenting on the pitiful foreign investment in South Africa, he shared a client perception of our beautiful continent: 'Africa – A series of Basket Cases!' More recently, *The Economist* (11 May 2000) cover story featured, 'Africa – The Hopeless Continent'.

The transform–perform relationship within this exciting and challenging environment comes together in an interesting way. The broader stakeholder environment (communities, informal housing settlements, organized labour, the previously disenfranchised) requires an additional contribution from business, not only globally competitive performance, as measured through conventional business ratios and performance indicators. South African organizations, in addition, have to *add value to the community* – alleviate, enhance or close the gaps associated with eradicating the injustices of the apartheid era.

Action learning is tailor-made for the awesome (some may view this as awful) challenges associated with this turbulent environment. Action learning addresses not only WHAT business must achieve, but simultaneously the WAY in which teams achieve and learn, from the process of performance improvement:

Behaviour and Results
Transform and Perform
Way and What

Leadership development: from individuals to teams

During the late 1980s, as an internal consultant with Eskom, a South African electricity utility recognized as one of the leading utilities in the world, I had the opportunity to facilitate the preparation of Eskom's leaders for this uncertain future. The key feature of these initial learning interventions was a philosophy of the 'best influencing the rest'. Learning designs included pre-work, an intense eight-day residential phase, followed by individual assignments and a 'graduation'. Eskom has a staff of 40 000 and the leadership interventions were targeted at delegates from the top 2000. The leadership programme involved not more than two groups a year with a group size not exceeding 50 delegates.

The leadership model deployed, although emphasizing CONTEXT, facilitated insights into SELF as well as the refinement of personal development

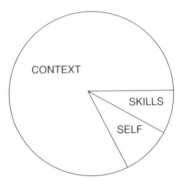

Figure 16.1   Leadership model emphases

plans related to further SKILLS development. A graphical depiction of the relative emphasis, or weightings, can be depicted as in Figure 16.1.

Leadership model

Botanists, ballerinas and business benchmark experts were chosen to stimulate the delegates. Customers and politicians challenged them. Colleagues and associates from neighbouring utilities also participated in the learning. The programme design peaked when it was co-designed with colleagues from Kenya and Tanzania and run as a learning event in Arusha, Tanzania in 1994: 25 South African delegates were joined by 25 delegates from 10 neighbouring countries from Southern Africa for a stretching and provocative development initiative.

The programme provided stimulating opportunities for individuals to metaphorically, *climb a high mountain* and *explore the mirages in the heat haze on the distant horizons*. The contextual objective was simple. Given the opportunity to explore, experiment and debate future scenarios in a stimulating, creative, yet low-risk learning environment, delegates were encouraged to make decisions and implement actions that would help their host organizations thrive in this uncertain world.

Positive reviews, solid impact analyses, programmes oversubscribed by 150 per cent, company accolades, conference presentations, involvement and support from chairmen and chief executives – a track record of success, and the temptation to be lulled into complacency – analyses back in the workplace highlighted the potential for real longer-lasting results.

Fred Neubauer from IMD in Lausanne made an observation relevant to South African executives, on Change. 'They know it all – they don't do it!'. Noel Tichy provided a further clue with his action learning approach that stresses the need to involve *teams* in achieving new approaches to problem-solving with an emphasis on fundamental organizational change.

Learn the way you work

Natural, or intact teams became the new learning unit. Networking and diversity was facilitated by involving up to four management teams from different regions in South Africa to facilitate insight and understanding of the unique peculiarities and challenges facing Eskom in different parts of the country, as well as teams drawn from different functional areas in the business, such as generation (production), finance, distribution or research. This facilitated a greater knowledge transfer and understanding of the business, and broader networking. A typical design could be depicted as in Figure 16.2.

The design included input for the 3¹/²-day residential phase from the Global Utilities Institute (Birmingham, Alabama) as well as from other key stakeholders within and outside the organization. Key to success was the inclusion of the Chief Executive of Eskom, who spent three days in Atlanta, as co-designer of the learning process. Major features of his input included insistence that the learning initiative should not only produce bottom-line business results but, in addition, should include objectives that would accelerate Eskom's business transformation and *provide for broader societal impact*.

This intervention known as the Chief Executive Programme, followed the earlier leadership initiative that focused heavily on context and awareness. This later learning process emphasized action and results, and eventually,

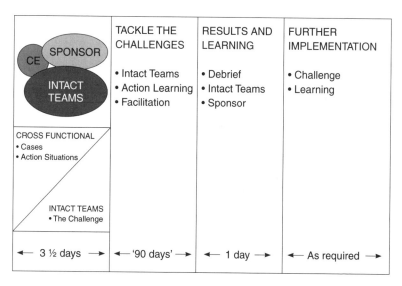

Figure 16.2   Chief executive programme outline

over 30 teams participated. Corporate specialists were linked to the teams for the entire duration of the 90-day action learning phase. This provided an opportunity for fresh input, a shift in perspective and dynamics and, of greatest importance, enhanced mutual respect and a deeper appreciation of the corporate specialists' role and contribution in relation to site-based core business teams.

Typical challenges issued to the teams are reflected as follows:

Management team, Kendal Power Station (3900 megawatts capacity)

Challenge

Develop suitable actions to enable Eskom to achieve values for availability, reliability, forced outage rate, thermal efficiency and plant reserve margin equal to the *average of the three best performing utilities in the world . . .*

Results

- Availability   90%
- Forced outage rate   3%
- Planned outage rate   7%
- Thermal efficiency   35%
- Reliability (trips per unit per year)   2
- Plant reserve margin   < 15%
- Availability improvement   (80–90%)
- R10 million per year 1994 rands

These results for the entire Generation group have been consistently exceeded since 1995, resulting in the 'saving' of a future planned power station – an impact exceeding R12 billion ($2^{1/2}$ billion).

Transmission

Challenge

Achieve a step change in the cost of an already planned/budgeted electrification project...

New structure and team composition for transmission field work . . . Do the fieldwork so much better that resources will be freed up to be seconded to electrification projects...

Results

'Weltevreden was planned at R4000 per connection, now at best R1540 per connection'.

Bloemfontein distributor

Challenge

Industrial Relations . . . develop the actions for your Distributor that will position your business in a new equilibrium (management and organized labour) that is more effective for all stakeholders.

Results

Mandays lost
June–August 1994   1093 days
    (before action learning challenge)
September–November 1994   14 days
    (after action learning challenge)

The Chief Executive's personal ownership was reflected in that not only did he personally invite each of the teams, he personally participated in the crafting of each of the action learning challenges for these teams. This, too, was complemented by his involvement during the residential phase of each programme.

Given the Chief Executive's focus on results, challenges were developed that highlighted opportunities for implementation by the teams themselves, hence the choice of natural or intact teams. Quantitative results were nothing short of spectacular. This echoed Rohlin's view that the return on investment of only *one* action learning challenge more than covers the entire front-end investment for the entire learning initiative.

During the residential phase of these programmes, facilitators or process consultants were introduced to each of the teams. The facilitators' role, metaphorically speaking, was 'to hold up the mirror' in order for:

'Managers to act and reflect so that they may learn

they reflect on learning so that they may act more effectively'

Only the best facilitators could be utilized for this role. The teams were typically senior (albeit multi-level), and it required accuracy, assertiveness, rapport and confidence to ensure that during the 90-day action learning challenge phase, the team dynamics were constructively impacted. Again the concept was simple – without a facilitator and/or specialists working with natural teams, teams would generally tackle a challenge with all their current habits and patterns in place. They would lose the opportunity for 'muscle-building', or enhancing their capabilities in order to tackle increasingly complex challenges in the future. The facilitators were required to ensure a balance as indicated in Figure 16.3.

BEHAVIOUR AND RESULTS

(process)   (content)

Behaviour Results

Action Learning Team

Behaviour   Results

Results   Behaviour

Task Group   Training Group

Figure 16.3   The balance of behaviour and results

Source: Partners for the Learning Organization (Warwick, Rhode Island) unpublished paper. See also Victoria Mersick *et al.* (1995), *ARL™ Inquiry. Life on the Seesaw: Tensions in an Action Learning Program*, Adult Education Conference Proceedings (pp 1–6), Edmonton, Alberta: University of Alberta.

A colleague and fellow process consultant, Jeff Lomey, used the iceberg approach to depict the process–content relationship (Figure 16.4), and Figure 16.5 indicates that teams were encouraged to spend time, during each meeting, addressing process-related issues.

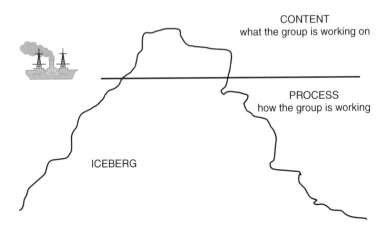

CONTENT
what the group is working on

PROCESS
how the group is working

ICEBERG

Figure 16.4   The process–content 'iceberg' relationship

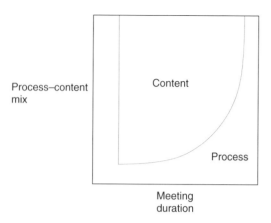

Figure 16.5   An action learning meeting graphically depicted a typical action learning meeting as shown in Figure 16.5

After the 90 days, all the attendees of the residential phase would reconvene for a one-day debrief on learning and results. The Chief Executive often delegated this role to an executive board colleague (known as the sponsor) fully empowered to decide appropriately on team proposals. The de-brief day emphasized the balancing behaviour and results practice, in that *equal* agenda time was given to content and process (Box 16.1).

Box 16.1   De-brief

08:00   1st group presentation, part 1 – the challenge (Team Leader and Group Members)

- The Challenge (highlight challenge goals)
- Achievements (underachieved/overachieved)
- Benefits to Eskom's customers
- Recommendations and next steps

08:45   Group questions

09:00   1st group presentation, part 2 – the process as a team member (each group member)

- Personal disappointments and highlights
- My commitment
- My learning about my colleagues
- How did we become aware of process learning points?
- Behaviour changes
- New personal insights
- How will this impact our future operation as a team?

10:00 (Executive board member) responds to results and process. A key feature of this design was that *each* team member was required to reflect personally on the learning during the 90 days.

Behaviour

A range of tools and instruments was introduced by different facilitators in order to de-brief behaviour and results on a regular basis. An example used by Rob Rörich included:

Goals and objectives	The team members understand and agree on goals and objectives.
Utilization of resources	The resources of all team members are fully recognized and utilized.
Trust and conflict resolution	There is a high degree of trust among team members, and conflict is dealt with openly and worked through.
Leadership	There is full participation in leadership; leadership roles are shared by team members.
Control and procedures	There are effective procedures to guide team functioning; team members support these procedures and regulate themselves.
Interpersonal communications	Communications between team members are open and participative.
Problem solving/decision-making	The team has well-established and agreed upon approaches to problem-solving and decision-making.

Experimentation/creativity	The team experiments with different ways of doing things and is creative in its approach.
Evaluation	The team often evaluates its functioning and process.

A self-assessment pattern for one of the teams over the 90 days is reflected in Figure 16.6.

Personal reflections included:

'Saw strengths (in colleagues) that I hadn't seen before.'

'Gave me insights into my own strengths and shortcomings.'

'The normal business suffered a bit (during the 90 days), but we have competent people and they ran the business.'

'There is recognition that all of us have broader knowledge over and above our functional knowledge.'

'During our first meeting we were all shouting, talking – now we can listen!'

'I learnt that I'm not a failure. I can ask for help.'

'We've learnt to challenge each other.'

'From colleagues, to building friendships'.

'The challenge was like asking an artisan to perform a heart by-pass operation.'

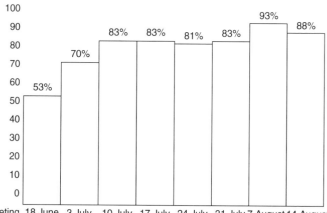

Figure 16.6   Trust and conflict resolution

'The added load was in excess of 1000 man hours – but the result is there – it was worthwhile.'

'From swearing at each other to holding hands.'

Action learning refinements

> A good shop steward, today, is one who can co-operate with management for the good of the company – gone are the days where the shop steward was the ringleader that showed the workers how to throw stones!
>
> Mnyamana Wandile, Shop Steward, Mercedes-Benz South Africa

Mercedes-Benz South Africa (MBSA) is a complex organization. During the 1980s MBSA often made local and, at times, international headlines, with regular reports on the 'war' between organized labour and management. This resulted in the manufacturing plant being closed for extended periods. Management practice today still reflects the painful legacy associated with that trying period in the country and the company's history.

In addition to its battle scars, MBSA is famous, too, for the production and delivery of the famous, 'Mandela car', a Mercedes-Benz passenger car built with loving care by the plant's workers in their own time. Soon after Mandela's release from prison, the keys to this beautiful gift were handed over to the President-to-be by the worker who came up with the idea for this special gesture.

Insight and understanding of action learning's potential in the South African environment culminated in an ongoing application recently implemented at MBSA. MBSA, owned by its German parent company, is a multi-product, multi-franchise operation. In addition to importing and manufacturing Mercedes-Benz commercial vehicles and passenger cars, the company provides products and components for Freightliner, Honda and Mitsubishi Colt (but see note on p. 229).

Added to the product range complexities, there are geographic and associated communication challenges emanating from the location of the manufacturing and assembly plant in the port city of East London, the parts and components operation situated in Pinetown, Kwazulu Natal, and the Head Office sited near Pretoria.

Globalization: intensified competition

South Africa's collapse of race barriers has been accompanied by the dismantling of the protective tariff and trade arrangements, and a marked shift is visible right across the automotive industry. Since the removal of sanctions, Volvo, Alfa Romeo, Renault, Peugeot, Saab, Hyundai, Daewoo, Daihatsu and Kia, to mention a few, have entered, or returned to the South African market. General Motors, Ford, Nissan, BMW and Fiat have recently announced significant or further investments in South Africa. Once again the South African motoring customer is again enjoying choice, price competitiveness, and ever-improving levels of after-sales service.

As part of MBSA's extensive reengineering linked to some of these international and national challenges, a focus on MBSA's leaders was elevated to impact performance in the recently reconfigured divisionalized business. Linked to the organization's transformation initiatives, the company had adopted the 'European Model for Business Excellence'. Leadership is a key component of this model and self-assessments indicated significant scope for improvement towards worldclass performance.

Building on the experience of the Eskom action learning application, a leadership intervention was jointly designed with MBSA staff, including input from shop stewards and the chairman over a period of 10 months stretching from 1996 through to early 1997. Clearly this extended diagnosis and design phase resulted in the required levels of *ownership* and understanding from the internal support staff. Conceptually the same CONTEXT, SELF and SKILLS model was applied, but the emphasis in design application reflected a more even focus as depicted in Figure 16.7.

Themes that served as the basis for the learning intervention included:

- The MBSA environment (technical, socio-political, international, regional, national);
- Customers (including winning back former customers);
- Business basics – the Vital Signs (interpreting MBSA's key numbers);

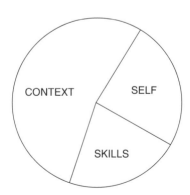

Figure 16.7   Leadership model

- Leadership (with an emphasis on leveraging diversity);
- Divisionalization (the basis for current strategies and structure);
- Quality, performance and accountability;
- Trust and courage

Residential learning: 'world class africa player to global network partner'

It has always been intriguing to listen to executive development experts from companies such as General Electric or AT&T share their expertise and learning related to in-house or corporate residential learning interventions. *Three or four week programmes away from the office* are not uncommon. South African executives, however, appear to have a slightly different view. It is not unusual for a leading executive to attend an overseas programme at an institution such as Harvard, Stanford or Wharton for periods varying from five to 12 weeks! Back in South Africa, however, it is *impossible* for these very same executives to vacate the office for three days!

Consequently, the designs typically include pre-work and *intense* residential programmes that vary from three and a half to seven days. 'Intense' implies starting at 06:00 most mornings with a varied physical/mental wellness-related intervention, and although not a 'boot camp' approach, the days close typically at 22:00 to 23:00 with evening programmes reflecting creative, edutainment components – orchestral metaphors, interactive customized industrial theatre, fireside chats, and the sharing of leadership stories (how I got to be here – my associated challenges, failures and successes).

Given the pressure related to minimum time away from the workplace, action learning fits snugly into the learning design as a process maximizing performance leading to behaviour change back in the working environment.

Action learning: building on the lessons learned

During the first half of 1997, MBSA ran the SIYPHAMBILI (moving forward together) Beyond 2002 Programme. One hundred and fifty seven MBSA executives, managers, shop stewards, professionals, artisans, administrators and team members participated in four residential leadership programmes comprising four teams per session, with each team receiving a 90-day action learning assignment from MBSA chairman, Christoph Köpke. Action learning challenges included some of the well-known attributes for stretching assignments:

- problems with no known solutions;
- complex;
- across boundaries/functions;
- strategic;

- challenges in which reasonable, knowledgeable team members would disagree regarding the outcome.

Christoph Köpke is an exceptional corporate leader. In fact, he is so passionate about DaimlerChrysler South Africa transforming (DCSA) into a serious globally competitive contributor that, at times, the intensity with which he pursues this vision can be quite intimidating. Before, during the residential and 90-day phases, and continuing after the leadership intervention, he spent considerable hours interacting, guiding, influencing, encouraging and recognizing the exceptional contributions of his teams.

The 16 intact, or natural work teams, together with their attached (for the residential and 90-day components) head-office specialist colleagues, tackled a range of assignments that were very varied, including reducing inventories, waste and lead times (order to dealer), enhancing quality in the sensitive paintshop area, reducing work in progress, enhancing on-time deliveries, and impacting a number of 'hard' customer-sensitive areas.

Not all the targets were met, but a number of exceptionally stretching targets were exceeded. Once again, the return on investment in learning was exceptional. One example will be used for illustration purposes: A purchasing action learning team led by a veteran German expatriate, highlighted that a focused $1 million investment on increasing the local (South African) content of C-Class Mercedes-Benz passenger cars would provide a conservative $5.5 million return on investment (savings to be obtained over the period June 1998 to May 1999).

Strength in numbers: the multiplier effect

While still at Eskom, a highlight in action learning was watching the Koeberg Nuclear Power Station executive team tackle an assignment that involved 'reducing outage time length, reducing outage costs whilst maintaining the commitment to being the safest nuclear power station in the world'. This gifted team had to reduce outage times from 84 days (currently at 42) to the benchmark of 26 days, for this type of French-designed plant. (During the benchmarking phase 13 questions were sent to utilities in 10 countries; the response rate was close to 100%.)

The Koeberg action learning team of 13 persons involved the entire power station staff in the brainstorming and data-gathering phase. The executive team generated 52 improvement ideas, while the staff provided over 600 ideas!

At MBSA, at least two of the teams followed this approach and embraced their colleagues who were unable to attend the residential programme. The paintshop team involved their 200 associated colleagues, while the Mercedes-Benz passenger car leadership team embraced 600 production line colleagues. Given the strained industrial relations circumstances over many years, this was particularly gratifying. Shop stewards initially invited to attend the residential programme as 'observers' generally became fully involved. This was despite the fact that on a national trade union level, trade union member participation endorsement was never obtained.

Action learning facilitators

As stretching as the results targets may be, the behaviour change component in the South African environment is even more demanding. It is probably not an unfair generalization that the corporate environments mirror the country environment. Trust, openness, fairness and interdependence are a few of the areas where the vulnerabilities and insecurities associated with the transform – perform concept can be impacted.

Experience has indicated that only the best, most courageous process consultants add value during the 90-day action learning phase. Eskom experience led to a recommendation that MBSA should use external facilitators exclusively. Even the best internal consultants might hesitate before directly confronting powerful senior executives in matters related to observed dysfunctional behaviour patterns. MBSA action learning teams typically met once a week or once per fortnight for a session dedicated to their challenge. Budget was provided for the external facilitators to attend the sessions on this basis. At least three of the 16 teams invested in additional facilitation time from their own departmental budgets. Prior to each residential programme, facilitators were carefully selected, briefed and matched, respectively, to teams and their associated challenges.

This professional, commercial (rather than organizational) relationship is given considerable credit towards the success of the leadership initiative. Subsequently a number of the facilitators were invited back by their teams, after the 90-day phase, for additional assignments.

Commitment

'In 15 years it's the first time i've seen maintenance guys come together and talk!'

'The company is there for us, we must keep it alive.'

'My team manager *listened* for the first time.'

'People volunteered – I will do that!'

One of the most moving examples of commitment and dedication was evidenced by a maintenance team leader who had resigned during the 90 day phase but returned to lead his team at the one-day debrief (results and learning) session. It was not uncommon for teams to meet after normal working hours, and sometimes teams even met off-site at the residence of one or other team member. This was articulated by an MBSA team member who said:

> I've never heard so many commitments made from the heart. I always respected my colleagues – but have since discovered many more hidden talents.'

Spreading the word: results and reflections

MBSA used a variety of media at their disposal, including in-house TV and in-house corporate and departmental newspapers and magazines, to publicize the successes and recognize the teams. Each team member received an award presented by the Chairman at the learning and results de-brief sessions. In addition, as indicated, the Chairman's follow-up and involvement continues, and plans were prepared to impact a larger group with the launch of further related initiatives from mid-1998.

Subsequent to the implementation of this leadership and action learning intervention, a further self-assessment with the 'European Model for Business Excellence' reflected a shift from a score of 273 to 317 (MBSA aims to reach + 600 – world class by 2002). The accountable executives ascribe this shift, almost exclusively, to the impact of the learning intervention.

Conclusion

Reflecting a few years later, both DaimlerChrysler South Africa and Eskom's nuclear business continue to use the action learning approach. DaimlerChrysler's results-emphasis has been relentless, and action learning was incorporated in a South African-based Insead Consortium programme.

Eskom's Koeberg Nuclear plant recently initiated a widespread leadership development initiative that will continue into 2001, whilst actions and processes from the 1997 initiative are still being implemented and benefits measured. The current initiative, led by the 1997 business leader Peter Prozesky, is more widespread. It is focused on enhancing the impact of supervisory leadership, aimed at breaking down 'silos', and hence challenges and teams are deployed in a cross-functional format. Each member of the executive leads and participates during the two-week residential phase and continues as action challenge sponsor for the 90-day problem-solving and learning phase.

Finally, each successive implementation process provides further opportunities for evaluation and self-reflection, resulting in tweaks and refinements to this basic action learning model. It has been a privilege in these early stages of the birth of a new democratic South Africa to participate in a process that impacts competitiveness *and* behaviour change.

Spectacular business performance improvement is gratifying, but what really moves the facilitator or process consultant is the opportunity to influence and witness the human shifts in attitude and action, hinting at the real promise of the 'Rainbow Nation'!

References

Hopeless Africa (2000), *The Economist*, 11 May (cover story).
Marsick, V. *et al.* (1995), *ARL™ Inquiry: Life on the Seesaw – Tensions in an Action Learning Program*. Adult Education Conference Proceedings. Edmonton, Alberta: University of Alberta, pp. 1–6.

Part IV

Action Learning in Asia Pacific

17
Action Learning in Korea

Taebok Lee

Introduction

In this unprecedented competitive business environment, companies in Korea have invested much energy and money to transform their organizations in order to become more competitive. The pressure to transform has increased in urgency as the world has become more complicated and markets have become globalized. As a result, 'transformation' and 'innovation' have become the latest buzz words in the business sector. The recent explosive interest in the digital economy, e-commerce and intellectual capital is accelerating change in the paradigm of management.

With these changes in the business environment and management paradigm, change in the paradigm of human resource development (HRD) has proven unavoidable. Many HRD practitioners agree that changes in the traditional mindset of human resource development are necessary. Four of the 'hot' issues in this area are: being digital, globalization, personal competitiveness and business results-oriented learning (Figure 17.1).

Upon entering the digital age, HRD systems in Korean companies are undergoing rapid change. In terms of content, they emphasize how they are transforming their companies into digital companies: in other words, how they can digitalize products, services, processes and culture. One company has a digital principle of 'one – ten – one hundred'. 'One' is that everyone should have his or her own home page; 'ten' is that everyone should post 10 pieces of information per month; and 'one hundred' is that everyone should identify at least 100 websites that can be used to access information.

Globalization creates a great obstacle for Koreans who are not familiar with Western business practices, their cultures and languages. Korean companies, however, cannot afford to delay globalizing their businesses if they are to survive, and globalization of business makes the globalization of

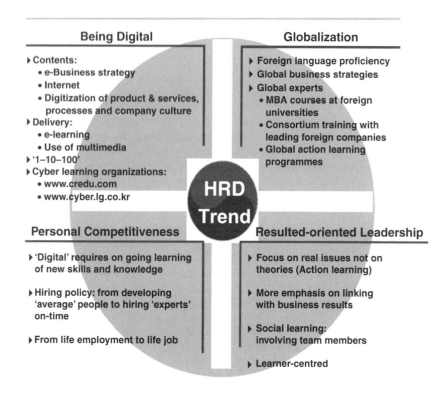

Figure 17.1   Major HRD issues for Korean multinationals

employees unavoidable. Therefore, one major focus for human resource development is developing the global capabilities of employees.

Even three or four years ago, most Koreans took lifetime employment for granted. Now they know that they cannot survive with this mental model, and therefore they have no option but to pursue lifetime learning to increase their personal competitiveness.

In Korean companies, many training courses take the quick-fix approach, focusing on short-term problem-solving. These kinds of courses are provided when unexpected problems arise. After the courses are provided, however, everyone forgets the content: they have little or no impact on improving business performance. Accordingly, many companies have recognized the limitations of traditional quick-fix training and are trying to shift their focus to business results-oriented learning. More and more leading companies have taken an interest in action learning as a vehicle to meet the needs mentioned above. With the belief that these programmes help people to develop their learning capabilities, it is also possible to contribute to business results because of the concurrence of learning and working.

In the mid-1990s, action learning programmes were designed and implemented by several companies including Samsung, Taepyungyang, SK and LG (Lucky Goldstar). The cases of Samsung, Taepyungyang and SK will be discussed in this article. These three companies have emphasized developing individuals and transforming their organizations with the aim of becoming worldwide leaders in their industries for the twenty-first century. The Samsung case will provide a look into recent innovations in their Training and Development System, as well as action learning. Samsung, Taepyungyang and Sunkyong agree on the philosophy that 'the best individual and organization development occur simultaneously'. Action learning and innovation in training and development are part of their efforts to assist the simultaneous occurrence of individual development and organizational transformation.

Action learning at SK

SK Group (former Sunkyong Group) is one of Korea's largest diversified manufacturing and service companies. Their business domain includes energy, chemicals, telecommunications, finance, engineering and construction, hotels and leisure, and logistics. SK Group has pursued a change initiative called Supex (Super Excellence) since 1979. The ultimate goal of Supex is to be the best company in the world. SK's top management saw that the greatest challenge in the course was the development of people and the creation of a global organization. They also agreed that realization of Supex required continuous employee development at all levels.

SK Group has developed the Executive Management Development System in order to identify and develop executives who will lead SK Group in the new millenium. The fundamental goals of this system are to establish criteria required for SK executives in the twenty-first century, to evaluate and select outstanding executives as well as high-potential executive candidates, and to systematically develop and train them for their future roles.

SK Academy (SK's Training and Development Center) took over the responsibility for developing personnel who would maintain a strong commitment to the vision of Supex. By the early 1990s, SK Group had increased their investment in the globalization of markets and employees, and with this new business focus, experiences of a global nature were increasingly needed. In order to meet the need for the globalization of business and employees, SK Academy decided to provide formal global development experiences for management and employees. Table 17.1 shows Senior Executive Management Development programmes provided by SK Academy.

Table 17.1   SK's senior executive management development programmes

Management level	Programme
CEO/Vice-Chairmen/business leaders	CEO Seminar
Vice-Presidents of each business/ senior executives	Senior Executive Programme
Executives	Global Executive Programme
New executives	New Executive Programme
General managers	SUPEX Leader Development Programme

SK Academy designed an intensive management development programme called the Global Executive Programme (GEP), which focused on expanding the global mindset, cross-cultural competency and global business capabilities of executives. It used action learning to provide greater challenges for the executives. In the course of designing the GEP, SK Academy visited and received information on action learning approaches from Motorola, DuPont and GE's Management Development Centre at Crotonville. Their aim was to integrate their best practices into SK's Global Executive Programme.

Overview of global executive programme

The Global Executive Programme was first launched in 1995 with teams of executives from different businesses within SK. The participants were selected from among executives with high potential for global business. During the programme, the teams travelled to different regions of China to investigate investment opportunities. This was an experimental and a learning-oriented programme; it focused on studying the regions of China and developing the global mindset of participants rather than solving any specific business issues. After the first GEP programme in China, the second GEP programme was run in India in 1996 to develop a more accurate operation that focused on investigating investment opportunities. With more experience and insight from these programmes, GEP was able to be held again, this time in Indonesia in 1996.

By 1997, the focus of the programme had shifted to solving real business issues in the regions where investments were in the early stages of development. Table 17.2 provides an overview of a GEP. As a result-oriented action learning programme, the participants were expected to develop specific strategies concerning problems proposed in their projects.

During the first four-day seminar (action learning seminar), the team was informed of the objectives and goals that the programme expected the GEP team to achieve and the way of performing action learning. The GEP

Table 17.2   Overview of a global executive programme

Programme objectives:

(1) To make a plan to disseminate and practice SK Management System/SUPEX Quest effectively in the USA with regard to SK's ABC project.

(2) Develop global business capabilities of executives

- Effective dissemination of basic business concepts

    * management perspectives
    * definition and objective of business management
    * principles of business management

- Localization of SUPEX Quest
- Adaptation of dynamic factors

    * human resource management
    * can-meeting execution

- Other recommendations for successful ABC project

Programme flow:

- Action learning seminar : 4 days/SK Academy

    * action learning in SK Group
    * CEO's expectations of the programme
    * ABC project introduction
    * team building
    * discussion on SK management system/Supex Quest
    * globalization of SK management system/Supex Quest
    * can-meeting: discussion on topic solving plan

- Global strategy and case studies: 4 days/SK Academy

    * framework for global strategy
    * strategy of US companies
    * HR features of US companies
    * localization cases in USA

- Action learning interim meeting: 4 days/SK Academy

    * survey techniques
    * cross-cultural awareness
    * team activity

        – discussion of draft plans
        – survey and study
        – study of visiting companies

- On-site visits : 11 days/USA

    * interviews with host companies and government officers
    * seminar
    * wrap-up meeting in USA

Table 17.2   continued

- Wrap-up meeting : 1 day/ SK Academy
  * preparation of the final report

- Presentation of the final report : 1 day
  * briefing the final report to CEOs and business leaders

---

included team-building, studying the host companies and business culture, case studies of 'globalizing' strategies of world leading companies, learning survey techniques, and so on. The GEP team was required to gather relative information and data, analyse and make a draft plan before site visits through intermediate meetings.

During the on-site visits, the teams had interviews with host companies and government officers that focused on the topic of their programme. They also held interim meetings to share the intelligence that each team had collected, and seminars were conducted on the topic. As a result of sending the questionnaires to the interview partners a month in advance, the interviews were productively focused and intense.

After the on-site interviews, the team held a seminar on the topic with relevant officers and executives with organizations in the USA. The team then returned to the SK Academy in Seoul to prepare their recommendations and make presentations to the CEO and business leaders. The CEO and business leaders, as well as the participants, concluded that the Global Executive Programmes were invaluable in both developing the participants' personal global leadership capabilities and global mindsets, and improving business performance. SK will evolve and expand the Global Executive Programme based on the experiences of participants todate.

Samsung: to develop competitive human resources in the twenty-first century using Action Learning

Samsung, established in 1938, is a very diversified company. Its continuous growth has been realized through its diversified business groups: electronics, machinery, chemical, finance and insurance and other Samsung companies. Samsung is also determined to become one of the world's top corporations in the early twenty-first century. They recognize that developing their employees' capabilities is one of the sure ways to realize this vision, which is why Samsung has emphasized developing human resources over the past few years and has spent more money on this than any other corporation in Korea. We can see their focus on human resource development in the management philosophy of Lee Kun-Hee, Chairman of the Board of Samsung, who states, 'I have made it my personal philosophy and commitment to establish a tradition of people-oriented management.'

Samsung has implemented many change initiatives to become one of the world's top corporations. Until late 1996, the change initiatives had been focused on 'quality' in every aspect of business, but by early 1997 Chairman Lee stated that Samsung would focus on 'speed', based on the quality that Samsung employees had in proactively dealing with and initiating change in the business environment. The four points of Samsung's 'speed' management are 'first', 'fast', 'timely' and 'frequent'. 'First' means rapidity in developing business opportunities and introducing new products faster than any other company; fast refers to the reduction of cycle-time in every business process, including decision-making; timely encompasses on-time delivery and zero inventory; and frequent underscores flexibility. Samsung applies this new management philosophy to every facet of their business. The Samsung HRD center has tried to embody this management philosophy in its strategy of employee education, summarized in Table 17.3.

Educational innovation at Samsung is based on the basic assumption that learning should make a direct contribution to increasing competitiveness. How can learning create a dynamic competitive advantage for business? In an economy where the only one sure source of maintaining a competitive advantage is knowledge, successful companies are those that consistently create new knowledge, disseminate it widely throughout the organization, and quickly embody it in new techniques and products. Samsung's HRD centre has studied how they can implement the idea of a learning organization or knowledge-creating company in Samsung. Regarding the learning organization, the HRD centre's major question is:

Table 17.3 Four points of 'speed' education at Samsung

First	Faster and more rapid than any other company in finding core competencies of employees for future business; developing, and implementing courses for developing these core competencies Proactive rather than passive education
Fast	Cycle-time reduction in programme planning, designing and development and implementing the cycle
Timely	JIT (just-In-time) education Granular training
Frequent	Perfect after-service Flexible education system where working and learning become the same activity

How can Samsung support the idea of a learning organization or knowledge-creating company in order to facilitate the processes of developing the world's best human resource programme at a fast speed and at the same time manage the creation of core knowledge related to business strategies?

They found that one answer to this question is in developing intellectual assets through the methodology of action learning, which is one of the key methodologies used to implement the idea of a learning organization (Samsung's HRD center uses the term 'action reflection learning'). They believe that there is no tool more effective in building a learning organization than action learning. It enables and forces organizations to continuously learn on an organization-wide basis, thereby allowing them to adapt to a continuously changing environment. To foster high performance and to actualize the potential of employees, the HRD centre tries to use the concept of action learning in planning, designing, implementing and evaluating its programmes.

One of the key implications of the idea of a learning organization for the field of human resources development is that it helps HRD move from a culture of training to a culture of learning, where everyone is responsible for his or her own learning. Shifting the paradigm from training to learning, Samsung's HRD centre has been reconceptualizing its roles and functions. They have placed considerable emphasis on continuous learning in the workplace, and the HRD centre believes that making clear boundaries between two activities will be outdated as learning and working become the same activity in developing human resources. They are shifting their focus from limited quick-fix training (in which the instructor merely pours information into the learner's head) to a process of developing a total learning culture.

Samsung's HRD center has designed and implemented action learning programmes to help Samsung employees become valuable intellectual assets. It is a major effort to redesign the existing training programmes into learner-centred programmes. The principles of action learning, which was created by Reg Revans and revised by Alan Mumford (1997), are: L (Learning) is the sum of Q1 (Question), P (Programmed Knowledge or Structured Learning Programme), and Q2 (Question). Based on these principles, Samsung's HRD centre applies action learning to its recruitment education (see Table 17.4). The three components of ARL are incorporated into a three-year programme: working on a project, formal structured learning, continuous discussions and reflection of concerns that arise as learners try out new skills; and continuously practicing to be lifelong learners.

With the advent of the knowledge economy and the information society, learning rather than training consists of a more coherent and central set of

Table 17.4 Application of action learning

Principles of ARL steps	Q1 – step 1	P – step 2	Q2 – step 3
Instructional strategies	• Pre-learning activities • Self-learning	• Formal structured off-job learning • Small group discussion • Presentation and facilitation	• On-the-job development • Structured learning environment
Main activities	• Social services • Acquiring basic information and knowledge necessary for being a 'Samsunger' • Computer skills	• Formal recruitment education • Exchanging ideas and lessons learned from pre-learning activities • Practical knowledge and skills related to real jobs	• Mastering two foreign languages • Work on a project as a team • Continuous discussions and reflections of concerns on the job that arise as learners try out new skills • Continuous learning to be a lifetime learner • Reporting and developing new job manuals • Project work in a foreign country
Terms	1/2 year	2 weeks	$2\frac{1}{2}$ years

processes. These will drive the organization forward and help develop strategic human resource programmes in the twenty-first century. Samsung's

HRD center continuously highlights how learning can identify wider patterns in the activities happening outside the organization and challenge what is happening internally.

Taepyungyang: visionary leadership course

Taepyungyang is one of the largest cosmetic and consumer product companies in Korea. In late 1997, this company felt the necessity to develop 'core leaders' who will lead it in the twenty-first century. In order to develop the leaders systematically and strategically, the human resource development center was determined to utilize the action learning approach. The programme, 'Visionary Leadership Course' was completed in May 1998, and first launched in July of the same year (Figure 17.2).

The programme lasts for six months and the participants do their projects part-time during the six-month period. During the process of solving the tasks, the participants have several seminars on specific topics such as business strategy, leadership, marketing and finance to improve their qualifications as future leaders. In order to broaden perspectives, each team is required to have approximately 80 interviews with competitors, customers, suppliers and best-practice companies, with all the interviews required arranged by themselves.

Each team is composed of three or four members and one coach. Coaches are executives who have knowledge and experience in specific tasks. One unique task is assigned per team: for example, if there are 10 teams there are a total of 10 different tasks. The tasks are selected by the CEO after a discussion with the coaches and include such topics as 'Analyzing the marketing strategies of its major competitor and developing a strategy to

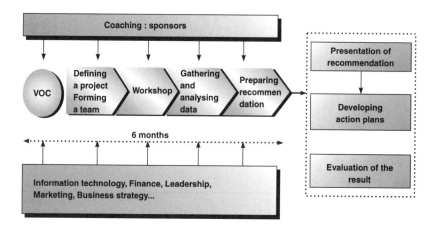

Figure 17.2   Visionary leadership course

compete with them'; 'A strategy for a systematic approach to In-Store Merchandising'; 'A strategy to establish Supply Chain Management'; 'A strategy to improve brand equity', and so on.

The Visionary Leadership Course has been conducted once a year since its first launch in 1998. Usually, it lasts for six months and the participants carry out the projects they are given while they are doing their original jobs. Every participant to date has emphasized the outstanding results they have achieved during the six-month part-time programme even though it provided many hardships which they had to overcome. For example, one of the tasks in 1999 was to develop 'a strategy to increase market share' in a specific area. In the process of completing the task, the team created many good ideas some of which were adopted even before the end of the programme. These made a great contribution to increasing market share in that area, and the president of the company who sponsored the programme said that the recommendations from the participants had been really helpful in developing their business plans. In reality, for the company, the Visionary Leadership Course is like an academy developing leaders. Since the programme was first implemented, all newly-promoted executives have successfully undergone this course.

Conclusion

Action learning was utilized by a few leading companies like Samsung, SK and LG in its early stages. For the past few years, more companies have been interested in the action learning approach and have conducted several action learning programmes to date. They have great confidence in its value, and more and more companies accept the necessity of action learning as a powerful tool in dealing with changes in the business environment. For example, in early 2002, POSCO, the no. 1 steel company in Korea, started utilizing the action learning approach to develop their leaders for the new millennium. I expect that in a few years more and more companies in Korea will use action learning both for personnel development and improvement of business results.

References

Mumford, Alan (1997) 'Action Learning as a Vehicle for Learning,' in A. Mumford (ed.), *Action Learning at Work*. Aldershot, UK: Gower, pp. 3–24.
Mumford, Alan (1997a) 'A Review of the Literature', in M. Pedler (ed.,) *Action Learning in Practice*. Aldershot, UK: Gower Press.

18
Business Driven Action Learning in Japan

Mika Nakano Honjo

Introduction

In the post-Second World War era from around the 1950s to the 1970s, Japan was driven by two main goals – that of improving its economy, and striving towards efficiency. Such a focus enabled Japan not only to merely recover its economy, but also to become an economic giant by the 1980s. In fact, Japan was able to accomplish an economic miracle by establishing the so-called Japanese-style management system according to its principles of lifelong employment and seniority system. Thanks also to this system, Japanese multinationals did not have to invest in executive education in contrast to Western multinationals that had to concentrate much of their spending in that area.

As the bubble economy burst around the beginning of the 1990s, however, serious problems surfaced, and with this came the need to review the traditional Japanese-style management and employment systems. Other factors that made the revision of the status quo necessary included the advancement of women in the workplace and the consequent lowering of the birth rate, the rapidly aging society, the globalizing business environment, as well as the new trends set by developments in technology and information.

Especially since late 1997, the business environment in Japan changed drastically with the bankruptcy of large-scale financial institutions such as Yamaichi Securities and the Japan Long-term Credit Bank. Putting an end to the myth that 'financial institutions never go under', their failure spurred the restructuring of various industries to meet the global standard. Some major examples are found in the auto and financial industries. In the former Mazda and Nissan came to be managed by foreign capital, whereas in the latter mega-mergers exceeding the framework of conventional corporate groups have taken place, as is represented by the new 'Mizuho financial group', the three-bank merger of the Dai-ichi Kangyo Bank, the Fujibank and the Industrial Bank of Japan.

Under such circumstances, Japanese multinationals today are being urged to shift their human resource management and human resource development (HRM/HRD) systems from seniority- to meritocracy-based. And with the pressing need to bring up next-generation leaders swiftly, more and more corporations are starting to actively invest in executive development. Hence, business driven action learning has gained notice over the past few years and is being examined by Japanese multinationals.

Action learning programmes in Japan

In this study, I would like to focus on the examples of two Japanese subsidiaries of major Western multinationals that have been rooted in Japan for many years. Their cases will first be scrutinized to examine the benefits and problems of the programmes for Japanese participants, and then considered as to whether or not action learning can become a truly effective means for Japanese multinationals.

The first example is a Japanese subsidiary of a major Western multinational. This Japanese subsidiary has recently started sending its employees to the executive programmes held by its headquarters in the United States. Introduced here is the evaluation made by the human resource staff of the Japanese subsidiary. The staff point out the benefits as well as the issues concerning the employees of the Japanese subsidiary who participated in the executive programme organized by the Headquarters.[1]

The second example is Texas Instruments Japan (TIJ). In addition to the executive programmes of the Texas Instruments Headquarters, of note is that TIJ has its own executive programmes that meet Japanese business conditions and the cultural/social reality. Highlighted is the explanation of the staff who actually designed the programmes at TIJ, including points noted upon programme design to meet TIJ's actual business conditions. The case of TIJ is likely to become a very good example for Japanese multinationals considering a full-fledged introduction of the action learning methodology to their respective organizations.[2]

An example of action learning

Programme outline

The executive programme of the first company is held twice a year in the spring and autumn. Each programme lasts eleven weeks, and its main goals are to learn ways to facilitate smooth operations, enhance cross-cultural understanding and build better communications with its overseas employees. The programme is designed for regional managers and/or regional manager candidates.

During the programme, participants attend lectures on topics such as finance, operations, distribution, human resources, marketing and sales.

They are also divided into teams, each team with about five persons of different nationalities.and assigned team projects on real business issues.

Benefits of the programme

How does the HR staff of the Japanese subsidiary evaluate this programme? Having already sent its regional manager to the 1998 autumn programme, the staff think the programme effective and hope to continue sending regional managers to the programme on a regular basis, probably one or two regional managers and/or regional manager candidates per year.

As for enhanced understanding of the Japanese market, the HR staff feel that the Japanese local staff should build a better communication network with staff in the USA and Europe.

Current issues

In spite of positive feedback on the programme, however, there are some problems to be overcome:

1   The regional managers in Japan have limited leadership and responsibility as compared to regional managers of other countries. For example, Japanese regional managers are not allowed to manage their nationwide finance or operations in contrast to those elsewhere. In Japan such issues are handled by a higher-level manager.
2   The regional managers of Japan are in their 50s, much older than those of other countries. This is due to the slow promotions in Japan stemming from its unique social and business culture.
3   There is a language barrier for Japanese managers, as well as for other Asian, non-English-speaking managers. All regional managers in Japan are locally employed, in contrast to most foreign regional managers working internationally.
4   The younger the participant, the more effective the learning from the programme. Hence, the HR staff think it crucial to reform the promotion system for the future dispatch of younger regional managers to the programmes. Ideally speaking, participants should at least be country-manager candidate level, as is the case with overseas countries that send foreign-division manager candidates.

Future issues

The Headquarters thinks that diversity training is very important, and that the understanding of a foreign language, culture and mentality are key points. Not only limited to this Japanese subsidiary, but also among many Japanese subsidiaries of Western multinationals, the 'language barrier', 'difference in age and business responsibilities of the trainees', as well as the 'discrepancies in mentality', tend to seriously affect the results of their respective action learning programmes. It is often the case that in spite of recognizing the effectiveness of action learning programmes organized by their headquarters, the programme results fail to be as remarkable or outstanding as in the West, due to the aforementioned reasons.

Executive training process at Texas Instruments Japan (TIJ)

Background

Texas Instruments Japan (TIJ) is another subsidiary with foreign capital having a more than 30-year history of operating in Japan. Its management and employment systems combine the methods of its US headquarters with the unique practices of Japan. As such, its young future leaders are not provided with much opportunity to acquire 'training while working' experience, which is much the case for many Japanese corporations. Therefore, the need arose at the company level to provide ample opportunities for young people with the potential to become leaders. At the same time, the drastic changes in the business environment urged TIJ to quickly design new executive programmes to bring forward high-quality executive candidates. Specifically, TIJ needed more leaders who would correspond to the rapid growth of business: better managers who could strengthen TIJ's global competitiveness, and executives who would have the ability to cope with diverse conditions for exploiting various new business opportunities.

Executive training process at TIJ

At TI groups other than TIJ, executive candidates are assigned on a one-by-one succession plan. But in Japan, it was considered more realistic to train a high-potential group of executive candidates and assign them to appropriate positions. Hence two programmes, MDC (Management Development Centre) and PLD (Professional Leader Development), were developed to train high-potential groups. Participants were expected to acquire a so-called 'helicopter' perspective and make higher-level management decisions. Though the contents were basically tailored to TIJ, the results were fed back to TI Headquarters through the human resources department and by the executives (see Figure 18.1).

The MDC programme was started in 1996 with 40 participants selected from various business divisions (middle manager class). The PLD programme, meanwhile, was started in 1997 to promote the diversity programme and bring up the next MDC candidates. According to a strong request from top management to also empower female high potentials, all participants of the 1997 PLD programme were females (female participants for the MDC programme amounted to only one in 1996 and two in 1998).

The MDC programme for fiscal year 1998 was conducted for 29 participants who were relatively younger and the same or lower-ranked than those of 1996.

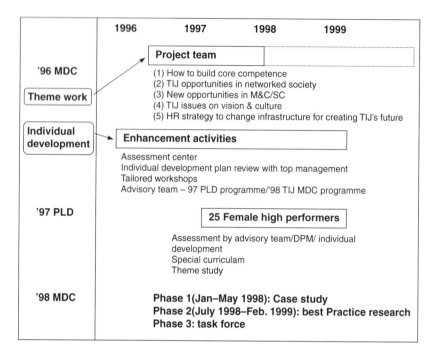

Figure 18.1   Core leader development activities

Described here are the 1996 and 1998 MDC programmes. Of note is that the three aforementioned programmes had a 'carry-over' effect. That is, the 1996 MDC programme participants served as advisers for the 1997 PLD and 1998 MDC programmes, while some selected persons from the 1996 and 1998 MDC programme participants formed a task-force to tackle real business issues.

1996 MDC programme outline

Since there was an urgent need to bring forward the next generation of leaders swiftly, the individual development programme (one year) and the theme work (1.5 years) were conducted simultaneously during the 1996 MDC programme. The main issue of the theme work was 'Creating TIJ's Future'. The specific question asked was 'What should TIJ do for the TI group to become the digital technology leader in the network society?'

Participants were divided into five teams, and each team made a proposal within 18 months on specific issues. In this case, executives served as facilitators for each group. The individual development programme included a two-day assessment centre, Where the 12 participants were evaluated by six consultants. The consultants evaluated each individual who role-played in a situation similar to the daily business scenes at TI such as e-mail exchange, participation in international conferences, and so on. Feedback was given to each participant immediately after the assessment, and a report was submitted by the consultants after one month. Then, a career plan was jointly created by the boss, the participant and the consultants and presented to the TI top management.

1998 MDC programme

Compared to the 1996 MDC programme, the participants were relatively younger and held the same or lower positions. Topics selected for the theme work focused, therefore, on more general issues as compared to 1996.

The 1998 MDC programmes contained three phases. Phase 1 was a six-month programme concentrating on the case study of business frameworks. To apply and use the theoretical learning obtained in phase 1, another six-month programme for phase 2 was designed to provide the participants with a 'real feeling' in actual business settings. Hence in phase 2 each group selected a specific theme such as factory management by themselves, and were asked to conduct 'best-practice research' through external company interviews. Through these interviews, the participants were expected to discover useful suggestions for their own company.

Phase 3 was planned as a task-force programme to tackle TIJ's management problems. This was be done by bringing together specially selected members from among the 1996 and 1998 MDC programme participants.

Key points

Points especially noted on programme design at TIJ are as follows:

1 *Big D (development), small S (selection).* In a matrix organization like TIJ, theme work is an effective training approach for a group of promising young staff selected from various business areas. Presentations made by the participants are also very useful for top managers to evaluate each participant. However, since proposals are difficult to materialize in a real business context, the programme first focuses on individual ability development (big D), and then promotes the staff who can actually turn their learning from the programme into real business results (small s).
2 *Participants' dissemination of learning and experience.* Programme learning can only be applied to real business by active follow-through, such as transferring staff to the strategic planning department or appointing the programme participant as a task-force member. But such personnel transfers require the unified consensus of top managers including the President.

   MDC programme participants are influential in being expected to utilize what they have learned and experienced at MDC. The participants are

also expected to become key members of important projects and programmes that contribute to TIJ's business and corporate growth.

3 *Sponsor's strong belief.* The sponsor's strong belief is crucial for the programme to succeed. The direction (objective, sponsor, budget) must also
be clarified to prepare the best content within the given parameters.

4 *Commitment of business managers.* In order to utilize the programme in
real business, the business manager should actually be the very person
who selects the participants and draws up the tasks. It is important to
stimulate the business manager's responsibility/awareness for the programme's success.

5 *Japanese in programmes, English in real business.* Japanese is preferable in
the programme, although the official language within TIJ is English. If
one person within the group cannot speak Japanese, however, then
everybody switches over to English.

6 *Clarification of the roles for the sponsor, agent and so on are vital for the success of a programme.*

7 *The programme must match the determined goal.* Clarity (theoretical frame)
and grounding (corresponding to the level of the participants) become
important.

8 *Fairness over equality.* The recent business trend of 'selection and concen-
tration' is starting to be reflected in individual career development:
'selecting capable people and concentrating investment (wages, education and promotion opportunity) on them'. Here, fairness is respected
over equality.

Conclusion: will action learning become an effective means for Japanese multinationals?

Action learning has gradually developed and is progressing among US and
European-based subsidiaries of Japanese multinationals such as Toyota and
Honda. Today, some Japanese multinationals are starting to introduce corporate executive programmes incorporating business driven action learning
methods to their organizations.

Thanks to Mr Aragon of Boeringer-Ingelheim, I had the opportunity to
interview the Japanese participants of the company's global High-Potential
Programme in Japan in June 1999. Although there were some obstacles,
such as the big difference in what the programme (global business scene)
requires, in contrast to what daily work (domestic business scene) demands,
I found that the Japanese young potentials were learning various things
from the action learning programme to become future global managers. As
time goes by, the Japanese participants are likely to absorb more from such
global programmes.

In the early stage, it may also be a good idea to start the programme in
Japanese by Japanese organizers who have a thorough understanding of

Western culture, as in the case with TIJ. Of course, the subsequent problem would be whether or not the programme learning can be applied to real global business situations in which case language and communication abilities would be required.

Finally, I would like to mention the two important differences between business-driven action learning programmes and executive programmes such as real business-oriented case studies and business-oriented theme works that are recently becoming popular among Japanese multinationals. One difference is how questions are asked: while business driven action learning addresses each question to the very person (for example: I, me), business-oriented case studies ask questions to the team or the company (for example: we, us), instead of each participant.

Another difference lies in how the themes are selected: while themes for business driven action learning are selected through a top-down process according to the sponsor's choice, themes of business-oriented theme work are often chosen by the participants themselves. In any case, Japanese multinationals today are already fully aware of the need to tackle real business issues. It is wrong, however, to think that business driven action learning is an approach similar or identical to the traditional Quality Control (QC) activities of Japanese corporations, or a business-oriented theme or a case study.

I personally think that now is the best timing for Japanese multinationals to introduce business-driven action learning. This is because the need to change is mounting on all levels including industry, corporate and executive levels and for each employee, in order to survive in the ever-diversifying global business arena. Although there may be a period of trial and error at the introductory stage, the experience of programme participants in the Japanese subsidiaries of Western multinationals is sure to serve as a good reference point.

As a conclusion, let me state that an action learning programme can become a truly effective means of developing managers for Japanese multinationals only when they fully recognize the fundamental difference between business-driven action learning and other already familiar methods.

Notes

1   Interview with the human resource development department of a Western multinational's Japanese subsidiary, Tokyo.
2   Interview with the ASP department, human resources, Texas Instruments Japan, Tokyo.

19

Tibetan Buddhism and Action Reflection Learning™ Philosophy

Lars Cederholm

Introduction

As I grow older, it has been increasingly important for me to strive to bring the different strands and activities of my life into one unified view, or *mandala* to use a Buddhist word. I lay no claim to have found the truth hidden behind this unified concept, but nevertheless it is important to me to continue the search. In this article I have attempted to describe the basic ideas in Tibetan Buddhism and Action Reflection Learning™ (ARL) and to highlight some similarities and connections. There are many differences. For one thing, Tibetan Buddhism is a religion. Action Reflection Learning philosophy and theory does not make that claim though some people may disagree with this assertion. There are many relevant and interesting parallels between Buddhist philosophy and Action Reflection Learning (ARL) as an approach to management and organizational development. The comparison to Tibetan Buddhism in this article will be to the approach, which goes under the name ARL as it is being practiced by the MiL Institute in Europe.

Development depends on role models and experience

During the last 16 years the author of this article has studied with the great Tibetan *Nyingma* Masters Khenpo Palden Sherab Rinpoche and his younger brother Khenpo Tsewang Dongyal Rinpoche. My gratitude to their love, compassion and patience with my turbulent mind cannot be expressed in words. During the same time span I have been a programme director, coach and special resource person to over 40 different ARL programmes. This article is very much based on my personal insights into what happens in programmes as well as my own experience as a Buddhist practitioner.

I also respectfully acknowledge the great professional support I have received during the last 17 years from Lennart Rohlin, the CEO and chief theoretician and guardian of MiL theory and values, and all my friends and colleagues at the MiL Institute.

Awareness of oneself and the environment is essential

Some years ago I was leading a workshop in New York City with a group of senior executives participating in an action (reflection) learning programme organized by the MiL Institute in Sweden. We were using the wonderful and complex web that is New York to evoke experiences out of the ordinary. Most of the situations confronting the participants required new ways of understanding or re-framing. One of the participants summarized his experience at the end of our week:

> In the past I have put restrictions on what I need to see to make sense of situations I am facing. This week has demonstrated to me that I am able to take in much more data without overwhelming myself and come out of the process with a better and more solid decision. To do this I realize that I need other people with whom I must have trusting relationships. I am not sure how to say this, but it feels like some kind of freedom!

What this person was describing comes close to the experience of my personal practice as a Buddhist and observations I have made conducting workshops and seminars in Action Reflection Learning programmes. The ability to calmly face complexity with inner and outer awareness is a core element of the practice. When we think we are overreaching our capability to process data, we tend to set boundaries, thereby diminishing the quality of information, analysis and decision-making.

Paradoxically one also needs to depend on other people to experience personal freedom. If this dependency is built on suspicion and mistrust between people, then personal freedom is difficult or perhaps impossible to attain. To be in the midst of a group of trusted fellow learners (the Buddhist *Sangha*, or participants in an Action Reflection Learning programme) is an important element to realize insights. In addition, to have a trustworthy spiritual friend (teacher or learning coach) is equally a key condition for progress in one's human development. If one can accept that all perceptions are ultimately a reflection of one's self, then the spiritual friend and fellow learners and the trust one feels in them can be transferred to the relationship to oneself.

Attitude will follow behaviour and vice versa

Change is mostly a gradual process but sometimes it is swift. Years ago, I was leading a workshop in team development. One of the participants (called the 'cobra' in his home organization) came with a reputation for his technical skills, business knowledge and ambition to succeed, but he was also known for his ruthless jungle tactics. In the ARL programme he was always first to answer, always first on the top of every hill ready to plant his victory banner. He seemed oblivious to the fact that his fellow programme participants were pulling away from him. During breaks he was often sitting by himself when he did not try to force himself into relationships with others.

One day he and I had the opportunity to sit down and I shared my observations with him. The result of our conversation was that he promised to experiment with some new behaviour for the next three days: wait for others, listen and take in others' views without arguments, recognize other people's contribution and actively seek feedback from his team-mates and other members of the staff and the programme. He became visibly disturbed facing the awkwardness of this new style but he promised to try. I suggested to him that he could always go back to his old self if he found the task impossible.

And it worked! Attitudes tend to follow behaviour. He was taken into the community of learners with open arms and, in fact, had a transformative and lasting experience. Tibetan Buddhism and the philosophy behind ARL are grounded in deep humanistic values and are both dedicated to explore the human potential, individually and in relationship to social interactions in the world in which we live.

Action Reflection Learning: we learn by doing and being in the world

The fundamental values for the design of an ARL programme is that the personal experiences and questions from the participants guide the content of what is under investigation. Theory is in principle discussed as a result of experience and not in anticipation of an experience. It is important that the participants use their own analysis and common sense first. The next step is to conceptualize the personal insights and compare it with available and relevant theory. The traditional classroom, case study or curriculum approach is underemphasized in favour of real strategic problems given to the programme by executives (the clients) in the participating company(s). The participants, mostly line managers with significant responsibilities, are divided into project teams of four to six participants according to certain principles.

The guide – someone who can support you and point out opportunities and pitfalls

A learning coach is assigned to each of the teams. Over time, periodic seminars of three to five days are held to discuss the opportunities of learning and the search for solutions to complex strategic questions. The process (how) of the project teams and the task (what) are investigated as the individuals, the teams and the whole programme group engage in the naturally-occurring events and questions which present themselves in the process of the work. The learning community of 20 or so participants is a central resource for personal development.

The learning coach is not restricted to making just process observations and on to guiding reflection, but may at times contract for periodic membership in the assigned team, always staying clear of the trap of assuming leadership over the team. The role is demanding and tricky and requires great maturity and personal grounding on the part of the learning coach. The learning coaches and the programme director take on the responsibility of making sure that the content of the programme does not develop into the more traditional cataloguing of knowledge. The focus is instead kept on creative problem-solving and the development of personally grounded change theories and team skills extracted from experience. It is not enough for the project teams to come up with a report of their investigations. The form is of minor importance. What is important is that the teams manage to have some demonstrable impact in the project host organization.

Programme goals

The programme goals are both to develop a personal and grounded leadership theory, as well as good results and organizational development for the client organization. In most cases the problems and opportunities given to the programme are addressed to the satisfaction of the clients. The participants also report significant growth in personally grounded management theory affirmed by the experience in the programme. After all, a manager who appears like a book or a clone of somebody else may have a credibility problem. Participation in the programmes is in principle based on invitation and free choice.

The fundamental principle of Tibetan Buddhism

What then is the essence of Tibetan Buddhism or for that matter any of the central schools of Buddhism now found worldwide? Is it a religion or is it a philosophical system to help us understand the world around us? The answer is that it is both. Tibetan Buddhism holds out a promise of a world free from the tyranny of the poisons of the mind. What we need to defeat are emotions such as anger, hatred, jealousy, fear, dualism and the clinging to our egos as if ego is something solid and separate from the natural world around us. These emotional poisons are consequences from actions during past and present lifetimes. Fortunately these poisons contain hidden transformative energies which, through diligent practice, will manifest themselves in both wisdom and compassion and kindness towards all life forms. Paradoxically, we can only become the masters of our own ego-centred world when we are willing to give it up or let go.

The true nature of the mind is love and compassion

Tibetan Buddhism is a vision of freedom and happiness. It is a view of the world built on faith in the unlimited vastness of the mind beyond literal, scientific reasoning. The foundation for this approach rests on the union between love and wisdom. Love being compassion and kindness and wisdom being the understanding of the relationships between all phenomena as well as a sharp understanding of every object and phenomenon in and of itself. It is said that love and kindness is what remains when we have removed all the filters that stand between us and the true mind.

Total focus on the secrets of the mind

For a time span of over 1300 years, Tibetan meditation masters have devised different practices to obtain the freedom and the favourable conditions of a human birth. When much of the rest of the world was busy with science and technology as means to explore the world order, Tibetan practitioners focused their efforts on the mind, sheltered from the pressures to admit 'mind' or 'experience' or 'intelligence' into the realm of hard sciences. The insights from their meditation practices in their isolated and unique environment are indeed worthy of serious investigation in this high-speed world of ours. It is important to add that other religions and philosophical systems have been developed with similar interests and motivations and have attracted huge followings through the power of the promise they hold. Tibetan Buddhism will never try to preach or diminish other's religious beliefs or life philosophies.

A long tradition based on faith and devotion

Tibetan Buddhism is both a practical guide for everyday life as well as a religion with devotion to the great and courageous Buddha and the great lineage masters of India and Tibet who have upheld the teachings for over 2500 years, ever since the time Siddharta became The Buddha (the enlightened one). To follow the Buddha's way, devotion and faith are vital elements. Using the intellect alone makes the teachings meaningless, unsustainable and brittle like a dry twig that can easily be broken. At the very root of the Buddhist faith is the possibility of enlightenment in this lifetime. Every one of us has the Buddha mind or the seed for enlightenment but this seed must be nurtured to realize its full potential. The notion that enlightenment is indeed possible rests on an unrelenting faith, devotion and various forms of meditation practices. Since conceptual understanding is not enough to harvest the fruit, one must strive to understand inner reality through a state of mind beyond the obvious world around us. This state of mind can only be personally experienced. Reading books and listening to learned teachers is not enough to get us to the goal.

Its right there in front of us

This understanding is said to be simple and perhaps humorously obvious. We can't see the truth simply because it is too close to us. Since it is beyond conceptual thinking it cannot be described for what it is by ordinary means. It is easier to describe the fruits of the Buddhist practice by what it is not, rather than what it is.

Tibetan, tantric Buddhism uses images of wrathful and peaceful deities far from Western imagery and rationality. All meditation practices on spiritual imagery must be understood as temporary structures, or representations of the psyche which are devised to help the journey towards enlightenment. They exist in the relative world but in the absolute sense they do not exist at all: another difficult paradox which cannot be understood by rationality alone. As the mind becomes gradually free from the cobweb of the five poisons (ignorace, hatred, pride, craving, envy), these helping structures are no longer necessary. After all, you don't need to carry the boat on your shoulder after you have crossed the river.

Understanding is your personal responsibility

Tibetan Buddhism has a morale code of conduct (*vinaya*), a philosophy (*abidharma*) and different systems to guide meditation (*sutras*). It is important to have an accomplished master/teacher to help guide the practitioner on the road towards the enlightened mind, although the discovery and realization of the great and hidden potential of the mind is up to each and every practitioner. Buddhism puts the responsibility squarely on the shoulders of the practitioner; there are no absolutes, no fundamentalism to rest on, and no external God or Devil to blame for one's possible misfortunes. Heaven and hell exist right here inside and around us and not in some imagined physical space in the afterlife. The law of *karma* is that the results of virtuous and unvirtuous actions are inevitable. If you plant corn you get corn, and not a rose. Likewise all actions, good and bad, will have consequences, if not right away then later.

Discipline and patience – practicing what you have learned

Buddhists need to practice diligently and positive results will definitely emerge. It is not enough to go to church or temple on holidays and be done with it. The practice must be moved into every aspect of one's life, even into the sleeping hours. The results of practice may initially be hidden from our view just like butter is hidden inside milk. The butter can not be seen just by looking at the milk but with the right understanding and action may be extracted from the milk. Action and reflection is necessary and Tibetan Buddhism without action is a road to nowhere. We learn through studies of the right view, and we take our insights into the world by being in the world with love, kindness and compassion. From this practical experience we go back to meditate and reflect on what we have learned and in this way we cycle through the development of our progress and realizations.

What do Tibetan Buddhism and ARL have in common?

Fresh environments promote learning

To create ideal conditions for learning (an inner environment) it is important to go away from the ordinary, everyday life to a physical place free from everyday distractions and habits. Seminars in ARL programmes are in principle held away from the home organization. In addition, the project teams are not working with familiar tasks, and each team member is assigned to a project team in an organization other than his/her own. In internal ARL programmes, participants work within the boundaries of the larger organizational context but in projects where the individual expertise is not directly applicable. All this is to promote fresh, out-of-the-box thinking and an active search for relevant information.

Trust is the basis for learning from each other

The participants themselves constitute a central support structure to help learning and promote understanding. In order to maximize the opportunity to learn from one another in action, a good deal of time has to be spent building trust in the learning philosophy as well as between the individual and fellow participants and programme staff. Good relationships and trust give rise to good information, analysis and decision-making.

Most practicing Buddhists periodically go on retreat and practice privately and together in groups. In Tibetan Buddhism this group support structure is called *Sangha* which is a set of personal relations and spiritual friendships coming together under a common vision to grow and learn and ultimately to seek enlightenment. In this environment (incubator) one has the opportunity to observe thoughts and emotions in one's self and others and practice love, compassion and understanding in accordance with the Buddha's teachings. To create ideal conditions for learning, Buddhists take refuge in the *Buddha* (he who had the courage and showed the way) the *Dharma* (the way) and the *Sangha* (fellow practitioners).

Awareness

The physical (outer) environment with its boundaries and limits has a deep influence on what we tend to pay attention to. What directs one's mind in New York City or on a Buddhist retreat in the mountains tends to be very different. In ARL programmes, participants learn to pay attention to personal traits and reactions to their thoughts and feelings as they become increasingly aware of the many boundaries in the programme. The boundaries and the way they are interdependent are many: between self and others, between the team and the client and his/her organization, between the different teams, between staff and participants, between the programme and invited resource persons, and between the formal and informal relationships which develop during the lifetime of the programme. The awareness of all these, mostly invisible, boundaries and the energy which develops at these boundaries tends to mobilize personal energy and interest in managing the social aspects of leadership. How can one create positive conditions for learning and understanding across all these boundaries? And how can insights be transferred to the work place and life in general? This is the challenge to each of the participants and the staff. To make the invisible visible is as central a task in Buddhist practice as it is in an ARL programme.

Sharpen your senses – be in the now and don't get caught

In Buddhist practice, awareness of the now is a central idea. The past consists of hazy memories and the future is merely speculative. The only real moment is awareness of the 'now' which *is* the Buddha. This is why just-in-time learning (JIT) is such a precious and powerful opportunity. What is happening in the 'now' is the opportunity to learn with all the senses present. The ability to stay suspended between different polarities such as good and bad, valuable and useless, ugly and beautiful, low and high without getting invested in either side gives a much broader view of the different forces at work. The art of staying neutrally alert in the present moment, that is not choosing sides before the whole picture is in focus, is a powerful tool in consultative management and facilitates access to the whole system. All complex situations confronting us have forces driving change and forces holding us back. To stay with both allows the positive to emerge. To push for premature closure will most likely create other types of problems later on, particularly in the way solutions are implemented.

In ARL project teams it is not uncommon that one or more team members 'know' the solution to the challenge posed by the client; they recognize the situation from past experience. The dilemma here is, of course, that they are often informed by old knowledge and blindfolded expertise. This type of 'knowing' leads to a tendency to ignore other people's points of view and thereby diminish the potential for team synergy. These attitudes tend to create conditions for conflict and power struggles. Awareness of the force-field of paradoxes and different perceptions increases sensitivity and the ability to tread lightly and kindly as one shows respect for the other side of the boundary. This is an important skill for change leaders as well as the Buddhist practitioner. The soft skills are indeed the hard skills.

Absolute and relative reality

The Buddhist practitioner realizes that boundaries are mostly artificial, social constructs and do not exist from an absolute point of view. Culture, as an example, is a set of social constructs. Nothing more than a set of collective agreements and habits designed to form group identity and security for its members. There is nothing to get attached to in reality but, as the Buddhist saying goes, respect the ways of the village. The practice on different levels of reality gives the Buddhist practitioner a chance to take a dispassionate look and not rush to get invested in 'this or that'. This is also at the core of the practice in an ARL programme. The stability and skill level of ARL programme directors and learning coaches are critical to the learning process. They must know when and how to slow down the action and reflect on the integration of task and process thereby helping participants to dissolve rigidity in the boundaries. In Tibetan Buddhism practitioners use teachers (*Lamas*) to help them be aware of how to walk patiently on the path in the right direction, one step at the time. Like the Lama, the learning coach must allow the participants to draw conclusions from personal experience even if it implies getting out of the way when the way is obviously leading away from the goal. The personal experience is sometimes more important than always doing the right thing. There is a striking similarity in roles between a good Buddhist teacher and the guiding role of the staff in ARL programmes.

Reflection – to understand our experience through meditation and periods of reflection

Reflection is closely related to learning and understanding. What did we do? How did we do it? Why did we make the choices we made? How can we improve? In any situation where there is pressure to complete the task (what), there is also a tendency to avoid reflection on how the system performs (the process). Time is a powerful player (time is money), and since reflection on the process requires time and often induces discomfort it tends to get pushed to the side at the expense of relevant data gathering, quality in analysis, decision-making and execution. Reflection and learning involve both the willingness and the skills of receiving and giving feedback. Without feedback, culture change is difficult or perhaps impossible. We are constantly challenged to handle the difficult paradox between navigating our lives based on old knowledge and safe methods on the one hand, and creation, renewal and change on the other. We need others to see how we make these choices since we are often unable to see the chair we are sitting on.

Reflection and feedback take place in all parts of an ARL programme. Individuals write in their learning logs. Teams take time out (often with the help of the learning coach) to reflect on both their accomplishments and their mistakes. The programme as a community is routinely taking time out to reflect using dialogue and conversation. Open dialogue is a kind of group meditation in the sense that every personal reflection is not to be countered and processed but rather deeply listened to until higher awareness and meaning is realized.

Meditation is reflection

Buddhist practitioners reflect through meditation and through dialogue and conversations with the *Lamas* and the *Sangha* members. The Buddhist practitioner receives feedback through observing the reactions and the behaviour of the teachers (*Lamas*), as well as receiving advice to support and make corrections in the practice. The *Sangha* has a similar role in helping the practitioner gain perspective on individual progress. Feedback must be given and received in the spirit of helping and caring for the growth and the development of the individual: a fundamental attitude in an ARL programme, as well as in a Buddhist *Sangha*.

To meditate is to sit on a chair or pillow and allow the mind to focus on certain objects or themes and to work without 'running' after every thought and emotion. The trick is to stretch the space between the different thoughts and emotions, thereby taming the mind to be stable. What happens in that process is private and defies explanation. The process in meditation and in an ARL programme may be described but the personal experience of changing perspectives is not readily expressed in words. One often hears the frustration of programme participants express the impact a programme has had on them. How do I put into words what fundamentally is a deep personal experience? The link between awareness, systems thinking and mind control cannot easily be put into a neat management model, and yet most people intuitively understand the importance for leadership. This 'lack of hard edges' is sometimes a source of frustration for CEOs and people in organizations who are responsible for management development. They often need hard statistical evidence and cost-factor analysis to justify the investment in managers and organizational development. People who come in contact with Tibetan Buddhism often experience similar frustration for the same reasons. Lack of dogmas and hard-edge prescriptions create uncertainty and confusion at first. In a world defined by order and strong structures, the impulse is to draw set boxes and concepts around whatever is hazy and hard to grasp.

We learn from action but also from theory

In Tibetan Buddhism, as in ARL programmes, practitioners do not rely on action as the only basis for learning. There is an extensive learning philosophy which is shared and discussed to give credence to ARL as an approach to management development. Participants are invited to discuss the theory and test it in relation to their own personal learning styles. Likewise in Tibetan Buddhism the study of theory (the view) precedes contemplation of meaning, followed by settling the mind in meditation on the meaning. This being said, practicing Tibetan Buddhism in action is where Tibetan Buddhism takes on its real meaning. The same is true for ARL.

Taming of the mind

The mind jumps around. Some people describe it as a constant, uncontrollable chatter or a chicken coop. When people start to practice meditation they are surprised and even scared to experience this chaotic state of the mind. To realize how little self-control we have shakes many self-perceptions, but that inner revolution is the doorway to deeper understanding. That is the Buddhist view. To find the diamond in the rough is to learn that the difference between suffering and happiness is really only one's own perspective. Just be aware, observe the stirrings of the mind and gently bring it back to the focus of the meditation.

Meditation on a specific object is called peace (*shamata*) meditation. This would come close to the personal reflection in the learning journal where reflection is focused on specific observations and related thoughts and emotions. Just allow thoughts to flow without too much editing. The aim is that the reflection will lead to insights into the difference between what is real and what is merely projections and fantasies which can be checked when sharing impressions with other participants: in other words the use of personal meditation and the support of the *Sangha*.

The more difficult and advanced type of meditation is called *vipashyana*, which unlike *shamata* meditation has no object: it is meditation on emptiness. Here emptiness must be understood as total freedom from grasping and attachments. The vast sky is the metaphor and the thoughts and feelings are passing through like white clouds across this vast emptiness. There is no need to hold on to or chase after these clouds. No matter how busy and cramped our physical world may seem to us, there is always the presence of the sky and the vastness of universe above. The object is to realize the absolute freedom of the mind once the practitioner can see that nothing is existing in and of itself: everything is interdependent. Perhaps dialogue where ARL participants stay alert and deeply listening, letting go of inner arguing, comes close to the idea of *vipashyana*. Let it come and let it go and new awareness and understanding will emerge.

Perspectives – the use of right view and systems thinking to frame the learning and understand the experience

The paper that this is written on is certainly just paper but on another level it is also water, soil, sun, pollinating insects, temperature, labour, machines, intentions, stockmarkets and so forth. To truly understand systems thinking one must understand the complex symphony of all phenomena. Upon close examination, there is no 'stand alone' reality. Likewise, the awareness of the complexity of an ARL programme and the immediate world around it as related systems will help participants to think in systems terms. This is also the purpose of meditation.

The realization of complex interdependencies will appear easier when one learns to relax the mind rather than forcing it to understand. One has to understand the importance of dissolving every thought to the freedom from grasping or holding on to any singular object and phenomena. The view is that nothing is reality in and of itself, and the resulting insight is freedom from the extremes. We must come to see that we as persons are not the solid centre of the universe but just a part of the ever-changing process of change. Every learning coach is well-aware of the danger of premature decision-making and the importance of staying in the middle of extreme views as long as possible. Perhaps ARL should be replaced by ARU, the U standing for understanding.

The dance of change – how change unfolds

From a Buddhist practice point of view everything, the whole universe, is constantly changing even if the movement cannot always be seen by ordinary perceptions. Every natural phenomenon is a constant dance of atoms. In fact, Tibetan meditation masters realized the existence of atoms and sub-atomic particles more than a thousand years ago. If one atom stops its dance the world would collapse since everything is ultimately related in the dance of change. The very nature of life is change and we find ourselves naturally in this ongoing dance. We must learn how to become masters of change and embrace it as a part of life itself.

One can argue that change management is the real purpose of an ARL programme even if different seminar modules appear under labels such as team-building, working with and through others, personal development, business savvy, strategic thinking, chaos theory and so forth. The participants learn to view change as opportunities rather than upsets. With increased information and understanding of the world around us, it is becoming increasingly clear to managers and leaders that we all need to learn about change as fast or faster than the rest of the marketplace. How we deal with change and how much we are able to drive change is as important to an ARL programme as it is fundamental to Buddhist practitioners.

Resistance to change

As much as people have to embrace change, it is equally important to come to terms with how change is resisted. Buddhist tantric masters as in other Buddhist meditation traditions recommend that one acknowledges or labels every feeling and thought before letting it go. One needs to be vigilant and nip compulsive thinking before it returns to the grooves of habitual thinking and feeling. If something causes resentment or anger then the practitioner stays briefly in the experience before releasing it back to freedom from grasping and holding on. Changing circumstance is not primarily what is happening in the world around a person, but change first and foremost implies a changing relationship to how someone experiences himself as a person. Facing change is often associated with feelings of fear, resentment, worry and hesitation. It is good to think of change as having smooth edges rather than sharp turns. The mind, much like the body, requires analysis and reflection before the possibilities are exhausted and right action is chosen. Our body demands that we chew our food before it is swallowed: it makes the work of the stomach easier and healthier and, besides, food tastes better that way. Change made in this fashion is more grounded and convincing.

ARL programme coaches must help participants to embrace and understand the nature of resistance. Change takes time and the work of understanding how change happens should ideally go from resistance or reality testing to understanding and commitment.

The quick-fix syndrome

There is a tendency in our modern society to talk about change as if it all exists in the same time/space continuum. In fact, the experience of the changing world around us is going on at a faster pace than change or adaptation on the personal level. This false view accounts for much of the quick-fix, hard-nosed demands on managers to sink or swim with all that is going on in the changing world around them. One can safely say that there is a tendency to stage one or two-day costly events, complete with motivational speakers, and leave the organizational investment in personal change at that. In truth, the basic condition for committed change is that the person involved in the change process experiences him/herself as being well-differentiated from others in terms of input and creativity. Long-term participation and change between programme activities and insights as well as back-on-the-job applications move the participants from compliance to commitment, as every member in an ARL team knows: alignment is the result of working in mutually respectful relationships. The work of the person considering change cannot be compared to an elevator ride, but rather a series of steps. Under normal circumstances, old habits should not be thrown out of the window, but rather coaxed down the steps. ARL programmes are designed over time to ensure that changes are analysed, well-grounded in the affected human system, and can be transferred to life outside the programme. In addition, much of the change around us is not under our control and will be a matter of our relationship to the inevitable. The Internet, globalization and the vanishing of political ideologies are examples of the times we live in to which we need to adapt rather than change. This is as true for the Buddhist practitioner as for the participants in an ARL programme.

In summary

This article has touched on some of the more obvious similarities between Action Reflection Learning™ and Tibetan Buddhism:

- The central role of the community of learners.
- The importance of a guide/coach/teacher to support reflection.
- Trusting relationships which enhance the quality of learning and understanding.
- The recognition of our vast human potential and inherent wisdom.
- Recognition and respect that each individual is unique and at different stages of readiness to change.
- The ultimate responsibility of the individual for inner work in relation to development.
- Recognition that opportunities are everywhere once we move away from bondage to the egocentric projected world.
- The central importance of understanding the world both in terms of relationships and also the ability to focus singular attention.
- The questions arising (rather than a preconstructed curriculum) as the key drivers for development.
- Without action no deeper understanding can be realized.
- Mindfulness of the impact of inner forces as well as outer events and relationships.
- The importance of reflection and meditation as a way to develop wisdom.

For me the investigation continues. I have more work to do in arenas where human interactions determine the quality of the outcomes of life in organizations. Some of the questions and paradoxes I will continue to focus on are:

- How can I best use my time in the compressed world of change and instant communication to find the right balance between learning from experts and learning from my own actions and reflections. I can't be everywhere and yet I must engage in actions to reflect and gain transferable understanding from them.
- How can I balance my need to bring my personal insights to some use in this tumultuous world and at the same time seek solitude and meditation away from that world.
- How can I simplify what seems turbulent, unbounded and chaotic.
  For me as a practicing Buddhist it has been a blessing to be able to bring my views and the fruits of my meditation to the work in ARL programmes. In fact, I am hard-pressed to find anything within these two perspectives that are in direct conflict with each other. I hope that you as a reader will get some thoughts and impulses from reading this material and, if you do, please share them with me.

20

Strategic Change Management at Merck Hong Kong: Building a High Performing Executive Team Using Action Reflection Learning™

Richard Pearson

This article recounts my experience introducing Action Reflection Learning (ARL)™ to Merck Sharp & Dohme in Hong Kong (wholly owned by Merck & Co., Inc., headquartered in Whitehouse Station, New Jersey, in the United States). It illustrates, from both a personal and professional perspective, the power of ARL and how it assisted both me and my clients to gain new awareness and move out of our traditional comfort zones. What is particularly significant is that this was my first application of ARL methodology. I was receiving coaching and going through the same learning process as my clients, reflecting one of the core principles of ARL: 'earning while learning'.

Looking back, I can unequivocally state that this assignment was the most profound learning experience of my professional career, opening up a whole new world of individual and organizational growth and development. I attribute this to several factors: the willingness of my primary Merck client to try new things and trust in the process; the coaching I received from Leadership in International Management (LIM); LIM's ARL process; and of course the Merck team who, through their patience, openness and trust, embraced a whole new way of being a team.

Setting the scene

In Asia, some of even the most progressive multinationals still operate on a more traditional hierarchical basis with the team leader or boss making most decisions and leading from the top. Sometimes this means people are not as open with their opinions and feelings – especially when the boss is in the room. This was certainly true of the Merck Hong Kong team when we first began working with them, which presented an interesting challenge to me. I had been living in Hong Kong for 12 years and working in the field of management training and development for eight of them, helping individuals, teams and organizations shift from a hierarchical, top-down management style to a more empowered, team-based culture. As always, the challenge was how to achieve ever better results for this new client.

My first meeting was with the managing director of Merck Hong Kong, who initially wanted executive coaching to help 'take her team to a higher level'. The context was change. As the pharmaceutical industry had been undergoing major consolidation and experiencing significant growth opportunities in Asia, a very different approach was imperative. Merck had engaged an internal consultant to facilitate the development of a new five-year strategic plan and the MD wanted her team to simultaneously develop the skills that would be necessary to implement their new plan. She wanted her team members to be more 'passionate' about their work, and to take more ownership and initiative – especially cross-functionally. Like many of the multinationals that we work with, the Merck Hong Kong executive team had strong technical (medical, professional, finance) backgrounds but less development on the people/business side of the business. Generating enthusiasm for a new 'soft' development initiative was no small challenge as the executive team was already performing at a very high level. Almost every CEO I deal with has shared this challenge when embracing such an initiative for meaningful change.

The initial contract

During my first interview with the MD it became apparent that the type of change she wanted could not come simply through executive coaching. We had to involve her team as well. This was quickly agreed and, as a first step, we conducted an analysis of the team's individual behavioural strengths using the Priority Profile, an effectiveness assessment developed by Priority Management in conjunction with Dr Peter Honey, a leading behavioural psychologist. This assessment measures effectiveness in eight key areas: defining purpose (values and vision); establishing goals; focusing resources (planning); managing priorities; measuring performance; taking ownership; influencing; and continuous improvement (change and learning). I had used this process many times with organizations across Asia and was confident in the outcomes it would produce. Typically, the areas of ownership and influencing are the areas most needing development.

Following a half-day debriefing on the results of the assessments, we also conducted one-on-one coaching with each member of the executive team to help them set personal development plans. This was also seen as an opportunity to introduce the idea of coaching to the team. While coaching was not new to the global Merck culture, it had not been used in Merck Hong Kong in a deep sense.

This approach worked well and initial feedback from the participants was positive. The results were as expected: the majority of the team showed strong opportunities for development in the areas of influencing and ownership. These two skills go hand in hand. A traditional directive influencing style (which is very prevalent in Hong Kong) tends to produce low ownership – people simply do not respond as well to being told what to do.

Phase two

Building on our initial success with the assessments and coaching, the stage was set to go to the next level. My client and I had considered several approaches. One was to offer modules within the team's monthly management meetings to provide training in the areas needing development. Another was to have me facilitate team problem-solving – a powerful feature of our TEC ('The Executive Committee') forum in Hong Kong where CEOs from non-competing industries meet on a monthly basis to help each other resolve strategic business issues. When I consulted my LIM colleagues at this stage, none of us could have anticipated how profoundly the assignment would evolve.

LIM's initial suggestion was to conduct a more in-depth Team Development Workshop using ARL principles to assist the team identify and begin developing the competencies of a high-performing team. The only problem was that I had never conducted such a workshop and had no exposure to ARL. Being an experiential learner, I usually work best when I can sit through a new workshop first and then do it on my own. I was not going to have that chance here, so I did the next best thing by getting long-distance assistance from my coaches.

After we designed and circulated a list of questions for the team to work on, a two-day workshop was scheduled. These questions were designed based on discussions with the head of Merck Asia Pacific (my client's boss) , my client and LIM. Individual team members were also encouraged to include questions that they felt were relevant, building their ownership of the process.

The questions were answered during personal interviews with me. To elicit candid feedback, I assured the interviewees that their views would be passed on anonymously. The interview process was also a good chance to get to know more about the individual members of the team and for them to develop their own comfort level with me. I was very encouraged by the outcome of these sessions and the level of participation from the team members.

The Team Development Workshop was held at an offsite venue where we all stayed the night. This proved to be important as discussions and meetings went on well into the evening after the first day. We kicked off the workshop with a rather innovative 'fishbowl' feedback of the results of the interview questions. To facilitate this, I had one of my associates interview me in front of the team about what I had learned during the interview process. Then we circulated my anonymous summary of their answers. After everyone had read it, we reflected on the questions that people now had based on what they had just heard and read. We used these new questions as the basis of the agenda for the balance of the workshop.

Although I believe in and practice 'situational facilitation', this type of totally 'unstructured' approach was new to me as well as the team. Through the ensuing discussions, we all learned a lot about ourselves and each other, and there was tremendous pressure to achieve the tasks of the meeting. The focus on 'process' was new to the team and was perceived to be slowing things down. Frustration was apparent – as was the learning.

On the evening of day one, I solicited written feedback from the team on the day's events. While half of the team members felt I needed to be more sensitive when dealing with difficult issues, the other half encouraged me to push them further. Clearly, the level of openness and disclosure experienced that day was well-beyond what the team was used to: it was also very new to me. I wrestled with how to add value as the process 'expert' while not interfering with the team's work. I got lots of coaching that evening, the advantage of having coaches on the other side of the world.

By the end of the workshop we had identified a list of high-performing team behaviours, clarified the vision for the team and learned a new set of tools and processes for team decision-making, reflection and dialogue. Their initial learning was recorded in individual learning journals. I remember feeling at the end of the workshop that this was the most meaningful work I had ever done. The level of learning using the ARL processes of 'stop and reflect' was far beyond what occurs in a normal debrief. We were all pushed out of our comfort zone and learned as our reward.

For me, this Team Development Workshop highlighted how ARL is a lot like fishing. A group of people set off in a boat with an objective – 'Let's head in this direction'. Then, when someone hooks a fish, everyone stops what they are doing, the boat slows and all energies are focused on catching the fish. So it is with ARL. The group forms with a direction or task in mind – usually, a business challenge or question they need to answer. Along the way, learning opportunities surface and it is necessary to interrupt the task to catch the fish. I quickly discovered that the ARL technique of 'stop and reflect' is a great way to 'catch fish', the gems of learning that would otherwise get away. Capturing these opportunities on a real-time basis is essential to becoming a 'learning organization', the goal of so many leading companies today.

The process of stop, reflect, write report is quite simple. At a time when there is a good chance to collect the team's input, we would take one minute to write down our answers to a particular question and then everyone shares what they have written. This method makes speaking out more objective and less personal – everyone has a chance to be heard and there is no judgment or criticism of what is said. I believe this has been a key element in transcending the typical Asian 'modesty' in relation to speaking openly. The other advantage is that the input of all members of the team is obtained – allowing the introverts time to think and the extroverts time to edit. Contrast a typical meeting where the extroverts dominate and the introverts (who often have valuable information) sit quietly.

Follow-up

We supported the workshop with additional one-on-one coaching. Much of what came up in these coaching sessions directly linked to the earlier discussions about the feedback from the Priority Profile assessments. While this was not surprising, it really helped reinforce the earlier feedback and gave it a practical context.

Through the process, the team realized they needed development in several key skills including influencing, coaching and taking ownership. A matrix of skills for development was conceptualized and mapped out by the team. This created the basis for further development both on the team and individual levels.

Based on the success of the process to date I was invited to join several of the ongoing strategic planning sessions being run by the internal facilitator. This posed a challenge as there was some concern that the team was getting behind in their work due to the processes they had learned in the Team Development Workshop. This highlighted the importance of aligning the different consultants working with a team. We worked with the internal consultants to integrate ARL within their process, to reinforce the team's learning of the new techniques as well as add value to the strategic planning process itself. This included using a very quick consensus-based decision-making tool we have called the 'fist – five' to check on the relative priority of items for discussion. We also carved out time from the planning process to reflect on what went well and could be improved at the end of each meeting. In addition, the team appointed a 'process checker' to ensure that the processes they had learned were being followed. This allocation of roles at a meeting is a very simple and powerful way to make meetings more effective and focused.

This point really reinforced one of the key elements of the ARL approach of 'earning while learning'. By integrating the learning with the team's actual strategic planning work, we were able to make the learning much more relevant and practical in the context of the team's current reality. This revealed the ARL 'just-in-time' versus 'just-in-case' approach. As traditional training programmes tend to be offered just in case a skill is needed, the subject matter often lacks immediate relevance for the attendees, which was highlighted for me on a personal level during this assignment. The year before I had attended an excellent four-day course on meeting facilitation in San Francisco. As good as the course had been, that binder had been collecting dust on my shelf ever since. Suddenly, with all this new work I was doing, I got very motivated to dust off the binder. The only problem was that I could not make any sense of my notes or the materials. The just-in-time learning provided through working on a real business issue and taking time to 'build-in' learning – supported with coaching – was proving to be much more effective for me and, I believe, the team members.

Recontracting

In the following months, I joined in several of the team's monthly meetings and we held several more one-on-one coaching sessions. All the while I had an uneasy feeling that the team, while benefiting from the process, was unclear about the direction or outcomes my client and I were looking for. This was reinforced by the completion of the strategic planning process which was ostensibly what I had been hired to support. On reflection, I realized that most of my contracting had been with my client directly and that, while she and I were comfortable with the *ad hoc* approach we were using, some of the team members were not.

This led us to dedicate some time in one of our next team meetings to the issue of contracting. I chose an innovative use of the fishbowl interview to have the team members assume the roles of my LIM colleagues, interviewing me about the progress, success and challenges with the Merck team. This led to a high level of disclosure from the MD and me which really helped the team understand where we were at and where we were going. It also created an opportunity for the team to offer their feedback and views, creating a much higher level of ownership and trust in all directions. I believe this trust and openness was principally achieved as a result of the process we used. The fishbowl interview is a great way to communicate information – it is genuine, real-time and based on their questions. Contrast this with someone making a presentation, a form of communication which is based on what the presenter wants to convey.

Based on this success and input from the team, we agreed on a series of next steps to include MBTI assessments, 360-degree feedback and further coaching and training in some specific areas such as coaching and influencing. This marked a significant breakthrough in our relationship and work together as now the team was taking ownership of what they wanted to learn and how they wanted to receive information and feedback. This is significantly different from many similar organizational development initiatives where, for example, 360-degree feedback is imposed on people when the necessary trust is not in place. This certainly contributes to the inability of many such initiatives to get the meaningful results they seek. The importance of contracting with both my client and the team was also highlighted – a key link to the team's ownership of the process.

Phase three

For this next phase, we shifted our informal monthly agreement to a retainer arrangement, allowing me to be more proactive with the team, both as a whole and one-on-one. Under this arrangement, team members were also encouraged to call me anytime to discuss specific issues they faced. Interestingly, the first person to call was one of the members from whom I had been sensing some resistance all along. We were able to make a breakthrough on what had been a key question within one hour.

Several initial successes were experienced in this next phase. Using an ARL process, each team member was invited to identify a specific business challenge they were facing. We then selected one person to share their issue with the team and the context for their learning in relation to the issue. The first person chose to share quite a sensitive issue which involved her desire to influence her boss to allow one of the members of another team to join hers. As that person's team leader was also an executive team member, this was potentially quite a hot point. To avoid conflict, I invited the boss (my client) to be an 'observer' of the discussion. The other team leader, who knew about the issue, felt comfortable enough to participate directly in the discussion.

The focal question, 'how can I influence my boss to accept my recommendation to shift this person to my team?' directly related to this person's development objective regarding influencing. The traditional way for her to do this would have been to go to her boss and present her argument. However, she intuitively knew that if she did this, her boss would likely push back. This is a natural consequence of two people with directive influencing styles adopting this style with each other – the effect is that they seem to be 'pushing' at each other. (To reinforce the point you only need to ask someone to stand up and hold out their hand. When you push against it they will resist. If you pull them towards you, it is easy.)

The team members helped process this issue and give the question owner a chance to identify and challenge her assumptions. In less than one hour she was able to gain considerable insight into the question and recognized some of her own learning about influencing. She was also able to resolve a key business issue and in the process actually received feedback from her boss that was very helpful. The team members all saw this as a very positive experience, especially as it had focused on a real business issue – 'earning while learning'.

Another success came through the debriefing of the MBTI assessment. We had chosen a half-day session during which each of the key dimensions was explained, after which each team member had a chance to 'validate' their results through feedback from their colleagues at the meeting. One of the team members commented that this type of open discussion would not have been possible six months earlier – a real testimonial to the progress the team had been making.

Next steps – organizational transformation

The next challenge is for the team to begin transferring the skills and learning to their own teams. As a first step, we recently facilitated the company's mid-year meeting using ARL principles to introduce the methodology and techniques to all 90 employees around the theme of change. This went very well, including a fishbowl personal interview with the MD in front of the whole company (instead of the usual Powerpoint presentation of the year's results). Again, this led to a high level of disclosure and trust on a personal level. At the end of the interview, participants were invited to do a stop/reflect on their questions based on what they had heard. They were then divided into cross-functional teams with the executive team as facilitators. After sharing their questions, each group chose one question to be the focal point of their discussion. At the end of this discussion, presenters from each group were asked to come up on stage to report. They all came equipped with notes to read. Sensing that this might be somewhat cumbersome with presentations from all eight teams, I modified the format to another fishbowl discussion, inviting the eight presenters to sit on the stage and discuss amongst themselves what they learned through their teams' discussions. This really shocked the participants as it was not what they had come prepared to do and, because of this, provided some powerful, just-in-time learning around change. In fact, the outcome of that impromptu, 30-minute group discussion was equal to the type of debrief I have seen from two or three-day workshops on change. All the participants commented how much they enjoyed this format even though they had been nervous at first. At the end of the day we included a 'campfire'-type reflection and dialogue session for all 90 people – a very innovative way for the participants to communicate with each other around the question 'based on what we have experienced today, what are the implications for me personally?'

From this session we then sat with the executive team to involve them in creating the vision and mapping out the steps for driving change throughout the entire organization. This will have to be the subject of another chapter as we are just initiating this process now.

Lessons learned

My experience with Merck Hong Kong demonstrated to me, quite unequivocally, that ARL can effectively substitute for traditional, expert-led training and support a meaningful commitment to change through just-in-time learning linked to real business issues. Furthermore, even though there is a traditional reluctance to give open feedback in Asian culture, ARL processes can facilitate a much deeper level of openness and trust than is normally possible. And, perhaps most importantly, the experience reaffirmed to me how true organizational change and individual growth of the type that Merck was seeking requires deep personal awareness.

I recently asked the Merck team members to reflect on the experience we had shared over the past months. Given the spectacular growth and development achieved by what was already a high-performing team, it is appropriate to give them the 'last word' on what they were able to accomplish with the help of ARL.

Q　As a consequence of our team development work together, how have you changed your thinking, attitude or behaviour – if any?

'How to exert influence on others and why we want to do it.'

'I have become more proactive in both thinking and behaviour. I begin to look at things not only from my own perspective and my own function, but from other team members' angle as well in a bid to achieve better integration.'

'Action reflection learning/Just-in-time learning can bring forth high-performance teams at all levels of an organization. Leadership is learned through effective action/reflection learning. All leaders should learn to take time out to reflect and spare time to have dialogue with their teams as a communication tool. These tools are very effective in achieving business goals.'

'I know my fears and weaknesses.'

'I now have a different view of my people and take a different approach on the possibility of influencing upwards.'

Q　How do you perceive that your team has changed?

'Better listening.'

'Increased respect for others' opinions.'

'We are now more open on the "undiscussables". We thought we were quite open but actually were not.'

'Most team members have changed a lot in leadership approach.'

'I think the process has made the team more mature, taking on more ownership, being more willing to open up and to share, and being prepared to pass the learning on to my team.'

'The team has changed so much. They display much stronger leadership. The team is now more aligned and integrated towards our company goals. As a company with a very strong culture and functional excellence, it has always been a challenge to align among ourselves, and since the kick-off with Action Reflection Learning, the team is working towards a High-Performance Team level. The team has also become more aware of the need to continuously raise the bar in leadership standard and see this as a competitive edge.'

Q   What has been the biggest challenge for you personally in relation to the Team Development Process?

'Facing my own weaknesses and helping others become aware of and face their own weaknesses in a constructive way.'

'Doing something when I don't really understand/see the motive or benefit of doing it (i.e. committing to do something when the whole picture is not clear). Maybe this is managing change.'

'For me, the biggest challenge has been the "requirement" to open up'.

'Getting buy-in among the team members to this change management process is quite a challenge, since we have always been successful as a company, and we don't see our blind-spot readily. Self-awareness was not high enough to bring about the need to change.'

Q   What did you perceive as your team's biggest challenge?

'I think it was integration and consideration.'

'Raising new heights in leadership standard was a challenge for the team. Also, asking the team to get out from their comfort zone was very difficult with this group since they are all very good at what they do functionally.'

'Continuous improvement in leadership development is a new challenge for us.'

'Facing one's personal fear and helping one's awareness of it in a team manner.'

Q   In what specific ways have I, in my role as a learning coach, been helpful to you and/or your team?

'Showing me that someone with a very different working style can also be effective.'

'Making me work with more flexibility.'

'As a coach, you have helped me to realize that change (for the better) is a must and we must keep on learning and improving ourselves in order to be more competitive. You have helped me to face the reality courageously and to take ownership.'

'Creating an environment and special circumstances where our fears can surface and be faced.'

'You are very effective in coaching us to gain ownership of the change management process. You understand our organizational issues, and you are able to assimilate the Action Reflection Learning tools into our culture, and ways of doing things around the team.'

Q   What would you hope the article I am writing would reflect/capture in terms of lessons learned about using Action Reflection Learning with Merck Hong Kong?

'Capture that different members of a team have different learning/adoption style. If the usual style used by a coach does not achieve the intended results, try another style or individualize the style to help everyone on board.'

'Having a top grade/High-Performance Team is no doubt a competitive advantage, but it requires serious commitment of the leader and the management team to drive it down to the whole organization.'

'Questioning is the most powerful awareness weapon.'

'Define the players in the team development process: include the leader, or not? If yes, leader must be on equal footing and be ready to be helped. If not, leader can just be a sponsor of the process, which is OK and equally important.'

'Respect is the platform of change and awareness.'

'Action Reflection Learning is an effective concept to drive team development. I highly recommend for any company, small or large, to adopt this concept.'

21

Building Internal Capacities for Change in China: Action Learning in the Public and Private Sectors

Lichia Yiu and Raymond Saner

China has pursued an 'Open Door' policy since 1979 which started the transformation of its economic system. Foreign companies were invited to invest in China and to participate in the construction of a socialist market economy with 'Chinese characteristics' and the Chinese government itself embarked on fundamental reforms of its administration. In the short time span of 20 years, China has transformed itself from being an isolated under-developed country to a country with significant economic prowess. Its GDP has quadrupled since 1979 and China is now enjoying a huge trade surplus with the United States. Major Chinese cities from Guanzhou and Shanghai to Tianjin and Beijing have gone through urban renewal and now boast a skyline dotted with skyscrapers forming the backdrop to bustling economic activities. Today, the major companies of the world can no longer afford to be absent from the China market.

This article reports on some of the fundamental changes which have taken place in the field of management and which are representative examples of how China has changed over recent years. The authors will present and discuss two examples where action learning was used as a stra-tegic instrument for collective learning and improvement of organizational performance in both the public and private sectors in China.

The first example describes a change project within China's public admin-istration where action learning was used to modernize the human resource development function throughout China's public administration. The sec-ond example describes a management development programme where action learning was used to rapidly develop local management personnel in order to support Motorola's fast business growth in China.

Modernization of the human resource development (training) function in China

Successive public administrative reforms took place in China in 1982, 1988, 1993 and again in 1998. One of the common features of these reform efforts was continual downsizing of the public administration. The number of cadres has since been reduced from 40 million cadres in 1980 to 4 million civil servants in 1998. The latest initiative by Premier Zhu was to reduce the size of administrative staff by 50 per cent from approximately 8 million civil servants down to 4 million.

While the downsizing of the public administration took place, the complexity and work requirements confronting Chinese civil servants increased significantly. Therefore, the continuous upgrading of the knowledge and skill level of government officials has been of paramount importance. Similar needs were also felt in the economic sector. Competition in the Chinese market has been steadily intensified since the 1980s due to gradual but continuous market opening and deregulation of China's market. The need to survive in a competitive transitional market has forced state-owned enterprises to reinvent themselves through financial restructuring and the upgrading of core competencies among their employees.

This task of reshaping and upgrading the leadership and managerial competence of Chinese government officials as well as the competence of the senior management of state-owned enterprises[1] has been the responsibility of a multitude of administrative cadre schools and party schools at the central, provincial and county levels. For the past decade, government officials have been told to undertake pre-assignment training ('Gong Chien Pei Xun'), requalification training and in-service training ('Sun Gong Pei Xun') at regular intervals as part of their career development steps. The duration of these training programmes varied from three months to one year depending on the rank and function of the trainees. These training activities focused mainly on the rationale and policies of economic reform and general management concepts applicable to a socialist market economy. The new emphasis on upgrading educational qualification and technical competencies constituted a major shift from the pre-Deng reform period (before 1979) and represented a major investment considering China's limited public resources. It was recognized that 'strengthening the training of the state civil servants is an effective measure and guarantee for the transition of the economic system' (Sheng, 1994).

China's in-service training institutions, along with the government's human resource development departments, however, were ill-prepared to respond to these growing demands for managerial training and development. Most of these institutions lacked the needed competencies to carry out these tasks and had no in-depth understanding of their customers' demands. Instead, these training institutions continued to churn out uniform training programmes which were strong on ideological fervour, but weak on skill development and management tools.

It was in this context that an international technical cooperation project was first conceived in 1987 and implemented in 1993–96 as a partnership project jointly financed by China and Switzerland.[2]

Objectives and key tasks of the bilateral project

The objectives of this Sino-Swiss bilateral cooperation project (SSBP) were to strengthen the in-service training and development function within the administrative system (training management) and to improve the efficiency and the effectiveness of China's training delivery system; that is, administrative cadre training schools, party schools and economic cadre training schools. It was envisioned that SSBP would contribute to the modernization of the Chinese central administration and help China's large state enterprises improve training management and management training capabilities. The Chinese participants ('trainees') of the project were to form the vanguard of a new generation of Chinese public management trainers and HRD managers after acquiring the concepts and techniques of modern management training and organizational development.

The intended target

The target population was defined on an institutional rather than on an individual basis. It included (a) provincial administrative cadre training institutes, and (b) provincial party schools and their respective supervisory bodies, such as the training departments of Provincial Organization Departments of the Chinese Communist Party. While the former institutions were responsible for management training programmes, the latter were responsible for the establishment of the overall training plan which included the training curriculum, training targets, duration and budget.

At the time of the SSBP project, the Chinese training system was organized into a matrix consisting of three-tier administrative levels (national, provincial and county) and three sectors (economic, public administration and political/party). The total number of training institutions within the party and the administrative sector was approximately 6000 nationwide (Yiu and Saner, 1998). Additionally, there were more than 2800 training institutions that catered to the needs of the economic sector. These figures, however, do not include training centres within the large state-owned enterprises and companies.

The architecture of the project design

A multi-level intervention was designed by the authors to tackle the specific characteristics of China's administrative system and to achieve a sustainable

performance improvement of these approximately 6000 cadre training institutions to help them conduct their core business.

A combination of action learning (AL) and action research (AR) methods
was used in order to accomplish the said objectives within a limited time
project life-cycle. These action-based approaches were novel in China[3] and
constituted a pioneering attempt at international know-how transfer. They
were meant to offer viable tools for developing internal capacity for
continuous improvement and for system-wide multi-level intervention.
Specifically, this Sino-Swiss bilateral project (SSBP) consisted of the following elements:

1   A train-of-trainer's (TOT) programme which formed the core of SSBP.
    Representatives from the different constituencies at the national and
    provincial levels were selected to attend the Train-of-Trainers pro-
    gramme (TOT) in Beijing. A total number of 60 upper middle-level offi-
    cials and faculty members were trained. Twenty provincial govern-
    ments together with the Ministry of Personnel and State Economic and
    Trade Commission were the sponsors of these trainees.
2   Two TOT cycles were organized at the developmental stage of SSBP in
    order to stabilize the basic design of SSBP.
3   Action research and action learning were used as learning methods in
    order to tackle systemic-level issues regarding HRD.
4   Clear delineation and involvement of the stakeholders of SSBP.
    The stakeholders of the project included the training institutions who
    were going to sponsor the trainees and also included the supervisory
    government organizations which directed and monitored these train-
    ing institutions (boundary definition).
5   Network formation at both trainee and institutional levels.
    Trainees were selected and grouped into learning cohorts. Members of
    these learning cohorts came either from related institutions, such as
    training institutions or the training departments within the respective
    administrative supervisory bodies. The assumption here was that these
    cohorts could form the nucleus of innovation once they returned to
    their job sites and region. Likewise, the participating institutions would
    also form the basis of a learning network which would spearhead the
    reform of the existing training function and training apparatus;
6   Two periods of work-based application as integral parts of TOT (see
    Figure 21.1).
    Trainees were given the assignment to conduct 'promotional' seminars
    at their home organization in order to share their newly-gained ideas,
    insights and methods. Participants of these seminars included peers,
    superiors and 'clients'.
7   Learning projects.

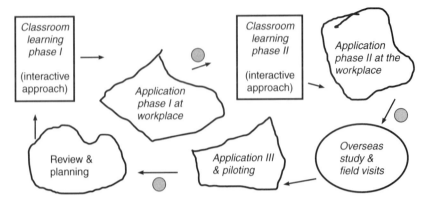

Figure 21.1   The TOT course design of the Sino-Swiss bilateral project, 1993–96
● = Learning conference

Source: Adapted from Yiu and Saner, 1998.

Projects were undertaken by the trainees with real and strategic issues relating to human resource development and management at their job site, such as the administration, training institutions or enterprises.

8   Conference-style learning reviews were organized at the end of each application phase.

9   The outputs were expected to be concrete and fitting to top-quality curriculum design, research reports on real leadership and management issues and problems, and training strategies and materials based on accepted adult learning theories and practices and Chinese case examples.

10   Bottom-up dissemination was conducted to sensitize the supervisory bodies and trainees' respective institutions in order to obtain political support for implementation of the recommendations from trainees' project work.

The TOT[4]

Programmed learning

This was structured into 10 basic units covering topics such as comparative public administration, human resource management, organizational theory and development, adult learning theories and methods, and training management. These topics were taught in the classrooms (learning phases I and II) by foreign experts in Beijing. Trainees were organized into learning groups for the entire duration of the TOT programme.

To ensure *workplace application* trainees from the same provincial or municipal administrative structures were given a group project to work on. Selection criteria of these learning projects were:

- It had to deal with substantial organizational and/or systemic issues or problems requiring resolution by the senior leadership of the trainee's own work organization.
- It had to be vital for the survival or effectiveness of trainees' work organization.
- It had to be a complex issue covering different aspects of the management task in today's China.

After consultation with the Chinese partner organization, CTCSPMO[5], learning projects were undertaken by the trainees which covered the following topics:

- Redesigning the existing management-development programmes for county magistrates (for example Gansu province), enterprise managers (for example Henan and Shangdong provinces) and senior party cadres (for example the Central Party School, Beijing).
- Developing training programmes for training managers working in the prefectural-level training institutions (for example Fujian province).
- Developing new training programmes on managing large infrastructural projects for public sector managers (for example the State Council).
- Conducting research projects on how to improve human resource management practices within the state-owned enterprises in order to improve employee motivation (for example the State Economic and Trade Commission).

Learning-set meeting

During these two application phases, a cohort of trainees from the same provinces or municipalities formed a learning set to work on a common project. They were assisted by a tutor and were instructed to meet every two weeks either physically or by phone. Due to the great physical distance even within the same province, face-to-face meetings were often beyond the financial means of these trainees.

Learning journal

Trainees were also asked to keep a learning journal to record their reflections while carrying out their action learning projects.

Learning conference

A learning conference was scheduled at the end of each application phase to review the project work and its findings and to exchange experiences working within a team. The Swiss advisers (authors) participated in these learning conferences to provide feedback and reflection.

Training of tutors (set advisers)

The tutors were selected from the existing training staff of counterpart organizations in China and affiliates who had received training abroad in the field of HRD and adult learning. The training inputs here were primarily concerned with action learning and action research methodologies and personal development as set advisers.

Action (1993–96) and reflection

During the initial preparatory phase (September 1993 to March 1994), the trainees were given intensive English language courses. Subsequent to the language learning, the first TOT cycle was implemented from March 1994 to July 1995. An in-depth review involving all actors and related stakeholders took place in the interim and the second cycle was implemented from March 1996 to December 1996.

Looking back, there were many challenges to be overcome and problems to be solved during the implementation of SSBP, and these challenges them-selves also represented valuable learning opportunities for all parties involved (see Table 21.1 and Table 21.2).

Table 21.1 Key challenges during the classroom learning phases (adopted from Yiu & Saner, 1998)

Actors	Learning challenges	Acquired learning
Chinese trainees	• To participate actively in the learning process and take responsibility for the relevance of their learning • To redefine the role of a 'good' trainer/teacher • To question each other and the trainer/teacher statements as 'facts', 'opinion' or 'truth' • To challenge the conviction that 'the bird who raises its head will be shot first' (equivalent to the Japanese saying of 'the nail that sticks out will be hammered in') • To perceive the social process and group dynamics of learning as being beneficial, not chaotic nor as lacking discipline	☑ Knowledge and associated techniques relating to training, human resources and organizations ☑ Greater understanding of the behavioural aspects of - organizational life ☑ Appreciation of the active training methodology in a safe environment ☑ Development of team work and confronting the 'group think' phenomenon

Table 21.1 continued

Actors	Learning challenges		Acquired learning
Chinese tutors	• To act as facilitators, not as 'administrators' or 'controllers' • To question the perception that 'teacher should know everything' • To support an open and trusting learning environment • To learn how to work as a team with experts from diverse cultural backgrounds	☑ ☑ ☑ ☑	On-the-job learning of participatory training approaches Gaining new professional knowledge Questioning established ideas Reducing psychological distance with 'foreigners'
Foreign Experts	• To question and to reflect on their own assumptions concerning organizations, human relations and management theories • To confront their own cultural stress in a foreign environment which had its own logic in getting things done • To find ways to work as a team with the Chinese tutors who had different ways of relating to students	☑ ☑ ☑ ☑ ☑	Experience of working in a Chinese cultural milieu Readjustment of one's own interactive style and role definition Dealing with ambiguity Dealing with indirect communication styles Dealing with consensus decision-making without necessarily being involved in the decision-making

Source: Adapted from Yiu and Saner, 1998.

Table 21.2 Key challenges and learning from application phases I and II when trainees undertook work-based learning projects

Actors	Challenges		Learning and benefits
Trainees	• To confront the pressures from their colleagues at home who wanted them to resume their regular job and tasks • To seek out additional financial and material resources for their project • To take responsibility for their own actions • To manage the client relationships • To question each other's assumptions • To manage the learning project	☑ ☑ ☑ ☑	Gaining better insights of Deng Xiao Ping's statement regarding China's reform process which should be based on the spirit of 'touching the stones to cross the river' (meaning learning by experimenting) Knowledge of the real world in the workplace and real issues outside of the classroom environment Testing Western management theories in the Chinese context Perceiving the management

and sustain their learning set

- To bridge the two worlds of conceptualisation, i.e., East and West
- To break the mode of communicating in abstractions and generalities.

issues in a more holistic and integrated manner
☑ Recognition from their

superiors and colleagues
☑ Strengthening their networking and selling skills.

Chinese tutors	• To actually facilitate the learning process over distance • To grasp the real issues in the workplace • To manage and administer multiple long distance learning projects with limited resources • To fully grasp the action learning and action research methodologies • To feel comfortable in offering process feedback.	☑ Observing 'action learning' and 'action research' in action ☑ Taking responsibility to solve problems ☑ Personal development regarding leadership skills ☑ Managing constituencies of these learning projects.
Client organiza-tions in the provinces and cities	• To stay open and receptive regarding the findings and recommendations • To Freally support the learning by providing needed resources • To implement the recommended changes.	☑ Getting feedback from their target population regarding training needs and existing programs ☑ Getting solutions in the form of new curricula, training materials and training methods.
Chinese project manage ment team	• To deal with the cultural and structural differences of the Chinese and Swiss environment • To deal with the boundary issues *vis-à-vis* the Swiss partner organization, participating institutions inChina, and internal organizations within CTCSPMO • To be open to learning opportunities • To avoid political blunders which would jeopardise future cooperation with outside world.	☑ Dealing with complex project organizational structure involving international partners, ☑ Dealing with project partners as equal instead of seeing them as contractors and therefore less than equal.
Swiss project manage ment team	• To challenge assumptions made concerning the Chinese partners and institutions; • To refrain from assuming responsibility for the Chinese partners • To facilitate rather than dominate	☑ Learning how to operationalize an action learning design through others ☑ Learning how to manage multi-level relationships and power structures ☑ Managing frustration.

Table 21.2   Continued

Actors	Challenges	Learning and benefits
	• To sustain the interest and commitment of the CTCSPMO and tutors to the action research and action learning approach; • To provide feedback in constructive fashion; • To deal with frustration.	

Source: Adapted from Yiu and Saner, 1998.

Reactions from *clients*, like the Deputy Directors of the provincial organization department of the CCP the Deputy Commissioner of the State Commission of the Nationalities, the Academic Dean of the Central Party School, the Directors of Training of the Ministry of Personnel and the State Economic and Trade Commission, and so forth, were in general positive. They found the results of the action research informative and the recommended solutions helpful. The rate of implementation of the recommendations was high which was later verified by a team of international independent reviewers. A final project evaluation was conducted in October 1997 which confirmed the initial positive assessment.

A second phase of the SSBP was agreed upon by the Chinese and Swiss governments. CSEND[6], represented by the authors transferred the implementation responsibilities to the University of Geneva.

Benefits and capacity-building effect

The Sino-Swiss bilateral project was designed to increase the institutional capacity of Chinese public administration in managing change. The strategy used was to train a small group of experienced training managers and trainers with the ability to apply scientific methods of inquiry, to make rational decisions, to learn new behaviour, and to carry out their roles and tasks with greater effectiveness. Lastly, they were expected to act as the catalyst to bring about the institutional development of their respective training institutions.

Activities designed to provide trainees with the opportunity to acquire and apply knowledge in practical situations and to learn via participatory learning methods have by and large been successful. Some of the spin-off activities (projects) of the SSBP project were:

- In 1996, the Provincial government of Fujian started a replication project for the training institutions of the lower administrative units, that is municipalities and counties[7]. The original design of SSBP was customized to fit with the existing training capacity and the strategic plan of Fujian. The objective of Fujian's project was to reorient its training system in order to support its strategic vision for the twenty-first century.

- In 1997, the Provincial Government of Gansu established a Training Centre for Senior Cadres (GTCSC) to provide modern management development programmes. This Centre has also established a cooperative arrangement with the School of Business Administration in Solothurn, Switzerland. GTCSC is just one of the 20 centres that were established in the provincial capitals of China after 1996, based on modern interactive methods.

Localization of mid-level managerial staff in China: the Motorola story

In the early 1990s, Motorola started to invest in China and rapidly expanded its operation in order to gain market share in China's nascent telecommunications market. In a short time span, Motorola China Electronics Limited (MCEL) grew from a sales organization to a vertically-integrated company in China. Its sales volume reached US$2 billion and it employed 3500 employees by 1994. MCEL has become one of the biggest global foreign-owned companies in China.

In 1998, Motorola's investment in China reached US$1.9 billion (Kevin, 1999) with plans to double its investment in the next few years. Its sales revenue reached US$3.1 billion from Greater China which includes Hong Kong and Taiwan. Billboard advertizing of Motorola products could be seen even in the most remote corners of China. It is also a common sight to see businessmen and government officials sporting Motorola pagers and cellular phones as part of their fashion apparel. Motorola enjoys one of the rare success stories in China while most of the FDI (foreign direct investment) in China struggles on (according to the survey of the European Chamber of Commerce, 1997).

How did MCEL manage to seize the market opportunity? How did MCEL develop its organizational capacity to respond to the market demands? The answer lies in the commitment and approach that MCEL took in developing its Chinese employees.

China accelerated management development (CAMP)

Due to China's unprecedented high economic growth of the last 20 years, the demand for people with management skills outstripped the available local talent pool. Not only were multinationals competing for this scare 'resource', local Chinese enterprises were also in search of such talent.

Whereas China's working population had always enjoyed the safety of an 'iron rice bowl' (that is, lifetime employment), voluntary and involuntary turnover had become commonplace by the 1990s. Increased mobility was most evident among the young, well-educated and English-speaking professionals. They were highly sought after considering that less than 7 per cent of the total population received university education. This tight labour market has had its effect not only on salary and compensation, but also on selection and recruitment, which was a phenomenon akin to the situation witnessed by firms in Taiwan, Singapore, South Korea and Hong Kong in the mid-1980s leading to high turnover rates and mounting salary scales by the late 1980s (Saner and Yiu, 1993).

In a fast-moving telecommunication and IT market, difficulties in staffing professional and managerial functions could have hampered Motorola's business growth and could also have caused significant loss of market share. In order to support the rapid growth of MCEL, Motorola Inc. pooled managerial talents and functional experts from both the headquarters in Schaumburg, USA and from the regions, especially from Asia. By the end of 1994, there were approximately 140 expatriates working at MCEL (Motorola Training and Education, December 1994/January 1995).

However, it was clear that a reliance on expatriates to support the growth of MCEL had obvious shortcomings and could only be a transitional solution. Drawing heavily on internal resources from Motorola's Asian subsidiaries had caused operational strains in places such as Singapore, Malaysia and Taiwan. Also, it was clear that relying on expatriates would have been too costly over time.

Motorola soon realized that the issue of staffing MCEL with the right talents and at the right price was a priority and required urgent solution. Buying local talents from external labour markets was no option either, since there were persistent supply shortages and increasing costs. However, bringing in 'mercenaries – expatriates' could only provide short-term solutions. Motorola, therefore, decided on a long-term solution that called for developing an internal talent pool with management skills. Hence, CAMP was born as part of this localization strategy. The ensuing education and training investment made by Motorola in China was also designed to show Motorola's long-term commitment to China and to Chinese stakeholders, that is the Chinese government and the community ('guanxi'[8] building).

The objectives

CAMP was an innovative approach to management development for Chinese high potentials. It was created in 1994 to expedite the localization process. The short-term objective of CAMP was to develop effective middle managers who could replace expatriates at comparable levels (Motorola, 1994/95).

The long-term goal of CAMP was to develop potential leaders for MCEL. It was estimated that by year 2000, MCEL would grow into a 10'000 strong company with sales volume reaching 3.5 billion US dollars (Avishai, 1995).

The intended target

The target population of CAMP consisted of Chinese nationals who were expected to satisfy the following selection criteria:

- Being employed long enough with Motorola to have an initial understanding of their group or sector's business;
- Having been assessed as a high-potential employee through the internal review process;
- Having demonstrated a high level of English proficiency;
- Holding a bachelor degree or equivalent;
- Having supervisory responsibility.

The 'graduates' of the CAMP programme were expected to strengthen the organizational capacity of their sectors or units. It was hoped that by 1996 there would be 100 Chinese managers developed from the CAMP process.

The architecture of CAMP

In order to help the graduates of CAMP become high-performing 'Motorolans', an action learning-based design was chosen and mixed with classroom learning, real business-driven projects, on-the-job mentoring and exposure to alternative approaches to Chinese traditional ways of managing. The choice of action learning was of critical importance since this approach required trainees to actually 'put to test' whatever theories they had learned. Similar to the SSBP case, the key challenges confronting the programme designers[9] at Motorola University and the consultant[10] were:

1 Ensuring on-the-job transfer of 'classroom' learning.
2 Installing in the minds of trainees the business culture of Motorola.
3 Reorienting the mindset of trainees away from that of a risk-aversive administrator to that of a self-starting entrepreneur and manager/leader.

Action learning was identified as the approach that would be best-suited for these challenges. By reflecting on their experiences and questioning the underlining assumptions, trainees had the opportunity to develop their critical thinking and analytic skills that were necessary for effective problem-solving and for responding to the changing needs of MCEL and the changing conditions of the Chinese market.

It was also recognized that without ongoing mentoring and social support, it would be very difficult for trainees to try out the newly-learned Western theories of organization and management since in many respects they ran contrary to Chinese practices and beliefs. Therefore, a mentoring component by senior expatriate managers was incorporated into the CAMP programme design. Specifically, CAMP had the following elements:

1   A team-building component to encourage trust and to foster a construct-ive learning environment;
2   A workshop-style classroom-learning component;
3   A learning project which dealt with real organization and/or manage-ment issues;
4   A one-on-one mentoring relationship;
5   A benchmarking exercise to make cross-border comparisons;
6   Time-limited job rotation to an overseas site.

The total learning cycle lasted approximately 14 months and was broken down into five phases (see Figure 21.2). Each phase reflected the AL princi-ples of action–reflection–generalization–application, and reinforced the learning and insights gained during the previous phases.

The programme

- *Programmed learning* was structured into topical learning which covered topics relating to general management and leadership principles, advanced management concepts, cross-cultural studies, problem-solving and communication skills, project management skills, leadership skills, macro-economics and market economy, and Motorola-specific topics.
- *Action learning* projects during phase II and phase IV had different foci. The first learning project was more focused on management aspects of business issues, while the second project dealt with more complex issues and had an organizational learning dimension.

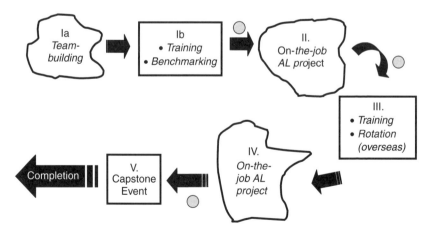

Figure 21.2   The basic design of the China Accelerated Management Programme (CAMP) – 10–12 participants were selected for each CAMP cycle

- *Learning-set project meetings* were held on a weekly basis to support individual and collective learning. Due to the fact that most of the CAMP trainees lived and worked in far-distant locations from Beijing and from each other, these meetings were held by teleconferencing and monthly face-to-face meetings in Beijing and Tianjin. The same applied to the case of set advisers who facilitated these meetings and who were also based mostly at different locations from their learning team members.
- *Benchmarking* was used to compare the work practices at different Motorola sites in Asia. The assumption was that through the benchmarking exercise, best practices would emerge and be transferred.
- *Mentoring* was seen as an integral part of the learning process, and trainees were coached on a regular basis by a senior expatriate manager. Each trainee was given access to his mentor for consultation regarding his action learning project or in general. A business *Simulation* was used toward the end of the CAMP training as a vehicle to help the trainees integrate different aspects of their business operation.
- *Workshop for the set advisers*. HR managers from different sites in China participated in this training effort as set advisers for the action learning groups during phases II and IV. A workshop focusing on AL principles and cultural adaptation, facilitation skills and implementation planning was conducted prior to the start of CAMP in Beijing.

CAMP started the first cycle in 1994 and has continued up to now, and remains one of the core features of the management development programme of Motorola University (Beijing).

Benefits

The challenges, which MCEL had to overcome during its early years of rapid growth, were many: however, the key ones related to the 'software' of the company, that is the human capital and the company culture of MCEL. CAMP has contributed to the development of human capital, as well as to safeguarding Motorola's corporate culture in its China subsidiaries. Graduates of the CAMP programme have not only enjoyed personal development, but have also become the cultural conduit or the change agent in transforming their colleagues and subordinates into true 'Motorolans'.

Although the investment made for each CAMP trainee was around US$50 000 per person (*USA Today*, 26 January 1999), the outcome of CAMP clearly shows favourable results both in terms of monetary and non-monetary outcomes. Six years after its initial offering, CAMP continues to be offered to the middle management of MCEL in a more condensed version of shorter duration.

CAMP was replicated in 1995 for India when Motorola speeded up its investment there. The prototype was customized to fit the specific context of India. The management development programme in India is called 'Leadership Accelerated Progarmme' and has been in operation since 1996.

Conclusion

Action learning has been recognized as being one of the most effective vehicles for management development. Some work has been reported regarding the application of action learning in developing countries, but only little has been reported about the potential for success and the need to adapt the action learning approach to the constraints in a developing country such as China. The examples reported here have attempted to demonstrate that the action learning methodology can be successfully applied outside an Anglo-American context.

Although these two cases are embedded in different operational environments – that is, one concerns the Chinese government, the other a global company – some common factors contributed to their success. The most striking was the use of action learning not only to solve business-driven issues, but also to develop an internal capacity for sustained management development.

In the case of SSBP, the Chinese government and the CCP were able to acquire cutting-edge know-how in management development and training, and at the same time they could review the various training programmes which were being provided for senior government officials, enterprise executives and party officials in China. Based on the findings from action learning projects, the training department of the CCP revised their training requirements, adjusted their training approach and added more skill-based topics to the curriculum.

In the case of CAMP, the goal of rapid localization was achieved despite phenomenal growth. MCEL, together with Hong Kong and Taiwan, has contributed 11 per cent of the consolidated revenue by 1996. Today, the 'Motorolans' of Chinese nationality are able to reach the quality standards required by Motorola's Six Sigma programme. They are sharing their best practices within the corporate family.

On demonstrated strength, Motorola will transfer more advanced technology to China by setting up another chip manufacturing facility in Tianjin and by fulfilling its promise to raise the standards of living in China via technological transfer.

Notes

1 There are approximately 70 000 state-owned enterprises in China according to the last count of the Chinese State Economic and Trade Commission (1999).
2 A modified version of the original design was transferred to the University of Geneva and continued until now.

3   The authors acted as advisers to a unit of the CCP's Organization Department which later on was established as a separate training institute called China Training Centre for Senior Personnel Management Officials (CTCSPMO). An initial institution-building phase of CTCSPMO was financed by United Nations Development Programme (UNDP) and both authors acted in the role of Chief Technical Advisers in 1987–90. The authors introduced CTCSPMO to AR which the client organization adapted and utilized for its policy seminars. These AR-related policy seminars have since become one of the backbone training activities of CTCSPMO which became the first governmental agency to use AR in all of China.

4   For detailed information, please refer to L. Yiu and R. Saner (1998) 'Use of Action Learning as a Vehicle for Capacity Building in China', *Performance Improvement Quarterly*, vol. 11(1), pp. 129–48.

5   CTCSPMO stands for China Training Centre for Senior Personnel Management Officials in Beijing. It reports to the Organization Department of the CCP.

6   CSEND stands for Centre for Socio-Eco-Nomic Development, Geneva. CSEND is a non-profit foundation specializing in process design and institutional reform. More details are available at *http://www.csend.org*.

7   A large county, or better known as prefect, could consist of up to 8–9 million inhabitants. This is equivalent to some of the smaller European countries.

8   'Guanxi' is the Chinese term for social capital.

9   Leo Burke and Rich Boucher from Motorola University (MU) Management Centre, Yeo Hiok Khoon and Patty Ide from MU China, and Wang Yi from China Human Resource.

10 Lichia Yiu, external consultant from Organizational Consultants Ltd, Hong Kong/Geneva.

References

Avishai, B. (1995) 'In China, It's the "Year of the Manager"', *Fast Company*, November. (*http://fastcompany.com/online/ 01/china.html*).

Centre for Socio Eco-Nomic Development, (1997) *The Sino-Swiss M.A.S.T.E.R.™ Project for Management Training and Organizational Development in the Public Sector of China 1994–1996*. Geneva: CSEND Working Paper.

Garratt, B. (1991) 'The Power of Action Learning', in M. Pedler (ed.), *Action Learning in Practice*, 2nd edn., Adlershot: Gower.

Gosling, J. and Ashton, D. (1994) 'Action Learning and Academic Qualifications', *Management Learning*, vol. 25(2), pp. 263–74.

Kevin, M. (1999) 'Motorola Stands by China', *USA Today*, Tech Report, 26 January.

Lawrence, W. G. (1977) 'Management Development: Some Ideals, Images and Realities', *Journal of European Industrial Training*, vol. 1, pp. 21–5.

McTaggart, R. (1992) 'Reductionism and Action Research: Technology versus Convivial Forms of Life', in C.S. Bruce and A.L. Russell (eds), *Transforming Tomorrow Today: Proceedings of the Second World Congress on Action Learning*. Brisbane: Action Research and Process Management Association Inc.

McTaggart, R. (1994) 'Opportunities: China Accelerated Management Program – An Innovative Approach to Management Development', *Motorola Training and Education*, vol. 11(7), December 1994/January 1995.

Ravens, R. (1991) 'Action Learning and the Third World', *The International Journal of Human Resource Management*, vol. 2(1), pp. 73–91.

Saner, R. and Yiu, L. (1993) 'Coping with Labour Turnover in Taiwanese Companies', *American Asian Review*. vol. 11(1), Spring, pp. 162–75.

Saner, R. and Saner-Yiu, L. (1996) 'Management Training and Organization Development in the Public Sector of the People's Republic of China: The Way Ahead, some Reflections and Suggestions', in Saner-Yiu, L. (ed.), *Compendium for the Best Management Development Practices: A Benchmarking Conference*. Geneva: CSEND.

Xun Zi (400 BC) 'Essay on the Evil of Human Nature', in *The Collection of Essays of Xun Zi*, Taipei: Taiwan Shang Wu Publications.

Yiu, L. and Saner, R. (1998) 'Use of Action Learning as a Vehicle for Capacity Building in China', *Performance Improvement Quarterly*, vol. 11(1), pp. 129–48.

Bibliography

Amdam, R. P. (1996) *Management Education and Competitiveness: Europe, Japan and the United States*. London: Routledge.

Argyris, C. (2000) *Flawed Advice and the Management Trap: How Managers Can Know When They're Getting Good Advice and When They're Not*. New York: Oxford University Press.

———.(1993) *Knowledge for Action: A Guide to Overcoming Barriers to Organizational Change*. San Francisco: Jossey-Bass.

———.(1992) *On Organizational Learning*. Oxford: Blackwell.

Argyris, C. and Schon, D. (1978) *Organizational Learning: A Theory of Action Perspective*. Reading, MA: Addison-Wesley.

Argyris, C., Putnam, R. and Smith, D. M. (1985) *Action Science: Concepts, Methods, and Skills for Research and Intervention*. San Francisco: Jossey-Bass.

Auteri, E. (1994) 'Fiat Revs Up the Engines of Change', *Personnel Journal*, May, vol. 73(5), pp. 107–13.

Baird, L., Holland, P. and Deacon, S. (1999) 'Learning from Action: Embedding More Learning into the Performance Process Fast Enough to Make Difference', *Organizational Dynamics*, vol. 27(4), pp. 19–32.

Balog, J. K. (1993) 'Chief Executive Peer Groups: A Case Study in Action Learning (Peer Group, Executive Education)', Dialog-Dissertation Abstracts Online, Dissertation Abstracts International, vol. 54/08-A; 3104 : Northern Illinois University, 141 pages.

Beaty, L., Bourner, T. and Frost, P. (1993) 'Action Learning: Reflections on Becoming a Set Member', *Management Education and Development*, Winter, vol. 24(4), pp. 350–67.

Becker, B. E., Huselid, M. A. and Ulrich, D. (2001) *The HR Scorecard: Linking People, Strategy, and Performance*. Boston: Harvard Business School Press.

Bellmann, M. (2000) 'Siemens Management Learning: A Highly Integrated Model to Align Learning Processes with Business Needs', in Y. Boshyk (ed.), *Business Driven Action Learning: Global Best Practices*. London and New York: Macmillan Business and St Martin's, pp. 140–51.

Bertsch, B. and Williams, R. (1994) 'How Multinational CEOs Make Change Programmes Stick', *Long Range Planning*, October, vol. 27(5), pp. 12–24.

Bibliography of Research on Experiential Learning and the Learning-Style Inventory (1985). Boston: McBer & Co.

Bierema, L. L. (1998) 'Fitting Action Learning to Corporate Programs'. *Performance Improvement Quarterly*. vol. 11(1), pp. 86–107.

Block, P. (1999) *Flawless Consulting: A Guide to Getting Your Expertise Used*. San Francisco: Jossey-Bass.

Bolt, J. F. (1997) 'Executive Development: A Strategy for Corporate Competitiveness'. Executive Development Associates.

Boshyk, Y. (2000) 'Beyond Knowledge Management: How Companies Mobilize Experience'. in Donald Marchand, Thomas H. Davenport, and Tim Dickson, (eds), *Mastering Information Management*. London: Financial Times-Prentice Hall; 51–58.

Boshyk, Y. and Weidemanis, M. (2000) 'What Did We Earn and Learn? Emerging Markets and Business Driven Action Learning', in Y. Boshyk (ed.) *Business Driven*

Action Learning: Global Best Practices. London-New York: Macmillan Business and St. Martin's, pp. 134–39.

———.(2000) 'Business Driven Action Learning: The Key Elements'. in Y. Boshyk, (ed.), *Business Driven Action Learning: Global Best Practices*. London–New York: Macmillan Business and St. Martin's, pp. xi-xvii.

Boshyk, Y. (2000) (eds). *Business Driven Action Learning: Global Best Practices*. London-New York: Macmillan-St. Martin's Press.

Bossert, R. (2000) 'Johnson & Johnson Executive Development: Getting Business Driven Action Learning Started', in Y. Boshyk, (ed.), *Business Driven Action Learning: Global Best Practices*. London-New York: Macmillan Business and St. Martin's, pp. 91–103.

Botham, D. and Vick, D. (1998) 'Action Learning and the Program at the Revans Centre'. *Performance Improvement Quarterly*, vol. 11(2), pp. 5–16.

Botkin, J. (1999) *Smart Business: How Knowledge Communities Can Revolutionize Your Company*. New York: Free Press.

Boulden, G. P. and Safarikova, V. (1997) 'Industrial Restructuring in the Czech Republic', in M. Pedler (ed.), *Action Learning in Practice*, 3rd edn. Aldershot: Gower, pp. 107–16.

Bova, B, and Kroth, M. (2001) 'Workplace Learning and Generation X', *The Journal of Workplace Learning*, vol. 13(2), pp. 57–65.

Braun, W. (2000) 'DaimlerChrysler: Leadership Development Using Action-Oriented and Distance-Learning Techniques', in Y. Boshyk, (ed.), *Business Driven Action Learning: Global Best Practices*. London-New York: Macmillan Business and St. Martin's, pp. 3–13.

Bray, J., Lee, J. and Smith, L. (eds) (2000) *Collaborative Inquiry in Practice: Action, Reflection, and Meaning-Making*. New York: Sage.

Brenneman, W. B., Keys J. B. and Fulmer, R. M. (1998) 'Learning Across a Living Company: The Shell Companies' Experiences', *Organizational Dynamics*, vol. 27(2), pp. 61–70.

Brooks, A. K. (1998) 'Educating Human Resource Development Leaders at the University of Texas at Austin: The Use of Action Learning to Facilitate University-Workplace Collaboration', *Performance Improvement Quarterly*, vol. 11(2), pp. 48–58.

Bruzzese, A. (1998) 'Learning Locomotion', *Human Resource Executive*, vol. 12(10), pp. 28–30.

Burgoyne, J. and Reynolds, M. (eds) (1997) *Management Learning: Integrating Perspectives in Theory and Practice*. London: Sage.

Casey, D. and Pearce, D. (eds) (1977) *More than Management Development: Action Learning at GEC*. New York: AMACOM.

Cell, E. (1984) *Learning to Learn from Experience*. Albany: State University of New York Press.

Checkland, P. (1999) *Systems Thinking, Systems Practice*. Chichester: Wiley.

Clover, W. H. (1991) At TRW, 'Executive Training Contributes to Quality'. *The Human Resources Professional*, vol. 3(2), pp. 16–20.

Crainer, S. and Dearlove, D. (1998) *Gravy Training: Inside the World's Top Business Schools*. Oxford: Captstone.

Cumming, J. and Hall, I. (2001). *Achieving Results Through Action Learning: A Practitioner's Toolkit for Developing People*. Maidenhead: Peter Honey.

Cunningham, I. and Easterby-Smith, M. (1995). 'Debate', *Organizations and People*, vol. 3(2), pp. 41–47.

Cunningham, I. (1987) 'Structuring Set Advisor Training Using Simulated Analysis', *Training and Management Development Methods*, vol. 1(1).

Cusins, P. (1995) 'Action Learning Revisited', *Industrial and Commercial Training*, vol. 27(4), pp. 3–10.

Davenport, T. H. and Prusak, L. (1998) *Working Knowledge: How Organizations Manage What They Know.* Boston: Harvard Business School Press.

De Geus, A. (1997) *The Living Company.* Boston: Harvard Business School Press.

De Loo, I. and Verstegen, B. (2001) 'New Thoughts on Action Learning', *Journal of European Industrial Training*, vol. 25(2,3,4), pp. 229–234.

Dennis, C., Cederholm, L. and Yorks, L. (1996) 'Learning Your Way to a Global Organization: Grace Cocoa', in Victoria J. Marsick and Karen. E. Watkins (eds), *In Action: Creating the Learning Organization*, pp. 165–177.

Dilworth, R. L. (1996) 'Action Learning: Bridging Academic and Workplace Domains'. *Employee Counselling Today.* vol. 8(6), pp. 48–56.

Dilworth, R. L. (1998) 'Action Learning at Virginia Commonwealth University: Blending Action, Reflection, Critical Incident Methodologies, and Portfolio Assessment', *Performance Improvement Quarterly*, vol. 11(2), pp. 17–33.

———.(1998) 'Action Learning in a Nutshell', *Performace Improvement Quarterly*, vol. 11(1), pp. 28–43.

Dixon, N. M. (1994) *The Learning Organziation.* New York: McGraw-Hill.

———.(1999) *Organization Learning Cycle.* Aldershot: Gower.

———.(2000) Talk, 'Authenticity and Action Learning in the Learning Organization: Dialogue at Work', *The Learning Organization: An International Journal*, vol. 7(1), pp. 42–47.

———.(1997) 'More than Just a Task Force', in M. Pedler (ed.), *Action Learning in Practice.* Aldershot: Gower, pp. 329–337.

Donahue, S. and Girard, K. (2000) 'Crash and Learn', *Business* 2.0. 11 July, pp. 166–87.

Donnenberg, O. (ed.), (1999) *Action Learning: Ein Handbuch.* Stuttgart: Klett-Cotta.

Dotlich, D. L. and Cairo, P. (1999) *Action Coaching: How to Leverage Individual Performance for Company Success.* San Francisco: Jossey-Bass.

Dotlich, D. L. and Noel, J. (1998) *Action Learning: How the World's Top Companies are Re-Creating their Leaders and Themselves.* San Francisco: Jossey-Bass.

Downham, T. A. Noel, J. L. and Prendergast, A. E. (1992) 'Executive Development'. *Human Resource Management.* vol. 31(1,2), pp. 95–107.

Drucker, P. (1996) *The Executive in Action.* New York: HarperBusiness.

Edvinsson, L. and Malone, M. S. (1997) *Intellectual Capital: Realizing your Company's True Value by Finding its Hidden Brainpower.* New York: HarperBusiness.

Engen, John R. (1994) 'Getting your Chinese Workforce up to Speed', *International Business*, Aug; vol. 7(8), pp. 44–48.

European Community. (1978) *Education in the European Community.* Brussels: EC.

Fitz-enz, J. (2001) *The E-Aligned Enterprise: How to Map and Measure Your Company's Course in the New Economy.* New York: American Management Association.

———.(2000) *The ROI of Human Capital: Measuring the Economic Value of Employee Performance.* New York: American Management Association.

Fitz-enz, J. and Phillips, J. (1998) *The New Vision for Human Resources: Defining the Human Resources Function by its Results.* n.p.: Crisp Publications.

Flynn, G. (1996) 'Think Tanks Power Up Employees', *Personnel Journal*, vol. 75(6), pp. 100–108.

Foley, G. (1999) *Learning in Social Action: A Contribution to Understanding Informal Education.* London: Zed Books.

Foy, N. (1977) 'Action Learning Comes to Industry', *Harvard Business Review*, vol. 8, April, pp. 48–56.

Freedman, N. J. (2000) 'Philips and Action Learning Programs: An Assessment', in Y. Boshyk (ed.), *Business Driven Action Learning: Global Best Practices.* London-New York: Macmillan Business and St. Martin's, pp. 123–133.

Friedman, S. D. (2001) 'Leadership DNA: The Ford Motor Story', *Training and Development*, vol. Mar; 55(3), pp. 22–29.

Froiland, P. (1994) 'Action Learning: Taming Real Problems in Real Life', *Training*, vol. 31(1), pp. 27–32,34.

Garratt, B. (1987) *The Learning Organization and the Need for Directors who Think*. Aldershot: Gower.

Garvin, D. A. (2000) *Learning in Action: A Guide to Putting the Learning Organization to Work*. Boston: Harvard Business School Press.

Gemelli, G. (1996) 'American Influence on European Management Education: The Role of the Ford Foundation', in R. Petter Amdam (ed.), *Management Education and Competitiveness: Europe, Japan and the United States*, London: Routledge, pp. 38–68.

Gibbons, S. (1999) 'Learning Teams: Action Learning for Leaders'. *Journal for Quality and Participation*, vol. 22(2), pp. 26–29.

Global Forum on Business Driven Action Learning. (2000) *Fifth Annual*, 30 May–2 June, 2000. *Proceedings on CD-Rom*. St. Louis: Boeing Leadership Center.

Global Forum on Business Driven Action Learning. (2001) *Sixth Annual*, 22–25 May, 2001. *Proceedings on CD-Rom*. Aitkin Hill, Melbourne, Australia: BHP Billiton Global Leadership Centre.

Goldberg, Marilee C. (1997) *The Art of the Question*. Chichester: Wiley.

Gordon, J. (1998) 'My Leader, Myself', *Training*, vol. 35(11), pp. 54–62.

Greville, M. R. (2000) 'Learning and Team Development During Business Driven Action Learning: Personal Experiences', in Yury Boshyk (eds), *Business Driven Action Learning: Global Best Practices*. London–New York: Macmillan Business and St. Martin's, pp. 189–197.

Guillon, P., Kasprzyk, R. and Sorge, J. (2000) 'Dow Chemical's Business Driven Learning', in Y. Boshyk (eds), *Business Driven Action Learning: Global Best Practices*. London–New York: Macmillan Business and St. Martin's, pp. 14–28.

Hanabury, E. (1998) 'A Catalyst for Change', *Human Resource Executive*, vol. 12(14), pp. 17–19.

Hankoff, R. (1993) 'Companies That Train Best', *Fortune*, Mar 22, vol. 127(6), pp. 62–75.

Hay, J. (1997) *Action Mentoring: Creating Your Own Developmental Alliance*. Watford, UK and Minneapolis: Sherwood Publishing.

Heron, J. (1999) *The Complete Facilitator's Handbook*. London: Kogan Page.

Ho, S. K. M. (1999) 'Japanese 5-S – Where TQM Begins', *The TQM Magazine*, vol. 11(5), pp. 311–321.

Honey, P. and Mumford, A. (1992) *The Manual of Learning Styles*. Maidenhead: Peter Honey.

Honjo, M. (1992). Cross–Cultural Education in Executive Development. *Gendai-no Esprit (in Japanese)*, March, pp. 172–181.

Honjo, M. (1993). Cross–Cultural Conflict Management in Corporations. *Gendai-no Esprit (in Japanese)*, March, pp, 172–181.

Hosta, R. (2000) 'IBM: Using Business Driven Action Learning in a "Turnaround"', in Y. Boshyk (eds), *Business Driven Action Learning: Global Best Practices*. London–New York: Macmillan Business and St. Martin's, 76–90.

Howard, R. (1993) (eds). 'The Learning Imperative: Managing People for Continuous Innovation', *Harvard Business School Press*.

Inglis, S. (1994) *Making the Most of Action Learning*. London: Gower.

Justice, T. and Jamieson, D. W. (1999) *The Facilitator's Fieldbook*. New York: American Management Association.

Katzenbach, J. R. and Smith, D. K. (1999) *The Wisdom of Teams: Creating the High Performance Organization*. New York: HarperBusiness.

Kember, D. (2000) *Action Learning and Action Research: Improving the Quality of Teaching and Learning*. London: Kogan Page.

Kennedy, A. A. (2000) *The End of Shareholder Value: Corporations at the Crossroads*. Cambridge, Massachusetts: Perseus Publishing.

Keys, L. (1994) 'Action Learning: Executive Development of Choice for the 1990s', *Journal of Management Development*. vol. 18(8), pp. 50–56.

Kiser, G. A. (1998) *Masterful Facilitation: Becoming a Catalyst for Meaningful Change*. New York: American Management Association.

Kissel, W. (2000) 'Hoffman La Roche and Boehringer Mannheim: Mission Impossible – Executive Development During a Takeover', in Y. Boshyk (eds), *Business Driven Action Learning: Global Best Practices*. London-New York: Macmillan Business and St. Martin's, 65–75.

Knowlton, J. Charles Jr. (1992) 'Action Learning: A Case Study of Hospital Managers'. Dialog – Dissertation Abstracts Online, Dissertation Abstracts International, vol. 53/09-A, p. 3082: University of Georgia, 142 pages.

Kolb, D. A. (1984) *Experiential Learning: Experience as the Sources of Learning and Development*. Englewood Cliffs, NJ: Prentice-Hall.

Krucky, H. T. (eds), (1999) *In Action: Measuring Learning and Performance. Sixteen Case Studies from the Real World of Training*. Alexandria, VA: American Society for Training and Development.

Lamm, S. (2000) 'The Connection between Action Reflection Learning and Transformative Learning: An Awakening of Human Qualities in Leadership', New York: PhD dissertation, Teachers College, Columbia University.

Lawrence, J. (1994) 'Action Learning – A Questioning Approach', in A. Mumford (eds), *Handbook of Management Development*. 4th ed. Aldershot: Gower.

LeGros, V. M. and Topolosky, P. S. DuPont. (2000) 'Action Learning in Practice', in Y. Boshyk (eds), *Business Driven Action Learning: Global Best Practices*. London–New York: Macmillan Business and St. Martin's, pp. 29–41.

Levy, P. (2000) 'The Role of the Country Coordinator in An Executive Development Action Learning Programme', in Y. Boshyk (ed.), *Business Driven Action Learning: Global Best Practices*. London–New York: Macmillan Business and St. Martin's, pp. 204–224.

Lewis, A. and Marsh, W. (1987) 'Action Learning: The Development of Field Managers in Prudential Assurance', *Journal of Management Development*, vol. 6(2), pp. 45–56.

Maital, S. (1994) *Executive Economics: Ten Essential Tools for Managers*. New York: Free Press.

Marquardt, M. J. (1999) *Action Learning in Action: Transforming Problems and People for World-Class Organizational Learning*. Palo Alto: Davies-Black.

Marsick, V. J. (1990) 'Action Learning and Reflection in the Workplace', in J. Mezirow et al. (eds), *Fostering Critical Reflection in Adulthood*. San Francisco: Jossey-Bass, pp. 23–26.

Marsick, V. J. and Cederholm, L. (1988) 'Developing Leadership in International Managers: An Urgent Challenge!', *The Columbia Journal of World Business*, vol. 23(4), pp. 3–11.

Marsick, V. J. and Sauquet, A. (2000) 'Learning Through Reflection', in M. Deutsch and P. Coleman (eds), *Handbook of Conflict Resolution: Theory and Practice*. San Francisco: Jossey-Bass, pp. 382–99.

Marsick, V. J. and Watkins, K. E. (1999) *Facilitating Learning Organizations: Making Learning Count*. Aldershot: Gower.

Marsick, V. et als. (1995), *ARL™ Inquiry: Life on the Seesaw–Tensions in an Action Learning Program*. Adult Education Conference Proceedings. Edmonton, Alberta: University of Alberta, pp. 1–6.

Marsick, V., and Volpe, M. F. (1999) (eds.). *Informal Learning on the Job. No. 2 in the series, Advances in Developing Human Resources*. San Francisco and Baton Rouge: Berrett-Koehler and the Academy of Human Resources.

McCauley, C. D., Moxley, R. S. and Van Velsor, E. (eds) (1998) *The Center for Creative Leadership Handbook of Leadership Development*. San Francisco: Jossey-Bass.

McGill, I. and Beaty, L. (eds) (1993) *Action Learning: A Practitioner's Guide*. London: Taylor & Francis.

McGill, I. and Beaty, L. (1995) *Action Learning: A Guide for Professional, Management and Educational Development*. London: Kogan Page.

McLaughlin, H. and Thorpe, R. (1993) 'Action Learning – A Paradigm in Emergence: The Problems Facing a Challenge to Traditional Management Education and Development', *British Journal of Management*. March, vol. 4(1), pp. 19–27.

Meister, J. (1998) *Corporate Universities: Lessons on Building a World-Class Workforce*. New York: McGraw-Hill.

Mercer, S. (2000) 'Checklist and Tools for Business Driven Action Learning Teams: The General Electric Perspective', in Y. Boshyk (ed.), *Business Driven Action Learning: Global Best Practices*. London–New York: Macmillan Business and St. Martin's, pp. 179–88.

———.(2000) 'General Electric and Executive Development Action Learning Programmes', in Y. Boshyk (ed.), *Business Driven Action Learning: Global Best Practices*. London–New York: Macmillan Business and St. Martin's, pp. 42–54.

Mezirow, J. (1991) *Transformative Dimensions of Adult Learning*. San Francisco: Jossey-Bass.

Miller, P. (2001) *Mission Critical Leadership: Getting You and Your Business Up To Speed in the New Economy*. London: McGraw-Hill.

Mollet, G. (2000) 'Volkswagen: Action Learning and The Development of High Potentials', in Y. Boshyk (ed.), *Business Driven Action Learning: Global Best Practices*. London–New York: Macmillan Business and St. Martin's, pp. 152–65.

Mumford, A. (ed.) (1997) *Action Learning at Work*. Aldershot: Gower.

———.(1997) 'Action Learning as a vehicle for learning, in A. Mumford (ed.), *Action Learning at work*. Aldershot, UK: Gower, pp. 3–24.

———.(1993) 'How Managers Can Become Developers', *Personnel Management*. June, vol. 25(6), pp. 42–5.

———.(1995) 'Making the Most of Action Learning', *Journal of European Industrial Training*. vol. 19(5):v.

———.(1995) 'Managers Developing Others Through Action Learning', *Industrial and Commercial Training*. vol. 27(2), pp. 19–27.

———.(1997a) 'A Review of the Literature, in M. Pedlar (ed.), *Action Learning in Practice*. Aldershot, UK: Gower press.

Nevins, M. D. and Stumpf, S. A. (1999) '21st Century Leadership: Redefining Management Education', *Strategy and Business* (Booz Allen & Hamilton). vol. 16 (reprint 99305), pp. 2–12 .

Nishizawa, T. (1996) 'Business Studies and Management Education in Japan's Economic Devlopment: An Institutional Perspective', in R. Petter Amdam (ed.), *Management Education and Competitiveness: Europe, Japan and the United States*. London: Routledge; 96–110.

Nonaka, I. and Takeuchi, H. (1995) *The Knowledge-Creating Company: How Japanese Companies Create the Dynamics of Innovation*. Oxford: Oxford University Press.

O'Neil, J. Arnell, E. and Turner, E. (1996) 'Earning While Learning', in K. E. Watkins and V. J. Marsick (eds), *In Action: Creating the Learning Organization*. Alexandria, VA: American Society for Training and Development, 153–64.

O'Neil, J. R. (1994) *The Paradox of Success: When Winning at Work Means Losing in Life*. New York: Jeremy P. Tarcher/Putnam.

O'Neil, J. and Lamm, S. L. (2000) 'Working as a Learning Coach Team in Action Learning', *New Directions for Adult and Continuing Education*. Fall, vol. 87, pp. 43–52.

O'Neil, J. and Smith, P. (2000) (eds), What Works Online, 'Action Learning: Real Work, Real Learning' Unpublished paper.

O'Reilly, B. (1993) 'How Execs Learn', *Fortune*, April 5; vol. 127(number 7), pp. 52(4).

Owen, H. (1997) *Open Space Technology: A User's Guide*. San Francisco: Berrett-Koehler.

Parkes, D. (1998) 'Action Learning: Business Applications in North America', *The Journal of Workplace Learning*, vol. 10(3), pp. 165–68.

Pedler, M. (1996) *Action Learning for Managers*. London: Lemos & Crane.

Pedler, M. Burgoyne, J. and Boydell, T. (1997) *The Learning Company: A Strategy for Sustainable Development*. London: McGraw-Hill.

Pedler, M. (ed.) (1997) *Action Learning in Practice*. 3rd edn. Aldershot: Gower.

Petersen, D. B. and Hicks, M. D. (1996) *Leader as Coach: Strategies for Coaching and Developing Others*. Minnesota: Personal Decisions International.

Pfeffer, J. and Sutton, R. I. (2000) *The Knowing–Doing Gap: How Smart Companies Turn Knowledge into Action*. Boston: Harvard Business School.

Putterman, B. (1999) 'Busy Executives Want Action When They Learn', *Training Director's Forum Newsletter*. vol. 15(3), pp. 7.

Raelin, J. A. (1993) 'The Persean Ethic: Consistency of Belief and Actions in Managerial Practice', *Human Relations*. vol. 46(5), pp. 576–621.

———.(1999) 'The Design of the Action Project in Work-Based Learning', *Human Resource Planning*, vol. 22(3), pp. 12–28.

———.(2000) *Work-Based Learning: The New Frontier of Management Development*. Upper Saddle, New Jersey: Prentice Hall.

Ramirez, R. (1983) 'Action Learning: A Strategic Approach for Organizations Facing Turbulent Conditions', *Human Relations*, August vol. 36, pp. 725–42.

Redwood, S., Goldwasser, C. and Street, S. (1999) *Action Management: Practical Strategies for Making your Corporate Transformation a Success*. Chichester: Wiley.

Reid, M. (1995) 'The Use of Written Reports in Action Learning Programmes or More Traditional Management Development Courses', *Training and Management Development Methods*, vol. 9(2), pp. 101–09.

Revans, R. (1987) *International Perspectives on Action Learning*. Manchester: Institute for Development Policy and Management, University of Manchester.

Revans, R. W. (1998) *The ABC of Action Learning*. London: Lemos & Crane.

———.(1984) 'Action Learning: Are we Getting There?', *Management Decision*, vol. 22(1), pp. 45–52.

———.(1986) 'Action Learning in a Developing Country', *Management Decision*, vol. 24(6), pp. 3–7.

———.(1983) Action Learning: 'The Cure is Started (at West Middlesex Hospital, Britain)', *Management Decision*, vol. 21(4), pp. 11–6.

———.(1983) 'Action Learning: The Forces of Achievement, or Getting it Done', *Management Decision*, vol. 21(3), pp. 44–54.

———.(1983) 'Action Learning: The Skills of Diagnosis', *Management Decision*, vol. 21(2), pp. 47–52.

———.(1971) *Developing Effective Managers: A New Approach to Business Education*. London: Longman.

———.(1982) *The Origins and Growth of Action Learning.* Bromley, UK: Krieger (Chartwell-Bratt).

———.(1966) *The Theory of Practice in Management.* London: Macdonald.

Rimanoczy, I. (2001) 'Action Reflection Learning in Thailand: Defying Cultural Differences', in S. Sankaran et als (eds.), *Action Learning and Action Research.* Lismore, Australia: Southern Cross University Press.

Rolland, N. and Chavel, D. (2000) 'Knowledge Transfer in Strategic Alliances', in C. Despres and D. Chauvel (eds.) *Knowledge Horizons.* Boston: Butterworth Heinemann, pp. 225–236.

Rolland, N. (2001) 'L'apprentissage organisationnel de connaissances managériales'. Doctoral disseratation. Université Pierre-Mendès France, Grenoble 2, 444p.

Rohlin, L., Skarvad P.-H. and Nilsson, S. A. (1998) *Strategic Leadership in the Learning Society.* Vasbyholm: MiL Publishers.

Rothwell, W. J. (1999) *The Action Learning Guidebook: A Real-Time Strategy for Problem Solving, Training Design, and Employee Development.* San Francisco: Jossey-Bass Pfeiffer.

Rothwell, W. J. and Cookson, P. S. (1997) *Beyond Instruction: Comprehensive Program Planning for Business Education.* San Francisco: Jossey-Bass.

Sadler, P. (ed.) (1998) *International Executive Development Programmes.* London: Kogan Page.

Savage, C. M. (1996) *The 5th Generation: Co-Creating through Virtual Enterprising, Dynamic Teaming, and Knowledge Networking.* Boston: Butterworth-Heinemann.

Schein, E. H. (1999) *The Corporate Culture Survival Guide: Sense and Nonsense About Culture Change.* San Francisco: Jossey-Bass.

Schwarz, R. M. (1994) *The Skilled Facilitator: Practical Wisdom for Developing Effective Groups.* San Francisco: Jossey-Bass.

Seibert, K. W., Hall. D. and Kram, K. E. (1995) 'Strengthening the Weak Link in Strategic Executive Development: Integrating Individual Development and Global Business Strategy', *Human Resource Management*, Winter; vol. 34(4), pp. 549–67.

Seibert, K. W. and Daudelin, M. W. (1999) *The Role of Reflection in Managerial Learning: Theory, Research, and Practice.* Westport, Connecticut-London: Quorum.

Semler, R. M. (1995) *The Success Story behind the World's Most Unusual Workplace.* New York: Warner.

Senge, P. (1990) *The Fifth Discipline: The Art and Practice of the Learning Organization.* New York: Currency Doubleday.

Senge, P. and Kleiner, A. *et al.* (1999) *The Dance of Change: The Challenges of Sustaining Momentum in Learning Organizations.* New York: Currency Doubleday.

Svelby, K. E. (1997) *The New Organizational Wealth.* San Francisco: Berret-Koehler.

Taylor, J. and Marais, D. and Heyns, S. (1998) *The Action-Learning Field Kit. Case Studies of Development Issues and Problems Faced by Development Workers in South Africa, the Caribbean, Latin and North America.* Capetown: Juta & Company.

Taylor, J. and Marais, D. and Kaplan, A. (1997) *Action Learning for Development. Use Your Experience to Improve Your Effectiveness.* Capetown: Juta & Company.

Tichy, N. (2001) 'No Ordinary Boot Camp', *Harvard Business Review.* April pp. 63–9.

Timpson, W. and Broadbent, F. (1995) (eds), *Action Learning: Experience and Promise.* Brisbane: The Tertiary Education Institute, University of Queensland.

Ulrich, D., Zenger, J. and Smallwood, N. (1999) *Results-Based Leadership: How Leaders Build the Business and Improve the Bottom Line.* Boston: Harvard Business School Press.

Ulrich, J. G. (1997) 'Non-Company-Based Training: The Eastern German Experience', *Education and Training.* vol. 39(8) pp. 309–15.

Van Buren, M. and Woodwell Jr. W. (2000) *The 2000 ASTD Trends Report: Staying Ahead of the Winds of Change*. American Society for Training and Development.

Vicere, A. A. and Fulmer, R. M. (1996) *Crafting Competitiveness: Developing Leaders in the Shadow Pyramid*. Oxford: Captsone.

———.(1998) *Leadership by Design: How Benchmark Companies Sustain Success Through Investment in Continuous Learnng*. Boston: Harvard Business School Press. (US version of the previous)

Vince, R. and Martin, L. (1993) 'Inside Action Learning: An Exploration of the Psychology and Politics of the Action Learning Model', *Management Education and Development*. Autumn; vol. 24(3), pp. 205–15.

Watkins, K. E. and Marsick, V. J. (1996) (eds), *In Action: Creating the Learning Organization*. Alexandria, VA: American Society for Training and Development.

Weinstein, K. (1998) *Action Learning: A Practical Guide*. Second edition. London: Gower.

Weisbord, M. R. (1992) *Discovering Common Ground: How Future Search Conferences Bring People Together to Achieve Breakthrough Innovation, Empowerment, Shared Vision, and Collaborative Action*. San Francisco: Berret-Koehler.

Wills, G. and Oliver, C. (1996) 'Measuring the ROI from Management Action Learning', *Management Development Review*. vol. 9(1), pp. 17–21.

Yoong, P. and Gallupe, B. (2001) 'Action Learning and Groupware Technologies: A Case Study in Group Support Systems (GSS) Facilitation', *Information Technology and People*. vol. 14(1), pp. 78–90.

Yorks, L., Lamm S. and O'Neil, J. (1999) 'Transfer of Learning from Action Learning Programs to the Organizational Setting', in L. Yorks, J. O'Neil and V. J. Marsick (eds), *Action Learning: Successful Strategies for Individual, Team, and Organizational Development*. Baton Rouge, LA: Berrett-Koehler, pp. 56–74.

Yorks, L., Marsick Victoria, J. and O'Neil, J. (1999) 'Lessons for Implementing Action Learning', in L. Yorks, J. O'Neil, and Victoria, J. M. (eds), *Action Learning: Successful Strategies for Individual, Team, and Organizational Development*. Baton Rouge, LA and San Francisco: Berrett-Koehler, pp. 96–113.

Yorks, L., O'Neil J. and Marsick, V. J. (1999) 'Action Learning: Theoretical Bases and Varieties of Practice', in L. Yorks, J. O'Neil and V. J. Marsick (eds), *Action Learning: Successful Strategies for Individual, Team, and Organizational Development*. Baton Rouge, LA and San Francisco: Berret-Koehler, pp. 1–18.

Yorks, L. (2000) 'The Emergence of Action Learning', *Training and Development*. January vol. 54(1), pp. 56.

Yorks, L., O'Neil, J. and Marsick, V. J. (eds), (1999) *Action Learning: Successful Strategies for Individual, Team, and Organizational Development*. No. 2 in the series Advances in Developing Human Resources, R. A. Swanson, Editor-in-Chief. Baton Rouge and San Francisco: Academy of Human Resource Development and Berrett-Koehler.

Zuber-Skerritt, Ortrun. (1993) 'Improving Learning and Teaching Through Action Learning and Action Research', *Higher Education Research and Development*. vol. 12(1), pp. 45–58.

Useful Websites

IFAL Worldwide is an organization established in 1977 in the United Kingdom to promote action learning on an international scale. IFAL's aim is to 'identify and encourage a network of enthusiasts to support and develop the work of action learning worldwide'. IFAL forms the structure under which national 'chapters' and their members can operate and interact. http://www.ifal.org.uk/ifalhomesi5.html is the official site of the International Foundation for Action Learning and is the most representative site of the Revan's 'classic' approach.

These web sites provide access to the researchers and professionals engaged in IFAL in the UK, Canada and in the USA. It provides links, research leads, networking, membership, conferences and interactive conversation. IFAL's mission is to advance research and learning about Action Learning.

IFAL UK   http://www.ifal.org.uk/.
IFAL Canada   http://www.tlainc.com/ifalcan.htm
IFAL USA   http://www.ifal-usa.org/

Revans Institute for Action Learning and Research http://www.salford.ac.uk/pgpros99/rese arch/55.html. The University of Salford, UK in 1995 established, within Continuing Education, a new Institute with the specific task of contributing to the development of action learning based on Reg Revans works.

Department of Management Learning at Lancaster University http://www.lums.lancs.ac.uk/manlearn/. This university department uses an approach to learning based on self-management.

IMC (International Management Centres) http://www.i-m-c.org/. IMC is a private, multinational business school and offers management development and qualification programmes. IMC developed MBA programmes with the use of the Internet. Programmes are based on the principles of action learning. The IMC website provides many useful links.

Action Learning Institute http://www.action-learning.org/. This site is the gateway sponsored by the International Management Centres.

University of Action Learning http://www.u-a-l.org/. Dedicated to providing Internet resourced Action Learning undergraduate and graduate programs. Linked with the Action Learning Institute.

The Dutch Action Learning Association http://www.actionlearning.nl/general.html. This association was founded in 1994 by people who have been actively using or studying Reg Revans's approach to Action Learning. It is aimed to help firms to realize a learning organization and for developing personal entrepreneurship.

A German Language Website on action learning with close links to the Dutch Action Learning Association is www.actionlearningnetzwerk.net

MiL Institute http://www.milinstitute.se/eng/. MiL Institute is a non-profit foundation founded by companies and staff members from Lund University in 1977. They have a wide network of 'action reflection'™ learning practitioners and hold an annual conference in Lund, Sweden.

American Society for Training and Development (ASTD) http://www.astd.org. Founded in 1944, ASTD is the world's premier professional association and leading resource on workplace learning and performance issues. ASTD offers information, research and analysis for its 70 000 members and acts as a clearinghouse and network for a wide range of topics

Global Executive Learning Network www.GELNetwork.com are a worldwide professional network of practitioners and researchers of business driven action learning. The website has information on the Global Forum on Business Driven Action Learning and Executive Development and recommended sources on all aspects and from all approaches to action learning.

Index